"Concise . . . to the point . . . got me my CCNA! . . . It provides good practical exercises and the practice tests are great!"

From Bookpool.com
Harry Velez, CCNA, Network Security Analyst
Augusta, Georgia

"Great reading for a tough exam. [Lammle's *CCNA: Cisco Certified Network Associate Study Guide*] is an excellent introduction to the world of Cisco routers. . . . The author's writing style is approachable and light, making the often-tough topic easy to learn. . . . The plethora of network-activity traces really elucidates certain concepts, especially for those who've dealt with trace analysis before. The questions included at the end of each chapter were very helpful in studying and reviewing the material just read."

From Bookpool.com
Remek Kocz, Network Administrator
Rochester, New York

"Todd Lammle has done it again! Lammle's [*CCNP: Advanced Cisco Router Configuration Study Guide*] is unquestionably better [than other ACRC study guides] for ACRC test preparation. . . . Compared to a 5-day ACRC course which costs $1900 in my area (and likely requires another week or more of study before testing), this book for less than a 50 spot is a staggering bargain. Buy it and spend ample time with it. . . . Todd, my pocketbook thanks you."

A reader from Amazon.com
Jackson, Mississippi

"[The *CCNA: Cisco Certified Network Associate Study Guide* is] a must for professionals wanting to learn about Cisco routers. I have gone through Todd Lammle's book a couple of times before certifying, and countless times afterwards to review and pick up additional detail. It is fantastic. He has put together excellent sections discussing the theory and then shows you how to actually do the work. . . . He not only knows the information, but knows how to present it for ease of learning. I have never had information given to me in such a smooth manner and retained it so well."

From Bookpool.com
Russell Kaufmann, Ph.D., MCSE+I, MCT, CCNA
Denver, Colorado

"Like talking to a buddy. [*CCNA: Cisco Certified Network Associate Study Guide*] was a very good book and very easy to read. . . . [It] gives very good information, and isn't as dry as those 'other' books. Todd Lammle knows exactly when to throw in little analogies and jokes that help the learning process along."

From Amazon.com
Roy Valdez Jr. from Houston, Texas

"[*CCNP: Advanced Cisco Router Configuration Study Guide* is] clear and concise, with great detail. . . . This ACRC Study Guide, is a great study tool for the exam, and explains in great detail the harder, advanced Cisco routing concepts."

A reader from Amazon.com

CCNP™
Remote Access
Study Guide

Robert Padjen

Todd Lammle

with Sean Odom

San Francisco • Paris • Düsseldorf • Soest • London

Associate Publisher: Neil Edde
Contracts and Licensing Manager: Kristine O'Callaghan
Acquisitions & Developmental Editors: Jeff Kellum, Linda Lee
Editors: Susan Berge, Rebecca Rider
Production Editor: Elizabeth Campbell
Technical Editors: Matthew E. Luallen, Mark Tashiro
Book Designer: Bill Gibson
Graphic Illustrator: Tony Jonick
Electronic Publishing Specialists: Judy Fung, Susie Hendrickson
Proofreaders: Nanette Duffy, Amey Garber, Laurie O'Connell, Mae Lum
Indexer: Matthew Spence
CD Coordinator: Kara Eve Schwartz
CD Technician: Keith McNeil
Cover Design: Archer Design
Cover Photograph: Tony Stone Images

Library of Congress Card Number: 00-105397

ISBŃ: 0-7821-2710-X

SYBEX and the SYBEX logo are trademarks of SYBEX Inc. in the USA and other countries.

The CD interface was created using Macromedia Director, COPYRIGHT 1994, 1997-1999 Macromedia Inc. For more information on Macromedia and Macromedia Director, visit http://www.macromedia.com.

Internet screen shot(s) using Microsoft Internet Explorer reprinted by permission from Microsoft Corporation.

This study guide and/or material is not sponsored by, endorsed by or affiliated with Cisco Systems, Inc. Cisco®, Cisco Systems®, CCDA™, CCNA™, CCDP™, CCNP™, CCIE™, CCSI™, the Cisco Systems logo and the CCIE logo are trademarks or registered trademarks of Cisco Systems, Inc. in the United States and certain other countries. All other trademarks are trademarks of their respective owners.

TRADEMARKS: SYBEX has attempted throughout this book to distinguish proprietary trademarks from descriptive terms by following the capitalization style used by the manufacturer.

The author and publisher have made their best efforts to prepare this book, and the content is based upon final release software whenever possible. Portions of the manuscript may be based upon pre-release versions supplied by software manufacturer(s). The author and the publisher make no representation or warranties of any kind with regard to the completeness or accuracy of the contents herein and accept no liability of any kind including but not limited to performance, merchantability, fitness for any particular purpose, or any losses or damages of any kind caused or alleged to be caused directly or indirectly from this book.

Manufactured in the United States of America

10 9 8 7 6 5 4 3 2

Dedicated to the memory of Julius Grosberg.—Robert Padjen

This book is dedicated to Erin for putting up with my hiding in my office and never coming out.—Sean Odom

Acknowledgments

We would like to thank Neil Edde, Linda Lee, and Jeff Kellum for helping to define and structure this book's contents. Thanks also to Rebecca Rider and Susan Berge for editing the chapters and to Matthew E. Luallen and Mark Tashiro for reviewing the chapters for technical accuracy. Elizabeth Campbell deserves a thank you for maintaining the schedule and keeping us on track. Thanks to Nanette Duffy, Amey Garber, Mae Lum, and Laurie O'Connell for proofreading the book and to Judy Fung and Susie Hendrickson for putting the finishing touches on the pages.
—Robert Padjen, Todd Lammle, and Sean Odom

It is unrealistic to thank my family for everything they have done for me. However, I will try, with gratitude to my mom and dad, wife Kristie, and boys Eddie and Tyler. Thanks to Sean and the Schwabbies for a unique and fun work environment, and to my new family at Callisma. Thanks to Natasha for bringing a bit of fun to the summer and our family (a break from writing), in addition to the Russian lessons—*spasiba bal'shoye*. In addition, I'd like to thank all the people at Sybex who work so very hard to produce these books, and the readers who provide us with valuable feedback to make our books stronger.
—Robert Padjen

There are a few people I wish to thank for getting me where I am today. First, Todd Lammle, for choosing me (the needle) out of the haystack (all the other Cisco writers) and letting my name grace the cover of a book with his name on it. Also, all those who hate my hiding place (office) since I started writing. In particular, Erin, Hillary, Sean Jr., Mikayla, and the rest of my family.
—Sean Odom

Contents at a Glance

Contents

Introduction

The new Cisco certifications reach beyond the popular certifications, such as the MCSE and CNE, to provide you with an indispensable factor in understanding today's network—insight into the Cisco world of internetworking. This book is intended to help you continue on your exciting new path toward obtaining CCNP and CCIE certification. Before reading this book, you should have at least read the *CCNA: Cisco Certified Network Associate Study Guide* (Sybex, 2000). While you can take the CCNP tests in any order, you should pass the CCNA exam before pursuing your CCNP. Many questions in the 640-505 exam are built upon the CCNA material. However, we have done everything possible to make sure you can pass the 640-505 exam by reading this book and practicing with Cisco routers.

Cisco—A Brief History

A lot of readers may already be familiar with Cisco and what they do. However, those of you who are new to the field, just coming in fresh from your MCSE, or those of you who have maybe 10 or more years in the field but wish to brush up on the new technology may appreciate a little background on Cisco.

In the early 1980s, Len and Sandy Bosack, a married couple who worked in different computer departments at Stanford University, were having trouble getting their individual systems to communicate (like many married people). So in their living room they created a gateway server that made it easier for their disparate computers in two different departments to communicate using the IP protocol. In 1984, they founded cisco Systems (notice the small *c*) with a small commercial gateway server product that changed networking forever. Some people think the name was intended to be San Francisco Systems but the paper got ripped on the way to the incorporation lawyers—who knows? In 1992, the company name was changed to Cisco Systems, Inc.

The first product the company marketed was called the Advanced Gateway Server (AGS). Then came the Mid-Range Gateway Server (MGS), the Compact Gateway Server (CGS), the Integrated Gateway Server (IGS), and the AGS+. Cisco calls these "the old alphabet soup products." In 1993, Cisco came out with the amazing 4000 router and then created the even more amazing 7000, 2000, and 3000 series routers. These are still around and evolving (almost daily, it seems).

Cisco has since become an unrivaled worldwide leader in networking for the Internet. Its networking solutions can easily connect users who work from diverse devices on disparate networks. Cisco products make it simple for people to access and transfer information without regard to differences in time, place, or platform.

In the big picture, Cisco provides end-to-end networking solutions that customers can use to build an efficient, unified information infrastructure of their own or to connect to someone else's. This is an important piece in the Internet/networking-industry puzzle because a common architecture that delivers consistent network services to all users is now a functional imperative. Because Cisco offers such a broad range of networking and Internet services and capabilities, users needing regular access to their local network or the Internet can do so unhindered, making Cisco's wares indispensable.

Cisco answers this need with a wide range of hardware products that form information networks using the Cisco Internetwork Operating System (IOS) software. This software provides network services, paving the way for networked technical support and professional services to maintain and optimize all network operations.

Along with the Cisco IOS, one of the services Cisco created to help support the vast amount of hardware it has engineered is the Cisco Certified Internetwork Expert (CCIE) program, which was designed specifically to equip people to effectively manage the vast quantity of installed Cisco networks. The business plan is simple: If you want to sell more Cisco equipment and install more Cisco networks, ensure that the networks you install run properly.

However, having a fabulous product line isn't all it takes to guarantee the huge success Cisco enjoys—lots of companies with great products are now defunct. If you have complicated products designed to solve complicated problems, you need knowledgeable people who are fully capable of installing, managing, and troubleshooting them. That part isn't easy, so Cisco began the CCIE program to equip people to support these complicated networks. This program, known colloquially as the Doctorate of Networking, has also been successful, due primarily to its extreme difficulty. Cisco continuously monitors the program, changing it as it sees fit, to make sure it remains pertinent and accurately reflects the demands of today's internet-working business environments.

Building upon the highly successful CCIE program, Cisco Career Certifications permit you to become certified at various levels of technical proficiency, spanning the disciplines of network design and support. So whether you're beginning a career, changing careers, securing your present position, or seeking to refine and promote your position, this is the book for you!

Cisco's Network Support Certifications

Cisco has created new certifications that will help you get the coveted CCIE, as well as aid prospective employers in measuring skill levels. Before these new certifications, you took only one test and were then faced with the lab, which made it difficult to succeed. With these new certifications, which add a better approach to preparing for that almighty lab, Cisco has opened doors that few were allowed through before. So, what are these new certifications, and how do they help you get your CCIE?

Cisco Certified Network Associate (CCNA) 2.0

The CCNA certification is the first in the new line of Cisco certifications and is a precursor to all current Cisco certifications. With the new certification programs, Cisco has created a stepping-stone approach to CCIE certification. Now you can become a Cisco Certified Network Associate for the meager cost of Sybex's *CCNA: Cisco Certified Network Associate Study Guide,* plus $100 for the test. And you don't have to stop there—you can continue with your studies and achieve a higher certification called the Cisco Certified Network Professional (CCNP). Someone with a CCNP has all the skills and knowledge needed to attempt the CCIE lab. However, because no textbook can take the place of practical experience, we'll discuss what else you need to be ready for the CCIE lab shortly.

Check www.routersim.com for a cost-effective Cisco router simulator.

Cisco Certified Network Professional (CCNP) 2.0

Cisco Certified Network Professional (CCNP), Cisco's new certification, has opened up many opportunities for those individuals wishing to become Cisco-certified but lacking the training, the expertise, or the bucks to pass the notorious and often failed two-day Cisco torture lab. The new Cisco certifications will truly provide exciting new opportunities for the CNE and MCSE who are unsure of how to advance to a higher level.

So, you may be thinking, "Great, what do I do after passing the CCNA exam?" Well, if you want to become a CCIE in Routing and Switching (the most popular certification), understand that there's more than one path to that much-coveted CCIE certification. The first way is to continue studying and become a Cisco Certified Network Professional (CCNP), which means four more tests, in addition to the CCNA certification.

The CCNP program will prepare you to understand and comprehensively tackle the internetworking issues of today and beyond—and it is not limited to the Cisco world. You will undergo an immense metamorphosis, vastly increasing your knowledge and skills through the process of obtaining these certifications.

Todd Lammle offers a hands-on Cisco seminar (www.1ammle.com) that provides two Cisco courses in one week of training. The Cisco CCNA/CCNP/CCDP seminars include CCNA/CCDA, Routing/Support, and Remote Access/Switching. Each course is six days long, and every student receives two routers and a switch to configure.

While you don't need to be a CCNP or even a CCNA to take the CCIE lab, it's extremely helpful if you already have these certifications.

What Skills Do You Need to Become a CCNP?

Cisco demands a certain level of proficiency for its CCNP certification. In addition to mastering the skills required for the CCNA, you should have the following skills for the CCNP:

- Installing, configuring, operating, and troubleshooting complex routed LAN, routed WAN, and switched LAN networks, along with dial-access services

- Understanding complex networks, such as IP, IGRP, IPX, async routing, AppleTalk, extended access lists, IP RIP, route redistribution, IPX RIP, route summarization, OSPF, VLSM, BGP, serial, IGRP, Frame Relay, ISDN, ISL, X.25, DDR, PSTN, PPP, VLANs, Ethernet, ATM

LANE–emulation, access lists, 802.10, FDDI, and transparent and translational bridging

To meet the CCNP requirements, you must be able to perform the following:

- Install and/or configure a network to increase bandwidth, quicken network response times, and improve reliability and quality of service.

- Maximize performance through campus LANs, routed WANs, and remote access.

- Improve network security.

- Create a global intranet.

- Provide access security to campus switches and routers.

- Provide increased switching and routing bandwidth—end-to-end resiliency services.

- Provide custom queuing and routed priority services.

How Do You Become a CCNP?

After becoming a CCNA, you must take four exams to get your CCNP:

Exam 640-503: Routing   This exam continues to build on the fundamentals learned in the CCNA course. It focuses on large multiprotocol internetworks and how to manage them with access lists, queuing, tunneling, route distribution, router maps, BGP, OSPF, and route summarization.

Exam 640-504: Switching   This exam tests your knowledge of the 1900 and 5000 series of Catalyst switches. Sybex's *CCNP: Switching Study Guide* (Fall 2000) covers all the objectives you need to understand to pass the Switching exam.

Exam 640-506: Support   This exam tests you on the Cisco IOS troubleshooting information available. You must be able to troubleshoot Ethernet and Token Ring LANS, IP, IPX, and AppleTalk networks, as well as ISDN, PPP, and Frame Relay networks. Sybex's *CCNP: Switching Study Guide* covers all the exam objectives.

Exam 640-505: Remote Access   This exam tests your knowledge of installing, configuring, monitoring, and troubleshooting Cisco ISDN and dial-up access products. You must understand PPP, ISDN, Frame Relay, and authentication. This book covers all the exam objectives.

If you hate tests, you can take fewer of them by signing up for the CCNA exam and the Support exam and then taking just one more long exam called the Foundation R/S exam (640-509). Doing this also gives you your CCNP—but beware, it's a really long test that fuses all the material listed previously into one exam. Good luck! However, by taking this exam, you get three tests for the price of two, which saves you $100 (if you pass). Some people think it's easier to take the Foundation R/S exam because you can leverage the areas that you would score higher in against the areas in which you wouldn't.

Remember that test objectives and tests can change at any time without notice. Always check the Cisco Web site (www.cisco.com) for the most up-to-date information.

Cisco Certified Internetwork Expert (CCIE)

You've become a CCNP, and now you fix your sights on getting your Cisco Certified Internetwork Expert (CCIE) in Routing and Switching—what do you do next? Cisco recommends that before you take the lab, you take test 640-025: Cisco Internetwork Design (CID) and the Cisco authorized course called Installing and Maintaining Cisco Routers (IMCR). By the way, no Prometric test for IMCR exists at the time of this writing, and Cisco recommends a *minimum* of two years of on-the-job experience before taking the CCIE lab. After jumping those hurdles, you then have to pass the CCIE-R/S Exam Qualification (exam 350-001) before taking the actual lab.

To become a CCIE, Cisco recommends the following:

1. Attend all the recommended courses at an authorized Cisco training center and pony up around $15,000–$20,000, depending on your corporate discount.

2. Pass the Drake/Prometric exam ($200 per exam—so hopefully you'll pass it the first time).

3. Pass the two-day, hands-on lab at Cisco. This costs $1,000 per lab, which many people fail two or more times. (Some never make it through!) Also, because you can take the exam only in San Jose, California; Research Triangle Park, North Carolina; Sydney, Australia;

Halifax, Nova Scotia; Tokyo, Japan; or Brussels, Belgium, you might just need to add travel costs to that $1,000. Cisco has added new sites lately for the CCIE lab; it is best to check the Cisco Web site for the most current information.

What Skills Do You Need to Become a CCIE?

The CCIE Routing and Switching exam includes the advanced technical skills that are required to maintain optimum network performance and reliability, as well as advanced skills in supporting diverse networks that use disparate technologies. CCIEs just don't have problems getting jobs; these experts are basically inundated with offers to work for six-figure salaries! But that's because it isn't easy to attain the level of capability that is mandatory for Cisco's CCIE. For example, a CCIE must have the following skills down pat:

- Installing, configuring, operating, and troubleshooting complex routed LAN, routed WAN, switched LAN, and ATM LANE networks, along with dial-access services

- Diagnosing and resolving network faults

- Using packet/frame analysis and Cisco debugging tools

- Documenting and reporting the problem-solving processes used

- Having general LAN/WAN knowledge, including data encapsulation and layering; windowing and flow control, and their relation to delay; error detection and recovery; link-state, distance vector, and switching algorithms; management, monitoring, and fault isolation

- Having knowledge of a variety of corporate technologies—including major services provided by Desktop, WAN, and Internet groups—as well as the functions; addressing structures; and routing, switching, and bridging implications of each of their protocols

- Having knowledge of Cisco-specific technologies, including router/switch platforms, architectures, and applications; communication servers; protocol translation and applications; configuration commands and system/network impact; and LAN/WAN interfaces, capabilities, and applications

- Designing, configuring, installing, and verifying voice-over-IP and voice-over-ATM networks

Cisco's Network Design Certifications

In addition to the network support certifications, Cisco has created another certification track for network designers. The two certifications within this track are the Cisco Certified Design Associate (CCDA) and Cisco Certified Design Professional (CCDP) certifications. If you're reaching for the CCIE stars, we highly recommend the CCNP and CCDP certifications before attempting the lab (or attempting to advance your career). These certifications will give you the knowledge to design routed LAN, routed WAN, and switched LAN and ATM LANE networks.

Cisco Certified Design Associate (CCDA)

To become a CCDA, you must pass the DCN (Designing Cisco Networks) test (640-441). To pass this test, you must understand how to do the following:

- Design simple routed LAN, routed WAN, and switched LAN and ATM LANE networks.

- Use Network-layer addressing.

- Filter with access lists.

- Use and propagate VLAN.

- Size networks.

Sybex's *CCDA: Cisco Certified Design Associate Study Guide* (1999) is the most cost-effective way to study for and pass your CCDA exam.

Cisco Certified Design Professional (CCDP) 2.0

If you're already a CCNP and want to get your CCDP, you can simply take the CID 640-025 test. If you're not yet a CCNP, however, you must take the CCDA, CCNA, Routing, Switching, Remote Access, and CID exams.
CCDP certification skills include the following:

- Designing complex routed LAN, routed WAN, and switched LAN and ATM LANE networks

- Building upon the base level of the CCDA technical knowledge

CCDPs must also demonstrate proficiency in the following:

- Network-layer addressing in a hierarchical environment
- Traffic management with access lists
- Hierarchical network design
- VLAN use and propagation
- Performance considerations: required hardware and software; switching engines; memory, cost, and minimization

For used Cisco gear, check out www.netfix.com.

What Does This Book Cover?

This book covers everything you need to pass the CCNP Remote Access exam. It teaches you how to use Cisco routers to connect remote LANs together using remote access devices and IOS software.

- Chapter 1 introduces you to Cisco's solutions to Remote Access. This chapter is a high-level overview of the IOS solutions we discuss throughout the book and will introduce you to the concepts needed to understand to pass the Remote Access exam.

- Chapter 2 discusses the asynchronous connection types and how to configure, verify, and maintain async connections in your network.

- Chapter 3 covers the Point-to-Point Protocol (PPP); the different protocols used within the PPP stack; and how to configure, maintain, and verify PPP in your network. This chapter discusses PPP authentication, but Chapter 5 covers the configuration of PPP authentication.

- Chapter 4 discusses the Windows 95/98 dial-up connection, how to configure a client, and how to verify the connection.

- Chapter 5 provides an in-depth discussion on ISDN and how to use it in your network. This chapter presents the beginnings of ISDN, how to configure and maintain ISDN, and how to provide security and verify your connections.

- Chapter 6 covers the 700 series router. If you are planning to take the Remote Access exam, you must be able to configure a 700 series ISDN router. If you are not planning to take the exam, you should skim this chapter, because the 700 series router is not typically used in production networks any longer.

- Chapter 7 provides you with an understanding of X.25 and Link Access Procedure, Balanced (LAPB) and how they relate to the Remote Access exam. It is unlikely you will install and maintain X.25 in the U.S. these days, but you must know a little about it to pass the Remote Access exam.

- Chapter 8 gives you an extensive background in Frame Relay technology. This chapter discusses the beginnings of Frame Relay, how it has progressed, how to configure and maintain it, and how to troubleshoot it.

- Chapter 9 discusses the queuing and compression methods available through the Cisco IOS.

- Chapter 10 covers Network Address Translation (NAT) and Port Address Translation (PAT) and how to configure them in your network.

- Chapter 11 provides the information you need for understanding authentication, authorization, and accounting (AAA) and how to configure AAA on Cisco routers. This is important information to know for your Remote Access exam.

- Appendix A is a practice exam. If you think you are ready for the CCNP Remote Access exam, see if you can get by this practice exam. A second practice exam is located on the CD as well.

- Appendix B lists all the Cisco IOS commands used in this book. It is a great reference if you need to look up what a certain command does and is used for.

- Appendix C contains a list of Web-based resources for network administrators. Here you'll find various users groups, standards organizations, certification study groups, and more.

- The Glossary is a handy resource for Cisco terms. This is a great tool for understanding some of the more obscure terms used in this book.

Each chapter begins with a list of the topics covered that are related to the CCNP Remote Access test, so make sure to read them over before working through the chapter. In addition, each chapter ends with review questions specifically designed to help you retain the knowledge presented. To really nail down your skills, read each question carefully, and if possible, work through the chapters' hands-on labs.

Where Do You Take the Exams?

You may take the exams at any of the more than 800 Sylvan Prometric Authorized Testing Centers around the world. For the location of a testing center near you, call (800) 755-3926. Outside the United States and Canada, contact your local Sylvan Prometric Registration Center.

To register for a Cisco Certified Network Professional exam:

1. Determine the number of the exam you want to take. (The Remote Access exam number is 640-505.)

2. Register with the nearest Sylvan Prometric Registration Center. At this point, you will be asked to pay in advance for the exam. At the time of this writing, the exams are $100 each and must be taken within one year of payment. You can schedule exams up to six weeks in advance or as soon as one working day prior to the day you wish to take it. If something comes up and you need to cancel or reschedule your exam appointment, contact Sylvan Prometric at least 24 hours in advance. Same-day registration isn't available for the Cisco tests.

3. When you schedule the exam, you'll get instructions regarding all appointment and cancellation procedures, the ID requirements, and information about the testing center location.

Tips for Taking Your CCNP Exam

The CCNP Remote Access test contains about 70 questions to be completed in 90 minutes. However, the amount of exam questions and time may vary.

Many questions on the exam have answer choices that at first glance look identical—especially the syntax questions! Remember to read through the choices carefully because "close enough" doesn't cut it. If you get commands in the wrong order or forget one measly character, you'll get the question wrong. So, to practice, do the hands-on exercises at the end of the chapters over and over again until they feel natural to you.

Unlike Microsoft or Novell tests, the exam has answer choices that are syntactically similar—although some syntax is dead wrong, it is usually just *subtly* wrong. Some other syntax choices may be right, but they're shown in the wrong order. Cisco does split hairs, and they're not at all averse to giving you classic trick questions. Here's an example:

`access-list 101 deny ip any eq 23` denies Telnet access to all systems.

This statement looks correct because most people refer to the port number (23) and think, "Yes, that's the port used for Telnet." The catch is that you can't filter IP on port numbers (only TCP and UDP).

Also, never forget that the right answer is the Cisco answer. In many cases, more than one appropriate answer is presented, but the *correct* answer is the one that Cisco recommends.

Here are some general tips for exam success:

- Arrive early at the exam center, so you can relax and review your study materials.

- Read the questions *carefully*. Don't just jump to conclusions. Make sure you're clear about *exactly* what each question asks.

- Don't leave any questions unanswered. They count against you.

- When answering multiple-choice questions you're unsure about, use the process of elimination to get rid of the obviously incorrect answers first. Doing this greatly improves your odds if you need to make an educated guess.

- You can no longer move forward and backward through the Cisco exams (except the CCIE written exam and the CCDA exam), so double-check your answer before moving to the next question.

After you complete an exam, you'll get immediate, online notification of your pass or fail status, a printed Examination Score Report that indicates your pass or fail status, and your exam results by section. (The test administrator will give you the printed score report.) Test scores are automatically forwarded to Cisco within five working days after you take the test, so you don't need to send your score to them. If you pass the exam, you'll receive confirmation from Cisco, typically within two to four weeks.

How to Use This Book

This book can provide a solid foundation for the serious effort of preparing for the Cisco Certified Network Professional Remote Access exam. To best benefit from this book, use the following study method:

1. Take the assessment test immediately following this introduction. (The answers are at the end of the test.) Carefully read over the explanations for any question you get wrong, and note which chapters the material comes from. This information should help you plan your study strategy.

2. Study each chapter carefully, making sure you fully understand the information and the test objectives listed at the beginning of each chapter. Pay extra close attention to any chapter where you missed questions in the assessment test.

3. Complete all hands-on exercises in the chapter, referring to the chapter so you understand the reason for each step you take. If you do not have Cisco equipment available, make sure to study the examples carefully. Also, check www.routersim.com for a router simulator.

4. Answer the review questions related to each chapter. (The answers appear at the end of the chapter, after the review questions.) Note the questions that confuse you, and study those sections of the book again.

5. Take the practice exam in Appendix A. The answers appear at the end of the exam.

6. Try your hand at the bonus practice exam that is included on the CD that comes with this book. The questions in this exam appear only on the CD. This will give you a complete overview of what you can expect to see on the real thing.

7. Use the products on the CD included with this book. The electronic flashcards, the Boson Software utilities, and the EdgeTest exam preparation software have all been specifically picked to help you study for and pass your exam. Study on the road with the *CCNP: Remote Access Study Guide* electronic book in PDF, and be sure to test yourself with the electronic flashcards.

The electronic flashcards can be used on your Windows computer or on your Palm device.

8. Make sure to read the "Key Terms" and "Commands in This Chapter" lists at the end of the chapters. Appendix B includes all the commands used in the book, including explanations for each command.

To learn all the material covered in this book, you'll have to apply yourself regularly and with discipline. Try to set aside the same time period every day to study, and select a comfortable and quiet place to do so. If you work hard, you will be surprised at how quickly you learn this material. All the best!

What's on the CD?

We worked hard to provide some really great tools on the CD to help you with your certification process. All of the following tools should be loaded on your workstation when studying for the test.

The EdgeTest for Cisco Remote Access Test Preparation Software

Provided by EdgeTek Learning Systems, the test preparation software prepares you to successfully pass the Remote Access exam. In this test engine you will find all the questions from the book, plus an additional bonus practice exam that appears exclusively on the CD. You can take the assessment test, test yourself by chapter, take the practice exam that appears in the book or on the CD, or take an exam randomly generated from any of the questions.

To find more test-simulation software for all Cisco and NT exams, look for the exam link on www.lammle.com and www.boson.com.

Electronic Flashcards for PC and Palm Devices

To prepare for the exam, you can read this book, study the review questions at the end of each chapter, and work through the practice exams included in the book and on the CD. But wait, there's more! Test yourself with the flashcards included on the CD. If you can get through these difficult questions and understand the answers, you'll know you're ready for the CCNP Remote Access exam.

The flashcards include more than 150 questions specifically written to hit you hard and make sure you are ready for the exam. Between the review questions, practice exams, and flashcards, you'll be more than prepared for the exam.

Dictionary of Networking and *CCNP: Remote Access Study Guide* in PDF

Sybex offers the Cisco Certification books on CD so you can read them on your PC or laptop. The *Dictionary of Networking* and the *CCNP: Remote Access Study Guide* are in Adobe Acrobat format. Acrobat Reader 4 with Search is also included on the CD. This will be helpful to readers who travel and don't want to carry a book, as well as to those who prefer reading from their computer.

Boson Software Utilities

Boson Software is an impressive company: They provide many free services to help you, the student. Boson has the best Cisco exam preparation questions on the market at a very nice price. On this book's CD, they have provided the following:

- IP Subnetter
- eeSuperPing
- System-Logging
- Wildcard Mask Checker
- Router GetPass

CCNA Virtual Lab AVI Demo Files

The *CCNA Virtual Lab e-trainer* provides a router and switch simulator to help you gain hands-on experience without having to buy expensive Cisco gear. The demos are AVI files that you can play in RealPlayer, which is included on the CD. The files will help you gain an understanding of the product features and the labs that the routers and switches can perform. Read more about the CCNA Virtual Lab e-trainer at http://www.sybex.com/cgi-bin/ rd_bookpg.pl?2728back.html. You can upgrade this product at www.routersim.com.

How to Contact the Authors

To contact Robert Padjen, e-mail him at `networker@popmail.com`. Robert provides consulting services to a wide variety of clients, including Charles Schwab and the California State Automobile Association.

You can reach Todd Lammle through GlobalNet System Solutions, Inc. (`www.lammle.com`)—his training and systems integration company in Colorado—or e-mail him at `todd@lammle.com`.

To contact Sean Odom, e-mail him at `sodom@rcsis.com`. Also check out his Web site: `www.TheQuestForCertification.com`.

Assessment Test

1. When you are setting up a long distance connection, which of the following is typically the lowest cost solution?

   A. Frame Relay

   B. ISDN

   C. Leased Line

   D. Analog dial-up

2. What is the default encapsulation for serial circuits on Cisco routers?

   A. PPP

   B. ATM

   C. HDLC

   D. SDLC

3. Which of the following is true regarding ISDN PRI in Europe and the United States?

   A. The standards are identical.

   B. Primary rate in Europe is equal to BRI in the US.

   C. The two are different due to Europe's E-1 based carrier. The US uses T-1.

   D. ISDN is not available in Europe.

4. The LZW algorithm performs what function?

   A. Error correction

   B. Compression

   C. Hardware flowcontrol

   D. None of the above

5. Which of the following does a UART perform?

   A. Compression

   B. Error correction

   C. Buffering

   D. Compression and error correction

6. What is the modemcap database?

   A. A table of modem configuration information

   B. A listing of hostnames

   C. A set of compression formulas

   D. None of the above

7. Which of the following is a valid DLCI for use on a serial interface?

   A. 0

   B. 15

   C. 1008

   D. 1023

   E. None of the above

8. You have one corporate office and many small remote offices that transmit only bursty data transfers. Which WAN technology should you consider?

   A. Frame Relay

   B. X.25

   C. Dedicated circuit

   D. TDM circuit

   E. Not possible

9. A Frame Relay switch is getting congested. What type of message would it transmit to the sender of the frame, indicating that congestion is occurring?

A. BECN

B. FECN

C. DE

D. CIR

E. CR

10. Which of the following commands is a valid map class?

A. RouterA# `frame-relay map-class name`

B. RouterA(config-if)# `frame-relay map-class name`

C. RouterA(config-if)#`map-class frame-relay name`

D. RouterA(config)#`map-class frame-relay name`

11. Which of the following enables traffic shaping on an interface?

A. RouterA(config-if)#`frame-relay class name`

B. RouterA(config)#`frame-relay class name`

C. RouterA(config)#`frame-relay traffic-shaping`

D. RouterA(config-if)#`frame-relay traffic-shaping`

12. The NRN server type only supports which one of the following?

A. IP

B. IPX

C. NetBEUI

D. All of the above

13. Token-based security solutions are sometimes called which of the following?

    A. Something you have and something you know

    B. Random key

    C. Lock and key

    D. IPSec

14. What does the MD in MD4 and MD5 stand for?

    A. Manual distribution

    B. Multilink datagram

    C. Message digest

    D. Message distribution

15. Packet mode connections usually

    A. Pass through the router

    B. Terminate at the router

    C. Require the use of PPP

    D. Either A or B

16. The command `aaa authorization if-authenticated` performs which of the following functions?

    A. Allows only authorized resources to attempt authentication

    B. Allows only connections via console connections

    C. Allows all functions, if the user is correctly authenticated

    D. None of the above

17. An administrator needs to configure compression on an AS5300 for a remote user pool that includes 1600 and 700 series routers. The administrator should use which of the following?

   A. MPPC

   B. Stac

   C. Predictor

   D. All of the above

18. An address pool or DHCP might be preferred to manual address allocation for which of the following reasons?

   A. Conservation of addresses

   B. Exhaustion of addresses

   C. Simplification of client configuration

   D. Complexity of client configuration

19. Can PPP support 802.1d and IBM bridging functions?

   A. PPP cannot support either function.

   B. PPP can only support 802.1d.

   C. PPP can only support IBM bridging.

   D. PPP can support both functions.

20. Which of these is not a characteristic of CHAP? (Select all that apply.)

   A. MD5 is used as the default authentication algorithm.

   B. It is a two-way handshake.

   C. C023 is the Authentication-Protocol.

   D. It uses TCP for Transport.

21. What protocol is used for signaling on ISDN?

   A. LAPB

   B. LAPD

   C. LAXD

   D. ITU I.430

22. Debug ISDN Q.931 provides information about which of the following? (Select all that apply.)

   A. TEI negotiation

   B. Bearer capability

   C. B channel ID

   D. B and C

23. What is the correct syntax for an ISDN dialer map?

   A. `dialer map ip 192.168.254.2 8358661`

   B. `dialer string 8358661`

   C. `isdn dialer map 192.168.254.2 name R2 8358661`

   D. `isdn dialer string 8358661`

24. What is the interface name for the D channel on a T1-based PRI?

   A. Port 0:d

   B. Interface ISDN PRI0/0

   C. Interface BRI0

   D. Interface Serial0:23

25. Does the Cisco 766M run the same IOS as the 2501?

  A. Yes.

  B. Yes, but only the IP version of the IOS.

  C. No, but its command syntax is identical.

  D. No, both the operating system and the command syntax are different.

26. Snapshot routing provides what benefit?

  A. Routing updates do not need to keep the ISDN BRI up, reducing access costs.

  B. Routing tables can be moved into the fast-switched cache.

  C. A single IP address can represent multiple hosts.

  D. Routes can be redistributed into another protocol.

27. The 700 series routers support which of the following?

  A. ADSL

  B. X.25

  C. ISDN BRI

  D. ISDN PRI

28. Which of the following is not a feature of the 700 series router?

  A. Caller ID

  B. BGP routing

  C. Four-port hub connection services

  D. Bonding

29. Which of the following is not an LAPB frame type?

   A. I-Frame

   B. S-Frame

   C. U-Frame

   D. D-Frame

30. Which of the following is used to assemble and disassemble X.25 frames when a terminal is too simple to interpret X.25 packets?

   A. Switch

   B. Router

   C. PAD

   D. Modem

   E. Transceiver

31. In which of the following DNIC zones would the United States reside?

   A. Zone 1

   B. Zone 2

   C. Zone 3

   D. Zone 4

   E. Zone 5

   F. Zone 6

32. Which of the following command syntaxes can be used with the x25 modulo command? (Choose the two best answers.)

   A. 8

   B. 64

   C. 128

   D. 512

33. Which of the following commands allows an X.25 interface to be unnumbered?

    A. x25 address

    B. x25 map

    C. encapsulation x25

    D. x25 modulo

34. What type of compression compresses only the data, not the header?

    A. Cisco

    B. IETF

    C. TCP header

    D. Payload

    E. Link

35. What compression method compresses both the header and data fields?

    A. Cisco

    B. IETF

    C. TCP header

    D. Payload

    E. Link

36. What type of queuing is the default for serial links under 1.544Mbps on Cisco routers?

    A. Link

    B. Payload

    C. WF queuing

    D. Header

37. Which of the following commands is correct for configuring a custom queue list that takes all packets received on ethernet 0 and places them in the first queue?

A. `queue-list 1 interface Ethernet0 1`

B. `interface ethernet 0 queue-list 1`

C. `queueing-list 1 ethernet 0 1`

D. `queue-list e0 list 1`

38. Which of the following commands will show the custom queues configured on your router?

A. `show custom`

B. `show all queues`

C. `show queuing custom`

D. `show queueing custom`

39. Which of the following types of entries in the NAT table indicates an IP address and port pair?

A. Simple translation entry

B. Extended translation entry

C. Global translation entry

D. Inside translation entry

40. True/False: NAT hides end-to-end IP addresses, rendering some applications unusable.

A. True

B. False

41. True/False: NAT allows you to increase or decrease the number of globally routable addresses without changing any hosts on the network, with the exception of the NAT border router.

   A. True

   B. False

42. True/False: You should implement an access list to deny all inside IP addresses so they do not filter through the router into the outside network.

   A. True

   B. False

43. True/False: Port Address Translation will deny traffic from all well-known port numbers, such as ports used by FTP by default.

   A. True

   B. False

Answers to Assessment Test Questions

1. A. Frame Relay provides the advantage of being distance insensitive, thus reducing its cost. For more information, see Chapter 1.

2. C. The HDLC encapsulation is used by default on Cisco's serial interfaces. For more information on serial encapsulations, see Chapter 1.

3. C. Europe's phone system was designed around a 2.048 Mbps E-1 carrier, which differs from the US T-1 standard. This difference is carried into the ISDN environment, which uses T-1 and E-1 for PRI interfaces and aggregation. For more information, see Chapter 1.

4. B. Limpel, Ziv, and Welch developed a compression algorithm. For more information, see Chapter 2.

5. C. A UART buffers incoming serial data. More advanced UARTs buffer outbound data as well. For more information, see Chapter 2.

6. A. The modemcap database contains modem configuration information that the router can send to the modem in order to interoperate. For more information, see Chapter 2.

7. E. Valid DLCIs assignments are 16-1007. For more information about Frame Relay see Chapter 8.

8. A. Frame Relay is perfect for companies with many remote sites that have burst data transfers. See Chapter 8 for more information on Frame Relay.

9. A. Backward Explicit Congestion Notification is used to tell a transmitting router that the frame switch is congested and to slow the transmit rate down. See Chapter 8 for more information on congestion control with Frame Relay.

10. D. To create a map class, use the `map-class frame-relay name` command. See Chapter 8 for more information on Frame Relay traffic shaping.

11. D. The interface command `frame-relay traffic-shaping` is used to enable an interface to accept map class parameters. See Chapter 8 for more information on traffic shaping with Frame Relay.

12. B. Only NRN supports the IPX protocol. For more information, see Chapter 4.

13. A. Tokens work like ATM cards—you have the card, but you still need the PIN (personal identification number) when you go to the bank. The other answers are intended to sound similar. For more information, see Chapter 4.

14. C. Message digest, type 4 and 5, is used to hash passwords in Windows dial-up networking. For more information, see Chapter 4.

15. A. While packet mode includes PPP, among others, these connections generally pass through the router. PPP is not required. See Chapter 11 for more information on packet mode connections.

16. C. The `authorization if-authenticated` command is quite powerful—it authorizes all authenticated connections. See Chapter 11 for more information.

17. B. Recall that the Cisco 700 only supports Stac, making this the only viable option. For more information, see Chapter 3.

18. A, C. DHCP can greatly simplify client configuration—in fact, DHCP can negate the need for any client configuration. In addition, DHCP can conserve addresses as only concurrent stations within the lease period require an address, as opposed to the total number of stations. To learn more about DHCP, see Chapter 3.

19. D. Both Spanning Tree and IBM bridging are supported. To learn more about PPP, see Chapter 3.

20. A. CHAP uses MD5 as its authentication algorithm. For more information about CHAP, see Chapter 5.

21. B. Link Access Procedure, D channel (LAPD) is used to carry ISDN signaling information over the D channel. For more information about LAPD, see Chapter 5.

22. D. Debug ISDN Q.931 provides information about Layer 3, including information about bearer capability and channel ID. For more information about Q.931, see Chapter 5.

23. A. A dialer map statement is used to map a destination IP address to a Dial Number or Username. For more information about dialer maps, see Chapter 5.

24. D. The PRI D channel on a T1-based PRI is channel 23. B channel numbers start at zero (0), with 23 being the 24th channel. For more information about PRIs, see Chapter 5.

25. D. The 700 series OS is very different from the rest of the Cisco router products' IOS. For more information, see Chapter 6.

26. A. Snapshot routing maintains a routing table without requiring constant updates. For more information, see Chapter 6.

27. C. The 700 series, as of this writing, only supports ISDN BRI and Ethernet. For more information, see Chapter 6.

28. B. The 700 series router does not support advanced routing protocols, including BGP. For more information, see Chapter 6.

29. D. There is no such frame as a D-Frame. The LAPB frame types are Information Frame, Supervisory Frame, and Unnumbered Frame. To learn more about LAPB frames see Chapter 7.

30. C. The packet assembler/disassembler (PAD) is used to collect data and output it to an X.25 packet that can be interpreted by an asynchronous or dumb terminal. To learn more about PAD see Chapter 7.

31. C. The United States would reside in Zone 3. To learn more about which continents reside in each DNIC zone, see Chapter 7.

32. A, C. The x25 modulo command configures the maximum number of packets allowable over a VC. To learn more about the x25 modulo command, see Chapter 7.

33. A. The x25 address command allows you to configure and the X.25 interface to be unnumbered. The x25 map command allows you to configure an IP address from the IP address pool, the encapsulation x25 defines the DTE/DCE encapsulation types, and the x25 modulo command allows you to configure an X.25 window size. To learn more about these commands, see Chapter 7.

34. D. Payload compression does not compress the header of a packet, only the data field. See Chapter 9 for more information on compression.

35. E. Link compression compresses the header and data fields of a packet. See Chapter 9 for more information on compression.

36. C. Weighted fair queuing (WFQ) is the default for serial links on Cisco routers. See Chapter 9 for more information on queuing.

37. A. The command is queue-list [#] interface [interface] [queue number]. See Chapter 9 for more information on queuing.

38. D. The command is show queueing custom. (Yes, *queuing* is misspelled.) See Chapter 9 for more information on queuing.

39. B. An extended translation entry into the NAT table indicates an entry with an IP address and port pair. The single translation entry indicates an inside IP address to globally routable IP address translation. For more information on NAT table entries, see Chapter 10.

40. A. Some applications that use IP addressing stop functioning when NAT is used because NAT hides the end-to-end IP address. This can be overcome by using fully qualified domain names or implementing static mappings. For more information on end-to-end IP addresses, see Chapter 10.

41. A. NAT is configured only on the router between the inside network and the outside network. NAT translates addresses for the inside network, and a simple configuration change in the NAT configuration on the NAT border router can change the global address pool without any manual change required on any network host. For more information on globally routable IP addresses, see Chapter 10.

42. B. Just the opposite is true. An access list should be created with a permit statement to allow the inside addresses to be handled by NAT for translation from the inside network to the outside network. This process occurs after policy routing is applied. For more information on how access lists work in conjunction with NAT and PAT, see Chapter 10.

43. B. PAT does not deny any traffic from well-known addresses by default. For more information on PAT and how PAT translates well-known IP addresses, see Chapter 10.

Chapter 1

Cisco Solutions for Remote Access

THE CCNP REMOTE ACCESS EXAM TOPICS COVERED IN THIS CHAPTER INCLUDE THE FOLLOWING:

- ✓ Defining remote access
- ✓ Choosing a Cisco remote connection product
- ✓ Cabling the WAN
- ✓ Assembling the WAN
- ✓ Introducing remote access technologies includes X.25, Frame Relay, and asynchronous dial-up

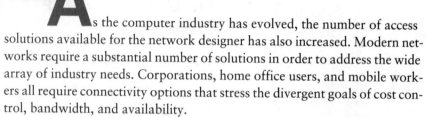

As the computer industry has evolved, the number of access solutions available for the network designer has also increased. Modern networks require a substantial number of solutions in order to address the wide array of industry needs. Corporations, home office users, and mobile workers all require connectivity options that stress the divergent goals of cost control, bandwidth, and availability.

Cisco has greatly augmented its product line to address some of these needs. The material covered in this book will focus on your ability to apply Cisco-centric solutions to the production networks of today. Architects and designers should always evaluate all vendors' solutions for each problem that they face; however, there is some merit to coming up with a strategic solution that maintains consistency along vendor and product lines. Many problems can arise from the interoperability issues that can result from the use of multiple vendors.

This text focuses on two goals. As with other study guides, the ultimate goal is to provide you with a substantial foundation of knowledge so you can successfully pass the Remote Access exam. The second goal is to provide you with information that relates to the live product networks that you will be challenged by every day. The benefit of this approach is that the live network experience you will encounter while reading will help you attain certification, and the certification will in turn provide you with a foundation to get experience with a live network.

This chapter begins with an overview of the fundamentals of remote access. In this section, you will learn about the various wide area network (WAN) connection types, WAN encapsulation protocols, and how to select a WAN protocol. In the next section, you will learn how to choose from among Cisco's remote connection products. And, in the final portion of this chapter, you will learn about WAN cabling and assembly issues. Developing a solid foundation in these topics is an extremely important part of your preparation for Cisco's Remote Access exam because it provides a framework for the subsequent chapters and the examination, not to mention real-world applications.

What Is Remote Access?

The term *remote access* is broadly defined as those services used to connect offices over a wide geographical area. These services are typically encompassed under the guise of a *wide area network (WAN)*. Traditionally, a wide area network uses a telecommunications provider to link distant locations; however, this definition is currently undergoing substantial change. Many providers are starting to offer Ethernet technologies over significant distances, although Ethernet is typically a local area network (LAN) technology. Unlike LANs, WANs usually use the telecommunications infrastructure—a group of services that are leased from service providers and phone companies.

Historically, the most common remote access installations have involved connectivity between fixed locations and a corporation's headquarters. Such installations are relatively simple once a design has been selected since the solution used for the first office is applicable to the hundredth. Designers need only concern themselves with scalability and availability—as long as the bandwidth needs of each office are comparable.

In the modern remote access design, the architect needs to focus on multiple solutions to address not only the branch office, but also the sales force (a typically mobile group) and telecommuters working from their homes. Residential installations usually have a different set of needs than office configurations, and T-1 and other high-speed access technologies are usually not available for home use.

With the deployment of Digital Subscriber Line (DSL) technologies, designers can provide the equivalence of T-1 bandwidth, and more, to the residential user. Actual T-1s are generally not available in residential settings, but they have been installed when the expense was warranted. This chapter will present a number of remote access technologies, including ISDN, Frame Relay, and asynchronous dial-up.

WAN Connection Types

The Remote Access exam is concerned primarily with five types of WAN connections. These are predominately older, more established technologies. The following are WAN connection types you can expect to see on the Remote Access exam:

- Asynchronous dial-up
- X.25
- ISDN
- Frame Relay
- Leased lines

Notably absent from this list are DSL-based systems, cable modems, Asynchronous Transfer Mode (ATM), wireless, and cellular technologies. Although the Remote Access exam was revised in early 2000, it does not yet address these, the newest trends in the marketplace.

Even though these are not covered yet, it is important to know a bit about these newer technologies. For instance, DSL and cable modem technologies have greatly enhanced the options available for home users. At present, neither is as flexible and universally available as asynchronous connections are, but both do offer substantial bandwidth at a relatively low cost. *Asynchronous Transfer Mode (ATM)* is a cell-based system similar in many respects to Frame Relay, although the use of fixed length cells can make ATM better suited to installations that integrate voice, video, and data. Wireless technologies include microwave, 802.11 LANs, laser and satellite systems, which typically require a fixed transmitter and receiver, although major strides are being made to add mobility. Cellular systems are very mobile, but they do not provide substantial bandwidth.

If you are a designer who is building a remote access solution, you will need to augment the technological material in this text in order to compose the best remote access solutions for your customer's needs.

For network architects and designers, it is recommended that you read the *CCDP: Cisco Internetwork Design Study Guide* by Robert Padjen with Todd Lammle (Sybex Inc., 2000) for more information on designing and integrating remote access solutions into the corporate network.

Asynchronous Dial-Up

Asynchronous dial-up is traditional modem-based access over the public analog phone network. The primary advantage of asynchronous dial-up is that it is available virtually everywhere. Unfortunately, its greatest limitation is bandwidth, which is currently limited to less than 56Kbps. In addition, asynchronous dial-up connections require a negotiation period, during which time traffic must be buffered and the user will experience delay.

Since hotels, homes, and customer sites are already supplied with the traditional level of connectivity, dial-up connections are primarily suited to those members in the workforce who are mobile. Such connections are a substantial benefit when compared to the other remote access technologies, each of which must be predefined or pre-provisioned.

Given the universal availability of analog circuits, most designers find that they still require dial-up installations to be a part of their remote access solution. Typically, Integrated Services Digital Network (ISDN) installations lend themselves to a dual role—as an ISDN PRI that can terminate 23 analog connections, or an assortment of ISDN B channels (user data bearer channels) and analog connections. This ability to service both ISDN digital connections and asynchronous dial-up connections can greatly ease facilities, configuration, and administration burdens.

Analog circuits are best suited for short-duration, low-bandwidth applications. Examples of this type of traffic would include terminal emulation and e-mail services. Limited file-transfer and client/server-based application activity could also use this connection.

In this study guide, you will see the terms asynchronous dial-up and analog used synonymously.

X.25

X.25 is a reliable Layer 2 and 3 protocol that can scale up to 2Mbps, although most installations stop at 56Kbps. The X.25 protocol was intended to provide reliable data transfer over unreliable circuits. Currently, X.25 is typically used for terminal emulation and small file transfers. Due to its low bandwidth and high overhead, X.25 is losing favor as a remote access technology. Originally, it was designed to address the higher error rates that were experienced on analog circuits. This high degree of overhead makes the protocol very inefficient but well suited to less-advanced telecommunications infrastructure, such as old carrier management systems.

Designers typically find that X.25 is one of the most widely available technologies on an international basis. This availability greatly adds to the desirability of the protocol. However, it is likely that demands for greater bandwidth and the proliferation of fiber-based networks will continue to erode X.25's market share. Although a migration to Ethernet has already begun, it is important to note that many telecommunications carriers continue to use X.25 for management of their switches and other systems.

Chapter 7 will explore the X.25 protocol in depth and describe its benefits and features.

Integrated Services Digital Network (ISDN)

Integrated Services Digital Network (ISDN) is the result of efforts to remove analog services from the network. In the 1960s, the American phone company, AT&T, realized that the network would be more efficient with digital services throughout. This included the residence, where most ISDN BRI (explained below) is found. However, the model scaled beyond this, and included aggregation and other interfaces that allowed efficient *MUXing*, or the consolidation of multiple small links into one large one.

There are two types of ISDN services available. The first, ISDN *Basic Rate Interface (BRI)*, provides for two 64Kbps channels (the bearer, or B, channels) and one 16Kbps channel (the D channel), which can carry user data. The second type of ISDN service is called *Primary Rate Interface (PRI)*, and it can provide 23 64Kbps channels for user data and one 64Kbps channel (D channel) for signaling.

Please note that the 16Kbps channel in ISDN BRI is used for signaling; however, many providers permit the transit of user data using this bandwidth. This is frequently marketed as "always-on" ISDN. ISDN PRI uses a single 64Kbps channel for signaling.

Some ISDN BRI installations limit each B channel to 56Kbps.

The primary advantage of ISDN is its ability to provide faster access than would be available from traditional asynchronous dial-up connections. Unfortunately, the service is not as widely available as traditional analog services, and it tends to be much more costly. ISDN is typically used in scenarios including low-bandwidth video, low-bandwidth data, and voice services. It is important to note that each of the two ISDN channels can provide the user with a traditional analog dial-up connection.

ISDN services are quickly being replaced in the United States by DSL services. Digital Subscriber Line connections are currently available at over one megabit per second and are becoming more widely available. However, substantial restrictions exist regarding the distance over which these connections can be set up (the maximum distance is 18,000 feet, or under three miles from the central office to the residence), and some sources predict that up to 40 percent of homes will be too far from the central office to receive the service.

ISDN is well suited for most applications, including file transfers. However, its high per-minute pricing makes it impractical when it is needed for more than a couple hours per day. Frame Relay, which you will learn about next, is typically a better solution for higher bandwidth, long duration connections.

Frame Relay

Frame Relay is a logical, low-overhead transport protocol that removes much of the overhead found in X.25. Frames are marked with a DLCI, or data link connection identifier, that provides direction to the switch regarding frame forwarding. As such, frames in Frame Relay are Layer 2 elements. In many companies, setting up Frame Relay services between central locations and remote offices is very popular. The primary benefit of Frame Relay is that it is traditionally tariffed to be distance-insensitive—this means that a connection that crosses the United States will be comparable in cost to that of a connection across town. In addition, Frame Relay services are available internationally from many providers.

Frame Relay, in addition to DSL, is becoming more accepted in the telecommuter workspace. Telecommuters are finding that connections are required for more than a few hours per day—a threshold that makes ISDN more costly than the other options. In addition, ISDN is incapable of expanding beyond 128Kbps without using PRI services. Frame Relay is available in a myriad of bandwidths, up to and including T-1. New variations on Frame Relay are increasing this performance characteristic.

Note that ISDN cannot scale beyond 128Kbps in user data on a single pair of B channels. Just as two B channels can be bonded together into a single logical data conduit, it is possible to bond multiple ISDN BRI circuits into a single logical data stream. Chapter 3 discusses bonding in greater detail.

For the network designer, there are two factors to consider when deploying Frame Relay: Frame Relay is available with a *Committed Information Rate (CIR)*, and Frame Relay allows multiple *Permanent Virtual Circuits (PVCs)* to terminate at a single connection point on the router. A PVC is a previously defined logical path through the network. The DLCI is used to determine which PVC is to be used. *Switched Virtual Circuits (SVCs)*, are alternatives to PVCs. SVCs are similar to PVCs, but they are not predefined and static. Before data can be transmitted using SVCs, a path must be established dynamically through the network.

The CIR is best thought of as a guaranteed amount of bandwidth available on a PVC. This figure may be substantially lower than the capacity of the circuit itself. The corporation will pay for the bandwidth guaranteed by the CIR, and any traffic that exceeds the CIR will be handled on a best-effort basis. Thus, a company can obtain better throughput than that for which it is being charged.

The ability of Frame Relay to allow multiple PVCs to terminate at a single physical connection point on the router is a powerful tool. This means that a designer need not purchase additional interfaces to accommodate multiple connections. In addition, there's a substantially lowered lead-time for new connections, and such connections can be provisioned without a visit to the remote location.

The Frame Relay protocol is primarily designed to encapsulate data on reliable connections. Its benefits include low overhead when compared to X.25, low cost when compared to point-to-point connections, and a single access point on the router that can terminate multiple virtual circuits (each of which can go to different destinations). This last benefit greatly reduces the costs associated with the router hardware. The Frame Relay protocol and its benefits will be explored in more detail in Chapter 8.

Due to its relatively low cost and high bandwidth, Frame Relay is well suited for higher bandwidth demands than other access technologies, including ISDN.

Leased Lines

Leased lines are commonly referred to as dedicated connectivity options. This means that the connection between the two endpoints is permanent in nature and 100 percent of the capacity is available to the end user. These connections are also called point-to-point links since the capacity of a leased line is dedicated to the corporation. Unfortunately, because bandwidths can not be shared, this type of connection is more expensive.

In addition, leased lines are also distance sensitive. Unlike Frame Relay, with leased lines, the telephone company will charge the end user for both the local loop and the transit network. For short distances, the differences in costs may be negligible, but for long distances, the costs increase dramatically. For example, a 200-mile Frame Relay connection may cost $200 a month, which would be the same as a 2000-mile Frame Relay connection. The lease line installation may also cost $200 a month for 200 miles, but most likely, it would cost $3000 a month for the 2000-mile link. The most common leased-line service available in the United States is called a T-1. This provides the corporation with 1.544Mbps of dedicated bandwidth. Older leased lines were digital data service circuits, or DDS circuits, and yielded up to 56Kbps of bandwidth. These connections were popular for mainframe connectivity at both the 9.6 and 56 Kbps levels.

New WAN Connection Technologies

As noted previously, there are many new technologies with which designers and administrators should be familiar, but they aren't covered on the Remote Access exam. These include Digital Subscriber Lines; their competitive counterpart, cable modems; Asynchronous Transfer Mode; and wireless and cellular services.

Digital Subscriber Line

Digital Subscriber Line (DSL) technologies were developed to be the magic bullet of the telecommunications industry. Primarily designed to add bandwidth to the home without installing fiber optics, the various DSL protocols, referred to in the generic as xDSL, have the potential to provide 52Mbps over already installed copper wire—a marked increase in performance. This feat is accomplished with special encoding of the digital signal. At present, DSL technologies are being used as a replacement for ISDN and analog Internet Service Provider (ISP) connections. However, as DSL technologies are accepted into the home and office, it is likely that they will be used for primary and backup data transfer and for high-demand services such as live video.

DSL technologies and cable modems are not included on the exam at present. This section is provided only as optional material for those readers interested in this technology.

The xDSLs provide for varying amounts of upstream and downstream bandwidth based on the equipment in use and the distances between this equipment. As a result of the distance sensitivity of xDSL, connections typically must terminate within three miles of the central office, but access technologies may be employed to extend the range. Access products connect a remote termination device to the central office via fiber optics, which greatly extends the reach of xDSL. Figure 1.1 illustrates a typical installation of DSL with and without an access product. As shown, a home four miles away cannot obtain xDSL access without an access product. Please note that most xDSL technologies support distances between 1,800 and 18,000 feet.

FIGURE 1.1   xDSL installations

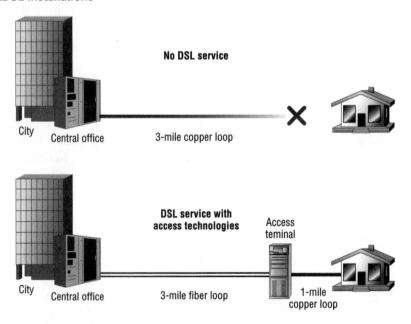

As of this writing, vendors are deploying DSL at fairly low speeds and as an Internet connectivity solution. Most vendors provide 1.544Mbps downstream bandwidth as viewed from the central office site, and 128Kbps to 384Kbps upstream. These bandwidths greatly surpass ISDN and analog offerings, but they cannot provide the multiservice goals of xDSL—primarily MPEG-2 video streaming. Table 1.1 shows the various xDSL technologies available.

TABLE 1.1 The Various xDSL Technologies

Standard	Characteristics
Asymmetric DSL (ADSL)	There are a number of flavors to Asymmetric DSL; the two most popular are G.dmt (discrete multitone) and G.lite. The G.lite specification provides 1.5Mbps/384Kbps bandwidth and typically invokes lower capital costs. The G.dmt specification can provide 8Mbps downstream and 1.5Mbps upstream.
High bit-rate DSL (HDSL)	HDSL is similar to SDSL, but it uses double and triple pairs of copper wire. Most other DSL technologies operate over a single pair, which can simplify installation compared to HDSL. HDSL typically provides distances reaching 15,000 feet.
ISDN-based DSL (IDSL)	ISDN-based DSL typically allows the greatest distances but it is limited to 144Kbps.
Symmetric DSL (SDSL)	Symmetric DSL provides 2Mbps bidirectional bandwidth over a single pair of copper wires. Distances are typically limited to 10,000 feet.
Very high bit-rate DSL (VDSL)	VDSL can provide up to 52Mbps downstream bandwidth, but its distance is limited to less than 4,500 feet. This is usually the shortest range DSL service.

Most vendors deploy one of the following two xDSL implementation models: ISP-based installation (Layer 3) and Remote LAN (RLAN, or Layer 2). The traditional ISP-based installation simply substitutes ISDN or analog dial-up for DSL. Because DSL is an always-on technology, there is no call setup or teardown process, and the connection to the DSLAM, or Digital Subscriber Line Access Multiplexer, is always active. There is a single link to the service provider, and all packets are routed to their destination. RLAN, on the other hand, places the DSL connection on par with Frame-Relay or point-to-point links in the WAN. This provides more secure connectivity that can support non-routable protocols. This solution is being deployed for telecommuters as opposed to interoffice connections. Ultimately, designers may find that the consumer level of support currently offered in DSL will be augmented, and the lower price for setup will encourage companies to replace Frame Relay and lease-line installations for interoffice traffic with DSL as well.

Both of these implementation methods can make a modern network design perform better. However, some caveats should be considered.

At present, most DSL vendors offer a single PVC with DSL installations. This limits connectivity options and makes redundancy difficult. A second PVC could provide a link to another head-end (Distribution Layer aggregation point), and most vendors have multiple DSLAMs in the central office. An SVC-based solution would also make a fault-tolerant design more successful.

Another concern with current DSL installations is that most products do not offer security solutions. The RLAN model greatly reduces this risk since the links are isolated at Layer 2, but all connectivity must be provided by the head-end, including Internet connectivity. For ISP Internet connections, the risk is significantly greater, especially when the bandwidth available for an attack and the use of static IP addresses or address pools are considered. A number of significant attacks have already occurred as a result of these issues, and while they should not deter the use of the technology, the risks should be addressed with firewall technology.

A third consideration in DSL is the installation delay compared to other technologies. Vendors are moving towards splitterless hardware so that the phone company does not have to install a splitter in the home. The splitter divides the traditional phone signals from the data stream and provides a jack for standard telephones—DSLs transports data and voice over the same twisted-pair wiring used for standard analog phone service. At present, because the circuit to the home and the installation of the splitter need to be validated, installations require weeks to complete.

Cable Modems

It would be unfair to present the DSL technologies without providing some space to discuss the alternative, cable modems. *Cable modems* operate over the same cabling system that provides cable television service; in other words, they use the same coax cable that is already used in the homes with cable television. Most cable installations will provide two cables, one for the television and one for the data converter, but the signaling and the system is the same. This is accomplished by allocating a television channel to data services. Bandwidth varies with the installation; however, 2Mbps in each direction is not uncommon.

Detractors of cable modem technology are quick to point out that these installations are shared bandwidth, similar to Ethernet, which results in contention for the wire among neighbors. This shared bandwidth also introduces a security risk, in that network analysis is possible, although vendors are working to address this concern with switching and encryption technology. This issue does not exist in DSL since the local loop connection to the home is switched. In DSL, traffic is not integrated until it reaches the central office, and at that point, the switch will forward only traffic destined for the end station based on the MAC (media access control) address. Basically, cable modems are a shared technology—similar to 802.2 Ethernet versus 10-BaseT. Along the same lines, a cable modem is really a broadband Ethernet bridge.

There is a lot of confusion in the marketplace regarding over-subscription and performance in the residential DSL and cable modem markets. DSL is usually oversubscribed 10 to 1 at the central office—if a DS-3 is used to link the DSLAM to the Internet, there could be as many as 300 homes connected to the DSLAM. None of those users would be oversubscribed on their connection to the DSLAM. Cable modems typically share bandwidth before the head-end. As a result, users contend for bandwidth both before and after the head-end (comparable to the DSLAM).

Network designers may wish to consider cable modems as part of a VPN deployment since the technology will not lend itself to the RLAN-type designs available in DSL. Recall that an RLAN requires Layer 2 isolation—a service not offered by cable modem providers at present. This may change in the future if channels can be isolated to specific users. This may be especially true in very remote rural areas, where cable is available and DSL is not.

Asynchronous Transfer Mode (ATM)

ATM does not relate in any way to asynchronous dial-up connections. Rather, it refers to the transmission of fixed-length cells and the transport of data, voice, and video services. The majority of the public telephone network has already converted to this technology for the aggregation of phone lines. Cells are fixed in length, and therefore, latency and delay can be determined and controlled accurately.

ATM is rarely used as a remote access technology in the context applied to the examination, and it would be best to think of it as a potential replacement for Frame Relay installations. Typically, residential ATM installations appear in the form of DSL—ATM being the underlying Data Link (Layer 2) technology.

Wireless and Cellular

Wireless technologies, including cellular systems, provide a mobile access method. Typically, these technologies offer substantially lower bandwidth than wireline services.

For remote access, wireless services might include radio, satellite, and cellular phone networks, or LAN-based systems based on the 802.11 standard. This last item is subject to some interpretation since 802.11 lacks the range of the other technologies. However, some companies have looked to 802.11 (capable of Ethernet type access) for linking uses in branch offices to the remote access router. Such a solution could work in the residence as well.

Radio-based systems are occasionally able to reach ranges of 17 miles at ISDN BRI bandwidths; however, most are restricted to 38.4Kbps or less, and distances that vary substantially. Mobility may also be restricted since the signal may need to remain stationary during the data transmission. Satellite systems usually share this limitation.

It is likely that the proliferation of Personal Digital Assistants (PDAs) will require additional wireless access; however, this would be over shorter distances than most remote access installations. The proliferation of PDAs and similar technologies will likely accelerate the needs to link remote access installations to wireless solutions.

Summarizing WAN Connection Technologies

Table 1.2 summarizes the WAN connection technologies discussed in this chapter in order to provide a comparison between them.

TABLE 1.2   Summary of WAN Connection Technologies

Connection	Max Throughput	US Availability	Relative Cost
Asynchronous dial-up 56K/DDS	56Kbps	Widely available	Low
Leased line T1/E1	1.544Mbps/ 2.048Mbps	Widely available	Medium

TABLE 1.2 Summary of WAN Connection Technologies *(continued)*

Connection	Max Throughput	US Availability	Relative Cost
Leased line T3/E3	44.736Mbps/ 34.368Mbps	Widely available	High
ATM	2488Mbps. However, it is virtually unlimited from a protocol perspective.	Moderately available	Very high
ISDN BRI	128Kbps for user, 16Kbps for control data and 48Kbps for overhead.	Moderately available	Low. However, per-minute tariffs can quickly alter this.
ISDN PRI	Around 2Mbps	Moderately available	Low
DSL	>128Kbps	Available in larger cities, becoming more available in rural areas	Low
Frame Relay	1.544Mbps or slower. However, new networks support DS-3 (45Mbps installations).	Widely available	Low

WAN Encapsulation Protocols

There are a number of WAN encapsulation protocols, which operate at Layer 2 to provide consistent transport at the Data Link Layer. It is important to note that some of these protocols extend into Layer 3, especially X.25. These protocols include the Point-to-Point Protocol (PPP), the X.25 link-access procedure, balanced protocol (LAPB), and the Frame Relay protocol. Additional WAN encapsulation protocols include the Serial Line

Internet Protocol (SLIP), the High-Level Data Link Control (HDLC) protocol, and Asynchronous Transfer Mode (ATM).

Again, the Remote Access exam omits a number of these protocols, both older and newer encapsulations. SLIP has been largely replaced by PPP, and ATM is quite common, but both are outside the scope of the exam. The omission of HDLC is significant if only because this protocol is the foundation for many other transports. In addition, it remains the default encapsulation for Cisco serial interfaces.

The encapsulations covered within the Remote Access exam and this text include the following:

- Point-to-Point
- X.25
- Frame Relay

In later sections of this chapter and in other chapters, you will learn about each of these in greater detail.

The current Remote Access exam does not include ATM, HDLC, or SLIP. Here you will find brief descriptions of these three protocols for reference only.

Asynchronous Transfer Mode (ATM)

You may be asking what the difference is between the technology and the encapsulation type. ATM as a technology is different from the protocol itself. Unfortunately, it would be inappropriate to go into significant detail regarding ATM in this chapter—both because it is functioning as an introduction and because this material is not on the exam. However, to understand ATM as an encapsulation type, you need to look at ATM adaptation layers (AAL) and cell header formats.

ATM is a cell-based service that breaks data into 53 byte packets. This fixed length allows processing to be handled in hardware, which reduces delay and provides for deterministic latency. ATM is primarily designed to integrate voice, data, and video services.

High-Level Data Link Control (HDLC)

High-Level Data Link Control (HDLC) is the encapsulation method used by serial links, and it is the default on Cisco serial interfaces. The protocol provides for a 32-bit check sum and three different transfer modes: normal, asynchronous

each HDLC is proprietary because each Vendor h an Twicked

response, and asynchronous balanced. Many point-to-point connections using Cisco routers continue to make use of the HDLC protocol.

Serial Line Internet Protocol (SLIP)

The *Serial Line Internet Protocol (SLIP)* is designed for point-to-point serial connections using TCP/IP. The Point-to-Point Protocol (PPP), which you will learn about next, has effectively replaced SLIP. Some installations, however, still rely on SLIP because of its simplicity.

Point-to-Point Protocol (PPP)

The *Point-to-Point Protocol (PPP)* is a standard, efficient Layer 2 technology designed for connections between two endpoints. As such, it doesn't include addressing functionality like Ethernet's MAC address, but it can be augmented to operate in point-to-multipoint installations. The PPP has effectively replaced SLIP, and is commonly found in lower bandwidth applications, although it is also used as a ubiquitous protocol for a wide range of higher bandwidth installations. One of the most innovative benefits of PPP is its support for multiple, upper layer protocols. This is accomplished by the use of the Network Control Protocol (NCP), which encapsulates the upper layers. The Link Control Protocol (LCP) is used to negotiate connections on the WAN data link, and in PPP, it provides for authentication and compression. Use of PPP permits the binding of connections, also called multilink.

PPP will be explored in more detail in Chapter 3.

The X.25 Protocol

The X.25 protocol is really comprised of a number of protocols, including Link Access Procedure, Balanced (LAPB) and X.25 itself, which is a Layer 3 protocol. X.25 also uses a number of standards, including X.121, X.75, and X.3, amongst others.

LAPB operates at Layer 2 of the OSI model, and is responsible for providing reliability. Specifically, LAPB provides windowing functions and detects missed frames.

Readers who wish to review the OSI model should refer to the *CCNA: Cisco Certified Network Associate Study Guide,* by Todd Lammle (Sybex Inc., 2000).

X.25 (which can be described as also belonging to Layers 1 through 3) was designed to catch errors, as it was developed to operate on poor quality telecommunications systems. At Layer 3, X.25 describes the formation of data packets and the methods to be used for connectivity, in addition to addressing.

Some consider the X.25 standards to be recommendations from the International Telecommunications Union-Telecommunication Standardization Sector (ITU-T). In practice, this can be accurate since private X.25 networks are free to operate over any methodology that works. However, the standards can simplify matters and become very important in public X.25 networking.

The most significant standard is X.121, which is the addressing specification. X.121 addresses are composed of a Data Network Identification Code (DNIC) and a Network Terminal Number (NTN). These numbers work similarly to the way area codes and phone numbers work—the DNIC is akin to an area code that is defined on a country basis. The NTN is a specific node identifier. X.25 will be presented in greater detail in Chapter 7.

Frame Relay

The Frame Relay protocol is quite simple compared to X.25 since the error correction functions have been removed. This allows the protocol to scale up to 45Mbps in currently available offerings, although this is more a practical limit than a technology-based one. The greatest benefit of Frame Relay is its availability and its low cost over long distances at high bandwidths.

The protocol itself is used to define virtual circuits, which adds an additional benefit to Frame Relay—a single physical port can terminate numerous logical virtual circuits. This can greatly reduce the hardware costs associated with an installation. Each virtual circuit is defined with a data link connection identifier (DLCI).

Frame Relay will be formally presented in Chapter 8, but in the context of this chapter, the protocols of this international standard should be noted. The specifics of the protocol are defined in the following standards:

- ANSI T1.617

- ITU-T Q.933

- ITU-T Q.922

To remember the function of each standard, look at the second digit of the ITU number. As could be inferred, Q.933 is a Layer 3 (OSI model) protocol, while Q.922 operates at Layer 2.

Selecting a WAN Protocol

There following list is composed of a number of factors for you to consider when selecting a WAN type:

- Availability
- Bandwidth
- Cost
- Manageability
- Applications in use
- Quality of service
- Reliability
- Security

As you can deduce from the list, many of these elements are common to any network design regardless of its WAN or LAN delineation. This section will define each of these factors and provide some guidance as to how they might apply to remote access deployments.

Availability

Unfortunately, not all of the WAN technologies introduced in this chapter are available in all locations. While this is frequently true in more rural locations, it may also be true on a country-by-country basis. Distance, technology, and infrastructure all play a role in determining what services will be available in a particular location. Table 1.3 summarizes the technologies and general availability throughout the world.

TABLE 1.3 Worldwide Availability of WAN Technologies

Technology	Availability
Asynchronous dial-up	Widely available
X.25	Widely available
ISDN	Moderately available
Frame Relay	Widely available
Leased lines	Widely available

Bandwidth

Applications may demand more bandwidth than is readily available with some WAN technologies. For example, an asynchronous dial-up connection is limited to 56Kbps. Should the application require the movement of more data than will fit in this constraint, the network architect will be required to select a different technology.

Frequently, selecting another technology will increase overall costs—a T-1 circuit will cost substantially more than a standard analog connection at a remote location. Some technologies provide high levels of bandwidth for relatively low cost. Frame Relay is an example of one such technology.

Table 1.4 compares available bandwidth of common WAN technologies.

TABLE 1.4 Bandwidth Comparison of WAN Technologies

Technology	Bandwidth
Asynchronous dial-up	Low
X. 25	Low
ISDN	Moderate

TABLE 1.4   Bandwidth Comparison of WAN Technologies *(continued)*

Technology	Bandwidth
Frame Relay	High
Leased lines	High

Handwritten annotations: HSSI — High speed interface Serial (module on router) (IMUX) (inverse multiplexer)

Handwritten: T3 = 45 MB

Cost

Cost is almost always the single most important criteria in the network design. As such, network designers and architects are required to weigh the relative cost of a WAN technology against the services that it provides. Again, Frame Relay frequently reduces the costs of a WAN circuit compared to a point-to-point leased line. The network architect needs to weigh this cost differentiation against the other factors used in determining the appropriate WAN protocol to use.

Table 1.5 compares the costs of various WAN technologies.

TABLE 1.5   Cost Comparison of WAN Technologies

Technology	Cost
Asynchronous dial-up	Low. However, per minute and distance charges can significantly increase total cost.
X.25	Low. However, per minute and distance charges can significantly increase the cost.
ISDN	Low. However, per minute and distance charges can significantly increase cost.
Frame Relay	Low
Leased lines	High

Manageability

The best networks cannot hope to operate without being manageable. In local area networks, this is fairly simple since the administrator controls everything from the wall jack to the server or WAN router. In remote access, these advantages no longer exist since the ability to physically access the remote end has been removed. When the connection is down or disconnected (reflecting the potential differences between dedicated circuits and on-demand connections), it is not possible to logically connect to the remote equipment either. Either of these limitations can greatly work against quick problem resolution.

For remote access manageability, the designer and administrator will frequently try to automate as many functions as possible. This can be accomplished with tools including DHCP (Dynamic Host Control Protocol), which automatically assigns IP addresses; and authentication servers, including TACACS+ (Enhanced Terminal Access Controller Access Control System), which can centralize the user authentication database. Administrators prefer this, instead of the alternative, which would require placing each user and password on every access resource manually. This centralizing of the security function will also make the network more secure—removing a single terminated employee will remove their access account from all entrances into the network.

Table 1.6 shows the difference in manageability of various WAN technologies.

TABLE 1.6 Manageability Comparison of WAN Technologies

Technology	Manageability
Asynchronous dial-up	Little
X. 25	Some, including congestion statistics.
ISDN	Some. However, most tools are lacking in obtaining and using this data.
Frame Relay	High
Leased lines	High

Remote Access in the Field: Manageability

The benefits of centralized access control cannot be over emphasized, but there is a certain amount of care that must accompany this process. Many older security products would store the password file in clear-text, which could be read by anyone with access to the server. This, coupled with no requirement to change the passwords on a regular basis, made centralized security less secure.

Obviously, the trick is to make sure that the central access control database and server are secure. This again yields a benefit to the administrator since this can be accomplished easily when there are one or two security servers (remember, redundancy is an important consideration). While the remote access devices will also demand a degree of security, it is far easier to protect a single resource than tens or hundreds—the basis for perimeter firewalls.

A note regarding forcing regular password changes—it can be taken too far. Consider an organization that requires monthly password changes. My first guess at everyone's password would be some combination of month and year—jun00, for example. Incremented passwords, such as Tyler7, Tyler8, and so on, would also be common—of course, substitute the name of your child, pet, or significant other in the string.

Applications in Use

Network designers are concerned with two specific characteristics of the traffic when selecting a WAN protocol. The first consideration relates to the upper layer protocol that will be used. For example, it is not possible to use SLIP with any other upper layer protocol except IP. In order to use a different protocol, the administrator would have to select another lower level protocol (PPP, for example) in order to transport native IPX packets. The second consideration has to do with the acceptability of delay on the part of the upper layer protocol. SNA, a mainframe protocol, traditionally cannot accept a high level of delay.

It is fortunate that most applications can make use of many transport protocols, and that most operate using IP. This allows the remote access solution to focus on supporting a single protocol in most cases, and it allows the use of a protocol that does not suffer significantly from the delay present in low-bandwidth and on-demand connections. Because of this, many vendors and designers will opt to use PPP as a transport protocol.

Quality of Service (QoS)

Unlike the marketing term "quality of service" that is based on packet shaping and control, this *quality of service (QoS)* refers to the reliability of the connection and its ability to process non-data traffic. This simpler view is controlled less by configuration and software and is more reliant on the physical and logical characteristics of the standard. There are two factors to consider when evaluating quality of service requirements on a WAN link. The first factor involves the type of application traffic that will traverse the link—will data and voice traffic both share the available bandwidth, for example. The second factor focuses more upon the reliability of the connection. For example, Dial-up analog connections are frequently considered less reliable than a point-to-point link. As a result, designers may wish to incorporate back-up technologies based on both the criticality of the data and the reliability of the selected WAN protocol. For instance, Frame Relay, though it is considered a reliable protocol, is frequently backed up with analog connections or ISDN.

Reliability

Reliability is a quality of service characteristic; however, it is relatively important and warrants separate consideration. As noted in the quality of service description, reliability is frequently a factor in determining whether or not a back-up link is required. Some designers will use multiple PVCs to provide a greater level of reliability when problems are anticipated in the WAN cloud; this differs from those situations when the designer is concerned with reliability in the local loop or in the last portion of the circuit. In these situations, a separate connection is warranted.

The designer may also wish to use separate components in remote locations to further augment reliability. This migrates the objective into the category of redundancy. It would require disparate routers, circuits, Data Service Unit/Channel Service Unit (DSU/CSU) terminations, and electrical systems to become fully fault tolerant, although it may also require placing the equipment in two separate telephone closets with different building entrances to different service provider's offices. Different providers would further add to the redundancy of the design and its ultimately survivability, which is synonymous to reliability. See Table 1.7 for a comparison of various WAN technologies.

TABLE 1.7   Reliability Comparison of WAN Technologies

Technology	Reliability
Asynchronous dial-up	Low
X. 25	High
ISDN	Middle
Frame Relay	Middle
Leased lines	Middle

Security

Security is an important consideration when selecting a WAN protocol—security relating to protection from corruption, theft, or misuse of digital transmissions. Some applications, such as financial ones, require a high-level of security. For example, many designers in the financial institution will select private point-to-point connections over fiber-optic cable. In installations that require less security, the designer may opt for a public connection, which frequently has a substantially reduced cost.

Remote access solutions can alter the security model of a corporation substantially. Implied with remote access is the concept that data will be remote. This immediately causes a security concern since a lost or stolen notebook can quickly lead to the release of corporate data. The network designer will typically be more concerned with the security requirements that will prevent unauthorized access to the network. This, again, is a fairly simple model since the majority of the security configuration will be placed on the remote access servers.

Virtual Private Networks (VPNs)

In recent years, the use of *virtual private network (VPN)* technology has entered into the remote access landscape. VPNs allow secure connections over public networks—typically making use of the Internet. Data is encrypted for transport in a virtual tunnel between source and destination, and its costs are greatly reduced without a substantial decrease in security. As such, a VPN is a system of these tunnels used to create a logical system of conduits that transport user data.

Although most VPN software is very solid, it is important to note that most companies bristle at the thought of using only basic software to secure data. In addition, the processing demands required by some encryption technologies are very high, and many implementations will likely require newer processors or coprocessed implementations. Coprocessors offload specific functions from the main processor—video adapters have used them for years to provide better graphics output. Encryption can benefit from this coprocessor design as well.

Choosing Remote Connection Cisco Products

Cisco offers a wide range of router products available for use in remote access solutions. Most of these fall into one of two general categories: fixed interface and modular interface. Fixed interface solutions are fairly common in remote deployments whereas modular interfaces are found in central locations. This placement relates well to their characteristics as well—fixed interface solutions are very limited and lack upgradeability. Modular routers are expandable and usually provide better performance.

In addition to the interface types, there are different software options available in the Cisco product line. Many products take advantage of the Cisco Internetwork Operating System (IOS), which simplifies administration and training expenses as administrators need only learn one operating system. Routers based on this software also support more features under most circumstances. Other Cisco routers make use of the Cisco Broadband Operating System (CBOS), which can be found on the 600 series products. The CBOS software is very limited in functionality, and many of its commands differ from their IOS counterparts. However, the 600 series routers may reduce the acquisition costs by more than half compared to an IOS-based platform—a substantial cost difference when magnified against the hundreds of routers that might be acquired in a large-scale remote access deployment.

The Cisco 700 series, presented in Chapter 6, is similar to the 600 series. More information regarding the differences in command syntax and structure are presented in that chapter.

Remote Access in the Field: Outsourcing Remote Access Solutions

Given the complexity of managing equipment in hundreds of locations internationally, many companies have selected to outsource their remote access solutions. This option provides a great deal of support flexibility since the outsourcing company can frequently provide technicians over a larger geographical area. As such, outsourcing provides a great deal of benefit since it can provide faster response times and free corporate support personnel from this responsibility of doing this themselves.

Outsourcing solutions can also provide cost savings in the form of leasing options for remote access equipment. While the final cost of leasing may be greater, many companies use this financing option as a means to reduce corporate taxes.

By no means should companies use outsourcing as a panacea. There are significant downsides, including the very real risk of outsourcing too many components of the network. Should the outsourcing company be unable to comply with service level agreements, or unable to provide a reasonable level of service, the remote users will suffer and the ultimate recourse will be to change outsourcing companies—a process that is very time-consuming and costly.

Company should seriously evaluate the benefits of outsourcing against their overall corporate strategy. Selective use of outsourcing, in addition to leasing, can greatly facilitate remote access solutions.

Fixed Interfaces

Early routers were little more than Unix workstations and PCs equipped with two Ethernet interfaces. The first fixed-purpose routers were typically fixed-interface as well—there was no provision for adding an additional interface or a new type of interface. As router products evolved, the capability to add modularity to the products increased. A fixed-interface router cannot be expanded, so one with two Ethernet interfaces will always have only two Ethernet interfaces. When you need a third, you must replace the router or augment it with another.

Fixed-interface routers typically reduce the costs associated with acquisition, which directly relates to the initial capital expense. Many organizations try to reduce the capital costs, even when this leads to ultimate replacement requirements. In addition, they are simpler to install, especially by less experienced staff and vendors. Fixed-interface equipment lacks an upgrade path, however. It is impossible to add features without requiring a complete replacement of the equipment. Replacing equipment can quickly offset the savings you made with the initial purchase. Because of this, designers should seriously evaluate the life span of the equipment and the growth potential for the environment before they make any irreversible decisions. Typically, sites with more than 30 users will quickly outgrow fixed-configuration routers, although different environments yield different thresholds.

Cisco offers two alternatives to the fixed router. The modular router allows cards to be installed by supplying the type and volume of interfaces needed; this is discussed in the next section. In addition, routers are also available for expansion with fixed interfaces and one or more modular ports. The Cisco 1600 is a good example of this hybrid router type, and it is discussed later in this chapter.

Modular Interfaces

The modular-interface remote access products provide the designer with a few benefits, including an upgrade path, and, typically, higher densities that are unavailable in the fixed interface models. Most of the time, this flexibility comes at a price; however, in most cases, the costs associated with the removal and replacement of network equipment easily offsets this initial cost difference.

The benefits of the modular router also lead to potential savings in the initial acquisition of the device. Sometimes the fixed-interface router provides a number of interfaces that are not needed—they still charge for the unused ports. While this is uncommon given the wide array of fixed-configuration routers in the Cisco product line, it is possible to find situations in which a high number of Ethernet ports also require a high number of serial ports on a fixed router, which greatly adds to the cost. Modular routers provide the following positives and negatives:

Pros	Cons
Defined upgrade path	Higher cost
Potentially lower total cost of ownership	More complex installation
	More difficult to stock spare equipment

Again, it is usually best to select modular router to avoid forklift upgrades in the future—ones that require the complete replacement of the chassis. However, the use of modular routers comes at a higher initial and support costs.

Product Selection Tools

Most designers find that the best information regarding Cisco's product line comes from their sales representatives. The sales force, though, relies upon information on Cisco's Web site. Cisco has provided a product selection tool that allows the designer to define the features that are needed for their particular WAN project. As of this writing, this service was available at `www.cisco.com/pcgi-bin/front.x/corona/prodtool/select.pl`; however, Cisco does change its site from time to time.

The end of this chapter provides a high-level presentation of the major remote access platforms provided by Cisco.

Cabling and Assembling the WAN

The cabling of the WAN will vary depending on the technologies used and the equipment locations. For example, central sites will typically make use of modular, high-capacity routers, while branch offices may typically use modular or fixed higher capacity routers. Typically, telecommuter equipment will entail fixed-configuration devices, and it will attempt to place all components of the Customer Premise Equipment (CPE) in a single chassis.

The cabling will also depend on the media to be used. For example, RJ-45 interfaces will typically be used to terminate Ethernet connections, while serial connections will typically be terminated with RS-232 or v.35 cables. The next section will supply an overview of the cable connections used with different WAN types.

In this section, you will learn about interfacing and terminating options for remote access equipment, identifying appropriate equipment, and verifying a network installation.

Subsequent chapters will expand upon many of the concepts introduced here, including ISDN, X.25, Frame Relay, PPP protocol, security, and the different types of telecommuters and specific equipment in the Cisco product line.

Internetworking Overview and Remote Access Interface Options

Selecting and determining the interoperability of interface types for the various cable connections are a couple of the most critical components used to construct an internetwork. While it is possible to perform media conversion for some interfaces, it is far easier to maintain consistency throughout the design. For example, if a fiber connection is needed to link the router to the switch, it is generally preferred to use a fiber interface on the router, as opposed to using a copper interface and then using a copper to fiber converter upstream. This is also applicable for serial connectors—it is far easier to manage the network when all cables and interfaces are the same and relevant to that provided by the vendors. In order to successfully design this standardization, it is important to know the functionality of each connection and how it may be used to terminate network interfaces; each of these connections will be discussed below.

Asynchronous or Analog Connections

Standard telephone service typically terminates with an RJ-11 interface, which connects the modem to the telephone company's jack. External modems are attached to a Cisco router with an RS-232 cable. This is also referred to as an EIA/TIA-232 cable. The router end of this connection uses the Cisco DB-60 connector, a 60-pin termination specific to Cisco routers, and a DB-25 connector, which interfaces to the modem. The DB-25 connector is quite common in telecommunications equipment.

ISDN BRI   *RJ4 5*

ISDN BRIs are very common in branch and telecommuter installations in which higher than asynchronous bandwidth is needed. The BRI specification avails two 64Kbps bearer channels (B channels) for use traffic, and it uses a single 16Kbps D channel for management and signaling. It is important to remember that these connections are circuit-switched, and that the data link protocol on the D channel is LAPD, or Link Access Procedure, Data. This differs from the X.25 protocol, which uses LAPB. The ISDN B channel is similar to a standard voice channel in terms of bandwidth, and because of this, most systems allow the use of a B channel for a traditional analog call. While the single channel is encoded digitally from the ISDN device to the switch—unlike an analog connection from a phone to a phone switch—the overall mechanics between them are similar.

Some installations of ISDN only allow 56Kbps for each B channel.

The ISDN BRI is terminated with a number of connections, but the network (phone company) is usually terminated with an RJ-11 or RJ-45 interface. According to the specifications, the termination should always be accomplished with an RJ-45, which provides for additional signaling and visually distinguishes the difference between the ISDN interface and analog connections. However, the exterior pins (1, 2, 7, and 8) of the RJ-45 are frequently unused, and for this reason, some providers use RJ-11 instead. If you can control this part of the installation, specify RJ-45 and use a specific color to differentiate it from Ethernet, T-1, and other connections.

ISDN PRI (North America)   *RJ4 5*

In North America, ISDN PRIs are provisioned over T-1 standards. The T-1 standard, also called DS-1, is capable of servicing 24 64Kbps channels—each channel being historically provisioned for a single voice connection. From this, 23 B channels are allocated, with the last 64Kbps channel used for D channel signaling.

The most important thing to note, in addition to the channels of ISDN PRI, is the fact that ISDN PRI operates over *channelized T-1* connections. This means that at its core, each B channel is one time slot in the T-1 specification, although clearly, there is additional functionality. As with BRI connections, PRI only requires two pairs of copper wire (the same as T-1);

however, all installations should use RJ-45. This provides a visual variance to RJ-11 ports, and typically RJ-45 provides a better, cleaner connection.

ISDN PRI (Europe)

The European telecommunications standard for T-1 services is called *E-1*, and it provides for 31 channels. The last channel is used as a D channel for signaling, yielding a total of 30 user bearer channels. As a significant aside, in Europe, the vendor typically provides the NT-1 network termination, while in the US, the customer usually provides it.

It is very important to understand the differences between the North American and European specifications.

Consult with the vendor to determine the proper termination for E-1 PRI terminations. These should differ little from American installations; however, there may be small alterations, which could include, for example, providing the demarcation point on a wiring block. ISDN remains popular in Europe and it is likely to continue as an access technology there for sometime. On a recent trip to Germany and Italy, I noted a number of advertisements for the service, but I didn't see any evidence of DSL proliferation.

Chapter 5 will address some of the differences in European ISDN specifications in greater detail, however, it is important to note that the middle channel of the E-1 circuit (16) is the D channel, contrasted with 24 in the T-1 specification. In addition, T-1 starts numbering at 0 and E-1 starts with 1. There is usually no channel 0 in European ISDN.

Frame Relay

Using Frame Relay is a very powerful way of getting remote access and WAN connectivity. As a packet-switched technology, Frame Relay operates at bandwidths up to 45Mbps, although older networks may limit this to 1.544 (DS-3 versus T-1). Sprint currently suffers from this limitation on one of their three Frame Relay networks—the highest port speed one can obtain is terminated with a T-1 circuit.

Frame Relay is supported on Cisco routers with EIA/TIA-232, EIA/TIA-449, V.35, X.21, and EIA-530 signaling, but the DB-60 serial cable is almost always used. The network side connection is RJ-45.

Identifying Company Site Equipment

One of the key challenges for the network designer is selecting the equipment that is appropriate to both the current and future demands of the network. This becomes even more difficult when cost constraints are taken into account.

Designers need to select equipment based primarily on the port type and density required for their application. *Port type* refers to the topology, interface, and protocol (T-1, PRI ISDN with an RJ-45 connector, for example). *Port density* is a simplified way of noting how many ports can be squeezed into a particular slot or chassis—frequently changing connectors will allow greater density; however, a larger chassis can also increase the density. As a result, equipment purchased for the central site will frequently require larger and more modular platforms. Equipment for remote locations tends to be simpler and less expensive—primarily to simplify administrative costs.

While the Remote Access examination is a relatively new test, some of Cisco's recommendations and questions may refer to end-of-life or end-of-sales equipment. Please consider this when deploying a production remote access solution, and consult the Cisco Web site, www.cisco.com, for the most current information.

Central Site

The central site has very different requirements compared to the remote branch and telecommuter locations. Unlike those locations, the central site is an aggregation point for all of the other links, and, as such, it requires greater bandwidth, larger equipment, and additional administration.

As of this writing, Cisco suggested four, high-end routers to meet the demands of the central site. Designers should consider protocols, interfaces, and scalability when selecting a piece of network equipment. The recommended platforms are as follows:

- The Cisco 3600
- The Cisco 4000

- The Cisco AS5x00

- The Cisco 7000/7500

It should be noted that each of these platforms is modular in nature. In addition, Cisco continually introduces new platforms into the product line and will most likely continue to do so as part of its AVVID initiative. *AVVID* stands for Architecture for Voice, Video, and Integrated Data, and while it is a marketing term, it will likely define an entire class of equipment for some time. Historically, remote access technologies have been centered on data transport, with support for voice—ISDN and the use of a B channel, for example. Demands will increase for video, voice integration, and data transport in the future—in fact, these demands are already surfacing today.

The following sections provide a more detailed overview of these platforms.

The Cisco 3600 Platform

The Cisco 3600 router platform is well suited to smaller aggregation point deployments, and it is currently available in the 3620, 3640, and 3660 models. The third digit in these numbers reflects the number of slots available for modules—two, four, and six, respectively. The 3600 was originally designed to address high-bandwidth services and integration of voice and video, along with traditional data services. Due to these characteristics, the platform is also well suited to the remote branch application.

Many production networks have deployed this system in the remote branch locations as well, when high-speed or multiple interfaces are required. The OC-3 ATM port adapter and the newer IMA (inverse multiplexing for ATM) adapter are benefits to the 3600 platform in remote branch installations. Prior to the release of the 3660, the 3600 series was limited to a single internal AC power supply, which reduced its acceptance in the data center or central site—the 3620 and 3640 routers were only provisioned with a single power supply. These boxes could, however, be outfitted with external DC-based redundant systems, but this solution was never clean from a wiring and simplifying perspective.

There are many differences in the equipment that can be used in the central site, but Cisco recommends the 3600 platform overall. As one of the newest routers, the 3600 does provide a solid service offering for designers. The AS5x00 platform is also well suited to ISDN and dial-up terminations in the central site.

While fairly advanced, the 3600 platform lacks certain features that administrators may be accustomed to. For example, the squeeze command, used to purge deleted files from flash, is notably missing from the platform. Designers may wish to purchase additional flash cards for this system in remote installations, particularly when using modules that are not supported in ROM based IOS—the ATM OC-3c module being most notable.

The Cisco 4000 Platform

There are effectively two versions of the 4000 series in the Cisco router line—the older 4000, and the 4500 and 4700 platforms. Both the 4500 and 4700 platforms can serve as remote access termination systems (the aggregation point of access in a dial-up network) in the central site. The routers can support two 16-port asynchronous port modules, or two single-port ISDN PRI modules.

The Cisco AS5x00 Platform

TACAS = Servers
RADIUS

The Cisco AS5x00 access servers are designed to terminate ISDN and analog dial-up connections. These systems differ substantially from other router platforms in the central site. The primary benefit of these systems is that the routing, switching, channel services, and modems are all integrated into a single chassis, which reduces the number of external connections and space requirements in the rack. These devices can terminate hundreds of connections.

The Cisco 7000/7200/7500 Platforms

Prior to the release of the GSR (Giga Switch Router), the 7000 series was the flagship of the Cisco router line. The 7000 series is still well suited to the task of remote access aggregation, which is typically less demanding than the high-speed ISP niche of the GSR.

The 7200 platform is most frequently used in new remote access installations. Cisco positions this box as a high-performance, high-density central site router for terminating LAN and WAN connections. Many companies use the 7500 (specifically the 7513) in their network cores, and the platform is still one of the most capable multi-protocol routers in production.

The GSR is beyond the scope of this text and is currently used in high-end data centers and ISP environments. It is designed to forward IP packets only.

Remote Branch

The concept of a remote branch is highly variable, depending upon the individual location and services needed. A branch office may contain two or a hundred users, and their demands may be substantial in terms of redundancy, bandwidth, and supportability.

Typically, the remote branch will service a population of users rather than a single user. In addition, the level of technical expertise in the remote location is usually limited. Platforms typically recommended for the remote branch include the following:

- The Cisco 1600 platform
- The Cisco 1700 platform
- The Cisco 2500 platform
- The Cisco 2600 platform

In addition to these platforms, many designers are now deploying the 1400 series router as part of a DSL migration. The 1417 router provides a single ADSL interface and an Ethernet connection. While DSL is beyond the scope of the Remote Access examination, it is important for designers to consider it, and the devices that support it, as part of a modern remote access solution. The cost savings and increased bandwidth available from DSL technologies make it fairly certain that it will replace ISDN by 2005.

The Cisco 1600 Platform

The Cisco 1600 provides an ISDN BRI termination in addition to a WAN expansion slot. This allows the router to accept a WAN Interface Card (WIC), which can be used for a serial connection or integrated T-1/fractional T-1 services. The WIC can also be used for Frame Relay terminations. The router is commonly deployed in remote branch facilities since it can link the Ethernet interface to a Frame Relay network with ISDN BRI backup.

This configuration does not provide router redundancy, but it can greatly augment circuit fault tolerance.

As an IOS-based router, the 1600 can support most features, including network address translation (NAT), access-list control, and multi-protocol support, including IP, IPX, and AppleTalk.

The Cisco 1700 Platform

The Cisco 1700 series routers provide two modular card slots for WAN interfaces, in addition to VPN features. This platform can support Ethernet and Fast Ethernet LANs. Expansion cards are interchangeable with other platforms in the Cisco line, including the 3600.

The Cisco 2500 Platform

Accelerator card

The Cisco 2500 series router is available in a wide array of fixed configurations, and depending on the model, it can support Ethernet, Token Ring, Serial, and ISDN BRI connections. Some models include an integrated Ethernet hub.

The Cisco 2600 Platform

The Cisco 2600 platform builds upon the 2500 series with the addition of two modular card slots for WAN interfaces, including T-1, ISDN PRI, and Frame Relay.

Telecommuter

In the real world, telecommuters fall into two distinct categories: remote users and telecommuters. The remote user requires access from multiple locations as they may be at home, at a customer's site, or in a hotel. Typically, these users make use of analog dial-up connections; however, it is likely that wireless technologies will become increasingly popular with these users. Most remote users are using a modem connected to their PC.

Telecommuters operate from a home office, or an otherwise fixed location. For telecommuters, the smaller, fixed-configuration routers are best suited to the task, and therefore, the technologies recommended by Cisco for remote access mesh well with their needs. These platforms include the following:

Set Base routing →
- The Cisco 700 series   CLIE
- The Cisco 800 series } IOS
- The Cisco 1000 series }

The primary characteristics of these platforms include simple options and fixed configurations, both of which can lower the cost of these systems.

The 700 Series

The 700 series was designed for telecommuters and supports ISDN. Routing services are provided for IP and IPX, and this router uses the Cisco IOS-700 software as opposed to the standard IOS. This can add to the training requirements for a corporation since the differences in syntax can be substantial.

Chapter 6 presents the 700 series routers in detail.

The main benefit of the 700 series is lower cost, and most remote users do not require the advanced features of the IOS-based platforms.

Product Selection and Outsourcing

When recommending a router product, I generally steer away from platforms like the 700 series. The limitations of the platform and the differences in command syntax generally add to the total cost of ownership, and the price difference, with discounts, is generally not that significant. Of course, when magnified over thousands of routers, a $200 difference per unit is suddenly $200,000 or more. Corporate budgets may bristle at that increase unless the consultant or designer can justify the extra expense with extra benefits.

One alternative that some companies choose is outsourcing their remote access platforms. This generally appears as a lease, which can be advantageous to the accountants, and off-load the support and repair functions from the staff.

The 800 Series

Cisco's lowest price IOS-based routers are found in the 800 series. For remote access, these routers offer ISDN BRI terminations and basic telephone service ports. Recall that ISDN BRI can be used for two traditional analog services.

Please be very careful with this statement—the 800 series is currently the *lowest* cost *IOS*-based router. This does not make it the cheapest router mentioned—the 700 series is generally the *lowest* cost router.

Please note that the recently released 827 router terminates DSL connections as opposed to ISDN. This likely illustrates future trends in both technologies, and provides designers with a lower cost alternative to the 1400 series.

The 1000 Series

The Cisco 1000 series routers are based around a fixed configuration; however, they provide for WAN options beyond ISDN. The Cisco 1005 router provides a traditional serial interface for expansion. Most corporations appear to be selecting other platforms than the 1000 series; however, there is no generally known reason for this.

Verifying a Network Installation

Verification of the network installation is encompassed in three different phases.

- Bit error rate tests and validation diagnostics
- Connection of customer premise equipment
- Configuration

The telephone company installer, who will usually perform bit error rate tests and other validation diagnostics, performs the first component of verification. The second phase of verification typically involves connecting the customer premise equipment—the router or Data Service Unit (DSU). Once connected, the installer may use the LED information to provide a high-level overview of the usability of the link. The third phase of verification makes use of an actual configuration. For example, the installer or network architect may configure one of the PVCs to carry an upper layer protocol for simple connectivity tests. For the purposes of the examination, Cisco is primarily interested in the use of the LED indicators.

Verifying the Central Site

As explained previously, Cisco recommends using its 3600 series routers for the central site, although a number of other platforms are also available. Because of this, the following text will focus on the verification steps for installation of the3600 platform.

As you will notice by looking at Figure 1.2, which shows the front of the 3600 router (in this case, it is a 3640 router), the router is fairly limited in the amount of diagnostic information it can provide. LEDs are limited in the same way idiot lights are more limited than gauges in an automobile—they can alert you when there is a problem, but full instrumentation (in a car this would include gauges and a tachometer) can provide details and advanced warning. However, it is a good place to start the process of troubleshooting, just as a oil warning light in the car helps you eliminate the brakes as a problem area.

FIGURE 1.2 The 3640 Router Front View

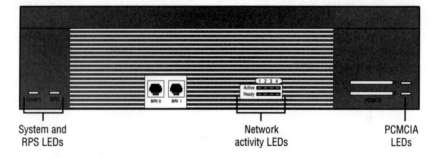

System and RPS LEDs   Network activity LEDs   PCMCIA LEDs

The front panel LEDs are presented as follows:

System The system LED is used to show both the system power and operation characteristics. When off, the router is not receiving power, while a solid green LED denotes proper, powered operation. An amber indicator shows that the router is not functioning correctly, but that power is connected. A blinking green light indicates that the router is powered and working properly, but that it is in ROM monitor mode. Alternating amber and green shows that the self-test is running. As indicated, a single LED can provide a great deal of information.

RPS The RPS LED denotes the status of the redundant power supply. On the 3640, only one power supply may be operational at a time. An off LED reflects that the RPS is not installed. A blinking green LED denotes that both the internal and redundant power supplies are operational—administrators should reconfigure the installation to run on one or the other system. A solid green LED denotes that the RPS is operational and amber shows that the RPS is installed but not in operation.

Network Activity   There are two sets of LEDs in the network activity section of the router. There are four LEDs per set, with one per slot. The ready LEDs illuminate to show that a module is installed in the slot and operational. An off LED indicates that nothing is installed in the slot or that it is not functioning. The active LEDs blink to indicate activity.

PCMCIA   The PCMCIA LEDs light up to show activity on that slot. This should serve as a warning to not remove the flash card when reading or writing data. Flashcards are also called PCMCIA memory cards, and they store the router's flash image.

The module LEDs vary widely depending on the type of interface; however, most include at least a link or enable the LED to denote connectivity. Many also include activity indicators—the serial module, for example, also includes clocking indicators to show the presence or absence of synchronization.

Verifying the Remote Branch

As noted previously, Cisco recommends the 1600 series router for remote branch installations. This platform provides an IOS-based system with expandability. Figure 1.3 illustrates the front of the Cisco 1600 router.

FIGURE 1.3   The Cisco 1600 LEDs

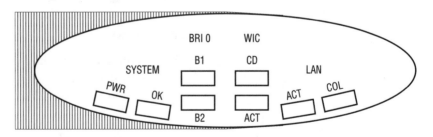

You should understand what each indicator means, as explained in the following list:

System PWR   The green system power LED illuminates to show that the system is on and receiving power.

System OK   The green system OK LED blinks during the boot cycle. Once the boot cycle is complete, this LED is steady.

BRI0 B1 and BRI0 B2 These LEDs display active connections on the BRI0 B1 and B2 channels, respectively. BRI 0 is the first ISDN BRI interface on the router.

WIC CD This LED denotes a connection on the WAN Interface Card. This indication can be helpful when troubleshooting DSU/CSU issues.

WIC ACT The WAN Interface Card activity LED can be used to indicate circuit use, although it is helpful to use the command line interface to see the direction and characteristics of the traffic itself.

LAN ACT The LAN activity LED is similar to the WIC activity LED, but it represents traffic on the Ethernet interface.

LAN COL The LAN collision LED indicates a collision on the Ethernet segment. It is yellow, unlike the other LEDs, which are all green.

Verifying the Telecommuter Installation

Cisco generally recommends the use of the Cisco 700 router in telecommuter installations. One example of this device is the 766 router. This device includes a substantial number of diagnostic LEDs, shown in Figure 1.4.

FIGURE 1.4 The Cisco 766 LEDs

These LEDs are read as follows.

RD The ready LED is illuminated when the router is operating normally. You may use it to verify that a successful power-on self-test (POST) has been completed and that power is available to the device.

NT1 For routers with an internal ISDN NT1, this LED displays the status of the ISDN connection. When steady, the ISDN switch and the NT1 are synchronized; when it is blinking the connection is attempting synchronization.

LINE The LINE LED indicates that framing between the router and the ISDN switch has been established.

LAN This light indicates that the Ethernet interface on the router is active and that a frame has been sent or received within the past 60 seconds. A link light on the back of the router denotes a valid connection.

LAN RXD The LAN received LED blinks upon receipt of a frame on the Ethernet interface.

LAN TXD The LAN transmitted LED blinks when frames are sent from the router onto the Ethernet link.

CH1 and CH2 These LEDs indicate the status of the two B channels on the ISDN BRI. They illuminate steadily when the connection is established and blink during the negotiation process.

CH1 RXD and CH2 RXD These LEDs reflect the receipt of packets on their respective ISDN BRI channels. Each packet generates a blink of the LED.

CH1 TXD and CH2 TXD These LEDs reflect the transmission of packets on the respective ISDN BRI channel. Each packet generates a blink of the LED.

PH1 and PH2 For routers so equipped, these LEDs provide information regarding the use of the plain old telephone system (POTS) ports on the router. These ports may be used for telephone, fax, or analog modem services.

Remember the significance of each LED, including its color, for the exam. This information can be helpful in live troubleshooting as well.

Summary

This chapter encompassed an overview of the services provided in remote access solutions and technologies used to interconnect offices. The chapter also defined the criteria used to select a WAN technology, and it defined the types of connections available to the network designer.

In addition, an overview of the WAN encapsulation protocols was provided. These protocols include ISDN, Frame Relay, PPP, and X.25. The chapter presented some of the issues that confront designers in the selection of these protocols, including cost, availability, and bandwidth.

The WAN technologies available from Cisco for use in remote access solutions were also presented. How they relate to the different types of offices in the modern corporation was discussed, including the central and branch offices, and the remote user operating from their home or mobile location.

Key Terms

Before you take the exam, be certain you are familiar with the following terms:

Asynchronous dial-up

Asynchronous Transfer Mode (ATM)

AVVID

Basic Rate Interface (BRI)

cable modems

channelized T-1

Committed Information Rate (CIR)

Digital Subscriber Line (DSL)

E-1

Frame Relay

High-Level Data Link Control (HDLC)

Integrated Services Digital Network (ISDN)

leased lines

MUXing

Permanent Virtual Circuits (PVCs)

Point-to-Point Protocol (PPP)

port density

port type

Primary Rate Interface (PRI)

quality of service (QoS)

reliability

remote access

Serial Line Internet Protocol (SLIP)

Switched Virtual Circuits (SVCs)

virtual private network (VPN)

wide area network (WAN)

X.25

Commands in This Chapter

In other chapters, you will find a list of commands that were used in this chapter here. You should make sure you are familiar with these commands and how to use them.

Written Lab

1. The system LED on the 3640 indicates _____.

2. A reliable protocol for poor quality circuits is _____.

3. A low overhead, low cost protocol is _____.

4. You believe that data is being received on the first B channel of a 700 series router. What would indicate this?

5. A modern alternative to ISDN is _____.

6. A common protocol for remote access is _____.

7. The most widely available remote access technology is _____.

8. The _____ series is the lowest model number IOS-based router platform.

9. The 7000/7200/7500 series routers would likely be found in the _____.

10. The 700 series router would likely be found in _____.

Hands-on Labs

In other chapters, you will find lab exercises that will reinforce the concepts of the chapter.

Review Questions

1. Which of the following remote access technologies is widely available?

    A. X.25

    B. ISDN

    C. Asynchronous dial-up

    D. Frame Relay

2. Which of the following remote access technologies provides the user with two 64Kbps channels for data traffic?

    A. Frame Relay

    B. Leased line

    C. X.25

    D. ISDN BRI

3. Which of the following is not a consideration in remote access design?

    A. Cost

    B. Availability

    C. Bandwidth

    D. Compression

4. Which of the following might be the best solution for use in an international remote access installation with poor cable quality?

    A. X.25

    B. ISDN

    C. Frame Relay

    D. Leased line

5. The administrator sees intermittent flashing on the CH1 RXD LED on a 700 series router. This most likely means

   A. That the asynchronous interface is bad

   B. That the first Frame Relay channel is receiving data

   C. That the first ISDN D channel is receiving data

   D. That the first ISDN B channel is receiving data

   E. That the first ISDN B channel is negotiating connectivity with the remote location

6. Of the following, which series offers the lowest priced IOS-based router?

   A. The 700 series

   B. The 800 series

   C. The 1600 series

   D. The 7000 series

7. Of the following, which router provides an Ethernet and ISDN BRI termination, in addition to a single WAN expansion slot?

   A. The 700 series

   B. The 800 series

   C. The 1600 series

   D. The 7000 series

8. The 700 series routers can support which of the following?

   A. AppleTalk

   B. IPX

   C. IP

   D. All of the above

9. The administrator observes that the power and OK LEDs are illuminated on a Cisco 1600 series router. From this, the administrator can deduce that

   A. The router is on.

   B. The router is on and successfully booted.

   C. The router is on and the Ethernet interface is receiving packets.

   D. The router is on and the ISDN interface is receiving packets.

10. An ISDN PRI in London, England provides which of the following?

    A. 23 B channels

    B. 30 B channels

    C. 23 D channels

    D. 30 D channels

11. Of the following, which series of router does Cisco recommend for use in central sites?

    A. The 700 series

    B. The 1000 series

    C. The 1600 series

    D. The 3600 series

12. Typically, which of the following connectors would be used to terminate an analog modem to a router?

    A. V.35

    B. 10-BaseT

    C. RS-232

    D. RS-449

13. According to Cisco, quick verification of a remote access installation can use which of the following?

   A. Router LEDs

   B. CiscoWorks

   C. Telnet

   D. Cable testers

14. The Data Link Layer of ISDN's D channel is which of the following?

   A. LAPB

   B. LAPD

   C. X.25

   D. PPP

15. ISDN is typically defined as a

   A. Packet-switched connection

   B. Cell-switched connection

   C. Circuit-switched connection

   D. Frame-switched connection

16. Modems are limited to a maximum bandwidth of

   A. 28.8Kbps

   B. 33.6Kbps

   C. 56Kbps

   D. 56Mbps

17. Which router is a high-performance, high-density LAN and WAN router positioned by Cisco for the central office?

A. The 700 series

B. The 1000 series

C. The 1600 series

D. The 7200 series

18. Which product is designed for designers looking for an access server that integrates the modem, switch, and router functions?

A. The 800 series

B. The 1600 series

C. The 4500 series

D. The AS5x00 series

19. What is one of the benefits of routers with fixed interfaces?

A. High cost

B. Lower cost

C. More flexibility

D. Harder configuration

20. Frame Relay is best suited for connections from the central site to which of the following?

A. Telecommuter homes

B. Hotel room access

C. Branch offices

D. All of the above

Answers to Written Lab

1. System power and operation characteristics

2. X.25

3. Frame Relay

4. The B1 RX LED

5. DSL

6. PPP

7. Asynchronous dial-up

8. 800

9. Network core

10. A small office or home office

Answers to Review Questions

1. C. Asynchronous dial-up is found in virtually every residential and business setting. It is the most basic of telecommunication services. It may be possible to install the other services many places, but asynchronous dial-up is the most ubiquitous connection type.

2. D. ISDN BRI provides two user channels of 64Kbps each.

3. D. While compression may be a desired feature, it is not a consideration in the design.

4. A. X.25 is widely available in international markets and was designed to operate on poor quality circuits.

5. D. Remember that the LED reflects the receipt of a packet, so the intermittent flashing will be faster under heavy loads and slower under idle periods.

6. B. The 800 series is the lowest priced IOS-based router. The 700 series uses a different operating system.

7. C. Make sure that you are familiar with the ports, slots, and modules of the Cisco router products. Of the choices, only the 1600 offers the configuration presented.

8. B and C. The Cisco 700 routers do not run the full Cisco IOS, and, because of this, they provide limited features.

9. B. Remember the significance of the colors and indicators on the LEDs.

10. B. European E-1 standards provide for 30 B + 1 D channel.

11. D. While Cisco recommends the 3600 for central sites, in reality, this decision should be based on requirements. Of the choices given above, however, the 3600 is the most scalable and best performing, and typically, it matches well with central site requirements.

12. C. The other choices are for Ethernet (B) or high speed serial connections (A, D).

13. A. The fastest and simplest way to check the status of a network device is to look at the LEDs. The other solutions require additional equipment and time. However, only high-level problems can be resolved using this method.

14. B. The easiest way to remember that LAPD is the correct answer is because it has a D at the end.

15. C. ISDN operates by establishing a circuit pathway for packets. There is no addressing information as part of the frame.

16. C. In the United States, the figure is actually 53Kbps due to Federal Communications Commission (FCC) regulations; however, the theoretical bandwidth is 56Kbps.

17. D. Of the choices provided, the 7200 router provides the highest density and performance. It is for these reasons that it is Cisco's recommended platform.

18. D. The AS series of products provides access services, which include modem terminations, routing and switching.

19. B. Fixed interface routers are cheaper to build, and thus have a lower cost. They are also generally easier to support.

20. C. Homes and hotels rarely provide the appropriate facilities for Frame Relay. Typically, only asynchronous dial-up is available; however, some hotels are providing T-1-based Internet connectivity from an office area or individual rooms.

Chapter

2

Asynchronous Connections

THE CCNP REMOTE ACCESS EXAM TOPICS COVERED IN THIS CHAPTER INCLUDE THE FOLLOWING:

✓ Reviewing asynchronous connections

✓ Understanding signaling, cabling, and modulation standards

✓ Configuring asynchronous connections

✓ Configuring modems—automatic and manual processes

As noted in Chapter 1, asynchronous (analog) remote access solutions are extremely popular, primarily because little preparation is needed on the remote side of the connection. Unlike Frame Relay, ISDN, and X.25, *asynchronous connections* (or *analog connections*) use standard phone lines and are available virtually everywhere. With cellular modems, these services are even available on a wireless basis. This wide availability provides a huge advantage over other remote access solutions and effectively mandates the inclusion of asynchronous connections in modern implementations. Unfortunately, analog-based modems suffer from low performance and relatively high cost per kilobyte.

The terms asynchronous and analog are used interchangeably in this text.

With a digital connection on one end, it is possible to provide up to 56Kbps of theoretical bandwidth to remote users; however, the FCC (Federal Communications Commission) limits this to 53Kbps in the United States. Also, asynchronous connections require a lengthy call setup time—sometimes more than one minute—which can substantially impact user and application performance.

Administrators frequently look for other technologies to replace asynchronous modems, or dial-up connections, in order to improve performance. Even with the proliferation of ISDN, DSL, cable modems, and other technologies, no system has yet successfully dethroned simple dial services.

Asynchronous Modems

Technically, *modems* are modulator/demodulators, but most people simply define them by their high-level function—modems connect devices to the telephone network. These devices connect the computer or router to the phone network and may incorporate a pass-though for an analog phone set. While the phone cannot be used while the computer is connected to a remote location, this does afford a non-concurrent role for the installation—only the phone or the data connection may be used at any given time.

Modems are considered Data Communications Equipment (DCE), while computers and routers are Data Terminal Equipment (DTE). The connection between the modems, or *DCEs*, is *analog* in nature, meaning that bits are defined by an analog waveform that is continuous and variable. *DTE* connections are *digital* in nature; this means that each bit has a clear zero or one voltage to denote the bit. It is important to remember that asynchronous refers to clocking and not a digital or analog transmission. *Clocking* is provided in asynchronous connections with start and stop bits, which results in 10 bits per byte of data—eight for the data byte and one each for the start and stop markers. Unlike asynchronous connections, synchronous connections have precise clocking to denote the start and stop bits; in these connections, bytes may only begin on the downbeat of the synchronous drum, for example. (There really isn't a drum in synchronous signaling. Rather, bits are sent in sync with the clocking pulse—similar to taking a dance step for every drumbeat, the dance step is the data. For an asynchronous connection, on the other hand, there are actually three distinct connections (DTE to DCE, DCE to DCE, and DCE to DTE), which are shown in Figure 2.1.

FIGURE 2.1   An analog connection

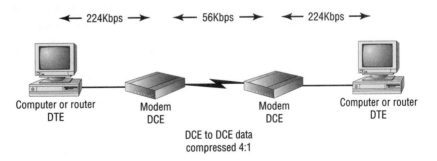

As shown in Figure 2.1, the DTE to DCE bandwidth is uncompressed and is four times that of the modem connection assuming optimum compression. Remember that this figure represents an optimal situation rather than a realistic one. Because of that, it is unlikely that either the DTE to DCE or DCE to DCE connections will normally see this level of performance. Some of this is attributable to the DCE to DCE limitations; however, there are also limitations in the serial interface from the PC to the modem, as described in the next paragraph.

Remote Access with Modems

When discussing the limitations of serial signaling, it would be remiss to not discuss the limitations of the public phone system and the analog technology available today. As noted earlier in this chapter, asynchronous connections are limited to 56Kbps, or 53Kbps by FCC order. Distance and line quality further limit this amount of bandwidth, possibly reducing throughput to 28.8Kbps or less. (I'm writing this in a Boston hotel room, where I can't get a reliable connection beyond 26Kbps.) In addition, connections may take a minute or more to establish and may be further impeded by load coils and analog-to-digital conversions between the home and the Central Office (CO). Load coils are amplifiers used to accommodate longer distances than normal, and analog-to-digital conversions are often used in new developments to convert the copper pairs to fiber, again extending the length of the link. It is far cheaper to run a few pairs of fiber to an access terminal (a small cabinet that sits in the neighborhood and converts the fiber to copper) where the copper runs, then extend into the home.

You need to remember that the plain old telephone service (POTS) is exactly that—old. It was developed from the same technology that Alexander Graham Bell developed in his lab over a hundred years ago and was never intended to address the needs of video and data. That's the first problem with analog connections—they were never designed to allow millions of bits of data to flow from one point to another.

The second problem with analog connections is their inefficiency. Voice is a very specific type of data and fits in a single 64Kbps channel. You may already be aware of the channels of voice aggregation, or T-1 circuits—where 24 voice signals (DS-0, digital signal) fit into a T-1 or DS-1. Data is unlike voice, however, which leads to inefficiency. Voice demands that the idle (or no data) points in the conversation be communicated as well, so there is always a constant flow of information. Data doesn't work that way—if no data is transmitted, there is little need for the bandwidth to be consumed. By only using the available bandwidth that is necessary, it is possible to service more connections with data than voice. You may have heard of convergence or time division multiplexing (TDM), two very different concepts that relate to this topic. *Convergence* is the concept of voice, video, and data all using the same network, whereas *TDM* is the old voice channel model—each channel always given the same amount of access to the network regardless of the need. Convergence will remove TDM from the network and place everything into packets that can then only use the required amount of bandwidth, as opposed to reserving more than is necessary.

However, convergence will also effectively eliminate the analog network (an event that has already occurred in the core of the telephone world). But before that comes to fruition, network administrators will need to contend with the problems of the current network, including long call-setup times, poor quality connections, and low bandwidths.

These problems, just for the record, already have solutions in many cases. While it is true that analog connections are the most prevalent in the world, the availability of DSL, cable, ISDN, Frame Relay, wireless, and long-distance Ethernet allows designers to incorporate alternatives into their installations and provides an indication of what will happen in the near future.

At the beginning of this sidebar, I noted problems with analog service and the phone network, and while discussing these problems, I failed to address what is possibly the most important problem—cost. Readers of the *CCDP: Cisco Internetwork Design Study Guide* (Sybex, 2000) will recall the emphasis on business concerns when designing the network. Cost is frequently the single biggest business factor, period. Business managers who do not understand bits and protocols certainly understand the benefits of a $40-a-month fixed cost per employee compared to a variable bill that could surpass $100 a month.

One last item—virtual private networks. Virtual private networks, or *VPNs*, are encrypted sessions between two devices over the public network, typically the Internet. These sessions are virtually private because the encrypted data is, conceptually, protected from snooping. Users, however, will still be affected by delay and bandwidth limitations that could be better controlled in private network installations. VPNs provide remote access designers with two benefits, however. The first is low cost, which, as noted in the previous paragraph, is a powerful business case argument. The second benefit is universality—or the ability to allow access from different technologies. With VPNs, the administrator no longer cares what technology is used on the remote side of the connection. The remote side only needs to connect to the Internet, or in some cases, an internationally accessible single-vendor network (which can provide service-level agreements and other service guarantees). Once connected, the connection traverses the network and is decrypted at the corporate access point, typically a T-1 or DS-3, depending on the bandwidth demands. For smaller support departments, this entire service may be outsourced so the maintenance of the VPN equipment and connections is not an additional burden on the team.

The *Universal Asynchronous Receiver/Transmitter (UART)* is a chip that governs asynchronous communications. Its primary function is to buffer incoming data, but it buffers outbound bits also. Most UARTs are limited to 115.2Kbps, which is insufficient for 56Kbps connections, and the most capable UART only provides for a 56-byte receive buffer and a 64-byte transmit buffer. Even this can be insufficient for maximum throughput.

In current computer designs, the UART is virtually disregarded as a component in the communications system. This is because most systems today provide sufficient buffering systems to address the volume of packets that come with 56Kbps asynchronous transmissions—specifically, the 16550 UART (16550 is a part number). In the early days of PCs, the most common chipset was the 8250 UART from National Semiconductor. It contained a single buffer of sorts—it could hold a single bit of data. Any transmission speed greater than 19,200Kbps was too fast for the UART to forward properly. This was a substantial cause of performance problems with the original deployments of 28.8Kbps modems.

Again, this issue is not of much consequence in modern communications systems. Unless you are installing a 386 or older computer, you should find that 16550 UARTs were used for the serial ports. Please note that most internal modem cards include either the 16550 UART or a proprietary buffering system.

Signaling and Cabling

The cables used in various asynchronous connections differ depending on the end equipment and the type and distance of the connection.

Modems typically use two different types of connectors—one for DTE and one for DCE. An RS-232C 25-pin connector typically provides the DTE termination; this RS-232C connector is now also called an ITU-232 connector. Both terms are still used, though the ITU terminology is more current. The DCE connection to the phone network is provided by a standard RJ-11 connector.

For the connection between the DTE and the DCE, there are individual wires used in the serial cable. These wires and their functions are shown in Table 2.1.

TABLE 2.1 DTE to DCE Signaling

Wire	Function
Tx	Transmits data from the DTE to the DCE. All serial connections send their data one bit at a time over a single transmission path. This differs from parallel transmissions that have multiple paths. Printers, for example, send a full octet per signaling window. Tx is on pin 2.

TABLE 2.1 DTE to DCE Signaling *(continued)*

Wire	Function
Rx	Receives data from the DCE to the DTE and is carried on pin 3. If there is a need to cross two serial ports together, as is the case in DTE to DTE connections, pin 2 is linked to 3 and vice versa.
Ground	The electrical ground provides a baseline for voltage changes on the Tx and Rx wires. It is on pin 7.
RTS	Request to send is one of the two hardware flow control wires. It signals that the DTE can receive data from the DCE. This depends on having sufficient buffers available.
CTS	Clear to send is the second hardware flow control wire, and it signals that the DCE is ready to receive from the DTE.
DTR	The data terminal ready wire is a modem control signaling wire, which signifies that the DTE can accept a call from the DCE.
CD	Carrier detection indicates that the DCEs have connected. It is also a modem control wire.

DCE is modem

The information in Table 2.1 is important to understand from a troubleshooting perspective; however, it is also nice to know for an overview of wiring. There are instances, such as the extension of a serial connection, in which it may be necessary to serially link two devices using Category 5 cable, for example. Hoods are available to make this link, and in fact, many Cisco connections use the fact that there are so few wires used in serial connections to terminate the console ports with RJ-45 connections. (Hood is a slang term that describes the plastic converter that covers the wiring as it changes from RJ to DB connections. Another term for this is media converter.)

Refer to the documentation that came with your router or switch regarding console connections. Cisco has been inconsistent with this implementation, sometimes requiring the use of rolled connection cables and at other times needing straight-through patch cords. A rolled connection places pin 1 on one end into the pin 8 position on the other end; thus, pin 2 falls into the pin 7 position, and so forth. Straight-through connections map 1 to 1 and 2 to 2.

Modulation Standards

Modulation defines the method used to encode the data stream between DCE devices. There are many different modulation standards, including several proprietary methods. Modems will negotiate the modulation standard to be used during connection, and newer modems will alter this negotiation during the connection, should line conditions permit. This can provide improved performance or prevent a connection from terminating, should the line condition degrade. Table 2.2 notes the common modem modulation standards.

TABLE 2.2 Modem Modulation Standards

Modulation	DCE to DCE Bandwidth	Status
V.22	1200bps	ITU standard
V.22bis	2400bps	ITU standard
V.32	9600bps	ITU standard
V.32bis	14.4Kbps	ITU standard
V.32 terbo	19.2Kbps	Proprietary
V.34	28.8Kbps	ITU standard
V.fast	28.8Kbps	Proprietary
V.FC	28.8Kbps	Proprietary

TABLE 2.2 Modem Modulation Standards *(continued)*

Modulation	DCE to DCE Bandwidth	Status
V.34 annex 1201H	33.6Kbps	ITU standard
K56Flex	56Kbps	Proprietary
X2	56Kbps	Proprietary
V.90	56Kbps	ITU standard

Most modems support all lower bandwidth ITU standards for backward compatibility, and many V.90 modems also support either X2 or K56Flex. Modems that shipped with X2 or K56Flex sole support—before the V.90 standard was ratified—can usually be upgraded in the field, frequently with software only.

The modulation standards also incorporate data compression and error correction specifications, which are detailed below.

Data Compression

Data compression allows the representation of the bit stream that substitutes repetitive data with fewer bits that will be interpreted, or uncompressed, on the other modem. Later in this book, we will present a more detailed example of data compression—for this introduction, it is sufficient to know that compression will allow fewer bits of data to represent the total number of bits needed to reconstruct the message accurately. One of the more common compression systems today is v.42bis, which is based on the theoretical works of Professors Ziv and Lempel at Technion University in Israel. I visited Technion in 1984 and was extremely impressed with the technical capabilities of their students and facility. At that time, they had perfected systems that could convert English text to Hebrew text and they could integrate both texts into a single document. In order to understand how impressive this was, consider that this was happening the same year as the first Apple Macintosh release.

The work of Ziv and Lempel was used by Englishman Terry Welch to develop the *LZW algorithm*, named to honor the three men. The LZW process uses two steps in order to parse character sequences into a table of strings; these strings are then represented with one of 256 codes. The parsing process works by constantly trying to find longer sequences that aren't part of the current 256 values. This allows the compression process to substitute longer and longer strings, which subsequently increases the benefits of the compression.

Error Correction

Error correction validates the integrity of the data and is frequently used with compression to verify that the compression process did not corrupt the data. The impact of a single-bit error can distort substantial amounts of compressed data—instead of just impacting a single bit, it might distort two or more bytes, which, in turn, may require retransmission of even more data. When one considers the overhead of asynchronous communications—the start and stop bits require two extra bits per eight-bit byte, or 20 percent—the added overhead that would result from errors involving compressed data only serves to further reduce the actual throughput. Detection of errors as quickly as possible can reduce the amount of data that needs to be retransmitted and, thus, improve total throughput.

The error correction process relies on a checksum value that validates the data. A simple example of this checksum would look like the following:

$$21+9+6+17+8+29+4+27=121$$

It is reasonably certain that the calculation on the left side of the equal sign is accurate because it does equal the value on the right side. However, it would also be possible for the 21 to be a 22 and the 9 to be an 8, which also yields an answer of 121. Error correction works on the same premise as this equation; however, most error correction algorithms work to allow for multiple errors and other distortions. Many error correction processes block the binary data and divide that value by a fixed value. This value is then added to the block of data and is transmitted with the user data. On the opposite end of the transmission, the checksum is calculated against the binary value of the data and the division of the same fixed value. If they match the data block, the result is considered true and forwarded. If the values do not match, the data is discarded.

Configuring Asynchronous Modem Connections

Asynchronous connections, like other connections, require configuration before they may be used. In applications using Cisco routers, this configuration can be supplemented with automatic functions, or it can be manual. As such, there are three possible configuration options.

- Manual configuration
- Autoconfigure
- Autodiscovery

Manual configuration requires knowledge of the commands required by the modem to establish the parameters that govern flow control, error control, compression, and the number of rings that will occur before the line is answered. Flow control is a function that uses the clear-to-send and ready-to-send pins on the serial cable to govern the bit stream, and it may be serviced by hardware or software.

Autoconfigure is used to automatically configure a modem from a router that has been given the modem type. The configuration information is stored in a database on the router.

The *autodiscovery* function detects the modem type and then supplies the proper initialization string information. This process works by first negotiating the baud, or data rate, and then sending queries to the modem to learn its identity. This is accomplished with standard attention (AT) command sequences based on the router's database. If there is no match, the autodiscovery function will fail.

Cisco routers provide two methods for preparing the modem for operation. These are manual and automatic, and within automatic configuration there are two options, a completely automatic process that learns the type of modem in use and a hybrid that relies on the administrator to define the type of modem connected to the router. This alternative removes the need for a negotiation process; however, it is still considered an automatic process. The modem's configuration must match the router so that communications between the two devices are properly coordinated.

Automatic Configuration

Most modern modems provide the ability to identify their type and specifications, which a computer or router can use to assist in the configuration process. Obviously, the benefit of automatic configuration is that it reduces the number of administrative tasks required during installation; however, the learning process can delay modem availability and can fail. The delay is the result of the interrogation process, and failure can occur if the router fails to understand the responses from the modem—this can happen if the modem is not in the modemcap database, discussed later in this chapter.

Commands for Automatic Configuration

This section will introduce the commands used for automatic configuration.

The *modem autoconfigure* Command

The modem autoconfigure command is used to instruct the router to use this feature. This feature will detect the type of modem connected to the router and then supply the initialization string to the modem—a process that can require up to five seconds. Automatic modem recognition is made possible by the modemcap database, which resides in the router. The *modemcap database* is a listing of modem configuration commands that provide basic information that will allow the modem to operate with the router in most instances. To show this database, use the show modemcap command. The output of this command is shown below. This output provides a list of the modem types that are defined in the database. This list is from a Cisco 2600 series router, and thus, it reflects those modem types that are included with that router image.

```
Router_A#show modemcap
default
codex_3260
usr_courier
usr_sportster
hayes_optima
global_village
viva
telebit_t3000
microcom_hdms
```

```
microcom_server
nec_v34
nec_v110
nec_piafs
cisco_v110
mica
```

Each modem type has a related AT command string sequence stored, which is shown with the show modemcap {modem type} command. From previous experience, you may recall that AT stands for attention and is the prefix for many modem commands. The output of this command, when used for the US Robotics Courier, is shown below.

```
Router_A#show modemcap usr_courier
Modemcap values for usr_courier
Factory Defaults (FD):  &F
Autoanswer (AA):  S0=1
Carrier detect (CD):  &C1
Drop with DTR (DTR):  &D2
Hardware Flowcontrol (HFL):  &H1&R2
Lock DTE speed (SPD):  &B1
DTE locking speed (DTE):  [not set]
Best Error Control (BER):  &M4
Best Compression (BCP):  &K1
No Error Control (NER):  &M0
No Compression (NCP):  &K0
No Echo (NEC):  E0
No Result Codes (NRS):  Q1
Software Flowcontrol (SFL):  [not set]
Caller ID (CID):  [not set]
On-hook (ONH):  H0
Off-hook (OFH):  H1
Miscellaneous (MSC):  [not set]
Template entry (TPL):  default
Modem entry is built-in.
```

This output is similar to what would happen if you manually sent the modem the sequence AT&FS0=1&C1&D2&H1&R2&B1. This sequence would instruct a Courier to reset its configuration and then answer in one ring, using hardware flow control with DTR dropping and Carrier Detect.

As denoted, this modem entry is included in the router's operating system—it is built in. Please note that the database entry must be complete and exact. As shown in the following output, the router will respond with an error message if the entry is abbreviated.

```
Router_A#show modemcap usr_cou
There is no record of modem usr_cou
```

In addition, the command modemcap entry modem_profile_name may be used to obtain an abbreviated version of the output.

The *modemcap edit* Command

To add entries to the modemcap database, the administrator may use the modemcap edit command. Commands are entered with the modemcap edit command followed by the database name using the format modemcap edit modem_profile_name. Configurations provided with the router cannot be modified. Administrators should create a similar user-created entry with their modifications.

Use care when removing modemcap entries. The no modemcap edit modem_profile_name command will delete the entire entry, not just a single line. To delete just a line from the profile, use modemcap edit modem_profile_name *attribute*.

It is generally recommended that administrators specify the type of modem that is connected to the router. This will reduce the probability of error and hasten the configuration process.

The *modem autoconfigure autodiscovery* Command

The command for discovering and automatically configuring the modems is modem autoconfigure discovery. As stated previously, the discovery process will try to learn the make and model of the modem automatically. The command is entered in interface mode, as shown in the following output:

```
Router_A(config)#line 1
Router_A(config-line)#modem autoconfigure discovery
```

This sequence will instruct the router, or access server, to send an AT command sequence to line 1 at varying baud rates until it receives an acknowledgment from the modem. *Baud* is a representation of the signaling speed, and it frequently corresponds to the bits-per-second capacity of the link. However, this assumes a modulation of one bit per signaling change—an inconsistent assumption given the wide variety of modulation protocols available in modern modems. Once it has determined the appropriate speed with which it should communicate to the modem, the router will attempt to determine the modem type with additional AT commands.

The modem entries in the modemcap database vary based on the version of IOS software and platform.

Automatic modem recognition can take up to five seconds, with a default setting sent to the modem after this timeout (six seconds). This will occur if there is no match found during the autodiscovery process, which means that a relevant entry was not found in the modemcap database. Specifying the type of modem and using the auto configure command should take less than two seconds for configuration.

Verifying and Troubleshooting the Automatic Configuration

Cisco provides a number of troubleshooting services to assist in the diagnostic process, and support for troubleshooting the automatic configuration service is no exception. However, before using the **debug** command and other troubleshooting tools, it is best to review the status of the installation and the connections between the modem and the router. Make sure to check for the following:

- The modem is turned on and it is receiving power.

- The cable is of the right type and is secured.

- The DIP switches or other physical options on the modem are set to known values or factory defaults. In this case, *known values* means settings that are known to work for this router and modem configuration in other installations—sometimes the factory defaults will not work. In addition, administrators may find that random guessing is required to find the proper settings.

- The modem is plugged into a phone jack and the dial tone is present.

After these steps are completed, it is appropriate to try *reverse Telnet* to communicate with the modem. To connect to the modem, the administrator would use reverse Telnet, which requires that the line interface will need a minimum of the `transport input all` and `modem inout` commands. These commands allow the port to accept input and transfer data to and from the modem. Note that reverse Telnet is not a command but, rather, a tool used to provide a connection to a reserved TCP port on the router, which maps to the asynchronous port. For example, port line 4 would map to TCP port 2004. As a result, the administrator may Telnet to the router and, by altering the port number (the default TCP Telnet port is 23), they can be connected directly to the attached device, such as a modem. TCP ports starting with 2000 are used for Telnet, whereas 4000 is the start of the range for non-Telnet specific TCP connections. Ports starting with 6000 are used for binary-mode Telnet. Of these, most administrators find it only necessary to use ports in the 2000 range.

Reverse Telnet is a powerful tool that has been required for practical demonstrations of Cisco expertise and certifications.

Manual Configuration

Manual configuration can eliminate the negotiation process required for automatic configuration, but it adds substantially to the configuration process, and it requires router changes if the modem is changed—possibly through an upgrade or replacement to a different vendor or model. Manual router configuration requires knowledge of the AT, or Hayes, command instructions.

The attention (AT) commands are used to configure the modem and, for most purposes, are used to create a standard operating system for modems, but there are differences from vendor to vendor in the function of each command. AT commands allow configuration and diagnostic services to become fairly advanced, including settings that report the modem's status, the quality of the network (phone company) connection, and the configuration of flow control and other modem functions. Software, including terminal software, will frequently provide these commands upon selection of a menu-driven function, which insulates the user from needing to learn and use the commands.

Please consult with the modem manufacturer regarding the appropriate codes for your modem.

Most modems have a number of commands in common, and many of these are quite useful for the administrator. These are outlined in Table 2.3.

TABLE 2.3 Common AT Commands

Command	Function
&F	The AT&F command resets most modems to their factory defaults.
&C	This command configures the modem-for-modem control (C is for Carrier Detect). C1 instructs the modem to use CD to reflect the actual connection status.
S0=1	There are a number of S series commands, of which S0 is the first. S0 controls the number of rings before the modem answers—in this case the modem will answer on the first ring. A setting of at least two is suggested for Caller ID installations, while some secure installations use fairly high values—perhaps 10 rings or more. This is because most "war dialers" (or automatic dialers) assume the line is not terminated after eight or more rings.
&D	The &D command relates to DTR. With a setting of D3, the modem will hang up the line when the DTR goes low. This is the normal configuration.
M0	This command turns off the audio output from the modem. This can provide a great benefit when you are not troubleshooting—the screeching of the modem connection sequence can be quite irritating.

TABLE 2.3   Common AT Commands *(continued)*

Command	Function
L1	The L commands control the volume on the modem speaker. L3 would turn the volume to maximum. Note that modems with external volume controls, such as the US Robotics Courier, will also require the physical knob to be turned.
&Q6	The &Q6 command is significant because it results in the DTE speed being locked. This is discussed in greater detail in Chapter 4, but basically, this means that locking the DTE speed can improve performance on lower quality circuits.

From the router's perspective, there are a number of commands that are necessary to configure an asynchronous connection. These are outlined in Table 2.4.

TABLE 2.4   The Asynchronous Router Commands

Command	Function
line N	Cisco routers refer to asynchronous ports as lines. *N* is equal to the number of the port and is used before the rest of the commands in this table.
login	The login command is required in order to permit a connection.
password	This command establishes the password to be used on the line.
flowcontrol	The flowcontrol command may be followed with hardware or software settings. Typically, hardware is allowed to provide control over the data flow. Software flow control is not recommended.

TABLE 2.4 The Asynchronous Router Commands *(continued)*

Command	Function
speed	The speed command establishes the maximum speed to be used between the modem and access server or router. It defines the speed of both transmit and receive, and it is noted in bits per second (bps). Note that the modem and access server can negotiate a slower speed or data rate.
transport input	The transport input command defines the protocol to use in reverse Telnet connections. This may be LAT, MOP, NASI, PAD, RLOGIN, Telnet, or v120; however, administrators typically use the all keyword to allow all connection types. This is potentially less secure, as a hacker could use one of these protocols to gain access or deny service to the router. For example, if there is no business need to use RLOGIN, why leave the access available to allow repeated access attempts from an outsider?
stopbits	Stopbits commands are sent in asynchronous connections in order to define the end of a byte. Typically, the stopbit value is set to 1 because there is little reason to send additional bits; however, values of 1.5 and 2 are also allowed.
modem	The modem command is used to define the type of call allowed. By default, the modem will allow dial-in, or incoming calls. However, for reverse Telnet or dial-out connections in addition to dial-in, the administrator would use the inout keyword.

It is important to note that each line (specified with the line command in Table 2.4) has an associated logical interface, defined by the router, an async interface. Configurations on async interfaces define the protocol characteristics of the connection. This would be used to define a protocol such as Point-to-Point Protocol (PPP) or the addressing mechanism to be used.

Configuration begins with the line command and the number of the interface. This is followed with the specific information that is needed—for example, the login capabilities and DTE to DCE speed. A typical configuration might appear as follows:

```
line 3
    modem inout
    stopbits 1
    transport all
    speed 56000
    flowcontrol hardware
    login
    password tplekprp
```

This configuration would allow calls in or out, with all protocols supported and login permitted. Hardware flowcontrol would be used. Flowcontrol is used to prevent buffer overruns and maintain an efficient flow of data by signaling the sender that it should slow down or speed up.

If there is a problem with manual configuration, it will be first noted when the administrator attempts to use the modem. Reverse Telnet, and use of the diagnostic commands associated with that modem, are most likely the best tools available for troubleshooting.

Summary

This chapter presented the foundation of asynchronous connections. It then built upon this foundation to provide examples of how designers and administrators configure and install asynchronous remote access solutions. This presentation included the following:

- Modems, including modulations, connections, and capabilities

- Automatic and manual router configuration

- Troubleshooting of automatic installations

This chapter also familiarized readers with the advantages and disadvantages of automatic and manual modem configuration, along with the AT command structure, which allows the modem to be customized for use in a remote access solution. In addition, as presented in the "Remote Access with Modems" sidebar, this chapter showed readers how to assess the appropriateness of an analog solution for their specific remote access needs.

Key Terms

Before you take the exam, be certain you are familiar with the following terms:

analog

analog connections

asynchronous connections

baud

clocking

convergence

data compression

DCE

digital

DTE

error correction

LZW algorithm

modemcap database

modem

modulation

reverse Telnet

TDM

Universal Asynchronous Receiver/Transmitter (UART)

VPN

Commands in This Chapter

Command	Meaning
line N	Cisco routers refer to asynchronous ports as lines. N is equal to the number of the port and is used before the rest of the commands in this table.
login	The login command is required in order to permit a connection.
password	This command establishes the password to be used on the line.
flowcontrol	The flowcontrol command may be followed with hardware or software settings. Typically, hardware is allowed to provide control over the data flow. Software flow control is not recommended.
speed	The speed command establishes the maximum speed to be used between the modem and access server or router. It defines the speed of both transmit and receive, which are noted in bits per second (bps). Note that the modem and access server can negotiate a slower speed or data rate.
transport input	The transport input command defines the protocol to use in reverse Telnet connections. This may be LAT, MOP, NASI, PAD, RLOGIN, Telnet, or v120; however, administrators typically use the all keyword to allow all connection types. This is potentially less secure, as a hacker could use one of these protocols to gain access or deny service to the router. For example, if there is no business need to use RLOGIN, why leave the access available to allow repeated access attempts from an outsider?

stopbits	Stopbits commands are sent in asynchronous connections to define the end of a byte. Typically, the stopbit value is set to 1 because there is little reason to send additional bits; however, values of 1.5 and 2 are also allowed.
modem	The modem command is used to define the type of call allowed. By default, the modem will allow dial-in or incoming calls. However, for reverse Telnet or dial-out connections in addition to dial-in, the administrator would use the inout keyword.

Written Lab

1. The command AT&F performs what function on many modems?

2. What command word is used to select hardware or software data control?

3. To set the maximum speed between the DTE and DCE, the administrator would use what command word?

4. What command is used to select configuration mode for port 5?

5. To define the number of bits that define the end of a byte in asynchronous communications, the command _____ is used.

6. The best theoretical analog modem DCE to DCE speed is ____.

7. In the U.S., the FCC limits DCE to DCE speed to no more than _____.

8. V.34 operates at _____.

9. Pin 7 in DTE to DCE signaling normally provides _____.

10. The connector for connecting to the public phone network from the DCE is typically _____.

Hands-on Lab

In this lab, you will configure the modem configuration with the AT commands.

1. Reverse Telnet into a modem connected to the router.

   `{Router Ethernet IP address} {port number}`

   Assuming 10.10.10.10, line 1, the command would be `10.10.10.10 2001`.

2. Using the modem's documentation, reset the modem's configuration, then instruct it to answer on the second ring, use CD, hang up on DTR low, and turn the speaker off.

```
AT&F
ATS0=1
AT&C1
AT&D3
ATM0
```

Note that the command could be entered on a single line as follows:

```
AT&FS0=1&C1&D3M0
```

The &F must appear at the beginning because it is the reset command. Placing it later in the string would erase any modifications made up to that point.

Review Questions

1. What is reverse Telnet?

   A. An encryption technique used by the Telnet protocol

   B. A method for connecting to directly attached asynchronous devices

   C. A function that is only available on the AS5x00 platform

   D. A function that is only available with internal modems

2. Modem-to-modem connections are which of the following?

   A. DTE to DTE

   B. DTE to DCE

   C. DCE to DCE

   D. Dependent upon the modulation used

3. Which of the following options represents the connection between the router and modem?

   A. DTE to DTE

   B. DTE to DCE

   C. DCE to DCE

   D. Analog

4. The UART provides which of the following services?

   A. Compression

   B. Encryption

   C. Error detection

   D. Buffering

5. What is the command to instruct a Cisco router to configure a modem automatically?

   A. modem auto-configure

   B. modem autoconfigure

   C. async modem autoconfigure

   D. modem configuration auto

6. To display the router's initialization string for a US Robotics Courier modem, what would the administrator type?

   A. show modemcap

   B. show modemcap modem usr_courier

   C. show modem usr_courier

   D. show modemcap usr_courier

7. Baud is roughly equivalent to which of the following descriptions?

   A. Bits per minute

   B. Bits per second

   C. Four to one encryption

   D. Analog-to-digital encoding

8. The protocol characteristics of the asynchronous connection are defined by which of the following?

   A. The line interface

   B. The Ethernet interface

   C. The asynchronous interface

   D. The modem interface

9. The administrator would use which command to configure a modem for both incoming and outgoing calls?

   A. modem answer

   B. modem inout

   C. allow modem dial in-out

   D. modem both

10. Which flowcontrol method is recommended for use by administrators?

    A. Hardware

    B. Software

    C. Varies with the speed of the modem

    D. Varies with the type of router

11. The speed command is applied to which of the following interfaces?

    A. Asynchronous

    B. Modem

    C. Line

    D. Port

12. The transport protocols do not include which of the following?

    A. Telnet

    B. rlogin

    C. v120

    D. FTP

13. What is the interface used to configure the router locally called?

A. Auxiliary

B. Virtual terminal

C. Console

D. Management

14. What is the command used to reset most modems to their factory defaults?

A. ATF&

B. Reset

C. AT&E

D. AT&F

15. What is the function of the ground wire?

A. To secure the modem to the router

B. To provide a reference signal for clocking

C. To provide a reference signal for voltage changes

D. To allow data bursts

16. The CTS and RTS wires are part of what modem function?

A. Modem control signaling

B. Hardware flow control

C. Data transfer

D. Compression

17. What is the result of the `modem autoconfigure discovery` command?

    A. The router will interrogate the modem at varying baud rates to automatically configure the modem.

    B. The modem will send an AT string to the router every five seconds following power on, which is used to configure the IOS.

    C. The router will send each of the AT command strings in the modemcap database until one receives an OK response.

    D. None of the above.

18. To permit a connection the administrator would enter which command in line configuration mode?

    A. `login`

    B. `access`

    C. `permit`

    D. None of the above

19. What is the command to have the modem answer on the second ring?

    A. S0=2

    B. AT=2

    C. AT&D2

    D. ATS0=2

20. What is a DIP switch?

    A. The act of hiring a new network administrator.

    B. A physical configuration pin on a modem.

    C. A logical configuration parameter accessed from AT commands.

    D. DIP is another term for DTR—it controls carrier detection.

Answers to Written Lab

1. It resets the configuration to the default.

2. flowcontrol

3. speed

4. line 5

5. stopbits

6. 56Kbps

7. 53Kbps

8. 28.8Kbps

9. Ground

10. RJ-11

Answers to Review Questions

1. B. While the term can be confusing, reverse Telnet links an IP port to a physical port on the access device. Thus, it is a method for connecting to directly attached devices.

2. C. Modems are regarded as DCE devices.

3. B. While the modem is a DCE device, the router is a DTE device.

4. D. UARTs provide a buffer for asynchronous ports.

5. B. Unfortunately, all of these answer choices seem plausible, and the difference between the first three options is minute. However, the command is `modem autoconfigure`, sans hyphen.

6. D. In practice, the administrator would likely use the built-in help function; however, the command to display the initialization string is answer D and is stored in the modemcap database.

7. B. The baud rate is usually parallel to the data rate in bits per second (bps).

8. C. The physical interface is responsible for the protocol characteristics.

9. B. Command questions can be the most difficult, and due to the inconsistencies of the IOS, most must be memorized. The `modem inout` command configures the interface to accept and place calls.

10. A. Hardware flowcontrol is recommended because it reduces the processing requirements incurred with software flow control.

11. C. The `speed` command is used to set the modem to DTE rate, and it is applied to a line interface.

12. D. FTP is not included in the transport protocols, which are best thought of as protocols that allow screen-based sessions, such as Telnet.

13. C. The console port is used to initially configure the router. The default data rate is 9600 baud.

14. D. The Hayes AT command &F resets the modem for compatible modems.

15. C. The ground wire provides reference voltage. Asynchronous connections do not rely on clocking, and no data is transferred on the ground wire.

16. B. Clear to send and ready to send provide hardware flow control functions.

17. A. Autoconfigure discovery starts by establishing a baud rate for further connectivity.

18. A. The login command is used to allow a connection. The other two commands are used for access lists and security.

19. D. If you answered A, you jumped the gun. All AT commands must be prefixed with the AT. While the S0=2 is the right variable, the command cannot stand on its own. &D2 is a DTR command.

20. B. A DIP switch is a physical switch used to alter a modem's configuration. Hope you chuckled at A; C infers a logical configuration change.

Point-to-Point Protocol

THE CCNP REMOTE ACCESS EXAM TOPICS COVERED IN THIS CHAPTER INCLUDE THE FOLLOWING:

- ✓ Learning the Point-to-Point Protocol
- ✓ Configuring access servers
- ✓ Working with PAP and CHAP authentication
- ✓ Configuring PPP servers for callback security
- ✓ Configuring PPP servers for compression and multilink services
- ✓ Verifying and troubleshooting PPP connections

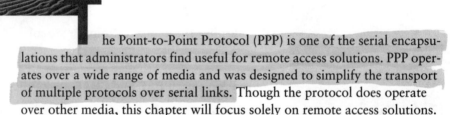

he Point-to-Point Protocol (PPP) is one of the serial encapsulations that administrators find useful for remote access solutions. PPP operates over a wide range of media and was designed to simplify the transport of multiple protocols over serial links. Though the protocol does operate over other media, this chapter will focus solely on remote access solutions.

With the intense demand for connectivity by salespeople, remote staff, and telecommuters, it becomes clear that consistent remote access solutions are required. The benefits of using PPP are that it is universal and efficient. PPP on Windows should be able to communicate with PPP on any access server, and the configuration demands on the client side are extremely small, thus resulting in fewer support issues. While HDLC, SLIP, and Frame Relay encapsulations are also somewhat standardized, the benefits of PPP and its low overhead, along with virtually universal media support, makes it an excellent choice for remote access.

This chapter will provide an overview of PPP and the commands and processes required in order to configure this protocol on Cisco access servers.

PPP Overview and Architecture

PPP is documented in RFC 1661 as a standard method for transporting multiple protocols over point-to-point links. This substantially improved upon the Serial Line Internet Protocol (SLIP). SLIP transports IP packets only across serial circuits.

While beyond the scope of this study guide, PPP has evolved to operate over Ethernet (PPPoE), as specified in RFC 2516, and PPP over ATM (PPPoA), as specified in RFC 2364. Packet over SONET also uses PPP-based encapsulations.

RFCs for Remote Access Networks

There appear to be two schools of thought on *requests for comments (RFCs)*—the documents that are used to establish and document standards in computer networking. Some believe that only geeks bother to memorize and recite the various RFC numbers, while others believe that such knowledge is critical to the proper design and administration of the network.

Regardless of your individual position, the various RFCs that document PPP are worthy of your time and attention. The various protocols are well documented and are invaluable in troubleshooting. Some of the RFCs that warrant specific attention include the following:

RFC 1334   Includes the PPP authentication protocols.

RFC 1661   Includes the current revision of the PPP protocol.

RFC 1990   Includes the PPP Multilink protocol, which will be discussed later in this chapter.

There are many RFCs that would augment this brief list, but their relevance is highly variable depending on the installation requirements. Appendix C lists several RFCs and Web sites to assist you in your studying. The IETF Web site provides links to all RFCs; however, there are other sources available as well.

PPP makes use of two primary protocols for operation. The first, *Link Control Protocol (LCP)*, is used when establishing, configuring, and testing the data-link connection. The second is actually a family of *Network Control Protocols (NCPs)*, which establish and configure different Network Layer protocols. PPP, LCP, and NCP are all considered Layer 2 protocols.

The PPP protocol adds a minimal amount of overhead to the packet, as shown in Figure 3.1.

FIGURE 3.1   The PPP frame structure

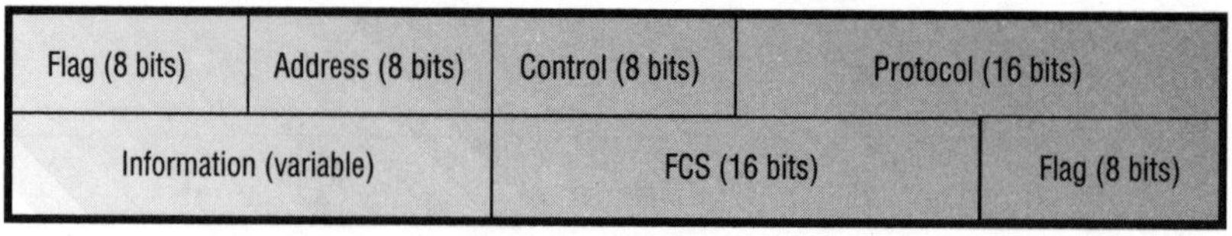

Flag (8 bits)	Address (8 bits)	Control (8 bits)	Protocol (16 bits)	
Information (variable)		FCS (16 bits)		Flag (8 bits)

The following sections describe each of the components found in the PPP frame.

The Flag Field

The *Flag field* is found at the beginning and end of each frame; it has unique pattern of 01111110. Generally, a single flag ends one frame and begins the next. But as can be seen in Figure 3.1, distinct start and end frames are also found. Both of these examples use the same pattern. *Bit stuffing* is used to make this pattern unique. Bit stuffing is a technique that alters other patterns that might appear, like the frame delimiter. For example, if the sequence 010101111110100 appeared representing two characters, the protocol would interpret this as the start of a frame—01111110. Bit-stuffing will re-represent the characters by altering this flow so that the 01111110 pattern remains unique.

The Address Field

The *Address field* is a single octet (8 bits) with the binary sequence of 11111111 (0xff hexadecimal). This is known as the All-Station Address since PPP does not assign individual station addresses. The field is included to allow addressing; however, as inferred by the term point-to-point, the destination is always the opposite end of the link.

The Control Field

The *Control field* is eight bits and contains the binary sequence 00000011 (0x03 hexadecimal), which is the Unnumbered Information (UI) command. This signifies that the following bits will provide information regarding the remaining data—as opposed to the data being part of the PPP protocol.

The Protocol Field

The *Protocol field* is 16 bits long and identifies the upper layer protocol. An upper layer protocol would include IPCP, or the IP Control Protocol. The more commonly assigned protocol fields, and their hexadecimal values, are listed in Table 3.1. This list is beneficial for two reasons: first, it shows the wide diversity of PPP; second, the list will supplement troubleshooting.

TABLE 3.1 PPP Assigned Protocol Fields

Value (in hex)	Protocol Name
0001	Padding Protocol
0021	Internet Protocol
0023	OSI Network Layer
0025	Xerox NS IDP
0027	DECnet Phase IV
0029	AppleTalk
002b	Novell IPX
002d	Van Jacobson Compressed TCP/IP
002f	Van Jacobson Uncompressed TCP/IP
0031	Bridging PDU
0035	Banyan Vines
0201	802.1d Hello Packets
0203	IBM Source Routing BPDU
8021	Internet Protocol Control Protocol
8023	OSI Network Layer Control Protocol
8025	Xerox NS IDP Control Protocol

TABLE 3.1 PPP Assigned Protocol Fields *(continued)*

Value (in hex)	Protocol Name
8027	DECnet Phase IV Control Protocol
8029	AppleTalk Control Protocol
802b	Novell IPX Control Protocol
803d	Multilink Control Protocol
80fd	Compression Control Protocol
c021	Link Control Protocol
c023	Password Authentication Protocol
c025	Link Quality Report
c223	Challenge Handshake Authentication Protocol

Notice that both Password Authentication Protocol (PAP) and Challenge Handshake Authentication Protocol (CHAP) are listed at the bottom of this table. These two protocols will be discussed later in the chapter; however, it is significant to note them here in the context of PPP's broad support for features. Authentication, multilink (the ability to bond different physical channels into a single logical connection), and compression are all supported in PPP and its associated upper layer protocols.

The Information Field

The *Information field* is also called the Data field. This field contains the data of the packet that has been encapsulated in PPP. It can be zero bytes or more, up to the length of the user data.

The Frame Check Sequence (FCS) Field

The *Frame Check Sequence field* is a 16-bit cyclic redundancy check (CRC), and it is used to validate the packet's integrity. This is also called a *checksum*.

Configuring Access Servers

While there can be differences in the configuration methodology needed for different platforms, the fact is that most steps are consistent and similar. Stated another way, commands for a Cisco access server are different than those for a Shiva LANRover, but the functions are similar.

Router ports on remote access devices can terminate standard terminal emulation (exec session)—sometimes thought of as a terminal or VT100 terminal—or a wide array of protocols including PPP, SLIP, and ARAP. The type of protocol used may be predefined by the administrator or automatically selected by the router. This feature uses the autoselect command. When autoselect is not enabled, the router will start an exec session on the line.

If autoselect is not used, the user may still start a session using one of the other protocols, but they will need to provide the command to start. With autoselect, the router can detect the protocol flag value—0x7E for PPP, 0x10 for ARAP, and 0xC0 for SLIP. A carriage return is interpreted as a request for an exec session.

For the remainder of this section the PPP protocol will remain our focus.

Configuring PPP

There are a few choices for the administrator or designer to consider when deploying PPP. These choices are above and beyond those that would be used with any other technology, such as IP addressing assignments (the actual addresses, not the method used) and the provisioning of routing protocols. This section will focus on some of the more common issues regarding PPP, including the selection of dedicated or interactive PPP, the implementation of Layer 3 addressing, and, in the subsequent sections, the selection of an authentication protocol and multilink technology.

Dedicated or Interactive PPP

To dedicate a line for use by SLIP or PPP, the administrator may use the async mode dedicated command. This command prevents the user from changing the encapsulation protocol, and it may augment security by restricting the method of access. The interactive option, configured with the async mode interactive command, allows the user to select any encapsulation for the session with a command entered in exec.

The default for each interface is no async mode. As such, neither PPP nor SLIP is available.

Interface Addressing Options for Local Devices

PPP configuration also requires attention to Layer 3 addressing. For this section, the IP addressing issues will be presented due to both their complexity and frequency. These include static, IP unnumbered, and dynamic addressing options:

Static Addressing   Clearly, the use of static addresses is the most basic IP addressing technique. Static addresses are entered on each interface manually and require administration and documentation. The benefit of static addresses is supportability—troubleshooting is simplified with statics; however, there is a substantial amount of administration overhead. Static addresses are well suited to the central office location or the remote access server.

IP Unnumbered   An alternative to static addressing is the use of IP unnumbered. This is not a dynamic solution, which will also be presented, but rather a feature that Cisco provides to allow a point-to-point link to share an IP address from another interface. For example, the remote client might be configured with a static IP address on its Ethernet interface, which would be used by the remote access interface as well. The downside of this solution is that the troubleshooting options are more limited. An alternative to using a physical interface is to use the loopback interface. Some argue that this interface is the best used with IP unnumbered because, theoretically, it can never go down.

Cisco documentation presents the loopback interface as one that can never go down; however, administrative errors can disable the interface. Overall, it remains a better alternative than a physical interface.

Dynamic Addressing   Dynamic addressing is an excellent solution in a number of installations, especially those that use modem attached workstations from a remote location. The administrator can configure a pool of addresses that are assigned on a per call basis rather than manually assigning a single IP address for each user. This greatly reduces the number of addresses that must be assigned, and it simplifies the administrative tasks. These assignments typically use DHCP, or Dynamic Host Control Protocol.

Configuring Dynamic Addressing

The commands to configure dynamic addressing are dependent upon the method used—while DHCP is one option (used as an example in the following text), there are other methods, including proprietary ones.

Before incorporating the dynamic addressing solutions, the first option is to configure manual addressing on the client. In Windows 95/98, this is accomplished with the Dial-Up Connection Properties menu, using the TCP/IP Settings dialog box. This dialog box is shown in Figure 3.2. Note that you must select Specify an IP Address to manually enter a selection.

FIGURE 3.2 Manual IP address configuration in Windows 95/98

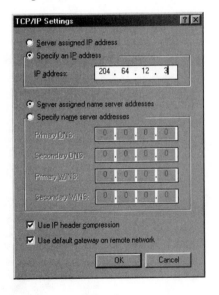

Windows will provide a warning if you attempt to use the Network Control Panel to configure the dial-up adapter, as shown in Figure 3.3. This is not permitted, but Microsoft has not explained why there is a different configuration method for dial-up configurations.

FIGURE 3.3   Configuring a dial-up adapter from the Windows Control Panel

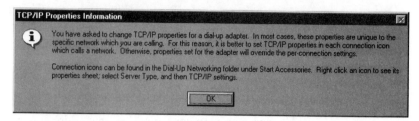

If you are configuring a router to provide the connection between the client and remote access server, you should use the standard Ethernet configuration commands. These entries are shown in Figure 3.4, and they include the IP address, subnet mask, default gateway, and name servers.

The configuration dialog box is accessed through Control Panel ➤ Network ➤ TCP/IP ➤ Adapter.

FIGURE 3.4   Ethernet based manual IP address configuration in Windows 95/98

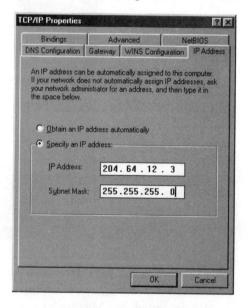

On the router, the configuration is straightforward, but it is dependent upon the role of the router and the type of dynamic assignment desired. The `async dynamic address` command allows the client to provide its address, but the `peer default ip address [ip-address | dhcp | pool poolname]` command is more often used. This command allows the administrator to select manual, DHCP, or pool-based address selection.

When selecting the DHCP option, the administrator must also configure the router for one of three choices.

- IP helper address
- IP DHCP server
- DHCP server on router

The IP helper address option is often found in router configurations, but without additional configuration, this option will forward all broadcast traffic to the *helper*. The helper is the server that provides the required service—DHCP in this example.

> **NOTE**
>
> It is important to remember that IP broadcast traffic will be forwarded to the helper regardless of the type of traffic by default; however, this can be blocked to only include DHCP datagrams.

A newer command is `ip dhcp server`, which the administrator can use to specify the address of the DHCP server specifically.

In addition, some routers may also provide DHCP server functionality. This should be considered for smaller installations only—routers are best suited to provide routing. However, this feature may be ideal for small office/home office installations.

To configure DHCP services on the router, the administrator must first decide if they wish to use a DHCP database agent to help manage the lease process. Cisco calls this feature *conflict logging*.

If conflict logging is desired, the administrator must also configure an FTP or TFTP server, which is defined with the `ip dhcp database` command. If the administrator does not wish to implement conflict logging, the command `no ip dhcp conflict logging` must be used instead. Note that there may be instances when the administrator must exclude an address from the DHCP pool. To do this, they must use the `ip dhcp excluded-address low-address {high-address}` command.

An entire configuration file for DHCP services is shown below.

```
service dhcp
ip dhcp database ftp://dhcp:cisco@10.11.1.10/dhcp
```

```
ip dhcp pool 0
 network 10.0.0.0  /8
 domain-name foo.com
 dns-server 10.2.20.51
 netbios-name-server 10.2.20.51

ip dhcp pool 1
 network 10.10.1.0 /24
 default-router 10.10.1.1
```

The previous configuration example uses an FTP server at 10.11.1.10 to capture information regarding the DHCP leases. The pool is for 10.10.1.0/24, and a default gateway of 10.10.1.1. The domain is foo.com, and DNS and WINS services are provided by 10.2.20.51. The service dhcp command used here is optional—the service is available by default. The FTP server username is dhcp with a password of cisco in the above output, however, obviously this is not a very secure option.

While this chapter focuses on Windows 95/98 configuration, readers should note that Windows NT and 2000 differ little in most regards. Figure 3.5 shows Windows 2000's dial-up networking configuration dialog box.

FIGURE 3.5   Windows 2000 dial-up networking

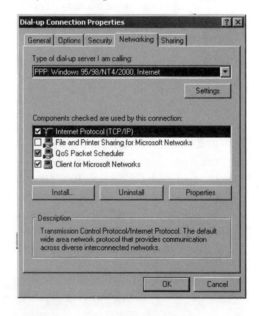

Static / tracking
= Security

How DHCP Works

DHCP is actually an open standard that is used by Unix and Macintosh clients as well as Windows-based systems. However, the protocol did not attain mainstream, corporate recognition until the server module was incorporated into Windows NT.

DHCP allows a host to learn its IP address dynamically. This process is termed a *lease* since the address assigned belongs to the host for an administratively defined time. On Windows implementations, this assignment is set for 72 hours by default.

DHCP leases are discussed in the following section.

From a router perspective, DHCP requires one of two components—a DHCP server on the local subnet, or a method for forwarding the broadcast across the router. DHCP requests are broadcasts, so the designer needs a DHCP server presence on each segment in the network. This clearly would not scale well and is impractical in most network designs, but it would provide addressing information to the clients.

The alternative is to provide a little help to DHCP. This is accomplished with the IP *helper address,* a statically defined address on each router interface that is connected to the local segment that needs the help; this segment in turn points to the DHCP server. Broadcast requests for addresses are sent to the helper address as unicasts or directed broadcasts, thus significantly reducing overall broadcast traffic.

Most DHCP implementations, including Microsoft's, can provide a great deal of information to the client as well, including time servers, default gateways, and other address-based services.

When designing for DHCP, most architects and administrators consider the DHCP lease length. When using the router as a DHCP server, there is generally less of a motivation to providing redundancy—whenever more than a handful of networks require addressing services, it is generally better to add a dedicated server. If the router is unavailable, it is unlikely that users will be concerned about the loss of a DHCP lease. If there are multiple networks, the likelihood of a single router point of failure is reduced, but there is also an increased load on the router from the number of leases that must be managed.

DHCP Lease Length

The length of the DHCP lease governs the amount of time a host "owns" the address. In order for the host to continue using the address, it must renew with the server before the lease expires. Designers must consider the overhead of this renewal traffic and the impact of failed or unavailable DHCP servers. In general, fixed configurations are appropriate venues for long leases, and short leases are applicable in more dynamic installations.

Consider a fully functioning network with a hundred workstations and a lease length of five minutes. This is an extreme example (DHCP typically sends a renewal request at an interval equal to one-half of the lease timer), but the overhead incurred would be 6000 requests per hour for just IP addresses. This is a high amount of overhead for information that should not change under normal circumstances.

In addition, when a lease expires, the host must release its IP address. Without a DHCP server, it will be unable to communicate on the network for want of an address. The alternative to a short lease is to make the lease very long. Consider the impact of a lease equal to 60 days. Should the hosts remain on a local subnet with very few changes, this would substantially reduce the volume of traffic. However, this would not be appropriate for a hotelling installation. *Hotelling* is a concept introduced years ago in which notebook users would check into a cubicle for a day or even a week. DHCP is a great solution for such an installation since the MAC addresses are constantly changing, but a long lease time would be inappropriate here. Consider a scenario in which each visitor connects once per quarter, or every 90 days. And, for this example, presume that there are 800 users of the service, and the pool is a standard Class C network of 254 host addresses. If the lease were long—90 days for this example—only the first 250 users would be able to obtain an address. Clearly, this is not appropriate to the type of installation—an important consideration for the designer.

As mentioned earlier, the default DHCP lease renewal interval (on NT) is 72 hours—DHCP attempts to renew the lease after one-half the lease duration, or 36 hours in the case of default NT.

The default lease on Cisco IOS-based DHCP servers is 24 hours.

This results in renewal requests every 36 hours (typically, this process begins at 50 percent of the lease period). For reference, the mechanism by which DHCP obtains an address is illustrated in Figure 3.6. Note that DHCP uses a system of discovery to locate the DHCP server—a phase that makes use of the helper function. Once the DHCP server is found, the offer is returned to the workstation, and the request is acknowledged or declined.

FIGURE 3.6 The DHCP process

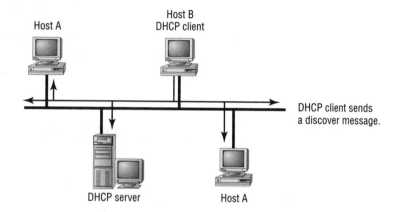

DHCP client sends
a discover message.

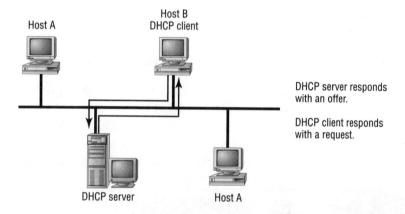

DHCP server responds
with an offer.

DHCP client responds
with a request.

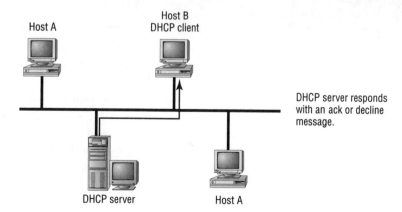

DHCP server responds
with an ack or decline
message.

DHCP operates in similar fashion when served from the router, as noted previously. Only the configuration process changes. As a personal aside, while it is a neat feature, the DHCP server option is really not practical in most installations. The need to maintain a separate FTP server for the database usually leads the administrator to opt for a more scalable option that involves installing a dedicated server.

PAP and CHAP Authentication

One of the key benefits of PPP is the ability to add authentication services, which are provided by PAP or CHAP. Authentication adds substantially to the security of the network and should be used. Even though PAP is presented in this section, its use is discouraged and administrators should configure their networks for the more secure CHAP.

Password Authentication Protocol (PAP)

Password Authentication Protocol (PAP) provides basic security authentication for connections. The username and password information, however, are transmitted in clear-text, which may be used by a hacker to compromise the network. Unfortunately, there are a few older systems that support only PAP, and not the more secure CHAP, which mandates PAP's usage.

PAP is defined in RFC 1334.

PAP usernames and passwords are transmitted in clear-text, reducing the security benefits of the protocol. Use CHAP whenever possible.

PAP operates by establishing a connection and then checking the username and password information. If the username and password information matches, an OK message is returned and the session is allowed to proceed. This is illustrated in Figure 3.7. Note that the username and password are transmitted in clear-text in PAP—a significant security risk.

FIGURE 3.7 PAP authentication

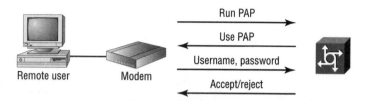

To configure PAP, the administrator needs to establish both the service and a database of usernames and passwords. The commands to do this are shown in the following:

```
encapsulation ppp
ppp authentication {chap | chap pap | pap chap |
    pap} [if-needed][list-name | default] [callin]
```

Usernames and passwords are added to the router with the `username` *name* password *secret* command.

There isn't much more to PAP—it works with a minimal amount of configuration, in large part due to its lack of security. Readers should be familiar with the existence of the protocol and the fact that it should not be used in current designs.

Challenge Handshake Authentication Protocol (CHAP)

The *Challenge Handshake Authentication Protocol (CHAP)* is significantly more secure than PAP. This is because of the mechanism used to transfer the username and password—CHAP protects against playback hacking (resending the packet as part of an attack) by using a hash value that is only valid for that transaction. When the attacker captures the CHAP session and replays that dialog in an attempt to access the network, the hash method will prevent the connection. The password is also hidden from the attacker—it is never sent over the circuit.

The hash shown in Figure 3.8 is valid for a relatively brief time, and no unencrypted information that would provide a hacker with needed information is sent over the link.

FIGURE 3.8 CHAP authentication

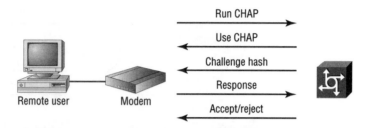

The commands to configure CHAP are very similar to those for PAP. Instead of selecting PAP in the `ppp authentication` command, the administrator uses the `chap` keyword. Notice that two additional options are also available—`chap pap` and `pap chap`. These keywords provide the administrator with a means of selecting both protocols, and they are attempted in order; thus, `chap pap` tries to authenticate via the CHAP protocol first. Typically, this configuration option is used only during transition since security would be compromised were PAP permitted it to be. The following commands are used to enable PPP, a requirement for CHAP, and to configure the router for CHAP authentication.

```
Encapsulation ppp
ppp authentication {chap | chap pap | pap chap |
    pap} [if-needed][list-name | default] [callin]
```

Usernames and passwords are added to the router with the `username name` password `secret` command.

In Windows networking, the administrator is given the choice of selecting password encryption, as shown in Figure 3.9. Note that this selection is unchecked, meaning that the user or administrator has not selected that passwords be encrypted.

FIGURE 3.9 Windows 95/98 password encryption

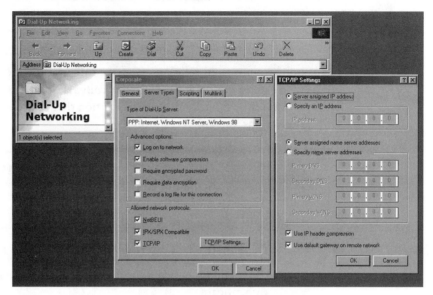

This configuration will work so long as PAP is not the only selected authentication method on the router. The Windows client will attempt to connect with MS-CHAP, a Microsoft proprietary version of the CHAP protocol. If the box is checked, meaning that the password must be encrypted, either PAP or CHAP will be used.

PPP Callback

Security in PPP can be further augmented with the use of *PPP callback*, which commands the access server to disconnect the incoming connection and reestablish the connection via an outbound dial. This security feature requires that the caller be in a single physical location and diminishes the impact of a compromised username and password. The service may also be used to control costs because all connections appear to be from the remote access server—allowing volume-based discounts.

PPP callback is documented in RFC 1570.

Clearly, this solution is not well suited to mobile users—callback to a hotel room would require repeated configuration and a mechanism to deal with extensions, for example. Some callback solutions allow the remote user to enter the callback number—a solution that removes the physical location restrictions and enhances mobility.

Cisco's callback feature does not permit remote users to dynamically enter the callback number.

Consider the security provided by a callback configuration:

- The remote client (user) must connect into the remote access server.

- Using an authentication protocol, such as CHAP, the user must authenticate.

- If authentication is successful, the session will terminate and the remote access server will call the remote client back. If the authentication fails the connection will terminate.

- Upon callback, the client and server can again perform a password verification.

Clearly, these extra steps could augment security.

To configure callback, the administrator needs to use the `ppp callback accept` command on the interface that receives the inbound call.

PPP callback will not make repeated retries to establish a return connection. This means that a busy signal or other impediment will require the client side to re-request the session.

PPP Compression and Multilink

It seems as though there is never enough bandwidth for the current user demand; however, PPP compression and multilink bonding can each provide a means of increasing the throughput between different locations.

Compression makes use of representation to remove bytes from the data stream. For example, if the word *the* is represented by an @ sign, the protocol could save two bytes per instance. Repeated hundreds of times for different strings, it is possible to save substantial amounts of bandwidth, which will improve performance. The overhead incurred with most compression is minor compared to the resultant savings.

Multilink works differently than compression. *Compression* makes use of the current connection and squeezes additional information across the link. *Multilink* takes the standard data stream and bonds multiple connections in order to increase the amount of bandwidth availed to the application. Thus, two or more circuits can be made to appear as a single large pipe. This will require greater expense than compression since each location will require two analog phone lines or ISDN circuits; however, the option does negate situations where more bandwidth is needed but no greater bandwidth technologies are available. This will ultimately improve throughput and reduce latency. Compression and multilink may be combined to further improve throughput.

Compression Configuration

Compression is available in the IOS software on virtually every Cisco router. However, despite its benefits, software-based compression places a significant load on the router's processor. Because of this, administrators must weigh the benefits of compression against the potential performance degradation that could result. In addition, monitoring the router's CPU is practically required, and the utilization of the CPU at any one time should not be allowed to exceed 65 percent. You can determine how much is being used by viewing it with the show process cpu command.

To configure compression, use the following commands:

```
encapsulation ppp
compress [predictor | stac | mppc [ignore-pfc]]
```

Note that both sides of the serial link need to be configured for the same compression method—different compression protocols are not cross-compatible. Designers should also consider the type of configuration that will be used when configuring, as described in this section:

Predictor The predictor option provides a useful benefit in that compressed data will not be *recompressed*—a process that typically increases the transmitted size and adds substantial delay. This is a good choice if there is a mixture of compressed and uncompressed data that will traverse the link. Predictor can be more memory intensive than other choices, but it does not burden the router's CPU substantially.

Stac   Most significantly, the Stac compression option is the only supported algorithm for the CBOS (Cisco Broadband Operating System)-based router platforms, including the Cisco 700 series. As with other compression mechanisms, Stac substitutes repetitive data sequences with brief, summarized values, which are decoded on the other end. The specific compression algorithm is called LZW, or Lempel-Ziv-Welch, the names of the creators.

MPPC   Microsoft Point-to-Point Compression is used when receiving compressed data from Windows clients. With this option, all data is compressed. Microsoft also supports TCP header compression with the IP header option. This type of compression is perfect for remote access ports that receive only direct client connections. It is also based on the LZW compression algorithm.

In addition, a fourth compression type is available to the designer—TCP header compression. Invoked with the `ip tcp header-compression` command, TCP header compression does exactly that—it compresses only the TCP header information (20 bytes). The specifics of TCP header compression, which is not unique to PPP, are documented in RFC 1144. This type of compression reduces the number of bytes required for each TCP packet and provides this reduction with a minimum amount of overhead. TCP header compression does not impact UDP or ICMP packets.

A Cisco 7000 series router is needed in order to offload the route processor from the burdens of compression. This makes use of the compression service adapter. When this card is present, the router will use the hardware-based compression that is running on this card. If the router contains VIP2 cards, the compression process can be *distributed*, which will move the overhead of compression away from the central processor. Interface functions on the card will be impacted, however. Without VIP2 technology or the compression service adapter, the router will default to software-based compression.

Compression is generally avoided beyond the 2Mbps level, and ideally, it is only used for links below 128Kbps. Review and consider your requirements carefully before selecting the type of compression—if traffic is truly that high, it may be a short time before additional capacity is necessary anyway.

Multilink Configuration

Like compression, multilink is fairly easy to configure. Figure 3.10 illustrates the desired configuration. Users or administrators simply configure the modem to be used and the phone number to be dialed. Multilink services require two or more modems and two or mode phone lines on the client side, which are bonded together into a single logical connection.

For further reference, the multilink PPP RFC is 1990.

FIGURE 3.10 Multilink installation

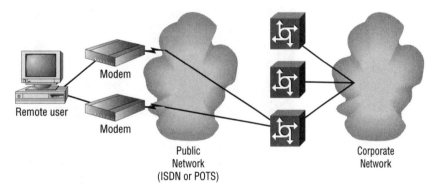

The commands for configuring asynchronous multilink or ISDN multilink differ little, and the primary commands only need to include the following.

```
encapsulation ppp
ppp multilink
```

Without multilink support, each individual ISDN B channel per port remains isolated. Modems (async connections) may also be used for multilink, and this standard (MP) is supported in Windows 95/98. The configuration is fairly straight forward, and the user or administrator defines the second access number under the multilink tab, as shown in Figure 3.11.

FIGURE 3.11 Windows 95/98 Multilink

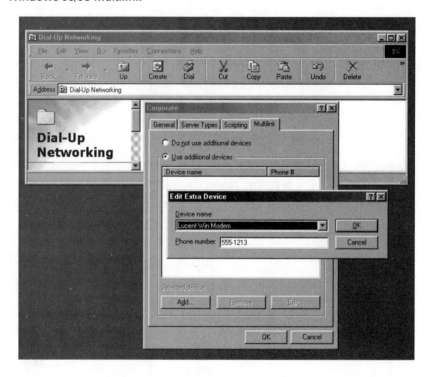

There is another multilink option available on Cisco routers and access servers—*Multichassis Multilink Protocol (MMP)*. This proprietary protocol allows the various bonded sessions to terminate on different access servers, as shown in Figure 3.12.

FIGURE 3.12 Multichassis Multilink Protocol

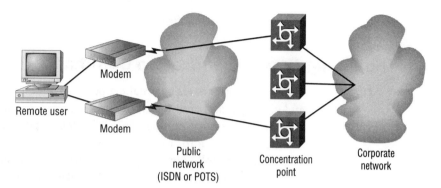

The benefit of this configuration is that single points of failure at the concentration point can be removed and port utilization can be optimized.

It is recommended that all PPP connections use authentication—PAP or CHAP. If authentication is not used, the telecommunications vendor will need to pass caller ID information for some services.

Verifying and Troubleshooting PPP

As with most troubleshooting on Cisco routers, administrators have a wide range of show and debug commands available to resolve problems that can occur with the Point-to-Point Protocol. Using standard troubleshooting methodologies, the administrator should be able to isolate physical problems quickly and then use these tools to locate and resolve logical issues.

Ideally, designers and administrators unfamiliar with PPP will implement a simple configuration before adding additional features such as authentication and multilink bonding; however, one or both of these services may be required as part of the initial installation. Debug and show commands will quickly help isolate the various issues.

This section will focus on the three most common debug commands:

- debug ppp authentication

- debug ppp negotiation

- debug ppp packet

The *debug ppp authentication* Command

Authentication failures can make a perfectly functional link appear faulty, and given the ease with which one can miss-enter a password or username, it is one of the most common issues. The debug ppp authentication command is very useful for resolving these issues.

Examine the following output from the debug session. The ISDN BRI attempted to connect, but the challenge failed and the link was disconnected immediately. The second packet attempted to restore the link (response id 8) and also failed. This type of output points to either a username or password problem—in this case the password was incorrect.

```
Router#debug ppp authentication
01:54:14: %LINK-3-UPDOWN: Interface BRIO:1, changed state
to up.
01:54:14: BRO:1 PPP: Treating connection as a callout
01:54:14: BRO:1 PPP: Phase is AUTHENTICATING, by both
01:54:14: BRO:1 CHAP: O CHALLENGE id 7 len 27 from
"Router"
01:54:14: BRO:1 CHAP: I CHALLENGE id 7 len 24 from "Top"
01:54:14: BRO:1 CHAP: O RESPONSE id 7 len 27 from "Router"
01:54:14: BRO:1 CHAP: I FAILURE id 7 len 25 msg is "MD/DES
compare failed"
01:54:15: %ISDN-6-DISCONNECT: Interface BRIO:1
disconnected from 18008358661 , call lasted 1 seconds
01:54:15: %LINK-3-UPDOWN: Interface BRIO:1, changed state
to down.
01:54:18: %LINK-3-UPDOWN: Interface BRIO:1, changed state
to up.
01:54:18: BRO:1 PPP: Treating connection as a callout
01:54:18: BRO:1 PPP: Phase is AUTHENTICATING, by both
01:54:18: BRO:1 CHAP: O CHALLENGE id 8 len 27 from
"Router"
01:54:18: BRO:1 CHAP: I CHALLENGE id 8 len 24 from "Top"
01:54:18: BRO:1 CHAP: O RESPONSE id 8 len 27 from "Router"
```

01:54:18: BRO:1 CHAP: I FAILURE id 8 len 25 msg is "MD/DES compare failed"
01:54:19: %ISDN-6-DISCONNECT: Interface BRIO:1 disconnected
from 18008358661 , call lasted 1 seconds
01:54:19: %LINK-3-UPDOWN: Interface BRIO:1, changed state to down.
01:54:22: %LINK-3-UPDOWN: Interface BRIO:1, changed state to up.
The debug ppp authentication command is most helpful in troubleshooting password problems.

As shown, the message I FAILURE id 8 len 25 msg is "MD/DEScompare failed" is a clear indication that the administrator should look at the password settings.

The *debug ppp negotiation* Command

The debug ppp negotiation command is useful for two reasons. First, it can augment the troubleshooting process on PPP links. Second, it provides a wonderful summary of PPP, including LCP and the upper layer protocols, including IPCP (IP) and CDPCP (CDP).

The following output shows the messages that might appear when using the debug ppp negotiation command.

Router#**debug ppp negotiation**
PPP protocol negotiation debugging is on
Router#**ping 10.1.1.1**
Type escape sequence to abort.
Sending 5, 100-byte ICMP Echos to 10.1.1.1, timeout is 2 seconds:
00:22:28: %LINK-3-UPDOWN: Interface BRIO:1, changed state to up
00:22:28: BRO:1 PPP: Treating connection as a callout
00:22:28: BRO:1 PPP: Phase is ESTABLISHING, Active Open
00:22:28: BRO:1 LCP: O CONFREQ [Closed] id 3 len 10
00:22:28: BRO:1 LCP: MagicNumber 0x50239604 (0x050650239604)
00:22:28: BRO:1 LCP: I CONFREQ [REQsent] id 13 len 10

```
00:22:28: BR0:1 LCP: MagicNumber 0x5023961F
(0x05065023961F)
00:22:28: BR0:1 LCP: O CONFACK [REQsent] id 13 len 10
00:22:28: BR0:1 LCP: MagicNumber 0x5.023961F
(0x05065023961F)
00:22:28: BR0:1 LCP: I CONFACK [ACKsent] id 3 len 10
00:22:28: BR0:1 LCP: MagicNumber 0x50239604
(0x050650239604)
00:22:28: BR0:1 LCP: State is Open
00:22:28: BR0:1 PPP: Phase is UP
00:22:28: BR0:1 CDPCP: O CONFREQ [Closed] id 3 len 4
00:22:28: BR0:1 IPCP: O CONFREQ [Closed] id 3 len 10
00:22:28: BR0:1 IPCP: Address 10.1.1.2 (0x03060A010102)
00:22:28: BR0:1 CDPCP: I CONFREQ [REQsent] id 3 len 4
00:22:28: BR0:1 CDPCP: O CONFACK [REQsent] id 3 len 4
00:22:28: BR0:1 IPCP: I CONFREQ [REQsent] id 3 len 10
00:22:28: BR0:1 IPCP: Address 10.1.1.1 (0x03060A010101)
00:22:28: BR0:1 IPCP: O CONFACK [REQsent] id 3 len 10
00:22:28: BR0:1 IPCP: Address 10.1.1.1 (0x03060A010101)
00:22:28: BR0:1 CDPCP: I CONFACK [ACKsent] id 3 len 4
00:22:28: BR0:1 CDPCP: State is Open
00:22:28: BR0:1 IPCP: I CONFACK [ACKsent] id 3 len 10
00:22:28: BR0:1 IPCP: Address 10.1.1.2 (0x03060A010102)
00:22:28: BR0:1 IPCP: State is Open
00:22:28: BR0 IPCP: Install route to 10.1.1.1
00:22:2.!!!
Success rate is 60 percent (3/5), round-trip min/avg/max =
32/38/48 ms
Router#9: %LINEPROTO-5-UPDOWN: Line protocol on Interface
BRIO:1, changed state to up
00:22:29: %LINK-3-UPDOWN: Interface BRIO:2, changed state
to up
00:22:29: BR0:2 PPP: Treating connection as a callin
00:22:29: BR0:2 PPP: Phase is ESTABLISHING, Passive Open
00:22:29: BR0:2 LCP: State is Listen
00:22:30: BR0:2 LCP: I CONFREQ [Listen] id 3 len 10
```

```
00:22:30: BR0:2 LCP: MagicNumber 0x50239CC8
(0x050650239CC8)
00:22:30: BR0:2 LCP: O CONFREQ [Listen] id 3 len 10
00:22:30: BR0:2 LCP: MagicNumber 0x50239CDA
(0x050650239CDA)
00:22:30: BR0:2 LCP: O CONFACK [Listen] id 3 len 10
00:22:30: BR0:2 LCP: MagicNumber 0x50239CC8
(0x050650239CC8)
00:22:30: BR0:2 LCP: I CONFACK [ACKsent] id 3 len 10
00:22:30: BR0:2 LCP: MagicNumber 0x50239CDA
(0x050650239CDA) 00:22:30: BR0:2 LCP: State is Open
00:22:30: BR0:2 PPP: Phase is UP
00:22:30: BR0:2 CDPCP: O CONFREQ [Closed] id 3 len 4
00:22:30: BR0:2 IPCP: O CONFREQ [Closed] id 3 len 10
00:22:30: BR0:2 IPCP: Address 10.1.1.2 (0x03060A010102)
00:22:30: BR0:2 CDPCP: I CONFREQ [REQsent] id 3 len 4
00:22:30: BR0:2 CDPCP: O CONFACK [REQsent] id 3 len 4
00:22:30: BR0:2 IPCP: I CONFREQ [REQsent] id 3 len 10
00:22:30: BR0:2 IPCP: Address 10.1.1.1 (0x03060A010101)
00:22:30: BR0:2 IPCP: O CONFACK [REQsent] id 3 len 10
00:22:30: BR0:2 IPCP: Address 10.1.1.1 (0x03060A010101)
00:22:30: BR0:2 CDPCP: I CONFACK [ACKsent] id 3 len 4
00:22:30: BR0:2 CDPCP: State is Open
00:22:30: BR0:2 IPCP: I CONFACK [ACKsent] id 3 len 10
00:22:30: BR0:2 IPCP: Address 10.1.1.2 (0x03060A010102)
00:22:30: BR0:2 IPCP: State is Open
00:22:31: %LINEPROTO-5-UPDOWN: Line protocol on Interface
BRI0:2, changed state to up
00:21:22: BR0:1 LCP: O ECHOREQ [Open] id 12 len 12 magic
0x5020C645
00:21:22: BR0:1 LCP: echo_cnt 1, sent id 12, line up
00:21:22: BR0:1 PPP: I pkt type 0xC021, datagramsize 16
00:21:22: BR0:1 LCP: I ECHOREP [Open] id 12 len 12 magic
0x5020C654
00:21:22: BR0:1 LCP: Received id 12, sent id 12, line up
00:21:22: BR0:2 LCP: O ECHOREQ [Open] id 12 len 12 magic
```

```
0x5020CD1B
00:21:22: BR0:2 LCP: echo_cnt 1, sent id 12, line up
00:21:22: BR0:2 PPP: I pkt type 0xC021, datagramsize 16
00:21:22: BR0:2 LCP: I ECHOREP [Open] id 12 len 12 magic
0x5020CD0D
00:21:22: BR0:2 LCP: Received id 12, sent id 12, line up
00:21:23: BR0:1 PPP: I pkt type 0xC021, datagramsize 16
00:21:23: BR0:1 LCP: I ECHOREQ [Open] id 12 len 12 magic
0x5020C654
00:21:23: BR0:1 LCP: O ECHOREP [Open] id 12 len 12 magic
0x5020C64500:21:23: BR0:2 PPP: I pkt type 0xC021,
datagramsize 16
00:21:23: BR0:2 LCP: I ECHOREQ [Open] id 12 len 12 magic
0x5020CD0D
00:21:23: BR0:2 LCP: O ECHOREP [Open] id 12 len 12 magic
0x5020CD1B
00:21:24: BR0:2 PPP: I pkt type 0x0207, datagramsize 15
00:21:25: BR0:2 PPP: I pkt type 0x0207, datagramsize 312
00:21:25: %ISDN-6-DISCONNECT: Interface BRI0:1
disconnected
from 18008358661 To p, call lasted 120 seconds
00:21:25: %LINK-3-UPDOWN: Interface BRI0:1, changed state
to down
00:21:107379488949: %ISDN-6-DISCONNECT: Interface BRI0:2
disconnected from 8358 663 , call lasted 120 seconds
00:21:25: %LINK-3-UPDOWN: Interface BRI0:2, changed state
to down
00:21:26: %LINEPROTO-5-UPDOWN: Line protocol on Interface
BRI0:1, changed state to down
00:21:26: %LINEPROTO-5-UPDOWN: Line protocol on Interface
BRI0:2, changed state to down
```

Notice that in this output, the first two ICMP packets (pings) failed due to the delay in bringing up the ISDN BRI. While faster than asynchronous connections, ISDN still introduces connection delay, which can impact user applications. In addition, the output from the debug ppp negotiation command shows the process by which a PPP session is activated.

This output does not make use of CHAP, compression, or multilink. Instead, as you can see, PPP starts and then LCP is activated. Once this occurs, the NCP negotiations begin, starting with CDPCP, followed by IPCP. *Cisco Discovery Protocol (CDP)*, is a proprietary advertisement protocol that sends router and switch information between Cisco devices. It operates over any physical media that supports SNAP (except ATM), and is independent of IP. The IP PPP protocol, IPCP, was started to transport ICMP pings that were sent from the router.

Remember that PPP sessions must undergo a negotiation process and that the debug ppp negotiation command will display upper level protocols such as IPCP, along with LCP and PPP.

The *debug ppp packet* Command

The debug ppp packet command reports real-time PPP packet flow, including the type of packet and the specific B channel used in the case of ISDN. Although this command generates a significant amount of output, it is quite useful for locating errors that involve upper layer protocols.

As with other debug packet commands, the debug ppp packet command records each packet that moves through the router using PPP. As such, the administrator can monitor traffic flows as if they had a protocol analyzer attached to the interface. This may be useful for troubleshooting Application Layer problems, but a formal protocol analyzer is highly recommended. In this output, there are both CDP packets (denoted with the CDPCP entries) and IP packets (denoting proper configuration of IP on the link):

```
Router#debug ppp packet
PPP packet display debugging is on
Router#ping 10.1.1.1
Type escape sequence to abort.
Sending 5, 100-byte ICMP Echos to 10.1.1.1, timeout is 2
seconds:
00:24:49: %LINK-3-UPDOWN: Interface BRI0:1, changed state
to up.
00:24:50: BR0:1 LCP: O CONFREQ [Closed] id 4 len 10
00:24:50: BR0:1 LCP: MagicNumber 0x5025BF23
(0x05065025BF23)
00:24:50: BR0:1 PPP: I pkt type 0xC021, datagramsize 14
```

```
00:24:50: BRO:1 PPP: I pkt type 0xC021, datagramsize 14
00:24:50: BRO:1 LCP: I CONFREQ [REQsent] id 14 len 10
00:24:50: BRO:1 LCP: MagicNumber 0x5025BF46
(0x05065025BF46)
00:24:50: BRO:1 LCP: O CONFACK [REQsent] id 14 len 10
00:24:50: BRO:1 LCP: MagicNumber 0x5025BF46
(0x05065025BF46)
00:24:50: BRO:1 LCP: I CONFACK [ACKsent] id 4 len 10
00:24:50: BRO:1 LCP: MagicNumber 0x5025BF23
(0x05065025BF23)
00:24:50: BRO:1 PPP: I pkt type 0x8207, datagramsize 8
00:24:50: BRO:1 PPP: I pkt type 0x8021, datagramsize 14
00:24:50: BRO:1 CDPCP: O CONFREQ [Closed] id 4 len 4
00:24:50: BRO:1 PPP: I pkt type 0x8207, datagramsize 8
00:24:50: BRO:1 IPCP: O CONFREQ [Closed] id 4 len 10
00:24:50: BRO:1 IPCP: Address 10.1.1.2 (0x03060A010102)
00:24:50: BRO:1 CDPCP: I CONFREQ [REQsent] id 4 len 4
00:24:50: BRO:1 CDPCP: O CONFACK [REQ.!!!
Success rate is 60 percent (3/5), round-trip min/avg/max =
36/41/52 ms
Router#sent] id 4 len 4
00:24:50: BRO:1 PPP: I pkt type 0x8021, datagramsize 14
00:24:50: BRO:1 IPCP: I CONFREQ [REQsent] id 4 len 10
00:24:50: BRO:1 IPCP: Address 10.1.1.1 (0x03060A010101)
00:24:50: BRO:1 IPCP: O CONFACK [REQsent] id 4 len 10
00:24:50: BRO:1 IPCP: Address 10.1.1.1 (0x03060A010101)
00:24:50: BRO:1 CDPCP: I CONFACK [ACKsent] id 4 len 4
00:24:50: BRO:1 IPCP: I CONFACK [ACKsent] id 4 len 10
00:24:50: BRO:1 IPCP: Address 10.1.1.2 (0x03060A010102)
00:24:51: BRO:1 PPP: O pkt type 0x0021, datagramsize 104
00:24:51: %LINEPROTO-5-UPDOWN: Line protocol on Interface
BRIO:1, changed state to up
00:24:51: BRO:1 PPP: O pkt type 0x0207, datagramsize 323
00:24:51: %LINK-3-UPDOWN: Interface BRIO:2, changed state
to up
00:24:51: BRO:2 PPP: I pkt type 0xC021, datagramsize 14
```

```
00:24:51: BR0:2 LCP: I CONFREQ [Listen] id 4 len 10
00:24:51: BR0:2 LCP: MagicNumber 0x5025C5EF
(0x05065025C5EF)
00:24:51: BR0:2 LCP: O CONFREQ [Listen] id 4 len 10
00:24:51: BR0:2 LCP: MagicNumber 0x5025C605
(0x05065025C605)
00:24:51: BR0:2 LCP: O CONFACK [Listen] id 4 len 10
00:24:51: BR0:2 LCP: MagicNumber 0x5025C5EF
(0x05065025C5EF)
00:24:51: BR0:2 PPP: I pkt type 0xC021, datagramsize 14
00:24:51: BR0:2 LCP: I CONFACK [ACKsent] id 4 len 10
00:24:51: BR0:2 LCP: MagicNumber 0x5025C605
(0x05065025C605)
00:24:51: BR0:2 PPP: I pkt type 0x8207, datagramsize 8
00:24:51: BR0:2 PPP: I pkt type 0x8021, datagramsize 14
00:24:51: BR0:2 CDPCP: O CONFREQ [Closed] id 4 len 4
00:24:51: BR0:2 IPCP: O CONFREQ [Closed] id 4 len 10
00:24:51: BR0:2 IPCP: Address 10.1.1.2 (0x03060A010102)
00:24:51: BR0:2 CDPCP: I CONFREQ [REQsent] id 4 len 4
00:24:51: BR0:2 CDPCP: O CONFACK [REQsent] id 4 len 4
00:24:51: BR0:2 PPP: I pkt type 0x8207, datagramsize 8
00:24:51: BR0:2 IPCP: I CONFREQ [REQsent] id 4 len 10
00:24:51: BR0:2 IPCP: Address 10.1.1.1 (0x03060A010101)
00:24:51: BR0:2 PPP: I pkt type 0x8021, datagramsize 14
00:24:51: BR0:2 IPCP: O CONFACK [REQsent] id 4 len 10
00:24:51: BR0:2 IPCP: Address 10.1.1.1 (0x03060A010101)
00:24:51: BR0:2 CDPCP: I CONFACK [ACKsent] id 4 len 4
00:24:51: BR0:2 IPCP: I CONFACK [ACKsent] id 4 len 10
00:24:51: BR0:2 IPCP: Address 10.1.1.2 (0x03060A010102)
00:24:52: BR0:1 LCP: O ECHOREQ [Open] id 1 len 12 magic
0x5025BF23
00:24:52: BR0:1 LCP: echo_cnt 1, sent id 1, line up
00:24:52: BR0:1 PPP: I pkt type 0xC021, datagramsize 16
00:24:52: BR0:1 LCP: I ECHOREP [Open] id 1 len 12 magic
0x5025BF46
00:24:52: BR0:1 LCP: Received id 1, sent id 1, line up
```

```
00:24:52: BR0:2 LCP: O ECHOREQ [Open] id 1 len 12 magic
0x5025C605
00:24:52: BR0:2 LCP: echo_cnt 1, sent id 1, line up
00:24:52: BR0:2 PPP: I pkt type 0xC021, datagramsize 16
00:24:52: BR0:2 LCP: I ECHOREP [Open] id 1 len 12 magic
0x5025C5EF
00:24:52: BR0:2 LCP: Received id 1, sent id 1, line up
00:24:52: %LINEPROTO-5-UPDOWN: Line protocol on Interface
BRI0:2, changed state to up
00:24:52: BR0:1 PPP: O pkt type 0x0207, datagramsize 323
00:24:52: BR0:2 PPP: I pkt type 0x0207, datagramsize 312
00:24:53: BR0:1 PPP: O pkt type 0x0021, datagramsize 104
00:24:53: BR0:2 PPP: I pkt type 0x0021, datagramsize 104
00:24:53: BR0:1 PPP: O pkt type 0x0021, datagramsize 104
00:24:53: BR0:2 PPP: I pkt type 0x0021, datagramsize 104
00:24:53: BR0:1 PPP: O pkt type 0x0021, datagramsize 104
00:24:53: BR0:2 PPP: I pkt type 0x0021, datagramsize 104
00:24:53: BR0:1 PPP: I pkt type 0xC021, datagramsize 16
00:24:53: BR0:1 LCP: I ECHOREQ [Open] id 1 len 12 magic
0x5025BF46
00:24:53: BR0:1 LCP: O ECHOREP [Open] id 1 len 12 magic
0x5025BF23
00:24:53: BR0:2 PPP: I pkt type 0xC021, datagramsize 16
00:24:53: BR0:2 LCP: I ECHOREQ [Open] id 1 len 12 magic
0x5025C5EF
00:24:53: BR0:2 LCP: O ECHOREP [Open] id 1 len 12 magic
0x5025C605
Router#
00:25:02: BR0:1 LCP: O ECHOREQ [Open] id 2 len 12 magic
0x5025BF23
00:25:02: BR0:1 LCP: echo_cnt 1, sent id 2, line up
00:25:02: BR0:1 PPP: I pkt type 0xC021, datagramsize 16
00:25:02: BR0:1 LCP: I ECHOREP [Open] id 2 len 12 magic
0x5025BF46
00:25:02: BR0:1 LCP: Received id 2, sent id 2, line up
00:25:02: BR0:2 LCP: O ECHOREQ [Open] id 2 len 12 magic
```

```
0x5025C605
00:25:02: BR0:2 LCP: echo_cnt 1, sent id 2, line up
00:25:02: BR0:2 PPP: I pkt type 0xC021, datagramsize 16
00:25:02: BR0:2 LCP: I ECHOREP [Open] id 2 len 12 magic
0x5025C5EF 00:25:02: BR0:2 LCP: Received id 2, sent id 2,
line up
00:25:03: BR0:1 PPP: I pkt type 0xC021, datagramsize 16
00:25:03: BR0:1 LCP: I ECHOREQ [Open] id 2 len 12 magic
0x5025BF46
00:25:03: BR0:1 LCP: O ECHOREP [Open] id 2 len 12 magic
0x5025BF23
00:25:03: BR0:2 PPP: I pkt type 0xC021, datagramsize 16
00:25:03: BR0:2 LCP: I ECHOREQ [Open] id 2 len 12 magic
0x5025C5EF
00:25:03: BR0:2 LCP: O ECHOREP [Open] id 2 len 12 magic
0x5025C605
```

The debug ppp packet command is most helpful in locating upper layer protocol errors. It filters out non-PPP output, resulting in a cleaner debug output than a regular debug ip packet command. Note that the magic numbers referred to in the above output are used to thwart playback attacks by maintaining a form of state for the session.

Summary

This chapter addressed some of the benefits that result from using the Point-to-Point Protocol and how the protocol can afford the designer with benefits in remote access networks. Some of these benefits included the following:

- Compression

- Authentication

- Multiprotocol support

- Multipoint support

In addition, this chapter addressed some of the diagnostic procedures that administrators will need in order to successfully implement and support PPP installations. This presentation included the configuration methods that are needed on Cisco access devices, including ways to allow users to select the encapsulation method.

At this point, readers should feel confident that they could support a recommendation to use PPP—a step that requires an understanding of the other possible protocols. Also, designers should come away from this chapter with an appreciation for how PPP interoperates with upper layer protocols, particularly IP. This should include configuration of IP on PPP clients, especially Windows 95/98 platforms.

Key Terms

Before you take the exam, be certain you are familiar with the following terms:

Challenge Handshake Authentication Protocol (CHAP)

checksum

Cisco Discovery Protocol (CDP)

compression

helper address

Link Control Protocol (LCP)

Network Control Protocol (NCP)

Password Authentication Protocol (PAP)

requests for comment (RFC)

Commands in This Chapter

Command	Meaning
compress [predictor | stac | mppc | [ignore-pfc]]	The compress command is used to select the type of compression desired on a PPP link.
debug ppp authentication	This command enables debug messages for authentication processes under PPP, including CHAP and PAP.
debug ppp negotiation	This debug command provides information about the PPP call establishment process.
debug ppp packet	The debug ppp packet command shows the administrator each packet that is encapsulated into PPP for transport.
default-router *ip address*	The default-router command configures the default gateway entry in DHCP leases.
dns-server *ip address*	Use the dns-server command to configure the name servers to be used by DHCP clients.
domain-name domain name	DNS servers are defined with this command.
encapsulation ppp	The encapsulation PPP command enables the PPP protocol on the interface.
ip dhcp database	The ip dhcp database command enters the database configuration mode.

`ip dhcp pool 0`	DHCP uses pools to categorize entries. This command example establishes the first pool, which generally contains global DHCP configurations.
`ip tcp header-compression`	This command enables TCP header compression services.
`netbios-name-server `*`ip`*` `*`address`*	This command configures the WINS server entry that will be forwarded in the DHCP lease.
`network `*`ip address mask`*	The `network` command within the `ip dhcp pool` command defines the scope for the DHCP process.

`ppp authentication {chap |`
`chap pap | pap chap | pap}`
`[if-needed][list-name |`
`default] [callin]`
	The `ppp authentication` command defines the type of authentication that should be used.

`ppp multilink`	This command enables multilink support.
`service dhcp`	The `service dhcp` command establishes a DHCP server on the router.
`username `*`name`*` password `*`secret`*	The `username` command places an entry in the router's user database.

Written Lab

In this lab, you will write in the answers to the following questions.

1. As the network designer, you've been asked to present a brief remote access solution for your company. The document need not concern itself with specific hardware, but it does need to focus on scalability, security, and availability. All of the users will be mobile, frequently operating from hotels. Two future locations will use ISDN for large file transfers, and all users require both IP and IPX support. Based on this chapter, please write a succinct overview of your solution.

2. The command to configure the router to act as a DHCP server is _____.

3. What command is used to enable PPP encapsulation?

4. To define a logical grouping of DHCP information, the administrator would use what command?

5. The administrator does not have an FTP or TFTP server available for the DHCP process. What command is required?

6. Microsoft Windows clients use which compression method?

7. Rather than sending the password, CHAP sends a ____ across the link.

8. The default lease on Cisco IOS-based DHCP servers is _____.

9. The default DHCP lease on Windows NT servers is _____.

10. Using an Ethernet IP address to define the serial IP address is called _____.

Hands-on Lab

In this section, you will perform one lab that requires a router with a serial and Ethernet interface and a single client that is attached to the Ethernet segment. This client should be configured for DHCP address assignment.

Lab 3.1: PPP and DHCP Configuration

1. Configure the router for an Ethernet interface address of 10.1.1.1/24.

   ```
   interface e0
   ip address 10.1.1.1 255.255.255.0
   ```

2. Configure a serial interface on the router for PPP encapsulation and an IP address of 10.2.2.1/30.

   ```
   interface s0
   ip address 10.2.2.1 255.255.255.252
   encapsulation ppp
   ```

3. Create a DHCP pool for the Ethernet interface with the following parameters. The domain is called company.com, and the default router is the Ethernet interface configured in step one. No FTP or TFTP server is available. The WINS server is at 10.20.2.10, and the DNS server is at 10.20.2.11.

   ```
   service dhcp
   no ip dhcp conflict logging
   ip dhcp excluded-address 10.1.1.1

   ip dhcp pool 0
    network 10.0.0.0  /8
    domain-name company.com
    dns-server 10.20.2.11
    netbios-name-server 10.20.2.10

   ip dhcp pool 1
    network 10.1.1.0 /24
    default-router 10.1.1.1
   ```

Review Questions

1. PPP improved upon SLIP by doing which of the following?

   A. Allowing the transport of only IP packets across Ethernet segments

   B. Allowing the transport of most protocols across serial segments

   C. Adding support for compression

   D. Adding support for AppleTalk to IP conversion

2. PPP uses which two protocols?

   A. LCP and NCP

   B. SLIP and SPX

   C. EIGRP and RIP

   D. LLC and IP

3. Which of the following compression methods can be used? (Select three.)

   A. Software

   B. Hardware

   C. Server

   D. Distributed

4. Which of the following is the command to use CHAP authentication?

   A. ppp authentication protocol chap

   B. authentication chap

   C. ppp authentication chap

   D. chap authentication

5. The `async mode dedicated` command configures which of the following?

   A. The port is locked to a single IP address.

   B. The port is locked to a single encapsulation, such as PPP or SLIP.

   C. The access server can only terminate asynchronous sessions.

   D. The session is encrypted.

6. Does the use of PPP require the administrator to use static IP addressing?

   A. No.

   B. Yes, unless CHAP is also used.

   C. Yes, unless PAP is also used.

   D. Yes, unless the `ppp dynamic` command is used.

7. What is the best choice for compression when the remote users will connect with Windows stations?

   A. Stac

   B. Predictor

   C. MPPC

   D. TCP

8. Which of the following is the best choice for compression when data is both pre-compressed and uncompressed?

   A. Stac

   B. Predictor

   C. MPPC

   D. TCP

9. The Cisco 700 router supports which of the following compression methods?

   A. Stac

   B. Predictor

   C. MPPC

   D. All of the above

10. Will the TCP header compression mechanism also compress UDP headers?

   A. Yes.

   B. No.

   C. Yes, but only with DHCP enabled.

   D. Yes, but only with DHCP disabled.

11. Does CHAP require the use of PPP?

   A. Yes, CHAP is a subprotocol of PPP.

   B. No, only PAP requires PPP.

   C. No, CHAP will work with any IP supported transport.

   D. No, CHAP only requires PAP.

12. Which command would be used to troubleshoot a suspected CHAP authentication problem?

   A. debug ppp negotiation

   B. debug chap protocol

   C. debug ppp chap protocol

   D. None of the above

13. As a general guideline, at what point should compression no longer be used?

A. 56Kbps

B. 128Kbps

C. 256Kbps

D. 2Mbps

14. What option is used when configuring a Windows 95/98 client for manual IP addressing on a dial-up adapter?

A. Control Panel, Network, Dial-up Adapter, TCP/IP address

B. Control Panel, Network, Ethernet, TCP/IP address

C. Dial-up Networking, Properties for the connections, Server Type, TCP/IP settings

D. The command `ifconfig -dial0 ip_address`

15. To configure an IP address for an Ethernet interface in Windows 95/98, the administrator would use which of the following?

A. Control Panel, Network, Dial-up Adapter, TCP/IP address

B. Control Panel, Network, Ethernet, TCP/IP address

C. Dial-up Networking, Properties for the connections, Server Type, TCP/IP settings

D. The command `ifconfig -hme0 ip_address`

16. When using DHCP for address assignment, what must the router be configured with?

A. A helper address

B. A DHCP server address

C. A configuration that makes the router provide DHCP services

D. Any of the above

17. To use a static pool of addresses for IP address assignment, the administrator would use which of the following commands?

A. `peer default ip address pool poolname`

B. `peer default ip address dhcp`

C. `async ip address pool poolname`

D. `async ip address dhcp`

18. Must compression and multilink PPP be used together?

A. Yes, administrators must configure the two to work together.

B. Yes, compression requires multilink, but multilink does not require compression.

C. Yes, multilink requires compression, but compression does not require multilink services.

D. No.

19. Is MMP an open standard for multilink bonding?

A. Yes. It is defined in RFC 2101.

B. Yes, however, MP is not an open standard.

C. Yes, however, it is not part of the PPP standard.

D. No, it is a Cisco protocol.

20. While troubleshooting a PPP session, the debug output reports CDPCP packets but no IPCP packets. What is the most likely meaning of this? (Select two.)

A. That IP is not configured for the link

B. That CDP has been disabled

C. That IP is not functioning on the link

D. That IP is functioning on the link, but with TCP header compression

Answers to Written Lab

1. It is proposed that the XYZ company use PPP for their remote access solution. This implementation should include the CHAP, which is more secure than PAP; however, given the remote nature of the users, PPP callback should not be used. In the future, PPP multipoint may be required for the ISDN connections; however, this is not critical to this recommendation. Universal support and flexibility makes PPP better suited than SLIP—especially considering the IPX requirement.

2. `service dhcp`

3. `encapsulation ppp`

4. `ip dhcp pool`

5. `no ip dhcp conflict logging`

6. MPPC, or Microsoft Point-to-Point Compression

7. Hash

8. 24 hours

9. 72 hours

10. IP unnumbered

Answers to Review Questions

1. B. Point-to-Point Protocol provides support for virtually all upper layer protocols, whereas SLIP is limited to IP only.

2. A. Unfortunately, this is a strict memorization question; however, choices B and C should be easy to eliminate. Answer D can also be eliminated because it infers a requirement for IP to support PPP.

3. A, B, D. Again, this is a memorization question, but server compression sounds awkward.

4. C. This question might be answered by the process of elimination—CHAP requires PPP, so the answer should include the ppp command; therefore it is easy to eliminate B and D. A and C are very similar, but A is noticeably verbose and incorrect considering "protocol" is already part of PPP.

5. B. As noted in the text, dedicated async mode instructs the port to terminate only async connections.

6. A. DHCP and other dynamic address assignment methods are available with PPP.

7. C. MPPC is the only option presented that is found in Windows software.

8. B. The Predictor compression method examines the data flow for compressibility and does not try to recompress already compressed data.

9. A. Remember that the Cisco 700 does not run the full Cisco IOS, and only supports Stac compression.

10. B. TCP header compression is based on the characteristics of the TCP header itself. UDP headers are different in format and protocol number.

11. A. This should have been easy. CHAP and PAP both require the use of PPP. This is one of few questions that uses the word requires and is also true.

12. A. Unfortunately, this is another case of needing to memorize the command. Remembering that CHAP is a function of PPP could help.

13. D. There are two reasons for this recommendation—first, the performance hit is quite high as bandwidth increases, and second, generally, there is no benefit to compression on E-1 or T-1 links. Note that this is a Cisco recommendation, and there is nothing that prevents the use of compression on higher bandwidth circuits. Note that while 2Mbps is the upper limit for compression, many administrators opt to not use compression beyond the 128Kbps point.

14. C. If you're a Windows user, hopefully, this was an easy question. The key is to remember that the dial-up adapter is different from the other network adapters. Unix administrators can use this tip also, however, it may be best to remember the steps.

15. B. Ah, a trick question. Remember that non-dial-up adapters are configured from the control panel and that this question is concerned with the Ethernet interface.

16. D. While one could argue that a local DHCP server negates each of these options, it is best to always think of answers in terms of scalability. Local DHCP servers on thousands of subnets would not be practical. Each of these options is valid—A and B providing more scalability and C is well suited to remote installations.

17. A. It would be nice to provide a cute and simple way to remember this, however, the command is a tad awkward. Of these choices, the best solution would be deduction—address assignment is not specific to async interfaces, and the use of the word pool in the question should negate choice B.

18. D. A common mistake is the belief that compression and multilink (MP or MMP) must be used together. The two are completely unrelated, and, in fact, it is usually best to choose one or the other. They may be used concurrently, however.

19. D. Remember that MP is an open standard limited to a single pair of devices, whereas MMP is a Cisco protocol for bonding to multiple destination switches.

20. A, C. Consider the parameters of the question. B is the opposite of the problem—CDP packets are present, so it wasn't disabled. D is unlikely since the IP header would still exist with TCP header compression. A is viable because CDP is protocol independent—IP need not be present. C is also eligible because a routing configuration error or other problem could prevent the transmission of IP packets.

Chapter

4

Using Microsoft Windows 95/98

THE CCNP REMOTE ACCESS EXAM TOPICS COVERED IN THIS CHAPTER INCLUDE THE FOLLOWING:

✓ Using dial-up networking (the term Microsoft uses to describe remote access connections)

✓ Configuring dial-up networking with Windows 95/98

✓ Verifying dial-up networking with Windows 95/98

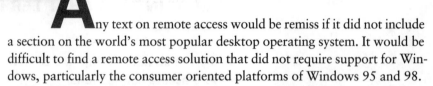

ny text on remote access would be remiss if it did not include a section on the world's most popular desktop operating system. It would be difficult to find a remote access solution that did not require support for Windows, particularly the consumer oriented platforms of Windows 95 and 98.

This chapter will focus on the configuration and support issues that surround this popular client software. Particular attention should be paid to the protocols that are supported and the configuration steps that are required on the client.

Reasons to Use Dial-Up Networking

Fortunately, not only is configuring and using dial-up networking in Windows 95/98 simple, but it also provides a broad base of services for remote users. These services include the following:

Automatic connection to Web sites   Once configured, the operating system will automatically establish a dial-up connection in order to connect with a remote Web server. If a user simply types a URL into Internet Explorer, the modem will dial the Internet Service Provider (ISP) and request the Web page.

E-mail   Mobile clients can connect with Microsoft Exchange or another e-mail service in the office. This provides an efficient way to communicate with colleagues.

File synchronization   Remote users can obtain file updates and post their files on a server in the office for local users. Although Microsoft provides the Briefcase application for this purpose, Symantec's pcAnywhere and other such programs may be desired by more demanding users.

Remote control   One alternative to high-bandwidth applications is remote control. Remote control software does exactly what it sounds like it does—keystrokes and mouse movements are sent to the host, and the host returns the image back to the remote user, allowing them to control the host. This solution allows only the screen images to be transferred, which can greatly reduce the required bandwidth for supporting the application.

Consider the following: a remote user on a dial-up connection needs to access a database that will result in 10 megabytes of data being transferred. With remote control, only the screen data will be sent for the session—with compression, this means that possibly less than 2 megabytes of data will be sent. Clearly, this bandwidth savings can be substantial. Note that remote control solutions must be connected to access data—unlike remote node solutions (where the modem acts as a slower network link), which use the remote user's local applications and data. Also, the bandwidth savings variance can differ significantly depending on the data demands of the application; in this context, remote control utilizes remote node solutions for transport, but the connection must be maintained for the duration of the remote control session.

Effectively, anything that a user can accomplish in the office is possible with dial-up networking. Unfortunately, the significantly lower bandwidth can make this impractical, depending on the application.

Configuring Dial-Up Networking with Windows 95/98

Dial-up networking in Windows 95/98 is extremely popular, perhaps for no other reason than that there are approximately 70 million clients that have it installed worldwide. From a client's perspective, the cost and effort needed to connect to the office remotely requires little more than a phone line and modem.

As you will see in this chapter, configuring and administrating a single Windows workstation for dial-up networking is very simple. Unfortunately, it is not as simple when you have to administer dial-up networking for thousands of remote users, and there are few existing tools that make this task easier.

Microsoft Windows 95 and 98 support remote dial-up networking with the protocols that provide transport for NetBIOS:

- NetBEUI
- IPX
- IP

transport Protocol

This is logical since Windows networking is still dependent upon the NetBIOS protocol and the name services that it provides. It is possible to add other protocols with third-party transport, but most designers find IP support to be sufficient, and they configure the client for PPP services.

See Chapter 3 for more information about the PPP protocol.

Configuring a Dial-Up Connection Client

The configuration of a Windows client for dial-up networking is a relatively painless process, although there are many different configuration options available, and good planning will greatly simplify an enterprise level deployment.

By default, the Windows 95/98 installation will include the basic files for installing and configuring a network connection. It is always a good idea, though, to have the original installation CD-ROM available since the setup program may need additional files to complete the installation. In addition, the latest service packs and updates should be installed—service packs contain many updates and problem fixes called *patches*. In general, the installation of patches is a benign event; however, before performing the upgrade, it is best to backup critical files and review the appropriateness of the patch. For multiple node upgrades, it is best to test the patch before you deploy it.

Check the Windows Web site at www.microsoft.com for the latest patches, service packs, and tips for configuring dial-up networking.

While there are many tools available for installing and configuring dial-up networking, this text will focus on the basic installation—PPP and TCP/IP protocols; however, multilink connections and scripting will all be presented.

The screen captures in this chapter, unless otherwise noted, are from Windows 98 Second Edition. While the screens will look similar, other versions of Windows may differ slightly.

Dial-Up Networking Application

To start configuring a dial-up connection, go to the Start menu and select Start ➤ Programs ➤ Accessories ➤ Communications ➤ Dial-Up Networking. This will open a dialog box similar to the one shown in Figure 4.1.

FIGURE 4.1   The Windows dial-up networking dialog box

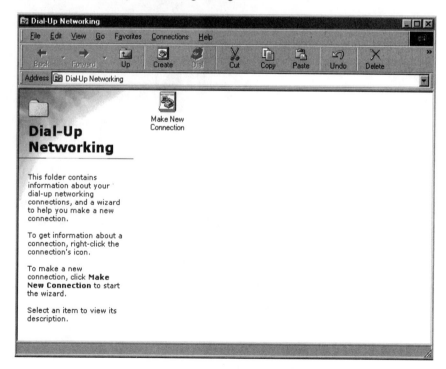

On the system shown here, this is the first dial-up connection, so Windows provides only a Make New Connection icon. This brings up the Dial-Up Networking wizard. If there were other connections available, the user or administrator could select them to initiate a call or to go into an already established connection in order to reconfigure options.

Make New Connection Wizard

After selecting the Make New Connection icon, Windows will begin the Make New Connection wizard. The first dialog box of this wizard is shown in Figure 4.2.

FIGURE 4.2 Making a new connection

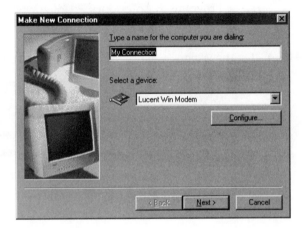

In this dialog box, you will select a name for the connection and set the type of modem that you will be using for the connection. If Windows did not detect and install a modem in the Select a Device box, you will need to correct this before continuing.

For instructions on installing a modem in Windows, please refer to the product documentation.

Note that in Figure 4.2, the Lucent Win Modem has been automatically selected, and the user has been prompted to provide a name for the connection.

Check the hardware compatibility list (HCL) to verify that your equipment is certified to operate in the Windows environment.

By default, Windows will insert the name My Connection; however, you should change this to a more descriptive name for the particular connection you are setting up.

FIGURE 4.3   Changing the dial-up name

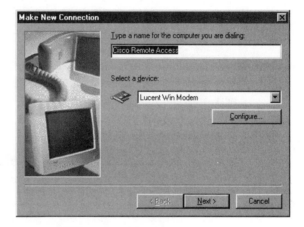

When you are finished renaming the connection and selecting the appropriate modem, click the Next button. The following dialog box (see Figure 4.4) will allow you to define the phone number that will be called. The default area code will be the area code defined when the modem was first installed. The country or region code drop-down list is used to define what digits would precede the area code. For example, if you were going to be making a call to somewhere in the United Kingdom, you would select it and insert country code (44) for the connection.

FIGURE 4.4 Defining the phone number

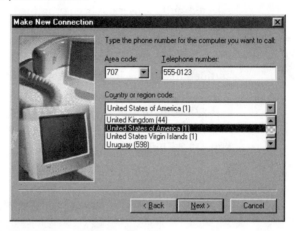

When you are finished, click Next. Windows will provide a confirmation similar to the one shown in Figure 4.5. An icon will be placed in the dial-up networking folder as well.

FIGURE 4.5 A successful connection defined

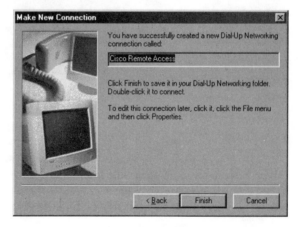

Connection Properties

Once this initial phase has been completed, you have the opportunity to select the icon and attempt a connection with the defaults, or you can right-click the icon to select the properties of the connection. Select the option you wish to edit, and the Connection Properties dialog box (shown in Figure 4.6) will appear. Note that there are four tabs: General, Server Types, Scripting, and Multilink.

FIGURE 4.6   Connection Properties dialog box

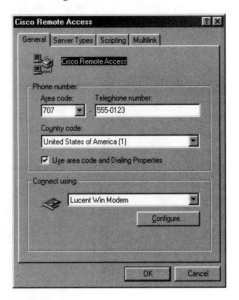

It is important to understand how to select and configure the properties on each of the four tabs.

The General Tab

The General tab displays the initial configuration information, including the name, phone number, country code, and modem that will be used. This tab is shown in Figure 4.6.

The Server Types Tab

You will find that the Server Types tab is the most important for remote access configuration. This section addresses protocols, encapsulations, addressing, compression, and encryption. You will need to match these settings to those on a Cisco remote access device in order to establish an efficient connection.

As shown in Figure 4.7, the first option available asks you to specify the type of dial-up server. There are a total of five options, although the pop-up menu shown in this figure has room to show only four. The types of servers are as follows:

- CSLIP: Unix Connection with IP Header Compression

- NRN: NetWare Connection Version 1.0 and 1.1

- PPP: Internet, Windows NT Server, Windows 98

- SLIP: Unix Connection

- Windows for Workgroups and Windows NT 3.1

You will learn more about each of these server types below.

FIGURE 4.7 The Windows dial-up networking server types

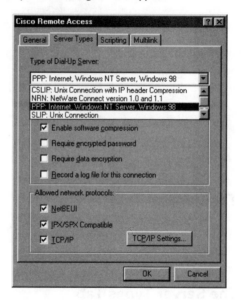

Note that the server types described here are not servers in the traditional sense, they are daemons or descriptions of protocols.

It is important to understand the distinctions between each of these server types:

CSLIP: Unix Connection with IP Header Compression   This server type is seldom used for the reasons outlined in Chapter 3—the SLIP protocol (Serial Line IP) is rarely used due to its sole support for IP. Legacy Unix servers, however, may still require the option. CSLIP stands for Compressed Serial Line Internet Protocol. This option only supports IP and does not support software compression, encrypted passwords, or data compression.

NRN: NetWare Connection Version 1.0 and 1.1   Just as SLIP and CSLIP will only support IP, the NRN connection will only support IPX/SPX. This option is provided for legacy installations of NetWare and most environments have migrated away from this platform.

PPP: Internet, Windows NT Server, Windows 98   PPP is not only the default dial-up server type, it is also the most recommended. As shown in Figure 4.7, it supports all protocols and features.

The PPP protocol is described in detail in Chapter 3.

SLIP: Unix Connection   As with CSLIP, SLIP only supports IP connections and does not provide advanced features. While PPP is both recommended and popular, there are a significant number of installations that only support SLIP. Migration from SLIP to PPP is highly recommended because of PPP's multiprotocol support.

Windows for Workgroups and Windows NT 3.1   This server type only supports NetBEUI and its upper layer protocol, NetBIOS. NetBEUI does not support routing, however. It is a very simple protocol and negates the need for addressing. For a single connection, NetBEUI may provide the best performance, but it cannot scale, and, given the demands on the network, it is probably best to use PPP.

The remainder of this section will focus on the rest of the information on the Server Types tab for a PPP server type.

Advanced Options

Microsoft considers optional functions to be advanced options. These options include settings to control compression and authentication protocols.

Under Advanced Options (see Figure 4.8), there are five choices that may be made by the user or administrator. These are documented following below. Figure 4.8 shows the default configuration for a PPP connection with the NetBEUI and IPX/SPX options unselected.

To improve performance, disable the NetBEUI and IPX/SPX compatible unless they are required.

FIGURE 4.8 Configuring PPP

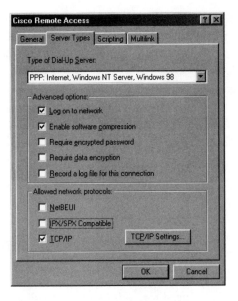

The five Advanced Option choices you can check are documented below:

Log On to Network If you are connecting to an NT domain, you would use this option to establish a network connection and to attempt to log in to the domain. Leave this option unchecked in order to improve performance on networks where this service is not required.

Enable Software Compression   Software-based compression is different from the modem-based compression features that were presented in Chapter 2. By selecting this option, you may improve throughput by enabling compression, but this depends on the type of data and equipment you use. By compressing with software, you are substituting a repetitious series of characters in order to reduce the amount of bandwidth required. When decompressing, the compressed data stream is translated back into an uncompressed form.

Require Encrypted Password   By selecting Require Encrypted Password, you are precluding the use of clear-text authentication. Microsoft supports a number of encrypted password options, including Shiva Password Authentication Protocol (SPAP), Data Encryption Standard (DES), CHAP, and MS-CHAP. MS-CHAP is based on RSA MD4 (message digest type four). On Windows NT or 95, this is enhanced to MD5 with Service Pack 3 or greater.

Remember when choosing your password that passwords are generally case sensitive.

Require Data Encryption   By checking this box, you are making sure that information passing through your connection will be encrypted. Unlike data compression, encryption protects the contents of the data during transmission. Even though this option provides relatively weak encryption, you may want to use it when you are transmitting critical data. Note that your performance will suffer slightly with this option as the encryption is processed in software.

Record a Log File for This Connection   When you check this box, a log file will be recorded. You may find that log files are useful for trouble-shooting purposes, but most administrators find the lack of information provided by this output frustrating. It may help to augment the diagnostic process, however. When used with caution, the Cisco debug commands provide substantially better troubleshooting output.

Viewing a Log File

The output below provides an example of the log output. Note that the software automatically recovered from an error condition found when hanging up the modem via hardware command by lowering DTR, or data terminal ready.

The log is a standard text file, and it may be viewed by selecting Connection ➤ Advanced from the modem's property dialog box (see Figure 4.9), and then clicking the View Log button in the following dialog box.

FIGURE 4.9 The View Log option

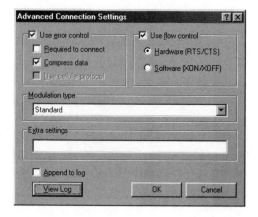

Below is a sample log file that shows the preliminary handshake with the modem. This identifies the INF, or information file, that is used, in addition to the status of connections, error control, compression, and hang-up characteristics. Note that in this case the modem did not respond to the lowering of DTR for the hang up and was disconnected with software. This may indicate a configuration problem with the modem; however, it is benign in this case:

```
02-15-2000 22:36:33.15 - Lucent Win Modem in use.
02-15-2000 22:36:33.16 - Modem type: Lucent Win Modem
02-15-2000 22:36:33.16 - Modem inf path: LTMODEM.INF
02-15-2000 22:36:33.16 - Modem inf section: Modem_PNP_DSVD
02-15-2000 22:36:34.80 - 115200,N,8,1
02-15-2000 22:36:34.80 - 115200,N,8,1
02-15-2000 22:36:34.80 - Initializing modem.
02-15-2000 22:36:34.80 - Send: AT<cr>
02-15-2000 22:36:34.81 - Recv: AT<cr>
02-15-2000 22:36:34.81 - Recv: <cr><lf>OK<cr><lf>
02-15-2000 22:36:34.81 - Interpreted response: Ok
02-15-2000 22:36:34.81 - Send: AT &F E0 &C1 &D2 V1
S0=0\V1<cr>
```

```
02-15-2000 22:36:34.85 - Recv: AT &F E0 &C1 &D2 V1
S0=0\V1<cr>
02-15-2000 22:36:34.85 - Recv: <cr><lf>OK<cr><lf>
02-15-2000 22:36:34.85 - Interpreted response: Ok
02-15-2000 22:36:34.85 - Send:
ATS7=60S30=0L0M1\N3%C1&K3B0B15B2N1\J1X4<cr>
02-15-2000 22:36:34.86 - Recv: <cr><lf>OK<cr><lf>
02-15-2000 22:36:34.86 - Interpreted response: Ok
02-15-2000 22:36:34.86 - Dialing.
02-15-2000 22:36:34.86 - Send: ATDT;<cr>
02-15-2000 22:36:37.38 - Recv: <cr><lf>OK<cr><lf>
02-15-2000 22:36:37.38 - Interpreted response: Ok
02-15-2000 22:36:37.38 - Dialing.
02-15-2000 22:36:37.38 - Send: ATDT#######<cr>
02-15-2000 22:37:10.81 - Recv: <cr><lf>CONNECT 26400
V42bis<cr><lf>
02-15-2000 22:37:10.81 - Interpreted response: Connect
02-15-2000 22:37:10.81 - Connection established at
26400bps.
02-15-2000 22:37:10.81 - Error-control on.
02-15-2000 22:37:10.81 - Data compression on.
02-15-2000 22:37:44.27 - Hanging up the modem.
02-15-2000 22:37:44.27 - Hardware hangup by lowering DTR.
02-15-2000 22:37:45.47 - WARNING: The modem did not
respond to lowering DTR.  Trying software hangup...
02-15-2000 22:37:45.47 - Send: +++
02-15-2000 22:37:45.55 - Recv: <cr><lf>OK<cr><lf>
02-15-2000 22:37:45.55 - Interpreted response: Ok
02-15-2000 22:37:45.55 - Send: ATH E1<cr>
02-15-2000 22:37:45.63 - Recv: <cr><lf>OK<cr><lf>
02-15-2000 22:37:45.63 - Interpreted response: Ok
02-15-2000 22:37:45.63 - 115200,N,8,1
02-15-2000 22:37:46.69 - Session Statistics:
02-15-2000 22:37:46.69 -                    Reads : 811 bytes
02-15-2000 22:37:46.69 -                    Writes: 2991 bytes
02-15-2000 22:37:46.69 - Lucent Win Modem closed.
```

Allowed Network Protocols

The Allowed Network Protocols section allows eligible protocols to be included or omitted from the dial-up networking connection. All three—NetBEUI, IPX, and IP—are allowed since PPP was selected. The TCP/IP settings button allows the user or administrator to choose DHCP assigned IP address information (the default), or the entry of static entries.

The Scripting Tab

Scripts allow the administrator or user to automate functions, including login or program execution. An example of a script would be a to-do list for getting ready in the morning—get up, brush teeth, get dressed, and so forth. Scripts should be approached with care since they are not stored in a secure manner and therefore, may present a security risk.

To select a script, enter the script name in the File Name text box (see Figure 4.10). The Step Through Script option (grayed out in this figure because a script file was not defined) may be useful for timing a script, or for general debugging, and the Start Terminal Screen Minimized option can be used to hide the script's execution from being displayed to the user.

FIGURE 4.10   The Scripting dialog box

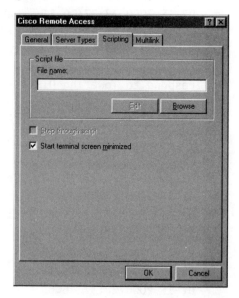

The Multilink Tab

You learned about multilink services and the Multilink Protocol (MP) in Chapter 3. Multilink provides the ability to create a single logical connection through two or more physical modems, which can provide greater aggregate bandwidth for a remote user. Note that Microsoft's multilink feature does not support the Cisco proprietary MPP protocol, only the standards-based MP. Users or administrators need only provide the phone number to configure the service, as shown in Figure 4.11. The dialog box shown in Figure 4.11 is provided when the user selects Use Additional Devices and clicks the Add button.

FIGURE 4.11 The Multilink dialog box

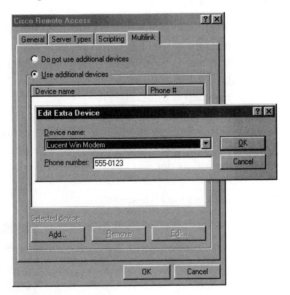

Additional Configuration Options

This section addresses two of the most common optional configuration options that administrators and users select in dial-up networking:

- Lock DTE speed
- Launch terminal windows

The first, lock DTE speed, is predominately used for troubleshooting or degraded circuits—circuits that are impaired due to line conditions. It is becoming less significant as phone line quality and termination equipment improves. The second option, launching terminal windows, is usually used for third-party authentication; however, it may also be used for manual control of the session. Unlike the previous options, both of these selections are grouped with the modem controls as opposed to the networking configuration. This is due to their relationship with the Physical and Data Link Layers—DTE speed and a terminal window are both independent of the Network Layer Protocol in use.

Lock DTE Speed

There may be times when the user will wish to lock the DTE speed or launch a terminal window in order to complete a connection. Locking the DTE speed can provide better performance on degraded lines if the speed is locked to a value lower than would otherwise be possible. For most connections, this step is unnecessary.

To lock the DTE speed, select the Only Connect at This Speed option in the Modem Properties dialog box, as shown in Figure 4.12. Recall that this is DTE to DCE speed, and as such, it should relate to the capacity of the DCE device, as defined in Chapter 2.

FIGURE 4.12 Locking the DTE speed

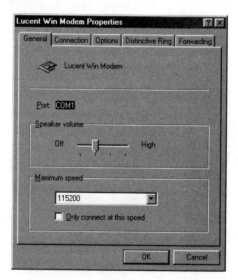

Launch Terminal Windows

Under the Modem Properties Option tab, the user is offered the option of launching a terminal window either before or after the connection is made. This option is frequently necessary for hard authentication options such as SecureID. This is shown in Figure 4.13.

FIGURE 4.13   Launching a terminal window

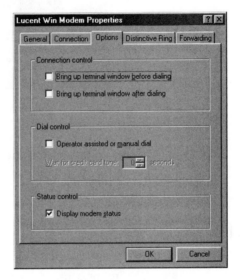

Typically, the terminal window is launched with a *challenge* sent from the SecureID or a similar third-party product. The challenge is a dynamically created value that is entered into a physical calculator that is programmed to generate the proper response. This response is only valid for the duration of the challenge—typically a minute—and it is a single-use password. These security solutions require physical possession of the token, or password generator, and the pin number that allows access. This security model is sometimes referred to as "something you have and something you know." Bank ATM cards use a similar principle.

Verifying a Dial-Up Connection

Dial-up connections work without a significant amount of troubleshooting under most circumstances. When they don't, Windows generally provides an indication of the error and a recommended course of action, as shown in Figure 4.14. This screen shows error 680, which means that there was no dial tone.

FIGURE 4.14 Dial-up networking error

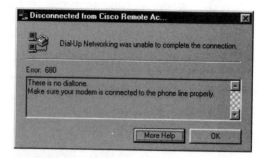

On the access server, the administrator may choose to use the show line command to view the status of the connection. Unfortunately, this requires that much of the connection is already established—a presumption that does not always coincide with troubleshooting.

Summary

This chapter presented how to configure and troubleshoot remote access for the popular Windows operating systems. It discussed the three supported protocols—IP, IPX, and NetBEUI—and it provided an overview of why an administrator would wish to configure dial-up networking—the remote access solution for Windows networks.

In addition, this chapter presented some of the methods used to troubleshoot these connections, including the log files and the locking of DTE speed to work-around degraded line conditions.

The information in this chapter is useful due to the proliferation of Windows clients in the enterprise; however, readers may note the lack of Cisco related material in the chapter. The Cisco portion of Windows connections is provided in Chapters 2 and 3 of this text.

Key Terms

Before you take the exam, be certain you are familiar with the following terms:

challenge

patches

scripts

Commands in This Chapter

Command	Meaning
show line	Shows the status of a line on an access server. Usually requires that the connection be established to provide useful diagnostic data.

Written Lab

1. What dial-up networking protocol does not support routing?

2. What dial-up networking protocol is a proprietary version of CHAP?

3. What dial-up networking protocol would be best used with Novell networks?

4. What three protocols are supported for dial-up networking?

5. What do the three supported dial-up networking protocols have in common?

6. Does Windows 95/98 dial-up networking support SLIP?

7. Windows 95/98 dial-up networking provides for _____ and _____ IP addressing.

8. The logical linking of two or more physical connections is called _____.

9. Ethernet configuration is selected from the _____.

10. Dial-up networking configuration is selected from the _____.

Review Questions

1. Windows remote access connections support which of the following protocols?

   A. IP

   B. IPX

   C. AppleTalk

   D. NetBEUI

   E. All of the above

2. The CSLIP server type supports which of the following?

   A. IP

   B. IPX

   C. NetBEUI

   D. All of the above

3. The Windows for Workgroups server type supports which of the following?

   A. IP

   B. IPX

   C. NetBEUI

   D. All of the above

4. The best reason to use PPP above all other server types is that it has

   A. Support for multiple protocols

   B. Integrated 128-bit encryption

   C. Enhanced AppleTalk support

   D. None of the above

5. To select an IP address for a dial-up network connection, the user would

   A. Use the network control panel.

   B. Select the icon from the dial-up networking folder.

   C. Either A or B.

   D. Neither A or B.

6. To configure a network connection between a Novell NetWare network and a Windows dial-up client, the server type would be set to which of the following?

   A. CSLIP

   B. SLIP

   C. PPP

   D. NRN

7. Which of the following would be a reason to launch a terminal window?

   A. To enable Cisco Discovery Protocol (CDP) packets on the link

   B. To set DTE speed after connection

   C. To use a third-party security solution

   D. When using dial-up DSL connections

8. Why might a user or administrator lock the DTE speed?

   A. To improve performance on degraded lines

   B. To alter the compression ratio

   C. To augment encryption on the line

   D. None of the above

9. To debug a script, the user or administrator might use which of the following?

   A. The `debug ppp script` command on the router or remote access device

   B. The protocol analyzer for POTS product

   C. The Step Through Script option

   D. The Windows 95/98 script debugger application

10. Does Microsoft supports Shiva's Password Authentication Protocol?

    A. Yes

    B. Yes, but only with EIGRP

    C. No

    D. Yes, but only with the Shiva add-in client

11. To debug a script, the administrator might use which of the following?

    A. The step through script option

    B. A protocol analyzer

    C. The `debug script` command

    D. None of the above

12. Which of the following is true?

    A. Passwords may be case-sensitive.

    B. PAP is less secure than CHAP.

    C. Microsoft supports the PPP protocol.

    D. All of the above.

13. To support only IPX, which of the following would the administrator select?

A. PPP

B. SLIP

C. NRN

D. None of the above

14. "Something you have" refers to which of the following?

A. A security token

B. A modem

C. A router

D. A computer

15. Which of the following are the NetBIOS protocols?

A. AppleTalk, IPX, and IP

B. IPX, IP, and EIGRP

C. IPX, IP, and NetBEUI

D. AppleTalk, NetBEUI, and IP

16. Which of the following are services that can use dial-up networking?

A. Electronic mail

B. Remote control

C. Automatic connections to Web sites

D. All of the above

17. To correct problems with dial-up networking, which of the following might the administrator first install?

    A. Multilink services

    B. Compression services

    C. A service pack

    D. None of the above

18. To create a new dial-up configuration, which of the following would the administrator or user run?

    A. The Make New Connection Wizard

    B. The Windows Installer

    C. The Cisco DUN Setup Program

    D. None of the above

19. Which of the following is not true regarding NetBEUI?

    A. It is supported by Windows.

    B. NetBIOS can operate over the protocol.

    C. It is routable.

    D. All of the following are true.

20. To improve performance on only remote IP sessions, which of the following should the administrator do?

    A. Disable compression

    B. Disable NetBEUI and IPX

    C. Disable multilink

    D. None of the above

Answers to Written Lab

1. NetBEUI/NetBIOS

2. MS-CHAP

3. IPX

4. IP, IPX, and NetBEUI

5. They all support NetBIOS.

6. Yes

7. Static, dynamic

8. Bonding or multilink

9. Network control panel

10. Dial-up networking folder

Answers to Review Questions

1. A, B, D. All protocols that support NetBIOS are allowed for remote dial-up networking. AppleTalk does not support NetBIOS.

2. A. Compressed SLIP only supports the IP protocol, the same as SLIP.

3. C. Windows for Workgroups used NetBEUI as the native transport for NetBIOS packets, which corresponds to this support.

4. A. Of the five server types, only PPP supports multiple protocols. It does not augment AppleTalk, nor does it include encryption.

5. B. The network control panel cannot be used for defining the IP address on a dial-up connection.

6. C or D. Both CSLIP and SLIP support IP only. This removes them from contention for IPX or Novell NetWare transport.

7. C. Launching a terminal window allows the user to key in a challenge/ response password. A, B, and D are all nonsensical options since they do not relate to the terminal window in any way.

8. A. On poor quality lines, the DTE may try to establish higher than acceptable speeds. Locking the speed prevents overrunning the line and typically leads to better throughput as there are fewer dropped packets.

9. C. While each of these choices, or a variation of them, could aid in debugging a script, only the Step Through Script option is legitimate. The others are not available as presented.

10. A. Microsoft's dial-up networking supports SPAP, in addition to PAP and CHAP. No add-in client is needed and EIGRP is not supported on Windows clients, making answer B bogus.

11. A. The step through script option will allow the administrator to find a faulty command in the script.

12. D. Each of these items is true.

13. C. While one could select PPP and only enable IPX protocol support, the NRN option is the best answer because it only supports IPX.

14. A. The security token is something you have as part of the security solution.

15. C. Windows dial-up networking supports the NetBIOS protocols, which are IPX, IP, and NetBEUI.

16. D. Dial-up networking can provide all of the listed services.

17. C. Service packs, which include bug fixes, can correct problems with dial-up networking. Multilink and compression would not correct these issues and might compound any problems.

18. A. The Make New Connection Wizard is used to define a new configuration.

19. C. NetBEUI contains no logical addressing information and is not routable.

20. B. Disabling NetBEUI and IPX can improve performance and reduce overhead. Multilink and compression can improve performance in some circumstances.

Integrated Services Digital Network (ISDN)

THE CCNP REMOTE ACCESS EXAM TOPICS COVERED IN THIS CHAPTER INCLUDE THE FOLLOWING:

- ✓ Understanding the basics of ISDN

- ✓ Configuring basic ISDN

- ✓ Describing the difference between BRI and PRI line types

- ✓ Describing the location and purpose of each ISDN function point

- ✓ Describing the different reference points in an ISDN network

- ✓ Listing the various ISDN protocols

- ✓ Understanding the ISDN setup and teardown mechanism

- ✓ Configuring ISDN authentication

- ✓ Understanding and configuring dial-on-demand routing (DDR)

- ✓ Understanding and configuring Bandwidth on Demand (BoD)

- ✓ Describing both channelized T1 and channelized E1

Integrated Services Digital Network (ISDN) has gained quite a following over the past few years. It offers a switched high-speed data connection that you can also use to support a voice, video, or fax call, making it an excellent choice for Small Office/Home Office (SOHO) users. However, Digital Subscriber Line (DSL) will probably replace ISDN completely within the next few years because DSL is cheaper and faster, which means it must be better, right? Maybe. DSL can also provide data, voice, and fax services to end users, just like ISDN. In addition, cable modems have also been around for a few years and provide a large amount of bandwidth for a neighborhood to the Internet, but these cable modems are really just composed of a large Thinnet network in which all your neighbors share the same bandwidth.

Now, you may be thinking, "Hey, I thought this was an ISDN chapter; what's with DSL taking over the discussion?" It is an ISDN chapter, and you do need to know about the topic. It won't be replaced overnight, though, and while DSL will probably replace it, it is possible that it won't. Remember about six or seven years ago when everyone was saying that ATM was going to take over the world? Pretty glad I didn't buy stock in that rumor. ATM is a contender, but the expense and difficult technical administration make it unpopular compared to Gigabit for the LAN and to DSL for the WAN. In defense of ISDN, it does have a few benefits over DSL and cable modems that I will describe in this chapter.

ISDN is still a good choice for WAN services because of its high speed (Cisco calls ISDN high speed). It can run anywhere from 56K to T-1 speeds (1.544Mbps). 128Kbps is the most common, though. While 128Kbps is not high speed to me, compared to a 33Kbps dial-up analog modem, it is.

ISDN is digital from end to end, instead of analog like a modem. Analog modems go from digital on the computer, to analog through the modem, then back to digital on the remote computer end. ISDN is more efficient and faster, and it also has a faster setup connection speed than an analog modem.

In this chapter, you will learn about ISDN, beginning with the Physical Layer and working up. Topics covered in this chapter will include the following:

- ISDN device types

- Layer 2 (Q.921)

- Layer 3 (Q.931)

- ISDN reference points (S, T, and U)

- Dial backup and Bandwidth on Demand configurations (legacy and dialer interfaces)

- Some commonly used show commands

- Useful debug commands

What Is Integrated Services Digital Network (ISDN)?

Integrated Services Digital Network (ISDN) has been under development for a couple decades but has been hampered by the lack of applications that can use its speed. It wasn't until recently that telecommuting, video conferencing, and *Small Offices/Home Offices (SOHOs)* have needed the capabilities ISDN presented. Another factor slowing the development of ISDN was that it was somewhat proprietary in nature. However, this ended when National ISDN-1 became available in 1992. National ISDN-1 is a standard switch type used by the ISDN providers. This now allowed vendors to interoperate between devices.

Before getting into what ISDN is and does, you first need to understand how our traditional, or *plain old telephone service (POTS)*, operates. Typically, you pick up the telephone receiver, you enter the number, and the party answers at the other end. Your voice—which is an analog wave—is converted into a digital signal through a process called *Pulse Code Modulation (PCM)*. PCM samples your voice 8000 times per second and converts the audio level into an 8-bit value. This 64Kbps channel, or DS0, is multiplexed with 23 other channels to form a T-1.

If you do the math, you'll notice that a T-1 is 1.544Mbps; however, 24 * 64Kbps is only 1.536Mbps. Where are the other 8Kbps? The 8Kbps are used by a single framing bit, which is added to every 24-channel block, which provides the 1.544Mbps called robbed bit signaling. *Robbed bit signaling* uses the lowest significant bit for signaling; this indicates whether the line is on or off the hook, leaving a practical channel bandwidth of 56Kbps. Robbed bit signaling is also called *in-band signaling*.

ISDN differs from POTS in a couple ways. First, ISDN starts off as digital signaling, so there is no analog-to-digital conversion. Second, call setup and teardown is accomplished through a dedicated 16Kbps channel also known as a D (data) channel. By using "out of band" signaling, we have the entire 64Kbps for data. This leaves one or two B (bearer) channels for your data or voice traffic that does not have an intrusion on the line for clocking or error control. ISDN then provides unadulterated bandwidth to end users.

ISDN benefits include improved speed over an analog modem, fast call setup (one second or less, typically), and lower cost than a dedicated point-to-point circuit. Digital Subscriber Lines (DSLs) and cable modems are replacing ISDN in some areas and will continue to do so as they fit the need for high-speed Internet access to the home. However, ISDN has some advantages over the newer, faster technologies like DSL and cable modems. Here is a list of the advantages that ISDN can provide:

- Ability to dial into many different locations simultaneously

- Dial-up services for traveling telecommuters at high speeds

- Fault tolerance of dedicated lines

- Remote SOHO connectivity

- Video conferencing

ISDN Line Options

ISDN is available in many different configurations or line options. In this section, you will learn about two of the most common—*Basic Rate Interface (BRI)* and *Primary Rate Interface (PRI)*. These flavors of ISDN vary according to the type and number of channels that carry data. Each option has one or more *DS0s* or *B (bearer) channels* and a *D (data) channel*. ISDN is characterized by the presence of a D channel, which carries control and signaling information, freeing up the B channels for voice and data transport.

Each DS0 is capable of carrying 64,000 bits per second of either voice or data. Telcos can provide ISDN on their current infrastructure with little additional work. Table 5.1 shows the relationship between the DS level, speed, designations, and number of DS0s per channel.

TABLE 5.1 North America Digital Hierarchy

Digital Signal Level	Speed	Designation	Channel
DS0	64K	None	1
DS1	1.544Mbps	T-1	24
DS2	6.312Mbps	T-2	96
DS3	44.736Mbps	T-3	672
DS4	274.176Mbps	T-4	4032

Different standards called Synchronous Optical Network (SONET) and Synchronous Digital Hierarchy (SDH) were developed for Fiber Optics Transmission Systems (FOTS). These standards are not covered in this course.

Another ISDN characteristic is the *Service Profile Identifier (SPID)*. A SPID identifies the characteristics of your ISDN line. SPIDs may or may not be needed, depending on the type of switch your service provider uses. ISDN National-1 and DMS-100 switches require a SPID for each B channel, whereas a SPID is optional with an AT&T 5ESS switch type. Please consult your ISDN provider if you are not sure whether you need a SPID. The format of a SPID is usually the 10-digit phone number, plus a prefix and possibly a suffix. For example, let's say that your telephone number is 212-835-8663.

Now add a prefix of 01 and a suffix of 0100. This gives you a SPID of 0121283586630100.

To place an ISDN call, you will also need a Dial Number, or DN. A DN is the actual number you would call to reach that B channel. In our example, the DN would be 2128358663 or 8358663. Knowing the SPID, switch type, and DN will speed up the configuration of your router. Your service provider should provide you with this information. Other than the dial number, the rest might be auto detected.

Basic Rate Interface (BRI)

A *Basic Rate Interface (BRI)* uses a single copper pair of wires to provide up to 192Kbps of bandwidth for both voice and data calls. A BRI uses two 64Kbps B channels and one 16Kbps D channel for framing the D channel. In addition, a 48Kbps channel is used for framing and synchronization. So, if each B channel is 64Kbps, that totals 128Kbps. Add the 16Kbps D channel, and the bandwidth for ISDN BRI is now at 144Kbps. Last, add the 48Kbps for framing and synchronization to get a total speed of 192Kbps.

Figure 5.1 shows the ISDN protocol layers.

FIGURE 5.1 ISDN protocol layers

DSS1 Q.931	IP/IPX
LAPD Q.921	HDLC/PPP/Frame/LAPD
1.430/1.431/ANSI T1.601	

Both the B and D channels share Layer 1. Layers 2 and 3 operate for the D channel, but the B channel operates in either an HDLC or PPP encapsulation mode to encapsulate the upper layer protocols instead of using Layer 2 and Layer 3 directly. As already mentioned, LAPD is the framing protocol used for the D channel data. The DSS1 (digital subscriber signaling system no. 1) is the Layer 3 protocol for the D channel. Only Q.931 is used here. B channels are used by the IP or IPX protocols for data transfer, and the D channel is used by dial-on-demand routing (DDR), which builds the connection over ISDN or analog links.

BRI Switch Options

There are several different BRI switch options available for configuring your router. These switch options vary according to geographic location. The available switch types are shown in Table 5.2.

*[handwritten: global command
ISDN switch-Type BASIC-NI]*

TABLE 5.2 ISDN BRI Switch Types

*[handwritten: INT BRI∅
no Shut
sh ISDN STATUS]*

Switch Type	Typically Used
basic-1tr6	1TR6 switch type for Germany
basic-5ess	AT&T 5ESS switch type for the U.S.
basic-dms100	Northern DMS-100 switch type
basic-net3	NET3 switch type for UK and Europe
basic-ni	National ISDN switch type
basic-ts013	TS013 switch type for Australia
ntt	NTT switch type for Japan
vn3	VN3 and VN4 switch types for France

One great benefit to a BRI is being able to make a voice call while maintaining your Internet connection. This is a great solution for SOHO deployments.

The D channel can also be used to transport packet-switched data communications, such as X.25. In fact, Cisco has enabled this feature in version 12 of its IOS software. The feature is called Always On/Dynamic ISDN (AO/DI). Basically, it allows the low bandwidth traffic to use the D channel and initiates a call using one or two B channels if the traffic warrants. This feature will be most useful for Point of Sale applications.

Primary Rate Interface (PRI)

Most Internet service providers use *Primary Rate Interface (PRI)* ISDN to connect to the PSTN. PRI allows users to provide service to analog modem users, digital modem users, and ISDN customers. The calls are routed to the different modems after the access server receives the calling number's bearer capability. ISDN also provides a means to deliver Calling Line ID (CLID), as well as Called Number or Automatic Number Identification (ANI). These features can be used to determine the correct authentication server for this customer.

PRIs have the following capacities:

- A T-1–based PRI has 23 B channels and one 64Kbps D channel, which equals a bandwidth of 1.536Kbps. An 8Kbps channel for framing and synchronization is used as well to get a bandwidth for a U.S. T-1/PRI of 1.544Mbps.

- An E-1–based PRI has 30 B channels and one 64Kbps D channel. An E-1 uses channel 15 for signaling (D channel). An E-1 has 2.048Mbps of bandwidth.

PRI Switch Options

Like with BRI, you have several switch types to select from. Check with your provider to get the correct one. Otherwise you may have to reboot your router for the change to take effect.

Table 5.3 shows the typical available switch types used with PRI.

TABLE 5.3 PRI Switch Types

Switch Type	Typically Used
primary-5ess	AT&T 5ESS switch type for the U.S.
primary-4ess	AT&T 4ESS switch type for the U.S.
primary-dms100	Northern DMS-100 switch type
primary-net5	NET3 switch type for UK and Europe
vn3	VN3 and VN4 switch types for France

T-1– and E-1–based PRIs use different line coding and framing schemes. A T-1–based PRI uses B8ZS encoding and ESF for framing. An E-1–based PRI uses High-Density Bipolar Order 3 (HDB3) for encoding and Cyclic Redundancy Check, level 4 (CRC-4) for framing.

ISDN Function Groups

It is important to understand the different function groups when you design and troubleshoot your ISDN network. By having a firm understanding of the following functions, you can more easily troubleshoot an ISDN line. Figure 5.2 shows the different function groups and their placement in an ISDN network.

FIGURE 5.2   ISDN function groups

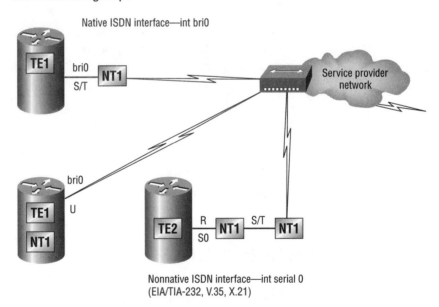

The following are definitions and examples of ISDN BRI functional groups as they relate to Figure 5.2.

Terminal Equipment 1 (TE1)   A device that understands ISDN digital signaling techniques. Examples of TE1 devices are digital telephones, routers with ISDN interfaces, and digital facsimile equipment. TE1 devices are 4-wire (2 pair) and need to be 2-wire (1 pair) to communicate with an ISDN network. A TE1 will connect into a Network Termination type 1 (NT1) to connect the 4-wire subscriber wiring to the 2-wire local loop facility.

Terminal Equipment 2 (TE2)   Equipment that does not understand ISDN signaling standards. Examples of TE2 devices are X.25 interfaces and serial interfaces on a router. TE2 needs to be converted to ISDN signaling, which is provided by a Terminal Adapter (TA). After that, it still needs to be converted to a 2-wire network with an NT1 device.

Network Termination type 1 (NT1)   This device is used to convert a 4-wire ISDN connection to the 2-wire ISDN used by the local loop facility.

Network Termination type 2 (NT2)   This device is used to direct traffic from ISDN devices (TEs) to an NT1. This is probably the most intelligent device in the ISDN network, provides switching and concentrating, and can sometimes even be a PBX.

Terminal Adapter (TA)   This device allows a TE2 device to communicate with the telco's network by providing any necessary protocol and interface conversion. In essence, a TA adapts the unipolar signal coming from a non-ISDN device into a bipolar signal used by the ISDN network.

Local Termination (LT)   The same device as an NT1 but is located at the provider's site.

Exchange Termination (ET)   The connection to the ISDN switch, typically an ISDN line card.

Both the LT and the ET are typically referred to as the local exchange (LE).

ISDN Reference Points

A *reference point* defines a connection point between two functions; you may also refer to it as an interface, though it does not represent an actual physical interface. The reference point is where data is converted between device types. Figure 5.3 shows the different reference points defined in an ISDN network.

FIGURE 5.3 ISDN reference points

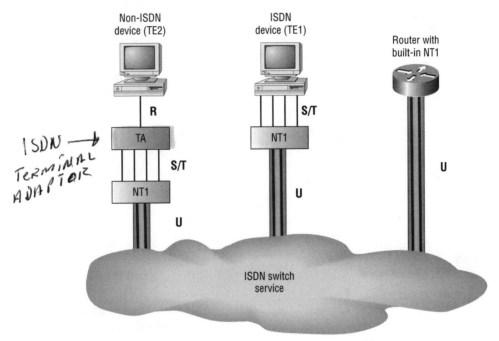

The reference points shown in Figure 5.3 are described in detail in the following list.

R reference point   This reference point defines the reference point between non-ISDN equipment and a TA. The R reference point allows a non-ISDN device to appear on the network as an ISDN device.

S reference point   The point between the user terminals and NT2 or, in other words, between a TE1 or a TA and the Network Termination (which is either an NT1 or NT2).

T reference point   This reference point defines the reference point between NT1 and NT2 devices.

S/T interface   As the name implies, the S/T interface combines both the S and T interfaces. This interface is governed by the ITU I.430 standard, which defines the connection as a 4-wire connection. The S/T interface is typically an RJ-45, with 8-pin cables using pins 3 and 6 to receive data and pins 4 and 5 to transmit data.

International Telecommunications Union (ITU) is a United Nations–sponsored organization formed in 1865 to promote worldwide communication systems compatibility. It has two groups, ITU-T and ITU-R. ITU-T deals with telecommunications and ITU-R is responsible for radio communications. You may visit their Web site at www.itu.int for more information.

U reference point This reference point is also known as a U (user) interface. This is a 2-wire connection between the NT1 and the telephone company (LE). Cisco routers are marked with an X if the interface is a U and a crossed-out X if the interface is an S/T. This is an ANSI standard used in the U.S., not ITU-T.

ISDN Protocols

ISDN protocols define how information is transferred between different devices in the network. Currently the ITU-T has established three types of protocols to handle this information transfer. The types of protocols are as follows:

- Protocols beginning with the letter E specify ISDN on the existing telephone network.

- Protocols beginning with the letter I specify concepts, terminology, and services.

- Protocols beginning with the letter Q specify switching and signaling. Two Q standards of interest are Q.921, which deals with Layer 2, and Q.931, which deals with Layer 3 interfacing.

Spending some time reviewing the Q standard will help us use a couple of the IOS **debug** commands we'll go over later in this chapter. As stated above, the ITU-T recommendations Q.921 and Q.931 handle switching and signaling. Q.921 uses *Link Access Procedure, Data (LAPD)* to communicate with other ISDN devices across the D channel. LAPD's primary purpose is to transport signaling information.

LAPD Frames

Layer 2 and 3 functions are handled with LAPD. Understanding the information contained in this frame will help you understand Q.921 and Q.931 debug outputs. Remember that LAPD is the framing protocol used for D channel data and that the D channel is used to build connections over either an analog or ISDN link.

An *LAPD frame* has six parts to it: Flag, Address, Control, Information, CRC, and a final Flag. Figure 5.4 shows the LAPD frame and the different fields within the frame.

FIGURE 5.4   Link Access Procedure, D channel

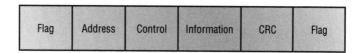

The following information describes the different fields within the LAPD frame:

Flag   This one-octet field starts and ends the frame with a value of 7E (0111 1110).

Address   This field is two octets long and contains some important information. This field identifies the TE using this link and has four parts: Service Access Point Identifier, Command/Response, Address Extension 0, and Terminal Endpoint Identifier.

Service Access Point Identifier (SAPI)   This field is six bits long. Table 5.4 shows the different SAPI values that can be used in an LAPD frame.

TABLE 5.4   SAPI Values

SAPI	Description
0	Call control procedures
1	Packet mode using Q.931 call procedures

TABLE 5.4 SAPI Values *(continued)*

SAPI	Description
16	Packet mode communications procedures
32–47	Reserved for national use
63	Management procedures
Others	Reserved for future use

Command/Response (C/R)   This is one bit long. This bit identifies the frame as either a command or a response. The user side always sends commands with this bit set to zero and responds with it set to 1. The network side is the exact opposite, sending a command with this bit set to 1, or a zero if it is responding.

Address Extension 0 (EA0 and EA1)   This is one bit long. Setting this bit to zero and setting EA1 to 1 identifies the frame as an LAPD frame.

Terminal endpoint identifier (TEI)   These values uniquely identify each TE on an ISDN S/T bus. A TEI can be either dynamically or statically assigned. Table 5.5 lists the values.

TABLE 5.5 Terminal Endpoint Identifier (TEI) Values

TEI	Description
0–63	Fixed TEI assignments
64–126	Dynamically assigned (assigned by the switch)
127	Broadcast to all devices

Control   This field has 11 available values, each one shown in Table 5.6, along with its application. You will see one of three types of information here: Information Transfer, Supervisory, or Unnumbered.

TABLE 5.6   Control Field Values

Format	Message Type	Control/Response
Information Transfer	I=Information	Control
Supervisory	RR=Receive Ready	Control/Response
Supervisory	RNR=Receive Not Ready	Control/Response
Supervisory	REJ=Reject	Control/Response
Unnumbered	SAMBE=Set Asynchronous Balanced Mode Extended	Control
Unnumbered	DM=Disconnected Mode	Response
Unnumbered	UI=Unnumbered Information	Control
Unnumbered	DISC=Disconnect	Control
Unnumbered	UA=Unnumbered Acknowledgment	Response
Unnumbered	FRMR=Frame Reject	Response
Unnumbered	XID=Exchange Identifier	Control/Response

Information   This field carries the Q.931 protocol data. Figure 5.5 illustrates how it is laid out. This is where the user data is carried.

FIGURE 5.5 Q.921/Q.931 information field format

Information Field							
1	2	3	4	5	6	7	8
Protocol Discriminator							
0	0	0	0	Length of CRV			
Call Reference Value (1 or 2 octets)							
0	Message Type (SETUP, CONNECT, etc.)						
Mandatory and Optional Information Elements (Variable)							

The following information describes the field format as shown in Figure 5.5.

Protocol Discriminator   Is one octet. Identifies the Layer 3 protocol.

Length   Is one octet. Indicates the length of the Call Reference Value.

Call Reference Value (CRV)   Is one or two octets. This value is assigned to each call at the beginning, is used to distinguish between other simultaneous calls, and is released after the call is torn down.

Message Type   Is one octet.

Mandatory and Optional Information Elements (variable length)   Are options based on the message type.

Layer 2 Negotiation

Understanding how Layer 2 negotiates and gets established will help you identify where a potential or real problem is occurring. One nice thing about Cisco equipment is the diagnostics available for finding ISDN problems. Knowing which side of the ISDN connection does what will help you identify a problem and start corrective action.

The first part of the process is TEI assignment, which is accomplished using this process:

1. The TE (Terminal Endpoint) and the network initially exchange Receive Ready (RR) frames, listening for an initiated connection.

2. The TE sends an Unnumbered Information (UI) frame with a SAPI of 63 (management procedure, query network) and TEI of 127 (broadcast).

3. The network assigns an available TEI (in the range 64–126).

4. The TE sends a Set Asynchronous Balanced Mode Extended (SABME) frame with a SAPI of 0 (call control, used to initiate a SETUP) and a TEI of the value assigned by the network.

5. The network responds with an Unnumbered Acknowledgment (UA); SAPI=0, TEI=assigned.

As you examine this partial output from a "Debug ISDN Q921," please refer to Table 5.7, which explains the meaning of the output.

```
ISDN BR0: TX -> SABMEp sapi = 0  tei = 77
ISDN BR0: RX <- IDCKRQ  ri = 0  ai = 127
ISDN BR0: TX -> IDCKRP  ri = 44602  ai = 77
ISDN BR0: TX -> IDCKRP  ri = 37339  ai = 78
ISDN BR0: RX <- IDREM  ri = 0  ai = 77
ISDN BR0: TX -> IDREQ  ri = 44940  ai = 127
ISDN BR0: RX <- IDREM  ri = 0  ai = 78
ISDN BR0: TX -> IDREQ  ri = 43085  ai = 127
ISDN BR0: TX -> IDREQ  ri = 11550  ai = 127
ISDN BR0: RX <- IDASSN  ri = 11550  ai = 79
ISDN BR0: TX -> SABMEp sapi = 0  tei = 79
ISDN BR0: TX -> IDREQ  ri = 65279  ai = 127
ISDN BR0: RX <- UAf sapi = 0  tei = 79
ISDN BR0: TX -> INFOc sapi = 0  tei = 79  ns = 0  nr = 0
i = 0x08007B3A0A30383335383636313031
ISDN BR0: RX <- IDASSN  ri = 65279  ai = 80
ISDN BR0: TX -> SABMEp sapi = 0  tei = 80
ISDN BR0: RX <- INFOc sapi = 0  tei = 79  ns = 0  nr = 1
i = 0x08007B3B028181
ISDN BR0: TX -> RRr sapi = 0  tei = 79  nr = 1
ISDN BR0: RX <- UAf sapi = 0  tei = 80
ISDN BR0: TX -> INFOc sapi = 0  tei = 80  ns = 0  nr = 0
i = 0x08007B3A0A30383335383636333031
ISDN BR0: RX <- INFOc sapi = 0  tei = 80  ns = 0  nr = 1
i = 0x08007B3B028381
```

ISDN BR0: TX -> RRr sapi = 0 tei = 80 nr = 1

TABLE 5.7 Debug ISDN Q.921 Details

Output	Meaning
ISDN BR0:	This is the interface.
TX ->	This router is sending this information.
RX <-	This router is receiving this information.
SABMEp	This indicates the SABME command, which is sent up N200 times until it is accepted or is confirmed with a UA response. This also resets or clears the exception conditions.
sapi=0 tei =77	Sapi will either be 0 (for call control procedures) or 63 (for Layer 2 management procedures). Here the router thinks it is using a TEI of 77.
IDCKRQ ri = 0 ai = 127	This indicates the Identity Check Request message type sent from the ISDN service provider on the network to the local router during the TEI check procedure. This message is sent in a UI command frame. A reference number (ri) identifies different devices requesting TEI assignment. Reference numbers range from 0 to 65,535, with 0 indicating that the message is sent from the network side and a reference number has not been generated. The action indicator (ai) is used to request that the network assign any TEI value. Here the value of 127 tells the router to check all the TEIs. The router rejects 77 and 78 before accepting 79 and 80.

TABLE 5.7   Debug ISDN Q.921 Details *(continued)*

Output	Meaning
IDREM	This indicates the Identity Remove message type sent from the network to the user-side layer management entity during the TEI removal procedure. This message is sent in a UI command frame. The message includes a reference number that is always 0, because it is not responding to a request from the local router. It is sent twice by the network to prevent a lost message.
IDKRP ri = 44602 ai = 77	This indicates the Identity Check Response message sent in response to an IDCKRQ message. The ai of 77 indicates that the router checked this TEI.
IDREQ	This indicates an Identity Request message sent from the local router to the network during the automatic TEI assignment.
Uaf	This confirms that the network side has accepted the SABME command previously sent by the local router. The final bit is set to 1.
INFOc	This is an information command. It is used to transfer sequentially numbered frames containing information fields provided by Layer 3.
IDASSN	This indicates an Identity Assigned message type sent from the network's ISDN service provider to the local router during the automatic TEI assignment procedure.
RR(x)	This indicates Receive Ready. If x=r, it is responding to an INFOc. If x=p, the router is polling the network side. And x=f means the network side has responded to the poll and the final bit is set.

ISDN Call Setup and Teardown

ISDN uses ITU-T Q.931 to establish and tear down calls. Call control and signaling information is carried over the D channel.

Figure 5.6 shows the Q.931 procedures.

FIGURE 5.6   ISDN call setup and teardown

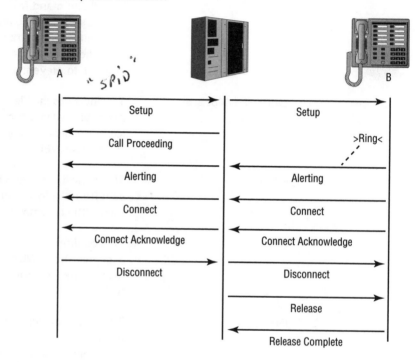

The process for ISDN call setup and teardown is as follows:

1. First a SETUP message is sent from device A. The SETUP contains information necessary to make the call.

2. Next the switch sends a CALL PROCEEDING back to device A.

3. An ALERTING message is sent back when device B is contacted. You may hear the phone ring at this point.

4. CONNECT and CONNECT ACKNOWLEDGE messages are sent to indicate that the call has been accepted.

5. Call teardown starts when one of the users hangs up. Here device A hangs up, and a DISCONNECT message is sent to device B. The switch now disconnects B and sends a RELEASE to A. A RELEASE COMPLETE message confirms the process.

Using "Debug ISDN Q931," we get the following output.

```
ISDN BR0: TX -> SETUP pd = 8  callref = 0x05 Bearer
Capability i = 0x8890 Channel ID i = 0x83
        Keypad Facility i = '8358662'
ISDN BR0: RX <-  CALL_PROC pd = 8  callref = 0x85 Channel
ID i = 0x89 Locking Shift to Codeset 5
        Codeset 5 IE 0x2A  i = 0x809402, '`=', 0x8307,
'8358662', 0x8E0B, ' TELTONE 2 '
ISDN BR0: RX <-  CONNECT pd = 8  callref = 0x85
ISDN BR0: TX ->  CONNECT_ACK pd = 8  callref = 0x05
ISDN BR0: TX ->  DISCONNECT pd = 8  callref = 0x05 Cause i
= 0x8090 - Normal call clearing
ISDN BR0: RX <-  RELEASE pd = 8  callref = 0x85
ISDN BR0: TX ->  RELEASE_COMP pd = 8  callref = 0x05
```

Table 5.8 describes the different output from the Q.931 command.

TABLE 5.8   Debug ISDN Q.931 Details

Output	Meaning
TX ->	This is the message originating at the router.
RX <-	This is the message received from the network.
SETUP	This is used to initiate a call. Either the network or the local router can send it.
pd = 8	This indicates the protocol discriminator. The protocol discriminator distinguishes messages for call control over the user-network ISDN interface from other ITU-T-defined messages, including other Q.931 messages.

TABLE 5.8 Debug ISDN Q.931 Details *(continued)*

Output	Meaning
Callref = 0x05	This indicates how many calls the router has processed. It increments every time a call goes out or comes in.
Bear Capability i = 0x8890	This is the request bearer service requested by the router. 88=ITU coding standard, unrestricted digital information 90=Circuit mode, 64Kbps 21=Layer 1, V.110/X.30 8F=Synchronous, no in-band negotiation, 56Kbps
Channel ID i = 0x83	This is the Channel Identifier. It indicates which B channel to use. 83=Use any channel 89=Use B1 8A=Use B2
Keypad facility	This is also known as "Called Party Number."
DISCONNECT pd = 8 callref = 0x05 Cause i = 0x8090 - Normal call clearing	Here the router is sending a DISCONNECT message to the network. The reason for this disconnect is "Normal call clearing 0x80". See "ISDN Switch Types, Codes, and Values" on CCO.

ISDN Configuration

To configure ISDN you need to understand that there are both simple and complex configurations. While you certainly can make more money by understanding the complex configurations, the simple ones are just as important. In this section, we will take a look at some benefits and drawbacks of two ISDN configuration types. The first is referred to as *legacy*, also known as the old way, and the second is referred to as *dialer profiles*. In this section, you will learn about one significant improvement that dialer profiles give you over legacy interfaces. First, though, you need to understand how the old and new ways differ.

The Old Way versus the New Way

Some of us may have grown up in a router world where we used dialer map statements to configure a dial session. But the times they are a-changin', and actually for the better. The basic configuration for a physical interface is entered under the actual interface, but the detailed configuration is placed under a virtual dialer interface. This is a really nice feature if you have a PRI that receives and makes calls to and from different locations (with different subnets).

Using a Legacy Interface

Under the old legacy way, you could have a main IP address under the interface, along with several secondary addresses. This worked fine, but you ran into problems if you were using a routing protocol because the physical interface always uses its primary address when sending out a packet.

Here is an example of a configuration using the old way. Notice the dialer map statements. This allowed an administrator to tell the router which number to dial based on IP packets received on one of the router's incoming interfaces.

```
Hostname R1
!
Serial 0/0:23
   Encapsulation ppp
   Ip address 192.168.250.1 255.255.255.0
   Ip address 192.168.251.1 255.255.255.0 secondary
   Dialer map ip 192.168.250.2 name R2 555-1212
   Dialer map ip 192.168.251.2 name R3 555-1234
Router ospf 100
   Network 192.168.250.1 0.0.0.0 area 0
   Network 192.168.251.1 0.0.0.0 area 0
!
End
```

```
Hostname R2
!
interface BRIO
    ip address 192.168.250.2 255.255.255.0
encapsulation ppp
    isdn spid1 91955512120100 5551212
    isdn spid2 91955512130100 5551213
dialer map ip 192.168.250.1 name R1 5551900
router ospf 100
    network 192.168.250.2 0.0.0.0 area 0
!
end

Hostname R3
!
interface BRIO
    ip address 192.168.251.2 255.255.255.0
encapsulation ppp
    isdn spid1 91955512230100 5551234
    isdn spid2 91955512350100 5551235
dialer map ip 192.168.251.1 name R1 5551900
router ospf 100
    network 192.168.251.2 0.0.0.0 area 0
!
end
```

In the above router configurations, both routers R2 and R3 will call into R1, but OSPF will only work between R1 and R2. This "source IP address" issue can be a real problem, but only if you are not aware of it. What is the solution to the primary IP address issue? Dialer interfaces.

Using a Dialer Interface

Using a dialer interface solves the primary IP address/secondary IP address problem because each interface can be assigned its own primary address. The `dialer map` command does not have to be used since each interface has its own IP address and dial number configured using the `dialer string` command.

A virtual interface must be associated with a dialer pool. The dialer is a group of one or many physical interfaces in charge of placing the call. Here is an example of a configuration using dialer interfaces:

```
hostname Router1
!
isdn switch-type basic-5ess
!
interface Ethernet0
 ip address 192.168.1.1 255.255.255.0
!
interface serial0/0:23
 no ip address
 encapsulation ppp
 dialer pool-member 1 priority 100
!
interface Dialer1
 ip address 192.168.250.1 255.255.255.0
 encapsulation ppp
 dialer remote-name R2
 dialer idle-timeout 300
 dialer string 5551212
 dialer load-threshold 50 either
 dialer pool 1
 dialer-group 1
!
interface Dialer2
 ip address 192.168.251.1 255.255.255.0
 encapsulation ppp
 dialer remote-name R3
 dialer string 5551234
 dialer load-threshold 150 either
 dialer pool 1
 dialer-group 1
!
Router ospf 100
```

(Handwritten annotations in margins:)

1st sling off?

BASIC-NI
INT BRI0
NO Shut
END
Sho ISDN STATUS
activates / deactivate

Layer 1 active
Layer 2 Multiple establish

ISDN SPID1
IP address
Dialer-Group
Dialer STRING
Dialer LIST

Conn V
Debug ISDN Q921
Layer 3
Debug ISDN Q931

```
network 192.168.250.1 0.0.0.0 area 0
network 192.168.251.1 0.0.0.0 area 0
!
dialer-list 1 protocol ip permit
!
end
```

Now OSPF will work properly because the source address on both sides of the link matches the network statement. The source address of a packet originating at a router is the primary address on the outgoing interface. Dialer interfaces are easy to configure. From global configuration mode, just type in the address you want to use. For example,

```
Config t
Inter dialer 2
```

Now, just create the configuration as you would under a physical interface. The dialer pool was created under the PRI interface of serial 0. The virtual interfaces are part of the dialer pool. The dialer-pool member is assigned to the physical interfaces, and the `dialer pool` command is used on the virtual interfaces.

Authentication

If you are using PPP encapsulation, you can also use *authentication*. Authentication allows you to verify who is connected and whether they are authorized to use this service. Note that this is optional and not required in any ISDN configurations.

You have two choices here: *Password Authentication Protocol (PAP)* and *Challenge-Handshake Authentication Protocol (CHAP)*. CHAP is preferred over PAP because of its inherent security features.

Password Authentication Protocol (PAP)

PAP uses a two-way handshake to establish the identity of the remote peer. This simple authentication protocol does not encrypt the password, making it somewhat insecure and subject to a playback attack. It is recommended that you use CHAP instead.

After the PPP link establishment, the optional Authentication-Protocol Option packet is sent. An Authentication-Protocol Option packet for PAP has three fields: Type, Length, and Authentication-Protocol. The Type field is eight bits long with a value of 3, Length is eight bits long with a value of 4, and Authentication-Protocol is 16 bits long with a value of c023.

PAP Packets

A PAP packet has four fields: Code, Identifier, Length, and Data. The Code field is eight bits long and can have one of three values:

- Authenticate-Request

- Authenticate-Ack

- Authenticate-Nak

The Identifier field is also eight bits long and contains values for matching authentication requests and replies. It changes every time an Authenticate-Request is sent. Length is an eight-bit field indicating the packet's length. The Data field varies in length depending on the packet type (Request, Ack, or Nak).

Authenticate-Request Packets

An Authenticate-Request packet is sent by the calling party to the called party. The Data field has four fields:

Peer-ID Length Eight bits long; indicates the length of the Peer-ID.

Peer-ID Zero or more octets long; contains the Username.

Passwd-Length Eight bits long; indicates the length of the Password.

Password Zero or more octets long; contains the plaintext password.

The called end will respond with either an Authenticate-Ack (Type 2) or Authenticate-Nak (Type 3) packet. Both packets have two fields as data. One is Msg-Length (eight bits), and the other is Message (one or more octets).

The following output is from a debug ppp auth command on a router that is authenticating using PPP with PAP.

```
BRO/0:1 PPP: Phase is AUTHENTICATING, by the peer
BRO/0:1 PAP: O AUTH-REQ id 3 len 14 from "r3"
BRO/0:1 PAP: I AUTH-ACK id 3 len 5
```

You can follow this debug PPP authentication router output by using Figure 5.7.

FIGURE 5.7 PAP authentication

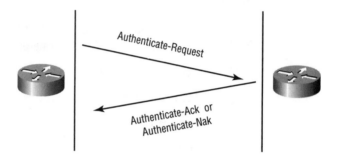

Configuring PAP authentication is a pretty straightforward process. Here is an example:

```
Config t
Username todd password cisco
Int bri0
Encapsulation ppp
ppp authentication pap
```

Challenge-Handshake Authentication Protocol (CHAP)

CHAP is used to periodically verify the identity of the remote peer using a three-way handshake. Normally this occurs immediately after the initial link establishment and before proceeding to the Network Layer phase. CHAP may also send a new challenge periodically to verify the remote node. All PPP authentications are optional. If you are using authentication, however, remember that both ends must be configured for it.

One CHAP packet is encapsulated in the Information field of a PPP packet, with the Type field set to 3, the Length field to 5, the Authentication-Protocol field to c223, and the algorithm to 5 (MD5). A CHAP Challenge packet is illustrated in Figure 5.8.

FIGURE 5.8 CHAP Challenge packet

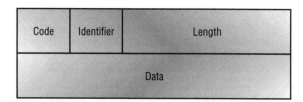

A CHAP packet consists of an eight-bit Code field, an eight-bit Identifier field, a 16-bit Length field, and a variable-length Data field. The *Code* field identifies the type of CHAP packet. Here are the four type options:

1. Challenge

2. Response

3. Success

4. Failure

The *Identifier* field contains an incrementally changing identifier, which the remote end copies into the response packet. Changing the identifier frequently provides protection against a playback attack. The *Length* field is 16 bits long and indicates the length of the CHAP packet including the Code, Identifier, Length, and Data fields. Octets outside the range have been added as padding and will be ignored. The *Data* field is zero or more octets and is determined by the Code field.

Configuring CHAP authentication is a pretty straightforward process. Here is an example:

```
Config t
username todd password cisco
int bri0
encapsulation ppp
ppp authentication chap
```

The `username name password password` command is used to set up the authentication between two or more routes. The username is the hostname of the router you want to connect to. The username of the remote route would be set to the hostname of the router it is receiving from. The passwords must be the same for this to work. For example, if I had a corporate router with a hostname of Acmecorporate and a remote router with a hostname of Acmeremote, the configuration of the corporate router would look like this:

```
Acmecorporate(config)#hostname Acmeremote password someone
```

The remote router's configuration would be this:

```
Acmeremote(config)#hostname Acmecorporate password someone
```

The Authentication Process

The authentication process between two routers occurs as follows:

1. Challenger sends a Type 1 (Challenge) to the remote end.

2. The remote end copies the identifier into a new packet and Responds (Type 2) along with the hashed secret. (The secret isn't transmitted, only the hashed value.)

3. The Challenger receives the Response and checks the hashed secret against its hashed secret. If they match, it sends a Success (Type 3) packet back. Otherwise it'll send a Failure (Type 4) packet back.

Challenge and Response packets have the following fields:

Code   Eight bits; value of 1 or 2

Identifier   Eight bits; must be changed every time a challenge is sent

Value-Size   Eight bits; indicates the length of the Value field

Value   Variable (eight-bit minimum)

Name   Variable (eight-bit minimum); identifies the system transmitting the packet

Success and Failure packets have these fields: Code, Identifier (which is copied from Response), Length, and Message. The Message field is one or more octets long and contains information that is readable by humans. Using debug PPP authentication, you can see each step that is taken. This **debug ppp auth** shows the PPP with CHAP Challenge and Response fields.

```
BR0:1 PPP: Treating connection as a callout
BR0:1 PPP: Phase is AUTHENTICATING, by both
```

```
BR0:1 CHAP: O CHALLENGE id 1 len 23 from "r2"
BR0:1 CHAP: I CHALLENGE id 1 len 23 from "r3"
BR0:1 CHAP: O RESPONSE id 1 len 23 from "r2"
BR0:1 CHAP: I SUCCESS id 1 len 4
BR0:1 CHAP: I RESPONSE id 1 len 23 from "r3"
BR0:1 CHAP: O SUCCESS id 1 len 4
```

Figure 5.9 shows the CHAP authentication process.

FIGURE 5.9   CHAP authentication

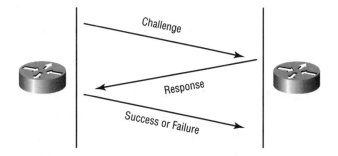

Dial-on-Demand Routing (DDR)

*D*ial-on-demand routing (DDR) is used to allow two or more Cisco routers to dial an ISDN dial-up connection on an as-needed basis. DDR is only used for low-volume, periodic network connections using either a Public Switched Telephone Network (PSTN) or ISDN. This was designed to reduce WAN costs if you have to pay on a per-minute or -packet basis.

DDR works when a packet received on an interface meets the requirements of an administrator-defined access list, which defines interesting traffic. The following five steps give a basic description of how DDR works when an interesting packet is received in a router interface:

1. Route to the destination network is determined.

2. Interesting packets dictate a DDR call.

3. Dialer information is looked up.

4. Traffic is transmitted.

5. Call is terminated when no more traffic is being transmitted over a link and the idle-timeout period ends.

Configuring DDR

To configure legacy DDR, you need to perform three tasks:

1. Define static routes, which define how to get to the remote networks and which interface to use to get there.

2. Specify the traffic that is considered interesting to the router.

3. Configure the dialer information that will be used to dial the interface to get to the remote network.

Configuring the Static Routes

To forward traffic across the ISDN link, you configure static routes in each of the routers. While you certainly can configure dynamic routing protocols to run on your ISDN link, the link will never drop. The suggested routing method is static routes. Keep the following in mind when creating static routes:

- All participating routers must have static routes defining all routes of known networks.

- Default routing can be used if the network is a stub network.

An example of static routing with ISDN is shown below:

```
RouterA(config)#ip route 172.16.50.0 255.255.255.0
172.16.60.2
RouterA(config)#ip route 172.16.60.2 255.255.255.255 bri0
```

What this does is tell the router how to get to network 172.16.50.0, which is through 172.16.60.2. The second line tells the router how to get to 172.16.60.2.

Specifying Interesting Traffic

After setting the route tables in each router, you need to configure the router to determine what brings up the ISDN line. An administrator using the `dialer-list` global configuration command defines interesting packets.

The command to turn on all IP traffic is shown below:

```
804A(config)#dialer-list 1 protocol ip permit
804A(config)#int bri0
804A(config-if)#dialer-group 1
```

The `dialer-group` command sets the access list on the BRI interface. Extended access lists can be used with the `dialer-list` command to define interesting traffic to just certain applications. We'll cover that in a minute.

Configuring the Dialer Information

There are five steps in the configuration of dialer information:

1. Choose the interface.

2. Set the IP address.

3. Configure the encapsulation type.

4. Link interesting traffic to the interface.

5. Configure the number or numbers to dial.

Here is an example of how to configure the five steps:

```
804A#config t
804A(config)#int bri0
804A(config-if)#ip address 172.16.60.1 255.255.255.0
804A(config-if)#no shut
804A(config-if)#encapsulation ppp
804A(config-if)#dialer-group 1
804A(config-if)#dialer-string 8350661
```

Instead of the `dialer-string` command, you can use a dialer map, which provides more security.

```
804A(config-if)#dialer map ip 172.16.60.2 name 804B
8350661
```

The dialer map command can be used with the dialer-group command and its associated access list to initiate dialing. The dialer map command uses the IP address of the next hop router, the hostname of the remote router for authentication, and the number to dial to get there.

Take a look at the following configuration of an 804 router:

```
804B#sh run
Building configuration...
Current configuration:
!
version 12.0
no service pad
service timestamps debug uptime
service timestamps log uptime
no service password-encryption
!
hostname 804B
!
ip subnet-zero
!
isdn switch-type basic-ni
!
interface Ethernet0
 ip address 172.16.50.10 255.255.255.0
 no ip directed-broadcast
!
interface BRI0
 ip address 172.16.60.2 255.255.255.0
 no ip directed-broadcast
 encapsulation ppp
 dialer idle-timeout 300
 dialer string 8358661
 dialer load-threshold 2 either
 dialer-group 1
```

```
isdn switch-type basic-ni
isdn spid1 0835866201 8358662
isdn spid2 0835866401 8358664
hold-queue 75 in
!
ip classless
ip route 172.16.30.0 255.255.255.0 172.16.60.1
ip route 172.16.60.1 255.255.255.255 BRIO
!
dialer-list 1 protocol ip permit
!
```

The BRI interface is running the PPP encapsulation and has a timeout value of 300 seconds. The `load-threshold` command makes both BRI interfaces come up immediately (If I am paying for both I want them both up all the time). The one thing you really want to notice is the `dialer-group 1` command. That number must match the dialer-list number. The `hold-queue 75 in` command tells the router that when it receives an interesting packet, it should queue up to 75 packets while it is waiting for the BRI to come up. If there are more than 75 packets queued before the link comes up, the packets will be dropped.

Optional Commands

You should configure two other commands on your BRI interface: `dialer load-threshold` and `dialer idle-timeout`. In conjunction with the `dialer load-threshold` command, you can use the `ppp multilink` command for multilink PPP (MP).

The `dialer load-threshold` command tells the BRI interface when to bring up the second B channel. The option is from 1–255, where 255 tells the BRI to bring up the second B channel only when the first channel is 100 percent loaded. The second option for that command is in, out, or either. This calculates the actual load on the interface either on outbound traffic, inbound traffic, or combined. The default is outbound.

The `dialer idle-timeout` command specifies the number of seconds before a call is disconnected after the last interesting traffic is sent. The default is 120 seconds.

```
RouterA(config-if)#dialer load-threshold 125 either
RouterA(config-if)#dialer idle-timeout 180
```

The dialer load-threshold 125 tells the BRI interface to bring up the second B channel if either the inbound or outbound traffic load is 50 percent. The dialer idle-timeout 180 changes the default disconnect time from 120 to 180 seconds.

MP allows load balancing between the two B channels in a BRI. It is non–vendor specific and provides packet fragmentation and reassembly, along with sequencing and load calculating. Cisco's MP is based on RFC 1990. The configuration would then look like this:

```
RouterA(config-if)#dialer load-threshold 125 either
RouterA(config-if)#dialer idle-timeout 180
RouterA(config-if)#ppp multilink
```

Not a tough configuration, but you want to use it nonetheless. This command will fragment packets and send them over both lines, which provides a load balancing effect on the data packet. You can verify that the multilink is working with the show ppp multilink command.

DDR with Access Lists

You can use access lists to be more specific about what is interesting traffic. In the preceding example we just set the dialer list to allow any IP traffic to bring up the line. That is great if you are testing, but it can defeat the purpose of why you use a DDR line in the first place. You can use extended access lists to set the restriction, for example, to only e-mail or telnet.

Here is an example of how you define the dialer list to use an access list:

```
804A(config)#dialer-list 1 list 110
804A(config)#access-list 110 permit tcp any any eq smtp
804A(config)#access-list 110 permit tcp any any eq telnet
804A(config)#int bri0
804A(config-if)#dialer-group 1
```

In the above example, you configure the dialer-list command to look at an access list. This doesn't have to be IP; it can be used with any protocol. Create your list, then apply it to the BRI interface with the dialer-group command.

Verifying the ISDN Operation

The following commands can be used to verify legacy DDR and ISDN:

Ping and Telnet Are great IP tools for any network. However, your interesting traffic must dictate that Ping and Telnet are acceptable as interesting traffic to bring up a link. Once a link is up, you can ping or telnet to your remote router regardless of your interesting traffic lists.

Show dialer Gives good information about your dialer diagnostic information and shows the number of times the dialer string has been reached, the idle-timeout values of each B channel, the length of cal, and the name of the router to which the interface is connected.

Show isdn active Shows the number called and whether a call is in progress.

Show ISDN status Is a good command to use before trying to dial. Shows if your SPIDs are valid and if you are connected and communicating with Layers 1 through 3 to the provider's switch.

Sho ip route Shows all routes the router knows about.

Debug isdn q921 Is used to see Layer-2 information only.

Debug isdn q931 Is used to see Layer-3 information, including call setup and teardown.

Debug dialer Gives you call setup and teardown activity.

Isdn disconnect int bri0 Clears the interface and drops the connection. Performing a shutdown on the interface can give you the same results.

Dial Backup

*D*ial backup, dial-on-demand routing (DDR), and Bandwidth on Demand (BoD) all use the same basic interface configuration. Dial backup and BoD also use interface backup commands to determine if, when, and how long an interface is to be activated. DDR is used for a temporary dial-up connection from a branch or home office.

Time to do some design work: Using Figure 5.10, let's design and configure both legacy and dialer interfaces. For the sake of this project, we'll assign some addresses to the interfaces on R2 and R3 in the figure.

Here is a list of the addresses we'll use:

R2/To0	172.16.2.0/24
R3/E0/0	192.168.252.0/24
ISDN cloud	192.168.254.0/24
Frame cloud	192.168.123.0/24

FIGURE 5.10 Network diagram

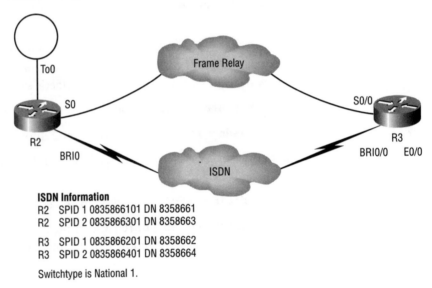

ISDN Information
R2   SPID 1 0835866101 DN 8358661
R2   SPID 2 0835866301 DN 8358663

R3   SPID 1 0835866201 DN 8358662
R3   SPID 2 0835866401 DN 8358664

Switchtype is National 1.

Setting Up Dial Backup

Our first project is setting up dial backup on the routers. We'll keep this fairly basic. R2 will call R3 when serial 0.202 goes down. The interesting traffic we'll designate is all IP. We will not use a routing protocol, so we'll have to put in a floating static route. A floating static route is used whenever a link that is not up comes up; a floating static route is also put into a routing table, then is removed when the link is down. Typically, floating static routes are used with DDR because they can be set to a higher administrative distance than the routing protocol being used. This allows the router to automatically bring up the BRI line if the main serial line were to drop.

In the configuration below, we issue a show ISDN status on Router 2 to verify that the configuration is working correctly.

```
r2#sh isdn status
The current ISDN Switchtype = basic-ni1
ISDN BRI0 interface
    Layer 1 Status:
        ACTIVE
    Layer 2 Status:
        TEI = 100, State = MULTIPLE_FRAME_ESTABLISHED
        TEI = 101, State = MULTIPLE_FRAME_ESTABLISHED
    Spid Status:
        TEI 100, ces = 1, state = 5(init)
            spid1 configured, spid1 sent, spid1 valid
            Endpoint ID Info: epsf = 0, usid = 1, tid = 1
        TEI 101, ces = 2, state = 5(init)
            spid2 configured, spid2 sent, spid2 valid
            Endpoint ID Info: epsf = 0, usid = 3, tid = 1
    Layer 3 Status:
        0 Active Layer 3 Call(s)
    Activated dsl 0 CCBs = 1
        CCB: callid=0x0, sapi=0, ces=1, B-chan=0
    Total Allocated ISDN CCBs = 1
```

As you can see, Layers 1 and 2 are up, we are using TEI 100 and 101, and the SPIDs and DNs are valid. This is one of the most important commands you can use. If the SPIDs are invalid or the configuration is wrong, you will see it in the show isdn status command.

Now we'll issue the backup interface bri0 under serial 0.202. This tells the interface s0.202 to use interface BRI0 if the serial interface loses DCD (Data Carrier Detect), which means the link is down.

```
r2(config-subif)#backup interface bri0
r2(config-subif)#
```

```
%ISDN-6-LAYER2DOWN: Layer 2 for Interface BRI0, TEI 100
changed to down
%ISDN-6-LAYER2DOWN: Layer 2 for Interface BRI0, TEI 101
changed to down
%LINK-5-CHANGED: Interface BRI0, changed state to standby
mode
%LINK-3-UPDOWN: Interface BRI0:1, changed state to down
%LINK-3-UPDOWN: Interface BRI0:2, changed state to down
```

As you can see, it places the main interface in Standby mode, effectively turning the interface down. This deactivates Layer 1 on the BRI0 interface. This can be verified by issuing a show ISDN status command at the router prompt.

r2#**show interface bri0**

```
The current ISDN Switchtype = basic-ni1
ISDN BRI0 interface
    Layer 1 Status:
        DEACTIVATED
    Layer 2 Status:
        Layer 2 NOT Activated
    Spid Status:
        TEI Not Assigned, ces = 1, state = 1(terminal
        down)
            spid1 configured, spid1 NOT sent, spid1 NOT
            valid
        TEI Not Assigned, ces = 2, state = 1(terminal
        down)
            spid2 configured, spid2 NOT sent, spid2 NOT
            valid
    Layer 3 Status:
        0 Active Layer 3 Call(s)
    Activated dsl 0 CCBs = 0
    Total Allocated ISDN CCBs = 0
```

Testing the Backup

After the configuration, it is important to test your backup link. You don't want to wait for an actual outage before discovering you made any errors. We'll test the backup by disabling one of the serial interfaces on R2.

When we tested this link, it took 11 seconds for the backup line to come out of Standby mode and another four seconds for Layers 1 and 2 to come up. The router output below shows this. Using a dialer interface can save you four seconds in this scenario.

```
00:46:22: %LINEPROTO-5-UPDOWN: Line protocol on Interface
Serial0, changed state to down
00:46:23: %LINK-3-UPDOWN: Interface Serial0, changed state
to down
00:46:23: %FR-5-DLCICHANGE: Interface Serial0 - DLCI 202
state changed to DELETED
00:46:23: %FR-5-DLCICHANGE: Interface Serial0 - DLCI 100
state changed to DELETED
00:46:23: %FR-5-DLCICHANGE: Interface Serial0 - DLCI 200
state changed to DELETED
00:46:23: %LINEPROTO-5-UPDOWN: Line protocol on Interface
Serial0.202, changed state to down
00:46:34: %LINK-3-UPDOWN: Interface BRI0:1, changed state
to down
00:46:34: %LINK-3-UPDOWN: Interface BRI0:2, changed state
to down
00:46:34: %LINK-3-UPDOWN: Interface BRI0, changed state to
up
00:46:38: %ISDN-6-LAYER2UP: Layer 2 for Interface BR0, TEI
107 changed to up
00:46:38: %ISDN-6-LAYER2UP: Layer 2 for Interface BR0, TEI
108 changed to up
00:46:59: %LINK-3-UPDOWN: Interface BRI0:1, changed state
to up
00:47:00: %LINEPROTO-5-UPDOWN: Line protocol on Interface
BRI0:1, changed state to up
00:47:06: %ISDN-6-CONNECT: Interface BRI0:1 is now
connected to 8358662
00:47:23: %LINEPROTO-5-UPDOWN: Line protocol on Interface
Serial0, changed state to up
```

```
00:47:24: %LINK-3-UPDOWN: Interface Serial0, changed state
to up
00:47:24: %FR-5-DLCICHANGE: Interface Serial0 - DLCI 202
state changed to ACTIVE
00:47:24: %LINEPROTO-5-UPDOWN: Line protocol on Interface
Serial0.202, changed state to up
00:48:24: %LINK-3-UPDOWN: Interface BRI0:1, changed state
to down
00:48:24: %ISDN-6-DISCONNECT: Interface BRI0:1
disconnected from unknown , call lasted 85 seconds
00:48:24: %ISDN-6-LAYER2DOWN: Layer 2 for Interface BRI0,
TEI 107 changed to down
00:48:24: %ISDN-6-LAYER2DOWN: Layer 2 for Interface BRI0,
TEI 108 changed to down
00:48:24: %LINK-5-CHANGED: Interface BRI0, changed state
to standby mode
00:48:24: %LINK-3-UPDOWN: Interface BRI0:1, changed state
to down
00:48:24: %LINK-3-UPDOWN: Interface BRI0:2, changed state
to down
00:48:25: %LINEPROTO-5-UPDOWN: Line protocol on Interface
BRI0:1, changed state to down
```

You can also note in the router output above that the backup line dropped one minute after the primary link came up. Changing the delay between primary failure and activation of the backup line can be modified by using Backup delay 10 60. The first number (10) is how many seconds to wait before using the backup interface, and the second number (60) is how long to stay up once the primary line comes back up.

Setting up a dialer profile involves two steps: configuring the primary interface and configuring the dialer interface. The primary interface only needs some basic information; for example, take a look at this configuration:

```
interface BRI0
 no ip address
 encapsulation ppp
 isdn spid1 0835866101 8358661
 isdn spid2 0835866301 8358663
 dialer pool-member 1
 !
```

Basically all we did was set up ISDN Layers 1 and 2, enable PPP encapsulation, and assign this interface to dial pool 1—pretty simple so far.

The next step involves the dialer interface. A dialer interface is *virtual*, meaning you add it by using the global command `interface dialer 1`. Your specific configuration commands are placed under this interface, including which dial pool to use. Again, it's not that difficult. Take a look at this configuration:

```
interface Dialer1
 ip address 192.168.254.2 255.255.255.0
 encapsulation ppp
 dialer remote-name r3
 dialer string 8358662
 dialer pool 1
 dialer-group 1
 ppp authentication chap callin
```

Now add the backup commands as discussed above. You will notice that the dialer interface goes into Standby, but the BRI interface doesn't. You can verify this using the `show ISDN status` command.

```
r2#show isdn status
The current ISDN Switchtype = basic-ni1
ISDN BRI0 interface
    Layer 1 Status:
        ACTIVE
    Layer 2 Status:
        TEI = 109, State = MULTIPLE_FRAME_ESTABLISHED
        TEI = 110, State = MULTIPLE_FRAME_ESTABLISHED
    Spid Status:
        TEI 109, ces = 1, state = 5(init)
            spid1 configured, spid1 sent, spid1 valid
            Endpoint ID Info: epsf = 0, usid = 1, tid = 1
        TEI 110, ces = 2, state = 5(init)
            spid2 configured, spid2 sent, spid2 valid
            Endpoint ID Info: epsf = 0, usid = 3, tid = 1
    Layer 3 Status:
        0 Active Layer 3 Call(s)
```

```
        Activated dsl 0 CCBs = 1
            CCB: callid=0x0, sapi=0, ces=1, B-chan=0
        Total Allocated ISDN CCBs = 1
```

The BRI interface is still active and not in Standby.

We'll introduce a nice diagnostic command here: show dialer. This output gives you a lot of information, such as dial reason, who you called or who called you, how long the interface has been up, how long it has been since it has seen interesting traffic, and how much more time remains until it hangs up.

```
r2#show dialer

BRI0 - dialer type = ISDN

Dial String      Successes    Failures    Last called
Last status
0 incoming call(s) have been screened.

BRI0:1 - dialer type = ISDN
Idle timer (120 secs), Fast idle timer (20 secs)
Wait for carrier (30 secs), Re-enable (15 secs)
Dialer state is data link layer up
Dial reason: ip (s=192.168.254.2, d=192.168.252.3)
Interface bound to profile Dialer1
Time until disconnect 105 secs
Current call connected 00:00:16
Connected to 8358662

Dialer1 - dialer type = DIALER PROFILE
Idle timer (120 secs), Fast idle timer (20 secs)
Wait for carrier (30 secs), Re-enable (15 secs)
Dialer state is data link layer up

Dial String  Successes Failures Last called    Last status
8358662      18        0        00:00:19       successful
```

The final configuration is shown below. R2 is set up to use a dialer inter-face; R3 is using legacy configuration.

```
r2#sh run
Building configuration...

Current configuration:
!
version 12.0
service timestamps log uptime
no service password-encryption
no service udp-small-servers
no service tcp-small-servers
!
hostname r2
!
enable password cisco
!
username r3 password 0 cisco
isdn switch-type basic-ni1
!
interface Serial0
 no ip address
 encapsulation frame-relay
 no fair-queue
!
interface Serial0.202 point-to-point
 backup delay 10 60
 backup interface Dialer1
 ip address 172.16.34.2 255.255.255.0
 frame-relay interface-dlci 202
!
interface BRI0
 no ip address
 encapsulation ppp
 isdn spid1 0835866101 8358661
```

```
 isdn spid2 0835866301 8358663
 dialer pool-member 1
!
interface Dialer1
 ip address 192.168.254.2 255.255.255.0
 encapsulation ppp
 dialer remote-name r3
 dialer string 8358662
 dialer pool 1
 dialer-group 1
 ppp authentication chap callin
!
ip classless
ip route 0.0.0.0 0.0.0.0 172.16.34.3
ip route 0.0.0.0 0.0.0.0 192.168.254.3 210
!
dialer-list 1 protocol ip permit
!
end

r2#

r3#sh run
Building configuration...

Current configuration:
!
version 12.0
service timestamps debug uptime
service timestamps log uptime
no service password-encryption
!
hostname r3
!
enable password cisco
!
```

```
username r2 password 0 cisco
ip subnet-zero
!
isdn switch-type basic-ni
!
interface FastEthernet0/0
 ip address 192.168.252.3 255.255.255.255
 no ip directed-broadcast
!
interface Serial0/0
 no ip address
 no ip directed-broadcast
 encapsulation frame-relay
 no ip mroute-cache
 frame-relay lmi-type cisco
!
interface Serial0/0.203 point-to-point
 ip address 172.16.34.3 255.255.255.0
 no ip directed-broadcast
 frame-relay interface-dlci 203
!
interface BRI0/0
 ip address 192.168.254.3 255.255.255.0
 no ip directed-broadcast
 encapsulation ppp
 dialer map ip 192.168.254.2 8358661
 dialer-group 1
 isdn switch-type basic-ni
 isdn spid1 0835866201 8358662
 isdn spid2 0835866401 8358664
 ppp authentication chap
 hold-queue 75 in
!
ip classless
ip route 172.16.2.0 255.255.255.0 172.16.34.2
ip route 172.16.2.0 255.255.255.0 192.168.254.2 210
!
```

```
dialer-list 1 protocol ip permit
!
end
```

As you can see, the configuration is not that complex. Having a good working knowledge of this will help you solve many dial backup scenarios. Of course, you may make this as complex as you'd like; we kept this example fairly simple as an illustration.

The command `dialer-list` creates the interesting traffic. The command `dialer-group` assigns the dialer list to an interface. The numbers must match. In the example above, both the dialer list and the dialer group are 1. The `hold-queue` command creates a buffer for incoming interesting traffic that is waiting for the BRI to be dialed. The 75 is the amount of packets that can be queued.

Bandwidth on Demand

What to do if you have more traffic than bandwidth? Wouldn't it be great if you could pull your magic router wand out and make the traffic go faster? You can approximate this magic by using Bandwidth on Demand.

Bandwidth on Demand (BoD) is an interface command, meaning you cannot apply it to a subinterface. Here is the syntax to assign a backup load to an interface: `backup load {enable-threshold | never} {disable-load | never}`. The threshold load is the percentage of interface load where you want the additional bandwidth dialed up. The disable load is the percentage of interface load where you want the extra bandwidth dropped.

At what point is the circuit congested enough to need extra bandwidth? Some people say 75 percent; yet others say queuing is needed. You will probably have to figure this out based on corporate policy, cost, sensitivity to slow responsiveness, etc. Since BoD is a dial-up feature, you may incur additional long-distance costs, so be careful about setting your thresholds.

Configuring BoD is almost the same as dial backup, except you're replacing the amount of backup delay with the amount of backup threshold. Here is an example:

```
Router#config t
```

```
Enter configuration commands, one per line.  End with
CNTL/Z.
Router(config)#int s0
Router(config-if)#backup interface BRI 0
```

The above configuration sets the interface serial 0 to use interface BRI0 as a backup as the main interface goes down. The configuration below shows how to configure the backup delay and the backup load.

```
Router(config-if)#backup ?
  delay       Delays before backup line up or down
transitions
  interface  Configure an interface as a backup
  load       Load thresholds for line up or down
transitions

Router(config-if)#backup delay ?
  <0-4294967294>  Seconds
  never           Never activate the backup line

Router(config-if)#backup delay 10 ?
  <0-4294967294>  Seconds
  never           Never deactivate the backup line

Router(config-if)#backup delay 10 60
```

The configuration above sets the backup delay to 10 seconds and 60 seconds. This means that the backup interface will not dial until serial 0 is down for 10 seconds, and it will drop the link once the serial link is back up for 60 seconds. The backup load command is shown below:

```
Router(config-if)#backup load ?
  <0-100>  Percentage
  never    Never activate the backup line

Router(config-if)#backup load 75 ?
  <0-100>  Percentage
  never    Never deactivate the backup line
```

```
Router(config-if)#backup load 75 35
Router(config-if)#^Z
```

The command above sets the router to dial the ISDN BRI0 interface if the bandwidth reaches a maximum of 75 percent and then to drop the link once the bandwidth is back at 35 percent. The interface configuration is shown below:

```
Router#sh run
[output cut]
interface Serial0
 backup delay 10 60
 backup interface BRI0
 backup load 75 35
 ip address 10.53.69.69 255.255.255.0
 no ip directed-broadcast
 --More-
```

Channelized T1/E1 (PRI)

Large businesses have typically used point-to-point connections with DSU/CSUs to connect two sites. In turn, these connected to low- and high-speed serial interfaces on routers—usually Cisco routers. The router backplane and the amount of interfaces the router could handle determined how well it supported a WAN connection.

The Cisco 7000 series of routers supports the Fast Serial Interface Processor (FSIP), which provides either four or eight serial ports, permitting the same amount of point-to-point connections to remote offices. The Cisco series of routers also supports the MultiChannel Interface Processor (MIP), which furnishes support for two full T1/E1 ports in the 7000 series and one port in the 4000 series.

T1s, which are called Primary Rate Interfaces (PRIs), run at 1.544Mbps, which uses 24 channels in contrast to E1s, which use 30 channels and run at 2.048Mbps. E1 is mainly used in Europe, and both T1 and E1 are considered wide-area digital transmission schemes.

Each port in the MIP can support 24 DS0 channels of 64Kbps each when using a T1, and 30 DS0 channels when using an E1. The MIP refers to each line as a subchannel, which allows each channel to be configured individually. Subchannels have all the characteristics and options of regular serial interfaces.

Configuring ISDN PRI

The serial links connect into either a private data network or a service provider's network. Both the line encoding and the framing must match the service provider's equipment. To configure a PRI on a serial link, you must supply the following information:

Channel type   Either T1 or E1.

Frame type   When using a T1, this can be either Super Frame or Extended Super Frame (ESF). Super Frame can also be referred to as D4 framing, which consists of 12 frames each with 193 bits. The last bit is used for error checking. ESF is an enhanced version of Super Frame that uses 24 frames each with 192 bits. ESF is typically used in the U.S.

Linecode   This will be either alternate mark inversion (AMI) or binary 8-zero substitution (B8ZS). B8ZS is typically used in the U.S.; however, most legacy phone systems still use AMI.

Which time slots the T1 uses   By using the `channel-group` command on your subchannel, you can define the subchannels associated with each time slot.

In the following example, we chose to configure Slot 1, Port 0 of the MIP card in our 7000 router, and we opted for ESF framing, with B8ZS line coding. The `pri-group 0 timeslots 1` indicates that circuit zero has only one time slot. Since no speed was specified, it's running the default of 56Kbps. Channel group 1 has six time slots running at 64Kbps. We could choose up to 24 DS0s but purchased only six from our provider. Here's a look at the output:

```
Router#config t
Enter configuration commands, one per line.  End with
CNTL/Z.
Router(config)#controller T1 1/0
```

from phone Co = Channel or 64 bit

```
Router(config-if)#framing esf
Router(config-if)#linecode b8zs
Router(config-if)#channel-group 0 timeslots 1
Router(config-if)#channel-group 1 timeslots 6 3,4,8-11
speed 64
Router(config-if)#^Z
```

An IP address and the serial encapsulation method (HDLC is the default) then needs to be assigned to each interface, as shown in the following example:

```
Router#config t
Enter configuration commands, one per line.  End with
CNTL/Z.
Router(config)#int s 0/1:0    = 1st channel
Router(config-if)#encap ppp
Router(config-if)#ip address 172.16.30.5 255.255.255.252
Router(config)#int s 0/1:1   = 2nd channel
Router(config-if)#encap hdlc
Router(config-if)#ip address 172.16.30.5 255.255.255.252
Router(config-if)#^Z
```

> **NOTE** When connecting two MIP cards, you must specify the clocking. This is done with the clock source command.

Configuring E1

The E1 configuration is similar to the T1 configuration but has a few different parameters.

Framing   The E1 framing types available are crc4, no-crc4, and australia. The default is crc4, and it specifies CRC error checking, with no-crc4 specifying that CRC checking is (surprise!) disabled. The australia framing method is used when configuring an E1 in (another surprise!) Australia.

Linecode   This is either AMI or HDB3 when configuring an E1, with AMI as the default.

In the following example, we specified Slot 0, Port 1 on our MIP card, and by using the crc4 framing type, we're actually specifying the ESF frame type. The provider has defined HDB3 as the linecode (AMI is the default) to match the carrier's equipment. Primary group 0 with a time slot of 1 specifies that there is only one time slot with circuit zero. However, primary group 1 is using 12 time slots, with up to 30 available if purchased.

```
Router#config t
Enter configuration commands, one per line.  End with
CNTL/Z.
Router(config)#controller T1 1/0
Router(config-if)#framing esf
Router(config-if)#linecode b8zs
Router(config-if)#channel-group 0 timeslots 1
Router(config-if)#channel-group 1 timeslots 12 12-23 speed
64
Router(config-if)#^Z
```

You then need to specify the IP address and encapsulation methods used, just as we did in the T1 example.

Summary

This chapter discussed the details of ISDN. Topics covered here included how Layer 2 is established between the router and the network and placing an actual call. You also learned about the differences between legacy ISDN configuration and the new dialer profile, as well as what benefits there are to both by using some useful IOS debug and show commands.

This chapter also went into more detail on PPP authentication by studying the packet format, process, and response codes used for both Password Authentication Protocol (PAP) and Challenge-Handshake Authentication Protocol (CHAP). And finally you reviewed the configuration of dial-on-demand routing, dial backup, and Bandwidth on Demand, verifying our configuration using more IOS show commands.

Key Terms

Before you take the exam, be certain you are familiar with the following terms:

authentication

B (bearer) channel

Bandwidth on Demand (BoD)

Basic Rate Interface (BRI)

D (data) channel

dial backup

dial-on-demand routing (DDR)

in-band signaling

Integrated Services Digital Network (ISDN)

plain old telephone service (POTS)

Primary Rate Interface (PRI)

reference point

robbed bit signaling

Service Profile Identifier (SPID)

Small Office/Home Office (SOHO)

Commands in This Chapter

Command	Meaning
backup delay	Used to set the amount of time that the BRI interface will dial the remote end after the primary interface drops. Also sets the amount of time before the secondary link drops when the primary link comes back up.
backup interface	Sets an interface to use a BRI interface if the main link fails.

`backup load`	Adds bandwidth to a primary link if it is saturated.
`channel-group`	Configures the amount of channels that are used on a PRI interface.
`debug isdn q921`	Shows the commands and responses exchanged during peer-to-peer communication carried over the D channel.
`debug isdn q931`	Displays information about call setup and teardown of ISDN network connections between the local router and the network.
`dialer hold-queue`	Specifies the length of the queue for packets waiting for the line to come up.
`dialer idle-timeout`	Tells a BRI interface to drop the line after a specified amount of seconds that interesting traffic is not found on the link.
`dialer load-threshold`	Specifies at what traffic load the BRI will bring up the second B channel. Also tells the interface when to bring down the second B channel. Used with multilink PPP.
`dialer map`	Describes to an interface what number to dial based on IP packet characteristics.
`dialer pool`	Binds a dialer interface to a dialer pool configured with the `dialer remote-name` command.
`dialer pool-member`	Tells a BRI interface that it is part of a dialer pool.
`dialer string`	Defines the destination router's phone number and supports optional map classes.

`dialer-group`	Configures a dialer list that defines interesting packet to trigger a call for DDR.
`dialer-list`	Creates a list of interesting traffic based on protocol type.
`encapsulation ppp`	Configures an interface to use PPP encapsulation.
`framing`	Configures a PRI interface with the type of framing that the provider's switch is using.
`interface dialer`	Creates a logical interface. Used instead of dialer map statements.
`isdn spid1`	Configures the first B channel on a BRI interface.
`isdn spid2`	Configures the second B channel on a BRI interface.
`linecode`	Sets the type of line coding in a PRI interface that the provider's switch is using.
`ppp authentication chap`	Configures an interface to use CHAP authentication.
`ppp authentication pap`	Configures an interface to use PAP authentication.
`ppp multilink`	Specifies that this dialer interface uses multilink PPP.
`show dialer`	Shows information statistics for incoming and outgoing calls.
`show isdn status`	Displays information about memory and Layer 2 and 3 timers as well as the status of the channels.
`username`	Sets the name and password used to communicate with authentication to the remote router.

Written Lab

In this written lab, you will write out the commands to configure a BRI interface.

1. Write the command to configure the basic-ni switch type on a BRI router.

2. Write the configuration of spid1 and spid2 on a BRI 0 interface and make the IP address of the interface 172.16.60.1/24. Make spid1 0835866101 8358661 and spid2 0835866301 8358663.

3. Specify interesting traffic to bring up the ISDN link. Choose all IP traffic.

4. Under the BRI interface, add the command that matches the dialer-list number and tells the BRI interface to be dialed if interesting traffic is found.

5. Configure the dialer information to dial 8358662.

6. Set the dialer load-threshold to bring up the second BRI at 50 percent bandwidth usage.

7. Set the BRI interface to fragment packets and load balance over both BRI channels.

8. Set the BRI channel to drop the connection if no interesting traffic is sent for 240 seconds.

9. Set the hold queue for packets at 75 for when they are found interesting and need a place to wait for the ISDN link to come up.

10. Write the command that will verify the ISDN connection by showing you your interface's Layer 2 and 3 information as well as if your SPIDs are valid.

Hands-on Labs

This section will provide two hands-on labs that you can use to gain the needed experience to pass your Remote Access exam.

In the first lab, you will configure two ISDN routers called 804A and 804B to dial ISDN between the networks 172.16.30.0 and 172.16.50.0, using network 172.16.60.0 on the ISDN BRI interfaces when interesting traffic dictates a DDR link. The second lab will have you configure PRI at a corporate office and BRI at a remote branch office.

For Lab 5.1, use Figure 5.11 as a reference for the network you are configuring.

FIGURE 5.11 ISDN lab

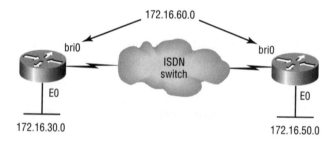

Lab 5.1: DDR

1. Go to 804B and set the hostname and ISDN switch type.

   ```
   Router#Config t
   Router(config)#hostname 804B
   804B(config)#isdn switch-type basic-ni
   ```

2. Set the hostname and switch type on 804A at the interface level. The point of these first two steps is to show that you can configure the switch type either through global configuration mode or at the interface level.

   ```
   Router#Config t
   Router(config)#hostname 804A
   804A(config)#int bri0
   804B(config-if)#isdn switch-type basic-ni
   ```

3. On 804A, set the SPID numbers on BRI0 and make the IP address 171.16.60.1/24. If you have either a real connection into an ISDN network or an ISDN simulator, put your real SPID numbers in.

```
804a#config t
804A(config)#int bri0
804A(config-if)#isdn spid 1 0835866101 8358661
804A(config-if)#isdn spid 2 0835866301 8358663
804A(config-if)#ip address 172.16.60.1 255.255.255.0
804A(config-if)#no shut
```

4. Set the SPIDs on 804B and make the IP address of the interface 172.16.60.2/24.

```
804A#config t
804A(config)#int bri0
804A(config-if)#isdn spid 1 0835866201 8358662
804A(config-if)#isdn spid 2 0835866401 8358664
804A(config-if)#ip address 172.16.60.2 255.255.255.0
804A(config-if)#no shut
```

5. Create static routes on the routers to use the remote ISDN interface. Static routes are recommended with ISDN DDR.

```
804A(config)#ip route 172.16.50.0 255.255.255.0
172.16.60.2
804A(config)#ip route 172.16.60.2 255.255.255.255 bri0


804B(config)#ip route 172.16.30.0 255.255.255.0
172.16.60.1
804B(config)#ip route 172.16.60.1 255.255.255.255 bri0
```

6. Specify interesting traffic to bring up the ISDN link. Let's choose all IP traffic. This is a global configuration mode command.

```
804A(config)#dialer-list 1 protocol ip permit


804B(config)#dialer-list 1 protocol ip permit
```

7. Under the BRI interface of both routers, add the command `dialer-group 1`, which matches the dialer-list number.

```
804A(config)#config t
804A(config)#int bri0
804A(config)#dialer-group 1

804B(config)#config t
804B(config)#int bri0
804B(config)#dialer-group 1
```

8. Configure the dialer information on both routers. This tells the BRI interface which number to dial when interesting traffic is found.

```
804A#Config t
804A(config)#Int bri0
804A(config-if)#Dialer string 8358662

804B#Config t
804B(config)#Int bri0
804B(config-if)#Dialer string 8358661
```

9. Set the `dialer load-threshold` and `multilink` commands, as well as the idle time percentage on both 804 routers.

```
804A#Config t
804A(config)#int bri0
804B(config-if)#Dialer load-threshold 125 either
804B(config-if)#Dialer idle-timeout 180

804B#Config t
804B(config)#int bri0
804B(config-if)#Dialer load-threshold 125 either
804B(config-if)#Dialer idle-timeout 180
```

The above commands set the BRI interfaces to bring up the second B channel when the first B channel is at 50 percent capacity from either inbound or outbound traffic.

10. Set the hold queue for packets when they are found interesting and need a place to wait for the ISDN link to come up.

804A#**Config t**
804A(config)#**int bri0**
804B(config-if)#**hold-queue 75 in**

804B#**Config t**
804B(config)#**int bri0**
804B(config-if)#**hold-queue 75 in**

11. Verify the ISDN connection.

Ping
Telnet
Show dialer
Show isdn status
Sh ip route

Lab 5.2: Configuring PRI and BRI

This lab will use Figure 5.12 as a basis for configuring a PRI interface on a corporate router and BRI on a remote branch router.

FIGURE 5.12 PRI to BRI configuration

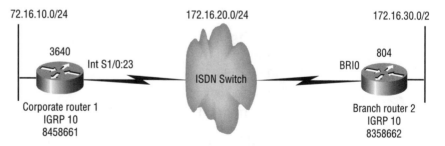

We'll start this lab by configuring the PRI interface on the corporate router.

1. Set the switch type on the router. Check with your provider to make sure you have the right switch type. Here is an example:

```
config t
isdn switch-type primary-5ess
```

2. Create a hostname for the corporate office router and the username and password for the remote router. Remember, this is the remote router's hostname. The passwords must be set identically on each router.

```
Config t
Hostname router1
Username router2 password cisco
```

3. Create an access list to identify the interesting traffic you want to bring up the ISDN link. At this point, keep it simple and use all IP traffic.

```
Config t
Dialer-list 1 protocol ip permit
```

4. Create a static route to the remote network.

```
config t
ip route 172.16.30.0 255.255.255.0 172.16.20.2
```

5. Configure the PRI (T1) interface with a linecode of b8zs and specify that the interface will click its transmitted data from a clock recovered from the lines receiving the data stream. Set the PRI framing as Extended Super Frame.

```
config t
int t1 0/1
linecode b8zs
clock source line
framing esf
```

6. Enable the PRI on your T1 interface with the channels you purchased. The example below will use all 24 channels.

```
Config t
Int t1 0/1
pri-group timeslots 1-24
```

7. Configure the D channel to use PPP with CHAP authentication.

```
config t
int serial 1/0:23
encap ppp
ppp auth chap
```

8. Add the IP address of the interface and add the command that will bring up the line when interesting traffic is found.

```
Ip address 172.16.20.1 255.255.255.0
Dialer-group 1
```

9. Configure the dialer idle-time.

```
dialer idle-timeout 180
```

10. Use a dialer map to set the number to dial.

```
config t
dialer map ip 172.16.20.2 name router2 8358662
```

11. Use a passive interface on the D channel to stop routing updates.

```
router igrp 10
passive interface serial 1/0:23
redistribute static
```

12. Configure the BRI interface of the remote branch router. Start by setting the switch type.

```
config t
isdn switch-type basic-5ess
```

13. Set the hostname of your router and the username and password of the corporate office.

```
Config t
Hostname router2
Username router1 password cisco
```

14. Create an access list to specify all IP traffic as interesting.

```
config t
dialer-list 1 protocol ip permit
```

15. Set the static routes.

```
config t
ip route 172.16.10.0 255.255.255.0 172.16.20.1
```

16. Configure the BRI interface with PPP encapsulation and CHAP authentication.

```
int bri0
encap ppp
ppp auth chap
```

17. Set the IP address of the interface, dialer-group, dialer idle-timeout, and dialer map statements.

```
ip address 172.16.20.2 255.255.255.0
no shut
dialer-group 1
dialer idle-timeout 180
dialer map ip 172.16.20.1 name router1 8358661
```

18. Set the passive interface so no updates bring up the ISDN link.

```
router igrp 10
passive interface bri0
redistribute static
```

19. Test the connection by pinging and telneting to the remote locations. Also, use the following commands:

```
show isdn status
show interface
debug q921
debug q931
```

Review Questions

1. What does an NT1 do?

    A. Converts non-ISDN devices into a compatible signal

    B. Acts as a point between and LE and TA that consolidates devices onto an ISDN line

    C. Provides the conversion between a bipolar and unipolar signal

    D. Converts the unipolar signal from the NT2 into a bipolar signal before sending it to the network

2. Which ISDN device refers to a non-ISDN device such as a POTS phone or fax machine?

    A. NT1

    B. NT2

    C. TA

    D. TE2

3. Which reference point is located between an NT1 and an NT2?

    A. R

    B. S

    C. T

    D. U

4. Which standard governs the S/T interface?

    A. ITU I.430

    B. ITU Q.931

    C. ITU I.225

    D. ITU E.911

5. How long is the SAPI field?

   A. One octet

   B. Two octets

   C. Three bits

   D. Six bits

6. What TEI value is used as a broadcast?

   A. Zero

   B. 127

   C. 64

   D. Z-1

7. Which ISDN call setup message may indicate a ring on the far end?

   A. Alerting

   B. Connect

   C. Connect Acknowledge

   D. Call Proceeding

8. Bearing Capability I=0x888F is which requested service?

   A. Unrestricted Digital Information

   B. Circuit mode, 64zkbps

   C. Layer 1, V.110/X.30

   D. Synchronous, no in-band negotiation, 56Kbps

9. Which ISDN switch type requires a Service Profile Identifier (SPID)?

   A. NTT

   B. 5ESS

   C. DMS-100

   D. NET3

10. An E1-based PRI uses which bits to handle its in-band communication?

    A. E bit

    B. There is no in-band signaling with an E1

    C. U bit

    D. D channel

11. Which of these is not a Primary Rate Interface (PRI) switch option?

    A. National-1

    B. DMS-100

    C. 4ESS

    D. NET5

12. An invalid username and password pair supplied in a PAP packet will result in which type of message?

    A. Code 4, Authentication Mismatch

    B. Authenticate-Ack

    C. Authenticate-Fail

    D. Authenticate-Nak

13. Which field carries the PAP username?

    A. Peer-ID

    B. Username

    C. Auth-Pair

    D. Peer-User

14. CHAP is identified by which Authentication-Protocol ID?

A. 0xFFF

B. 0xC223

C. 0xEFF

D. 0x89

15. CHAP response code type 4 indicates what?

A. Successful Authentication

B. Retransmit Password

C. Failure

D. Success

16. Which command verifies ISDN Layer 3?

A. Show ISDN status

B. Debug ISDN Q.931

C. Show Dialer

D. Show IP Interface Brief

17. Which command is used to verify ISDN Layer 2?

A. Show ISDN status

B. Debug ISDN Q.931

C. Show Dialer

D. Show IP Interface Brief

18. A Basic Rate Interface D channel does what? (Select all that apply.)

A. Carries low bandwidth traffic

B. Provides out-of-band signaling

C. Determines which B channel to use

D. Is a 20Kbps channel that provides out-of-band signaling

19. What is the format of the LAPD flag?

    A. 7E

    B. AF

    C. FF

    D. 9D

20. What is the channel configuration of a BRI?

    A. 1 B channel, 2 D channels

    B. 2 B channels, 1 D channel

    C. 23 B channels, 1 D channel

    D. 30 B channels, 1 D channel

Answers to Written Lab

In this written lab, you will write out the commands to configure a BRI interface.

1.

```
Config t
Isdn switch-type basic-ni
or
Config t
Interface bri 0
Isdn switch-type basic-ni
```

2.

```
config t
int bri0
isdn spid 1 0835866101 8358661
isdn spid 2 0835866301 8358663
ip address 172.16.60.1 255.255.255.0
no shut
```

3.

```
Config t
dialer-list 1 protocol ip permit
```

4.

```
config t
int bri0
dialer-group 1
```

5.

```
Config t
Int bri0
Dialer string 8358662
```

6.

```
Config t
Int bri0
Dialer load-threshold 125 either
```

7.

```
Config t
Int bri0
Ppp multilink
```

8.

```
Config t
Int bri0
Dialer idle-timeout 240
```

9.

```
Config t
Int bri0
hold-queue 75 in
```

10. Show isdn status

Answers to Review Questions

1. C. An NT1 converts the telco's 2B1Q signal into a bipolar signal that the NT2 can understand. It also acts as a loopback device for network testing. An NT1's output is also known as the T interface.

2. D. A TE2 is a POTS telephone or fax machine. This device requires a TA to interface with the ISDN network.

3. C. The T reference point is between an NT1 and an NT2.

4. A. Physical interfaces on an ISDN device are governed by ITU standard I.430.

5. D. The SAPI field is six bits long. The values transported in this identify the type of information in the packet.

6. B. The broadcast value TEI is 127, or all ones.

7. A. The Alerting message is returned to indicate the call is proceeding.

8. D. This value indicates the bearing capability is unrestricted digital information. Other options include 0X90, circuit mode, and 0x21 Layer1, V.110/X.30.

9. C. National-1 and DMS-100 switches require a SPID for each B channel; a SPID is optional with an AT&T 5ESS.

10. B. A PRI and BRI do not use in-band signaling. Instead this information is carried over the D channel.

11. A. National-1 is a BRI standard.

12. D. You will receive an Authenticate-Nak if the username/password pair is incorrect. You will receive an Authenticate-Ack if it is a good pair.

13. A. Peer-ID carries the username, and password carries the password.

14. B. CHAP is identified as Authentication Protocol c223, which is carried in the Information field of a PPP packet.

15. C. The four CHAP packet types are 1. Challenge, 2. Response, 3. Success, and 4. Failure.

16. C. `Show Dialer` will verify that ISDN Layer 3 is working. This is indicated by Success under Last Status.

17. A. You may view Layer 1 and 2 information using the `Show ISDN status` command. Layer 1 will be active, while Layer 2 will have valid TEIs.

18. A, B, C. The D channel carries call setup and teardown information as well as low bandwidth traffic. (This is a new option.)

19. A. A LAPD frame starts with 7E.

20. B. A BRI is also known as a 2B+D, for 2 B channels and 1 D channel.

Chapter

6

Cisco 700 Series

THE CCNP REMOTE ACCESS EXAM TOPICS COVERED IN THIS CHAPTER INCLUDE THE FOLLOWING:

✓ Selecting a suitable 700 series router

✓ Configuring Cisco 700 features, including DHCP and IP routing

✓ Troubleshooting the 700 series router

It would be nice if the Cisco 700 series routers used the standard Cisco IOS command structures and syntax. It would be nice. Unfortunately, Cisco acquired the 700 series platform, which uses a different operating system for the configuration and administration of these useful access node devices. The *Cisco 700 series platform* is well suited to the individual home telecommuter, although it can also support a small office. This chapter will address the features of this platform, in addition to the information required to configure and integrate the product into production networks. Due to the familiarity most readers already have with the IOS-based routers, this chapter will also compare the two platforms.

Readers will most likely find that they accept or hate the 700 platform—a few might actually prefer it to the IOS. For the real world, each environment will have to assess the suitability of the platform and, based upon that, evaluate the relevance of this chapter. If you are preparing for the Remote Access exam, this chapter is important for your overall success.

700 Series Overview

The 700 series routers were integrated into the Cisco product line to provide inexpensive, basic services for small and remote offices. As with many Cisco products, when they were acquired, they retained their original operating system, which differs substantially from the IOS. For all the differences in the software between the 700 platform and the other Cisco products, there are minor similarities beyond the generic routing functions. For example, like the other router platforms, Cisco provides light emitting diodes (LEDs) to aid in the troubleshooting process.

Chapter 1 described the LEDs of the 700 series (766) router in detail—if you skipped that chapter you may wish to refer to it now. As shown in Figure 6.1, LEDs are provided on the front of the router for Ethernet and ISDN interface status, in addition to a power (ready) LED.

FIGURE 6.1 The 700 series router

Various models in the 700 series are currently available, as outlined in Table 6.1. While it is always a good idea to check current data before ordering in production networks, you should remember the port types, features, and model numbers in order to meet the exam objectives.

TABLE 6.1 The Current Cisco 700 Series Routers *do not Have hull Ios And may set Base*

Model	Features
762M	Provides a built-in NT1 and an ISDN type U port, in addition to an external S/T port for additional ISDN devices.
765M	Supports call waiting, call hold, and call retrieve if provided by the ISDN vendor. Includes two RJ-11 analog interfaces for use with telephones and fax machines.
766M	Provides a built-in NT1 and an ISDN type U port, in addition to an external S/T port for additional ISDN devices. Supports call waiting, call hold, and call retrieve if provided by the ISDN vendor. Includes two RJ-11 analog interfaces for use with telephones and fax machines.
771M	Contains a built-in 4-port Ethernet hub.

TABLE 6.1   The Current Cisco 700 Series Routers *(continued)*

Model	Features
772M	Contains a built-in 4-port Ethernet hub. Provides a built-in NT1 and an ISDN type U port, in addition to an external S/T port for additional ISDN devices.
775M	Contains a built-in 4-port Ethernet hub. Supports call waiting, call hold, and call retrieve if provided by the ISDN vendor.
776M	Contains a built-in 4-port Ethernet hub. Provides a built-in NT1 and an ISDN type U port, as well as an external S/T port for additional ISDN devices. Supports call waiting, call hold, and call retrieve if provided by the ISDN vendor.

The M suffix reflects that these routers have 1.5MB of system RAM.

Cisco also markets the 700 series routers under the CiscoPro label. These platforms are identified with the CPA750 product number and are available in different configurations. This product also ships with ConnectPro, which is a Windows-based application for router configuration.

It is important to note that some companies refuse to deploy the 700 series because of its lack of standard IOS features. Sometimes this prevents utilization of more advanced features that the corporation requires; however, at other times, the corporation simply doesn't feel that the capital cost savings is worth the complexity of supporting multiple router operating systems. The 700 series is sometimes likened to Unix more than the IOS, perhaps in part due to its use of a directory structure metaphor for configuration commands. We will explore these commands later in this chapter; however, first we should identify some of the features available in the 700 series.

> Please refer to the Cisco Web site for the latest information regarding the Cisco 700 product line. Currently, the 800 series is the lowest model router that supports the IOS.

Features of the 700 Series

The Cisco 700 series supports IP and IPX routing, with support for other protocols through transparent bridging. The platform provides termination of the ISDN connection via an RJ-45 connector—recommended over RJ-11 connectors because of their compliance with the ISDN specifications and the typically higher-quality wire. It is unlikely that the platform will be expanded as significantly as the 800 series has been—for example, the 827 router was recently (as of this writing) introduced and brings DSL services to the 800 model. However, for ISDN BRI terminations, the 700 series may make sense, especially given its lower cost.

In keeping with its market position as a *simpler* router, Cisco provides several relatively simple programs, including ClickStart and Fast Step, to help with installation and monitoring. ClickStart software allows for the configuration of the 700 series through a Web browser. This can be a powerful tool for configuring the router, but it is important to know and verify the configuration manually via the *Command Line Interface (CLI)* to check for errors and omissions. For this reason, many administrators prefer to just use the CLI.

Fast Step is a configuration and monitoring software package for Windows 95 and NT that can quickly configure a 700 series router via Ethernet or serial cable. This tool may be better suited for multiple configurations, and administrators in enterprise situations should consider using it. However, many prefer to use the CLI, and knowledge of it is required for the examination objectives.

The 700 series also supports the following features:

DHCP Relay This can forward DHCP client requests to an off-subnet DHCP server. DHCP provides automatic IP addressing, which can greatly reduce the administration overhead of manual addressing.

DHCP Server This feature allows the 700 series router to provide the DHCP server function as opposed to forwarding DHCP requests to an external server.

While this feature may have some benefits, most large corporations prefer to use a centrally located and administered server and leave the routing function to the routers.

Port Address Translation (PAT)   This is an interesting feature for the designer and administrator to consider. It can significantly conserve address space because all devices share a single IP address to the outside network. The route alters the port number and maintains a dynamic one-for-one relationship between the source IP address and port and the altered port assignment. Unfortunately, PAT and its associated feature Network Address Translation (NAT) do not function correctly with protocols that embed the IP address, including NetBIOS packets. This makes these features difficult to implement in Windows installations that rely on NetBIOS functions.

Compression   The 700 series routers can compress data using the Stacker compression algorithm when communicating with Cisco IOS-based routers. You may recall from Chapter 2 that compression is a method by which computing devices substitute longer strings of repeated sequences with token or symbolic notation—the net result is a reduction in the number of bits required to send data. There is a performance penalty because the routers must compress and decompress the data stream; however, this is negligible in lower-bandwidth instances.

IPX and IP routing   All 700 series routers support IPX and IP packet routing. Bridging is offered for support of other protocols. This is not a major issue for many corporations because IP is easily the dominate protocol; however, it does mean that Macintosh environments that have not migrated to IP will likely wish to select another platform.

Bonding   The Cisco 700 series routers support *Multilink Protocol (MP) bonding*, which allows for the aggregation of two or more channels into a single logical connection. Bonding can be used to improve the throughput when only low bandwidth links are available.

Management   SNMP (Simple Network Management Protocol) management is available with routers in the 700 series. This allows for pooling and trap alarm messages. Some organizations do not opt to manage their remote equipment (home based) due to the volume of false error messages and the sheer number of devices.

Multinational support The 700 series routers support both North American and international applications, including most major ISDN switches. The platform is certified for use in over 25 countries. Administrators should check with the Cisco Web site or their sales representative for a current listing of countries and remember to verify power requirements for their installation.

Support for telephone services Specific models of the Cisco 700, including the 765, 766, 775, and 776, provide telephone services over ISDN, including call waiting, call hold, and call retrieve. The telecommunications service provider must make these services available.

Snapshot routing The *Routing Information Protocol (RIP)* is a fairly chatty protocol, sending a full update every 30 seconds. *Snapshot routing* resolves the problems that would result from using RIP on an ISDN circuit—because ISDN is tariffed on a per-minute basis in most installations, it would not be cost effective to have the circuit open all the time just for routing updates. Snapshot routing examines the real routing update and maintains it in the table even when the link is down.

Routing and WAN Features

The Cisco 700 series routers are well positioned for use in the Small Office/Home Office (SOHO) marketplace. On the connectivity side, the platform supports ISDN Basic Rate Interface (BRI) connections, providing 128Kbps of bandwidth on two B channels. The platform also supports IP and IPX traffic routing, which meet the needs of most modern remote access solutions. Bridging is also provided to allow other protocols. *Bridging* is a Layer 2 process that allows for protocol independence.

Given the switched nature of ISDN, the router is also well suited for installations in which multiple connection points are required. Distinct connections may be defined so that a single 700 router may terminate multiple dial-on-demand sessions.

One area where the 700 series falters due to its non-IOS architecture is support for routing protocols. RIP is effectively the only dynamic routing protocol for the 700, although it does support both versions that are currently available. The use of RIP version 2 allows for variable-length subnet masks (VLSMs), or non-classful routing. The exclusive support of RIP is typically not a significant problem because these connections are usually designed as a single gateway with a single Ethernet on the remote end. It does, however, preclude configuration as an extension of an Interior Gateway Routing Protocol (IGRP), Enhanced IGRP (EIGRP), or Open Shortest Path First (OSPF) domain. (The use of the term "domain" here is synonymous with autonomous system.) Redistribution of RIP or static learned routes becomes the only option.

Make sure that you are familiar with the differences between RIP versions 1 and 2. This is imperative for the routing examination and helpful for the Remote Access exam. *RIP version 2* transmits the subnet mask, which allows classless routing or VLSMs. Version 1 does not offer this service.

As noted in the previous section, one consideration in using RIP with ISDN circuits is the chattiness of the protocol. IP RIP normally sends an update every 30 seconds, which would effectively keep an ISDN circuit up all the time. Since ISDN is normally tariffed for per-minute usage, the goal of the designer is to keep the connection down unless *user* data is being transmitted. The technical term for this is snapshot routing, where each router captures a routing update and presumes that the state of the routing table will be unchanged for a period of time. This window is substantially longer than the normal timeout values of the RIP protocol. As a result, the router does not concern itself with receiving a RIP update every 30 seconds and presumes that networks learned while the ISDN circuit was up will remain up and reachable. The router is then free to bring the ISDN connection down and watch for interesting packets that are destined for networks held in the routing table from the snapshot. This will trigger the router to raise the ISDN circuit for a period of time, until no additional user data is being sent. During this window, the router can update its routing table, and it may also receive Internet Control Message Protocol (ICMP) unreachable messages for networks that are no longer active.

It is important to keep in mind that RIP is somewhat limited as a routing protocol, lacking support for VLSMs (version 1) and other advanced features. In addition, some users will connect to non-hub-based routers with a crossover cable, which will down the interface if the connected PC is shut down. A crossover cable is used between devices when neither internally flips the transmit and receive pairs in the 10BaseT connector. The loss of the Ethernet link and the resulting loss of downstream connections, where applicable, could significantly alter the routing table.

Designers should consider the flow of data in response to this issue. If all connections are spoke-to-hub, or traditional client-server, where a remote user is accessing a central server, then this issue is generally not a problem. However, if the use of the network is more workgroup-centric, then administrators will likely wish to use hub-based 700 series routers (which keep the interface and route active) and mandate that workstations in the field not be shut down. In best practice, companies should not employ remote access solutions that distribute data in the workgroup model. This is from both a security perspective and an operational one. It is easier to secure and back up centrally stored data than to try to keep data in someone's home. An additional risk is the theft of resources in the home.

Snapshot routing is both a routing and a WAN feature; however, there are other components in the WAN arena for the 700 series router. The most notable of these is the telephony support noted in the features matrix. *Telephony support* is an underlying feature of ISDN BRI services; in the case of the 700, however, the router augments it.

Stepping back a moment, it is important to note that ISDN was the first great hope for the American phone company in the 1960s. The concept was that everyone would have a digital connection into their home that would provide advanced phone services. This was the first attempt to push intelligence into the far end of the telecommunications network—normal POTS (plain old telephone service) analog services place all the network intelligence into the switch at the central office, with the analog phone instructing it based on pulses or tones that are then converted into commands. This is evidenced by the fact that phones do not even know their own number, nor do they understand SS-7 signaling. *SS-7 signaling* is the international standard for telephone switch communications, and it provides call setup, teardown, billing, and other functions for phone companies.

ISDN was intended to improve quality and to allow for greater capacity per pair of copper wires. The grand scheme was to have ISDN-terminated phones in the house, which would allow for a digital end-to-end connection. History shows us that this plan did not work, and building on some of the backwards compatibility of ISDN, the vendors altered the model and incorporated analog-to-digital, or POTS-to-ISDN, interfaces on their equipment in the home. As noted before, some 700 series routers include POTS interfaces that will allow an analog phone to connect over an ISDN B channel. In most public ISDN systems, the *SPID (Service Profile Identifier)* relates to the standard 10-digit phone number, and because of this, the port assumes the number for the phone.

The ability to offer voice and data services over the same cable is very important in SOHO installations, because the corporation can provide data and phone services with a single bill and a single installation. This can yield substantial savings, and along with phone company value-added features, it can bring many Public Branch Exchange (PBX)–based options into the home. For example, in California the provider offers Centrix ISDN, which can reduce costs and add call waiting, call notification, and extension dialing to groups of users in the same general area. Extension dialing and integrated voicemail can make it seem as though the remote user is actually in the office with the traditionally located workers.

Readers may note that this chapter has given very little attention to Novell IPX; however, it is supported in the 700 series and should be mentioned. Cisco supports IPX routing and IPX spoofing. *IPX spoofing* allows a disconnected resource, such as a NetWare server, to remain in the SAP table of the remote network; users remain unaware of the fact that the ISDN connection is down. This, like snapshot routing, allows the ISDN BRI to be connected only when user data is present. This chapter will not dedicate more space to this protocol because its importance in the exam and production environments is waning. Virtually all remote access installations would benefit from adoption of an IP-only policy.

ISDN and Telephony Features

In large part, the Cisco 700 is well suited to the home office because of its included interfaces. Models include two standard telephone jacks in addition to the ISDN termination. This allows the corporation to provide a single ISDN BRI in the home and gives the user the ability to use the B channels for data or voice services.

As described in the previous section, the 700 series allows for the termination of traditional telephone services in addition to the service of ISDN BRI data connections. Until recently, ISDN was one of the highest bandwidth technologies available for the residence—it was usually cost prohibitive to install a T-1, even if the circuit was available. DSL technologies have changed that substantially.

Remote Access with DSL and Cable Modems

It is unfortunate that Cisco chose to focus so much energy on the 700 series routers for the remote access examination because the platform will not, by all indications, service cable or DSL connections. In addition, its lack of true IOS support makes the platform appear to be an afterthought in the marketplace. As noted in Chapter 1, ISDN will remain on the technology spectrum of remote access for a specific period of time; however, it will be replaced by newer, cheaper, and better routers. While not as universally available, DSL will absolutely be one of those technologies.

Readers preparing for the examination should read this chapter carefully. Unless the 700 series is currently installed in your environment, the rest of you can skim the chapter because it likely adds little value. This is because, while the test is new, most shops will avoid the platform for new deployments and choose the 800 series—which now supports DSL—and other true IOS-based routers instead. A reasonable guess is that Cisco included the 700 series in their scope for the remote access materials because it does offer one possible solution for remote access installations, and because the platform's limited offerings can simplify the understanding of available features. For example, one can review the 700 series feature-set without needing to be concerned with EIGRP or OSPF.

Readers would be well advised to learn about DSL and cable modems. Appendix C includes several links that can augment the technical understanding of both services, and most vendors offer a high-level tutorial on their offerings via their Web pages. Review of this material is important if only to understand the limitations of your provider's capabilities.

In addition to the specific technologies, designers of remote access solutions will find that the industry trend is for outsourced services or universal entry points, such as those found in VPN (virtual private network) terminations. In a VPN, dial-up, cable, DSL, ISDN, and Frame Relay connections can all be terminated by the communications vendor, and access to the network, forgoing redundancy, can be provided by a single pipe—perhaps a DS-3 connected to a managed or unmanaged VPN termination device. In a managed installation, the corporate network staff might only see a Fast Ethernet connection into their firewall, with the circuit, remote technologies, and remote user support completely outside their scope.

This solution clearly provides benefits since the only risk is poor support from the outside vendor. On the plus side, the corporation no longer needs to provide an end-to-end solution, nor is it compelled to install more ports for expansion or negotiate with multiple providers. In addition, if a user lives in a location where DSL is not available, they can quickly install a VPN-based cable modem solution and be working in a very short time.

Profiles

The concept of a *profile* in the router is akin to a profile of a person or thing. For example, a profile of Michael Jordan might include tall, athletic, and from South Carolina. Additional details might be included, such as six-foot-six and lives in Illinois; however, all elements are descriptive of something—in this case, a famous basketball player.

Through the use of profiles, the relationship between the remote access port and the end user can be modified to enhance security. This might be through caller ID, or it may assign a specific characteristic to the connection, such as a callback number. Profiles can also be used to configure filters, passwords, demand thresholds, and parameters (which govern load characteristics and link relationships).

There are 16 available user profiles in the 700 series router. Four additional profiles, which cannot be deleted, are also used for defining connections. These four, documented below, may be modified by the administrator or user.

Profiles are stored in the router's NVRAM (non-volatile random access memory) and are loaded when the router is powered on. There are four profiles that are included with the router and cannot be deleted, although users may make modifications to them. They are

Internal   When routing is enabled, the internal profile is responsible for determining the flow of data between the routing engine (IP and IPX) and the bridging engine (used for other protocols).

LAN   The LAN profile governs the Ethernet interface of the router and is involved in the routing process.

Standard   The standard profile provides a default for ISDN connections that are not associated with a specific profile. This profile should be examined to provide security for unknown callers.

System   The system profile governs system-level configuration parameters. There are also system parameters that may only be changed at the system-level prompt and are not part of the profile. The system prompt is shown with the name of the router and a greater-than sign, or *router>*.

In the upcoming configuration section you will work with profiles as they relate to the installation of a 700 series router.

Configuring the 700 Series

The Cisco 700 series routers divide the configuration process into three distinct elements: system, LAN, and user. This section describes the components of each.

Many references to the Cisco 700 router's operating system use the term IOS, per Cisco's naming convention. The software is not based on the IOS software associated with the Cisco 800, 1400, 2500, 2600, 3600, and 7500 series.

Unix and Catalyst switch commands and the 700 series routers share many similarities. Like Unix, the 700 series uses the concept of directories to access configuration elements and, like the Catalyst, the router uses set commands to enter configuration elements. In addition, many commands are similar to their IOS-based counterpart in at least the root word. For example, set ip address is similar to ip address in the IOS router configuration. As always, it is best to consult the documentation that comes with your equipment and software version for the latest options and syntax. The following section documents the entire command syntax in the 4.0 Cisco 700 OS.

Cisco 700 Help

The help system in the 700 series is similar to the IOS-based routers and will parse the commands based on keywords. In reality, however, most administrators find the 700 commands much more akin to the Catalyst 5000 series switches. For example, there is no enable in the 700 router—all commands are equal and configured with a set command word.

Typically, we would not print the entire command list for a router, and you will note that the remainder of this chapter will only highlight some of the commands. We include them here for two reasons—first, to illustrate the differences between the more familiar IOS commands and the 700 series router. Second, the help output is included in this form so that those readers who don't have access to a 700 series router can see the entire syntax of the platform, including those commands that are not highlighted in the chapter. Readers should note that this output denotes the abbreviation syntax for each command as well. These uppercase letters reflect the fewest number of characters that are needed to invoke the function. So, for example, the command to configure callback services—set callback on–can be entered as se ca on. Please also note the limited number of root, or key, words, including set, show, and reset.

```
CAll [ C# | L# | # | C#/L# | C#/# | #/# ]   [ P# | CH# |
P#/CH# ] [<number>]
```

where

C#	indicates a Connection number
# or L#	indicates a Link number
C#/L# or #/#	indicates Link of a Connection
P#	indicates Port
CH#	indicates Channel
P#/CH#	indicates Channel of a Port

CD [<username>]

DEmand [<link>] [THreshold=kb/s] [DUration=<seconds>]
[SOurce= WAN | LAn | BOth]

DIsconnect [C# | L# | # | C#/L# | C#/# #/# | P# | CH# |
P#/CH# | ALl]

where

C#	indicates a Connection number
# or L#	indicates a Link number
C#/L# or #/#	indicates Link of a Connection
P#	indicates Port
CH#	indicates Channel
P#/CH#	indicates Channel of a Port

EStablish [<spid id>]

<Q> and <enter> to Quit or <enter> for MORE

HElp [<cmd> [<modifier>]]

LOg

LOg NOne | CAlls | MEssage | STate | ERrors | IPx [TIme]
[VErbose]

LOg [LAN | <connection>] PAckets | TRaffic [CHannel =
<channel>] [VErbose [INbound | OUtbo

LOGIn <ipaddress> | <ethernetaddress> | REmote

LOGOut

PIng <ip address>

REBoot

RELease [<spid id>]

REset ADdress = <address> | ALl

REset CALLBackreceive <number> | ALl

REset CALLIdreceive <number> | ALl

REset [<id>] FIlter = [ALl]

REset IP FIlter <filter ID> | ALl

REset IP ROute ALl

REset IP ROute DEstination <network>[/ <bits>] [GAteway <next hop>]

REset IPX GAteway

REset IPX ROute ALl | DEstination=<netnum> GAteway=<net:node>

REset IPX SAp HElper

<Q> and <enter> to Quit or <enter> for MORE

REset IPX SErvice ALl | NAme=<service-name> TYpe=<service-type>

REset [<connection> | LAN] PACkets [ALl]

REset PAssword [ALl]

REset [<patternname>] PATtern = [ALl]

REset SNmp TRaphost <ip address> | ALl

REset TYpe = <type> | ALl

REset USer < Username >

SEt ACtive [<username>]

SEt ADdress = <address>

SEt AGe = <seconds> | OFf

SEt [<link>] AUto = ON | OFf

SEt BAudrate 300 | 1200 | 2400 | 4800 | 9600 | 19200 | 38400

SEt BRidging ON | OFf

SEt BIlling SPc <number> | TImelink | NOne

SEt CAllback ON | OFf

SEt CALLBACKId ON | OFf

SEt CALLBACKReceive <number>

SEt CALLErid ON | OFf

SEt CALLIdreceive <number>

<Q> and <enter> to Quit or <enter> for MORE

SEt COmpression STac | OFf

SEt CPp NEgotiation ABort <DIsconnect | PReset>

SEt CPp | PPp NEgotiation COunt <attempts>

SEt CPp | PPp NEgotiation INtegrity <seconds> | OFf

SEt CPp | PPp NEgotiation REtry <milliseconds>

SEt CPp PRotocol HDlc | ORdered | FRagmented

SEt DAte MM/DD/YYYY

SEt DEfaults

SEt [<link>] DELay = <seconds>

SEt DHcp SErver | RElay <ip address> | OFf

SEt [<spid id>] DIrectorynumber = <number> [<.subaddress>]

SEt ECho ON | OFf

SEt ENcapsulation PPp | CPp

SEt <id> FIlter [<patternname>]^8 [BLock | ACcept] |
[IGnore | DEmand]

SEt GAteway <ip address>

SEt INactive [<username>]

SEt IP <ip address>

SEt IP ADdress <ip address>

SEt IP COst <value>

<Q> and <enter> to Quit or <enter> for MORE

SEt IP FIlter [<type>] IN | OUt [SOurce = [NOT]<address>]
     [DEstination = [NOT]<address>] BLock | ACcept

SEt IP FRaming EThernet_II | NOne

SEt IP NEtmask <mask>

SEt IP PRopagate ON | OFf

SEt IP RIp REceive BOth | V1 | V2 | OFf

SEt IP RIp SNapshot CLient ACtive <time> QUiet <time>
UPdate OFf | ON

SEt IP RIp SNapshot SErver ACtive <time> UPdate OFf | ON

SEt IP RIp UPdate PEriodic | LInkup | DEmand | SNapshot |
OFf

SEt IP RIp VErsion 1 | 2 | BOTH

SEt IP ROUTE DEstination <network>[/<bits>] GAteway
<nexthop>
     [PRopagate ON | OFf] [COst <value>]

SEt IP ROUTIng ON | OFf

SEt IPX FRaming EThernet_II | 802.3 | 802.2 | SNap | NOne
| UNKnown

SEt IPX GAteway <net:node> USer <username>

SEt IPX NETBios ACcept | BLock

SEt IPX NETWorkaddress <network number>

SEt IPX RIp REceive OFf | ON

```
SEt IPX RIp SNapshot CLient ACtive <time> QUiet <time>
UPdate OFf | ON
<Q> and <enter> to Quit or <enter> for MORE
SEt IPX RIp SNapshot SErver ACtive <time> UPdate OFf | ON
SEt IPX RIp UPdate = PEriodic | DEmand | SNapshot | OFf
SEt IPX ROUTE DEstination=<netnum> GAteway=<net:node>
               [HOps=<hops>] [COst=<ticks>]
SEt IPX ROUTIng ON | OFf
SEt IPX SAp HElper <net:node>
SEt IPX SErvice NAme=<service-name> TYpe=<service-type>
               ADdress=<net:node:sock> [HOps=<hops>]
SEt IPX SPoofing <minutes> | OFf
SEt IPX TRace <length> | OFf | ON
SEt LEarn ON | OFf
SEt LOcalaccess ON | PArtial | PRotected
SEt LOGout <time>
SEt [ <connection> ] LOOpback ON | OFf
SEt [ WAN | LAn ] MOde = ANy | ONly
SEt MUltidestination ON|OFF
SEt [<link>] NUmber = [<number> <.subaddress>]
SEt PASSThru ON | OFf
SEt PAssword HOst | SYstem | CLient
<Q> and <enter> to Quit or <enter> for MORE
SEt <patternname> [ PAttern = < hexpattern >
<binarypattern> <decimalpattern> ]
               [ OFfset = <number> ]
               [ FRom = BEGINNING | TYPEFIELD ]
               [ PATTERNName = <patternname> ]
SEt PLan NOrmal | INternational | NAtional | SUbscriber |
       UNknown_isdn | ABbreviated | CEntrex | NEtwork
SEt PPp AUthentication INcoming [ CHap ] [ PAp ] [ NOne ]
SEt PPp AUthentication OUtgoing [ CHap ] [ PAp ] [ NOne ]
SEt PPp CAllback REQuest | REPly ON | OFf | ALways
SEt PPp MUltilink ON | OFf
SEt PPP <PAssword | SEcret> <HOst | CLient>
SEt PPp TErmreq COunt <attempt>
```

SEt PROFile [POwerup=ACtivate|INactive]
[DIsconnect=DEactivate|KEep]
            [USer=<new profile name>]
SEt PROFile ID <ethernet address>
SEt PS1detect ON | OFf
SEt REmoteaccess OFF | PArtial | PRotected
SEt [<spid id>] RIngback [<number>]
SEt SCreenlength <lines>
<Q> and <enter> to Quit or <enter> for MORE
SEt SNmp COntact " contact string "
SEt SNmp LOcation " location string "
SEt SNmp TRap [COldstart = ON | OFf] [WArmstart = ON |
OFf]
 [LInkup = ON | OFf] [LINKDown = ON | OFf] [
AUthenticationfail = ON | OFf]
SEt SNmp TRAPHost <ip address>
SEt SPeed 56k | 64k | AUto | VOice
SEt [<spid id>] SPId = [<SPID number>]
SEt SUbnet <ip address mask>
SEt SWitch 5ESS | DMS | NI-1 | PERM64 | PERM128
SEt SYstemname [<Systemname >]
SEt TIme HH:MM:SS
SEt <link> TIMEOut [<seconds> | OFf]
SEt TYpe = <type> [ACcept | BLock] [IGnore | DEmand]
SEt UNicastfilter ON|OFF
SEt USer [<username>] [INcoming | OUtgoing]
SEt VOicepriority NEver | COnditional | ALways | DIsable
SHow
SHow [<connection>] ADdress
SHow COnfig | NEgotiation | SEcurity [ALl]
<Q> and <enter> to Quit or <enter> for MORE
SHow CONNections | DEmand | ETher | VOicerouting | STatus
| TImeout
SHow DHcp Config
SHow [<id>] FIlter
SHow IP COnfig | FIlter | ROute [ALl]
SHow IP RIp SNapshot [ALl]

```
SHow IPX COnfig | ROute | SErvice [ALl]
SHow IPX CONNections| DEmand | STatistics
SHow IPX RIp SNapshot [ALl]
SHow MEmstats | SNmp | TYpe
SHow [ <connection> | LAn ] PAckets
SHow [ <patternname> ] PATtern
SHow PRofile | USers
SWl
SWl [ TFTP ]
TEst  [ STop | REsult | ETher ]
TEst [ <connection> ] [ WAn | ALl ]
TEst MAxpkts <bytes>
TEst MInpkts <bytes>
TEst RAte <pps>
<Q> and <enter> to Quit or <enter> for MORE
TImeout <link> [THreshold=<kbs>] [DUration=<seconds>]
[SOurce= WAn | LAn | BOth]
UNlearn [<connection>]
UNset [<link>] AUto
UNset CAllback | CALLBACKId | CALLErid | COmpression
UNset [CPp] PAssword CLient
UNset [<link>] DEmand | TIMEOut
UNset LEarn | PRotocol | PASSThru | SPeed | BRidging |
ENcapsulation
UNset [<link>] NUmber | RIngback
UNset PPp AUthentication
UNset PPp CAllback
UNset PPp PAssword HOst
UNset PPp SEcret HOst
UPload
VErsion
Cisco> show configu
End-of-Line found, more input expected
SHow
SHow [<connection>] ADdress
SHow COnfig | NEgotiation | SEcurity [ALl]
```

```
SHow CONNections | DEmand | ETher | VOicerouting | STatus
| TImeout
SHow DHcp Config
SHow [ <id> ] FIlter
SHow IP RIp SNapshot [ALl]
SHow IPX RIp SNapshot [ALl]
SHow MEmstats | SNmp | TYpe
SHow [ <connection> | LAn ] PAckets
SHow [ <patternname> ] PATtern
SHow PRofile | USers
```

 Readers should consult their router's documentation for the specifics regarding these commands and their applicability.

Configuration Output

To further illustrate the differences in the 700 series routers, this section focuses on the configuration output. Accessed with the show config command, and as shown in this output, an entire configuration file is not provided, which is the biggest difference between the IOS and the 700 series. Rather, this command provides a summary of the system parameters and the ISDN parameters as shown, including the number of lines per screen (screen length), the SPIDs, and information related to the current profile.

```
Cisco> show config                    Same as Cat 55
System Parameters
    Environment
        Screen Length           20
        Echo Mode               ON
    Bridging Parameters
        LAN Forward Mode        ANY
        WAN Forward Mode        ONLY
        Address Age Time        OFF
    Call Startup Parameters
        Multidestination        OFF
    Line Parameters
```

```
        Switch Type              DMS
        Svc Profile ID           51237246200101
51237246210102
        Voice Priority           ALWAYS
        Call Parameters          Link 1              Link 2
        Retry Delay              30                  30


Profile Parameters
    Bridging Parameters
        Bridging                 ON
        Routed Protocols
        Learn Mode               ON
        Passthru                 OFF
    Call Startup Parameters
        Encapsulation            CPP
    Line Parameters
        Line Speed               AUTO
        Numbering Plan           NORMAL
    Call Parameters              Link 1              Link 2
        Auto                     ON                  ON
        Called Number
        Ringback Number
```

This output also provides the ISDN switch type configured—in this case, a DMS-100.

ISDN Switch Type Commands

One of the most important commands in any ISDN router is the switch type configuration command. This relates to the type of ISDN switch used by the telephone company to terminate your connection. As a global command, set switch may be one of the first commands that an administrator issues at the router—however, we recommend naming the router first, if for no other reason than to give it some personality!

NOTE Latest versions of the 700 series code may auto-negotiate the switch type for you. We recommend that you define this setting whenever the switch type is known—it is usually provided with the SPIDs and other information from the phone company.

To set the switch type, the administrator issues the `set switch` command as shown in Table 6.2. Without the proper configuration of the switch type, the router will be unable to establish a connection.

TABLE 6.2   The `set switch` Command

Command	Function
set switch 5ess	Sets the 700 router to work with AT&T basic rate switches (U.S.)
set switch dms	Sets the 700 router to work with Nortel DMS-100 switch (North America)
set switch ni-1	Sets the 700 router to work with National ISDN-1 (North America) switches
set switch net3	Sets the 700 router to work with switches found in the United Kingdom and other European countries

System-Level Configuration Commands

System-level configuration includes global parameters such as the system name and SPID/number information. Chapter 5 explains these ISDN concepts in greater detail. The system-level commands are outlined in Table 6.3.

TABLE 6.3   System-Level Commands

Command	Function
set systemname *name*	This command configures a name for the router.

TABLE 6.3 System-Level Commands *(continued)*

Command	Function
`set 1 spid` *spid-number*	This command defines the number to be associated with the first BRI channel. The number 2 would be substituted for the second BRI channel.
`set 1 dir` *directory-number*	The directory number is usually the last seven digits of the SPID number, not including the service bits. It may also be regarded as the prefix and identifier of the number in the North American Dialing Plan (NADP). This command defines the phone number of the connection, which may differ from the SPID.
`set default`	This command clears the router. It is similar to the `write erase` command in the IOS.

LAN Profile

The LAN profile is accessed with the `cd lan` command and is used to define parameters related to the Ethernet interface and functions. For example, the IP address and network mask would be defined in this mode, in addition to enabling routing or bridging. Table 6.4 outlines the commands that are used in this mode.

TABLE 6.4 LAN Profile Commands

Command	Function
`set default`	This command is the same as `write erase` in the IOS—it clears the configuration from NVRAM. Unlike the IOS, a reload command is not required after NVRAM is cleared.
`upload`	This command views the saved configuration of the 700 series router.

TABLE 6.4 LAN Profile Commands *(continued)*

Command	Function
`cd lan`	This command enters LAN configuration mode.
`set bridging off`	This command disables bridging services. As with most commands presented, the opposite keyword is used to reverse the setting—set bridging on, for example. This differs from the IOS, which typically uses the no prefix.
`set ip routing on`	This command enables IP routing.
`set ip address 192.168.2.1`	This command sets the IP address for the Ethernet interface to the value provided, in this case, 192.168.2.1.
`set ip netmask 255.255.255.0`	This command configures a 24-bit Netmask for the previously entered IP address. The IOS combines this with the `ip address` command.

Creating a User Profile

User profiles might be best compared to dialer-maps on the IOS-based routers, although their implementation and functionality is somewhat different. User profiles on the 700 series routers store information regarding the remote entity, including the IP address, host, user, name, the encapsulation type, and static route entries.

User profiles are created with the `set user profile_name` command. This command enters user mode and provides the database, or profile, with a reference name. Additional commands are then entered to populate the information specific to that profile. Table 6.5 outlines some of these commands.

TABLE 6.5 User Profile Commands

Command	Function
`set user profile_name`	This command enters user mode and defines the profile name.

TABLE 6.5 User Profile Commands *(continued)*

Command	Function
set active *profile_name*	This command configures a profile to be active. The reverse of this command is set inactive *profile_name*.

Caller ID

The telephone company provides caller ID to identify a call's originating number. It operates by sending an encoded data stream between the first and second rings. In a non-router application, the user would attach a decoder to the phone line, which would interpret this encoding and display it on the screen of the decoding device. The data stream is fairly simple, and it incorporates the number of the originating caller.

Once a user profile is defined in the router, it is possible to take the caller ID information and verify that the call originated from the proper telephone number. This can augment other security restrictions and passwords; however, it is important to note that caller ID information can be spoofed if the attacker has knowledge of and access to the phone company switch. It should be considered as part of an overall security policy.

Two commands enable security functionality based on caller ID, as shown in Table 6.6.

TABLE 6.6 Enabling Caller ID

Command	Function
set caller id on	This command allows receipt of caller ID information on the interface. It is important to note that this service must be provided by the local phone company. In addition, it is possible to block caller ID information—it is recommended that administrators install and test the connection without ID services and then add it to a working configuration.

TABLE 6.6 Enabling Caller ID *(continued)*

Command	Function
set callisdnreceive *number*	This command ensures that calls from the specified number will be authenticated. The corollary is also true—calls from other numbers will not be authenticated.

PPP Callback

Point-to-Point Protocol (PPP) callback is a powerful security feature available with the 700 series routers. This option allows the administrator to define a callback number used following an authenticated dial-in session. It allows the administrator to permit access from a single phone number, which, forgoing a hack of the phone system, guarantees that the caller is in a single physical location. This can be very useful in making sure data is not compromised.

Consider two possible ways in which callback can improve security. The first, perhaps obvious, way is that the phone line is in a locked building or room. A hacker's task is much more difficult if they must access a single physical location from which they can dial—however, if they don't, the access point will not grant access, even with a valid password. In addition, the caller knows the dial-in number to start the connection and must have the proper username and password for that location. The second concerns eavesdropping. How many times have you allowed someone to inadvertently look over your shoulder while you typed on an airplane or in a public place? While this is usually harmless, there are instances when it could lead to the release of critical data. By controlling the physical endpoint of where access can originate—a person's home, for example—the administrator can reduce this risk. It is unlikely that unauthorized persons would be allowed to look over the CEO's shoulder at home, and when they do, they are usually more interested in having Mom or Dad get off the machine so they can play Star Trek!

Of course, callback does introduce a problem—there is a downside to virtually everything. The user *must* be in a fixed location (disregarding wireless access modems). This makes callback impractical for workers staying in hotels, support staff that needs emergency dial-in access while at dinner, or other mobile connections. Once a single user has non-callback access, the entire security model is altered too, since that account now becomes a target for attacks. There is a benefit to limiting the number of such targets—a hacker will have fewer opportunities to find two accounts out of a thousand, for example, but the accounts exist and the hacker is back to needing only a number, a username, and a password to gain entry.

IP Traffic with CHAP between a 700 Series and an IOS-based Router

As noted in Chapter 3, *Challenge-Handshake Authentication Protocol (CHAP)* is the preferred authentication method in remote access. It is considered more secure because the password is not transmitted as clear-text, or readable text. In order to use CHAP between a 700 series router and an IOS-based router, such as the 3600 series, the administrator must first configure the 700 series router for CHAP authentication. This is a typical configuration need.

The commands for instructing the router to use CHAP authentication are straightforward and all start with the prefix command set ppp. This makes sense, because CHAP is a function of the PPP protocol.

Below is a partial configuration file, which shows the relative ease with which CHAP is enabled. The first two commands define CHAP in each direction of data flow—i.e., both routers will authenticate and receive authentication. While it is possible to only perform authentication in a single direction, it is less secure than allowing each side to verify the identity of the opposing party. The following two commands are the password configuration commands; note that the router will prompt for the password twice in response to each command. The first password, client, is for the client password, or the password that is hashed to send to the opposite device. The secret host password defines the password that is expected to be sent.

```
Router700>set ppp authentication incoming chap
Router700>set ppp authentication outgoing chap

Router700>set ppp secret client
    Enter new Password:<password>
    Re-Type new Password:<password>



Router700:>set ppp secret host
```

```
Enter new Password:<password>
Re-Type new Password:<password>
```

Table 6.7 describes the commands used in CHAP authentication.

TABLE 6.7 Configuration of CHAP Authentication

Command	Function
`set ppp secret client`	This command sets the client CHAP secret password.
`set ppp authentication incoming [chap | pap | none ]`	This command enables CHAP authentication for incoming connections when the chap keyword is used. All the options may be used, which will operate in the order chap, pap, and none.
`set ppp authentication outgoing [ chap | pap | none ]`	This command enables CHAP authentication for outgoing connections. This is an optional item.
`set ppp secret host`	This password must match the secret client of the opposing router. Host is used to authenticate to the remote router.

Readers should always consider CHAP authentication for security services and should use difficult passwords to thwart attackers.

Dynamic Host Control Protocol

In Chapter 3, we discussed the benefits of Dynamic Host Control Protocol (DHCP) and how it is used with Windows installations. The 700 series router can also facilitate DHCP installations, either by providing helper services or by acting as a DHCP server. Recall from Chapter 3 that helper services forward the DHCP broadcast to another subnet. Helper services are also called DHCP relay agents.

In the 700 series routers, the following commands are used to configure and define a DHCP scope to be served by the router. This is shown in Table 6.8.

TABLE 6.8 Cisco 700 DHCP Server Commands

Command	Function
set dhcp server	This command enables the DHCP server functionality on the Cisco 700 router.
set dhcp address *10.20.30.2 254*	This command defines the starting and ending addresses in the DHCP pool. In this case, addresses from 10.20.30.2 through 10.20.30.254 are part of the scope.
set dhcp netmask *255.255.255.0*	This command specifies the subnet mask for the pool.
set dhcp gateway primary *10.20.30.1*	This command defines the default gateway to be assigned as part of the DHCP lease.
set dhcp dns primary *10.10.1.51*	This command specifies the DNS address for DHCP clients.
set dhcp wins primary *10.10.1.51*	This command defines the WINS server to be used by DHCP clients.

The preceding commands use the same machine for DNS and WINS services, and the default gateway is part of the same subnet as the DHCP lease address.

Instructing the 700 series routers to provide DHCP relay functionality is very simple by comparison. There is a single command. The command set dhcp relay ip_address will forward DHCP requests to the address defined in the command.

Port Address Translation (PAT)

Port Address Translation (PAT) is an efficient method for conserving IP address space. In version 4 of IP (the currently used version), the allocation of addresses did not anticipate the explosive growth of the protocol and the demands that would be placed on it.

PAT operates by using a single IP address on the outside to serve all IP devices on the inside. This is accomplished by altering the source port information of the packet and using it to create a table that can be used to redefine the IP address when the receiver responds to the packet. For example, consider a typical Web (HTTP) session that uses port 80 for the destination and greater than 1023 for the source, as shown below:

Source IP	Source Port	Destination IP	Destination Port
10.10.10.5	1026	204.4.116.10	80

This packet cannot traverse the public Internet as it uses RFC 1918/RFC 1597 address space, or private address space. This is one of the ways PAT conserves IP addresses—private addresses may be used within the organization, eliminating the need to assign hundreds of addresses to the internal hosts.

NOTE NAT and PAT translations are established for a specific duration and are stateful. Because of this, once a NAT or PAT translation is established, it is important to maintain the same route through the network. A packet entering the network via another router would not receive the same translation—an important factor in planning redundancy.

When the packet is dispatched from the router into the public Internet (based on the local routing table), the router substitutes its IP address for the source of the packet. From a TCP perspective, the session is between the router and the Web server, while another independent session is between the client and the router. As shown below, the router may also alter the source port of the packet to maintain a unique port number for each session.

Source IP	Source Port	Destination IP	Destination Port
207.14.81.66	5620	204.4.116.10	80

While there are theoretically 65,000 port numbers that may be used in PAT, the practical limit is based on the processing power of the router and is generally less than 500 sessions. This guideline works well with the 700 series routers, as there are generally fewer than 10 users connected to the device.

To the Web server at 204.4.116.10, it appears that a browser at 207.14.81.66 is connected directly to it via port 5620. It is unaware of the PAT process and the fact that the user is actually at 10.10.10.5.

Table 6.9 shows the commands used for PAT.

TABLE 6.9 PAT Commands

Command	Function
`set ip pat udptimeout 5`	This command defines the timer used by the router to age UDP sessions—the router will remove the entry from the PAT table if no packets matching the entry are seen in the timeout window.
`set ip pat tcptimeout 30`	This command defines the timer used by the router to age TCP sessions—the router will remove the entry from the PAT table if no packets matching the entry are seen in the timeout window.

Cisco 750 series routers running version-4 code will not offer these options.

Troubleshooting the 700 Series

As we noted in Chapter 1, the LEDs on the front of the router are a good, albeit limited, first step in the troubleshooting process. Via the LEDs, the administrator or user can view the status of power, connection, and data flow characteristics without needing to log in to the router to view configuration information. This can be used to isolate the faulty element and make troubleshooting more efficient.

Unlike the IOS-based routers, the 700 series lacks a debug command and function set. Readers must remember that this product, originally developed outside of Cisco, was intended for small, simple remote access connections with limited field support. However, there are some commands, particularly the show commands, that can provide some insight into the workings of the router. The commands that validate IP routing are in the following section and are called out because routing is a frequent issue that cannot be troubleshot effectively with other means. For other functions, readers are advised to first review the configuration of the router—a leading cause of problems is a misconfigured SPID or dial-up number.

Advise users to *not* unplug or disconnect the 700 series router from the ISDN circuit. Many users view this connection as a fancy asynchronous modem, not realizing that the D channel is always active. When power is lost or the cable is disconnected, the telephone company may receive an alarm and shut down the interface. When power is restored, the user, or administrator, will need to call the provider to have them reenable the circuit.

Monitoring IP Routing

Diagnostic support for the 700 series routers is much more limited than for the full IOS platforms. However, the administrator has a few methods available to troubleshoot connections. It is important to consider that most installations will be in remote, home-office situations, and as such, the administrator will need to describe the screens and configuration setting options to a remote user. This is best accomplished by having a similar router available for following along—improved by having the same version of code installed.

The primary commands to monitor IP routing are shown in Table 6.10. These commands show the current status of the IP configuration and the IP route table.

TABLE 6.10 Commands for Monitoring IP Routing

Command	Function
`show ip configuration [all]`	With the all keyword, this command displays the IP configuration for all profiles. Without the keyword, the current profile's IP configuration will be displayed.
`show ip route [all]`	With the all keyword, this command displays all static IP routes. Without the keyword, the current profile's routes will be displayed.
`show ip filter [all]`	While not a routing command, many times routing problems will appear as a result of an IP filter, or an access list in IOS terms. This command will display the filter for the current profile or, with the all keyword, all configured filters.

The following output screens display the parameters for IP routing and IP configurations. As shown, there is only one IP route in the router's table. This route is for the local Ethernet interface of 10.4.12.0/24.

```
Cisco> show ip route all
Profile  Type Destination Bits Gateway Prop Cost Source Age
Internal NET  10.4.12.0   24   DIRECT  ON   1    DIRECT 0
```

The IP configuration is easy to understand in the context of the route table. The administrator here has assigned an IP address of 10.4.12.1/24 to the router's Ethernet port. RIP version 1 is defined, but the router does not send or receive updates, as shown.

```
Cisco> show ip config
Profile Routing Frame IP Address Netmask
        RIP TX  RX  Prop Cost
Internal   ON  ETH2  10.4.12.1  255.255.255.0
        V1  OFF OFF ON    1
```

By using the route and configuration commands, the administrator can examine the IP parameters of the router.

Summary

The Cisco 700 series is an inexpensive solution for providing remote access solutions. However, because the platform is not consistent with the Cisco IOS, configuration can be more difficult. This chapter addressed the differences between the Cisco 700 platform and the Cisco IOS, including the configuration commands to install and provision a 700 series router in a remote installation.

Readers should be familiar with some of the more advanced elements of this chapter as they relate to the Cisco 700 series IOS, including

- CHAP and PAP authentication

- DHCP services

- IP routing

Key Terms

Before you take the exam, be certain you are familiar with the following terms:

bridging

Command Line Interface (CLI)

IPX spoofing

Multilink Protocol (MP) bonding

Point-to-Point Protocol (PPP) callback

RIP version 2

Routing Information Protocol (RIP)

snapshot routing

SPID (Service Profile Identifier)

SS-7 signaling

Commands in This Chapter

Command	Meaning
cd lan	This command enters LAN configuration mode.
set 1 dir *directory-number*	The directory number is usually the last seven digits of the SPID number, not including the service bits. It may also be regarded as the prefix and identifier of the number in the North American Dialing Plan (NADP). This command defines the phone number of the connection, which may differ from the SPID.
set 1 spid *spid-number*	This command defines the number to be associated with the first BRI channel. The number 2 would be substituted for the second BRI channel.
set active *profile_name*	This command configures a profile to be active. The reverse of this command is set inactive profile_name.
set bridging off	This command disables bridging services. As with most commands presented, the opposite keyword is used to reverse the setting—set bridging on, for example. This differs from the IOS, which typically uses the no prefix.

`set caller id on`	This command allows receipt of caller ID information on the interface. It is important to note that this service must be provided by the local phone company. In addition, it is possible to block caller ID information—it is recommended that administrators install and test the connection without ID services and then add it to a working configuration.
`set callisdnreceive` *number*	This command ensures that calls from the specified number will be authenticated. The corollary is also true—calls from other numbers will not be authenticated.
`set default`	This command is the same as `write erase` in the IOS—it clears the configuration from NVRAM. Unlike the IOS, a `reload` command is not required after NVRAM is cleared.
`set dhcp address` *10.20.30.2 254*	This command defines the starting and ending addresses in the DHCP pool. In this case, addresses from 10.20.30.2 through 10.20.30.254 are part of the scope.
`set dhcp dns primary` *10.10.1.51*	This command specifies the DNS address for DHCP clients.
`set dhcp gateway primary` *10.20.30.1*	This command defines the default gateway to be assigned as part of the DHCP lease.
`set dhcp netmask` *255.255.255.0*	This command specifies the subnet mask for the pool.

`set dhcp server`

This command enables the DHCP server functionality on the Cisco 700 router.

`set dhcp wins primary`
`10.10.1.51`

This command defines the WINS server to be used by DHCP clients.

`set ip address 192.168.2.1`

This command sets the IP address for the Ethernet interface to the value provided, in this case, 192.168.2.1.

`set ip netmask 255.255.255.0`

This command configures a 24-bit Netmask for the previously entered IP address. The IOS combines this with the `ip address` command.

`set ip pat tcptimeout 30`

This command defines the timer used by the router to age TCP sessions—the router will remove the entry from the PAT table if no packets matching the entry are seen in the timeout window.

`set ip pat udptimeout 5`

This command defines the timer used by the router to age UDP sessions—the router will remove the entry from the PAT table if no packets matching the entry are seen in the timeout window.

`set ip routing on`

This command enables IP routing.

`set ppp authentication`
`incoming [chap | pap | none ]`

This command enables CHAP authentication for incoming connections when the `chap` keyword is used. All the options may be used, which will operate in the order `chap`, `pap`, and `none`.

`set ppp authentication outgoing [chap	pap	none]`	This command enables CHAP authentication for outgoing connections. This is an optional item.
`set ppp secret client`	This command sets the client CHAP secret password.
`set ppp secret host`	This password must match the secret client of the opposing router. Host is used to authenticate to the remote router.
`set switch 5ess`	Sets the 700 router to work with AT&T basic rate switches (U.S.).
`set switch dms`	Sets the 700 router to work with Nortel DMS-100 switch (North America).
`set switch net3`	Sets the 700 router to work with switches found in the United Kingdom and other European countries.
`set switch ni-1`	Sets the 700 router to work with National ISDN-1 (North America) switches.
`set systemname name`	This command configures a name for the router.
`set user profile_name`	This command enters user mode and defines the profile name.
`show ip configuration [all]`	With the `all` keyword, this command displays the IP configuration for all profiles. Without the keyword, the current profile's IP configuration will be displayed.

show ip filter [all]

While not a routing command, many times routing problems will appear as a result of an IP filter, or an access list in IOS terms. This command will display the filter for the current profile or, with the all keyword, all configured filters.

show ip route [all]

With the all keyword, this command displays all static IP routes. Without the keyword, the current profile's routes will be displayed.

upload

This command views the saved configuration of the 700 series router.

Written Lab

1. What command defines the hostname for CHAP authentication?

2. What command defines the name of the router and alters the prompt?

3. To define the SPID for BRI 1 to number 4085551213, with trailing numbers 0101, the administrator would type what command?

4. What is the command to turn off bridging from LAN mode?

5. What is the command to enter LAN configuration mode?

6. What is the command to enable IP routing?

7. What command is used to allow receipt of caller ID information?

8. What command is used to authenticate calls using caller ID?

9. What is the command to configure a user profile to be active?

10. What is the command to view the configuration of a 700 series router?

Hands-on Lab

In this lab, you will configure a 700 series router. If you wish, please expand upon the lab provided here and add an ISDN switch and second 700 series router to connect the two and test the connection.

1. Connect the router to a power source and connect the Ethernet cable to your workstation using a crossover cable.

2. If you have an ISDN simulator, connect the BRI0 interface to it. Obtain the SPIDs for your connection. Fill in this information below (in pencil) or record it on a separate sheet of paper.

   SPIDs: _____

3. Connect a console cable to the router and clear the configuration file using the `set default` command.

4. Configure the router as follows or using a convention architected for the classroom.

This configuration keeps the link up for IP RIP updates. Production networks would likely use snapshot routing or static routes without IP RIP to keep the ISDN BRI interface down.

Parameter	Value
Ethernet IP address	10.10.1.1/24
BRI0 IP address	10.1.1.1/24
Protocol	IP
Hostname	(Your initials)700
Bridging	Off
IP routing	On
Encapsulation	PPP
ISDN switch type	DMS-100
SPID 1 (if one is not assigned on the simulator)	41555512120101
SPID 2 (if one is not assigned on the simulator)	41555512120102
RIP version	1
Profile name	Remote
Remote dial number	17075551212

```
RP700>set systemname RP700
RP700>set switch dms
RP700>set 1 spid 41555512120101
RP700>set 2 spid 41555512120102
RP700>cd lan
RP700:LAN>set ip address 10.10.1.1
RP700:LAN>set ip netmask 255.255.255.0
RP700:LAN>set ip routing on
RP700:LAN>set ip rip update periodic
RP700:LAN>cd
RP700>set user REMOTE
RP700:REMOTE>set ip address 10.1.1.1
RP700:REMOTE>set ip netmask 255.255.255.0
RP700:REMOTE>set ip routing on
RP700:REMOTE>set ip rip update periodic
RP700:REMOTE>set ip rip version 1
RP700:REMOTE>set encapsulation ppp
RP700:REMOTE>set number 17075551212
RP700:REMOTE>set bridging off
```

5. Make the REMOTE configuration active.

```
RP700:REMOTE>set active REMOTE
```

Review Questions

1. Which of the following is true regarding the Cisco 766M?

   A. Contains 1.5MB of system RAM

   B. Has an internal, 4-port, Ethernet hub

   C. Supports call waiting and call hold features

   D. All of the above

2. The Cisco 700 series supports which of the following?

   A. Bridging

   B. IP routing

   C. IPX routing

   D. All of the above

3. Which of the following protocols may be routed with a 700 series router?

   A. IPX

   B. AppleTalk

   C. OSI

   D. IP

4. Can the 700 series router support AppleTalk?

   A. No. Only IP and IPX are supported.

   B. Yes, but only with an IP tunnel.

   C. Yes, but only with bridging.

   D. Yes, but addressing must be based on Phase 1 AppleTalk.

5. Which of the following models provides a built-in hub?

   A. Any model with an M suffix

   B. Any 77*x* model

   C. Only the 761EH

   D. None of the above

6. When using DHCP and a 700 series router, which of the following is true?

   A. The router can provide DHCP forwarding.

   B. The router can act as a DHCP server.

   C. Both A and B.

   D. Neither A nor B.

7. Which feature that conserves IP addresses is provided on the 700 series routers?

   A. Bonding

   B. PAT

   C. CHAP

   D. None of the above

8. Which of the following offer simplified configuration services without requiring the command line on 700 series routers?

   A. ClickStart

   B. FastStart

   C. ClickFast

   D. Fast Step

9. The Cisco 700 supports which of the following protocols in version 4.*x*?

   A. CHAP

   B. PAP

   C. PPP

   D. All of the above

10. Why does the author contend that the 700 series router and an ISDN solution for remote access services are undesirable?

    A. The 700 series is not an IOS-based router, which can increase support complexities.

    B. Managed solutions, including DSL technologies, can provide more flexibility and better service.

    C. The author doesn't contend that the 700 series and ISDN are undesirable.

    D. A and B.

11. What is the command to review IP route information on the 700 series routers?

    A. show ip routing

    B. show ip route all

    C. show routing

    D. show routed all

12. What service might best serve an administrator who is limited on the number of non-RFC 1918 IP addresses available?

    A. DHCP relay

    B. PAT

    C. Compression

    D. Bonding

13. To reduce the need to maintain a link for routing updates, the 700 series routers employ which of the following?

   A. Buffered routing

   B. Port router protocol

   C. Snapshot routing

   D. Policy routing

14. The update interval for IP RIP is normally how long?

   A. 10 seconds

   B. 30 seconds

   C. 60 seconds

   D. 180 seconds

15. Which of the following is true regarding CHAP on the 700 series router?

   A. PPP is required.

   B. CHAP may be defined in each direction independently.

   C. The password must be entered twice into the router's configuration.

   D. All of the above.

16. The 700 series router supports which of the following?

   A. DHCP relay

   B. DHCP server

   C. Both A and B

   D. None of the above

17. Which of the following are all features available on the 700 series routers?

A. AppleTalk routing, compression, and CHAP

B. IP routing, EIGRP, and PPP

C. IP and IPX routing, bonding, and compression

D. IP bridging, AppleTalk routing, and telephony services

18. The 700 series supports which of the following?

A. Bonding

B. Management

C. IP routing

D. All of the above

19. What is the command to define a name for the 700 series router?

A. `set system console name name`

B. `set routername name`

C. `configure name name`

D. `set systemname name`

20. The 700 series router is best suited for which of the following?

A. Central offices

B. Home offices

C. Branch offices

D. SMDS circuits

Answers to Written Lab

1. `set ppp clientname`

2. `set systemname`

3. `set 1 spid 40855512130101`

4. `set bridging off`

5. `cd lan`

6. `set ip routing on`

7. `set caller id on`

8. `set callisdnreceive number`

9. `set active profile_name`

10. `upload`

Answers to Review Questions

1. D. The 766M is perhaps the most feature-rich 700 series router, providing a 4-port hub and advanced ISDN services. The M denotes that the router has 1.5MB of system RAM.

2. D. The Cisco 700 series routers support bridging, which may be the only way to support non-IP and non-IPX protocols with the platform. IP and IPX are routed.

3. A, D. It is important to note that the 700 series will not support non-IP and non-IPX traffic without bridging. While this can significantly reduce the perceived functionality of the platform, in practice this is not a significant limitation.

4. C. The 700 series does not support advanced functions such as IP GRE tunnels; however, bridging may be used to support AppleTalk. Most current installations are architected to support IP exclusively.

5. B. Unfortunately, this question requires rote memorization. It is, however, fairly easy to retain the information. An M denotes memory functionality, and models with built-in hubs have a seven as the middle digit (771). Non-hub models have a six (761, for example).

6. C. One of the advanced features available in the 700 series is support for DHCP forwarding and services. This can simplify management in remote locations, which typically do not have trained staff to administer network devices or workstations.

7. B. Port Address Translation allows all nodes behind the router to use a single IP address when communicating with remote networks. CHAP is an authentication protocol and does not impact IP addressing.

8. A, D. Cisco is not beyond slight alterations in spelling when asking questions regarding product names or command syntax. Unfortunately, this is another memorization question.

9. **D.** It is helpful to remember that Cisco uses their exams, like other vendors, as marketing fodder in addition to technical assessments. Most questions like this will include all listed options—why note those things that aren't supported? However, it is clearly preferred that you remember the features.

10. **D.** While the 700 series and ISDN are a possible solution, the author presents a strong case for the use of IOS-based systems and leaving the option open for integration of non-ISDN-based services, including DSL and cable.

11. **B.** The command `show ip route all` is used to view the routing table.

12. **B.** Port Address Translation is the best answer to this question, as it implies the need for Internet-traversable addresses through the use of RFC 1918. DHCP relay would be best suited if addresses in general were not available. Compression and bonding are not applicable to addressing.

13. **C.** Snapshot routing is used to maintain a routing table even when the ISDN link is down.

14. **B.** IP RIP sends a full routing update every 30 seconds.

15. **D.** CHAP requires PPP and is direction independent. The 700 series router will prompt the administrator for the password twice.

16. **C.** The 700 series routers can act as a helper or server for DHCP services.

17. **C.** The 700 series does not support AppleTalk routing or EIGRP.

18. **D.** The 700 series supports MP bonding, SNMP management, and IP routing.

19. **D.** The command `set systemname name` is used to define the router name.

20. **B.** The limited features and fixed configuration of the 700 make it impractical for services beyond basic home office installations.

Chapter

7

X.25 and LAPB

THE CCNP REMOTE ACCESS EXAM TOPICS COVERED IN THIS CHAPTER INCLUDE THE FOLLOWING:

✓ Configuring an X.25 WAN connection

✓ Assigning X.121 addresses to router interfaces

✓ Mapping higher-level addresses to X.25 addresses

✓ Verifying the X.25 configuration

✓ Configuring LAPB

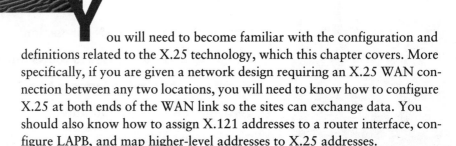

Y ou will need to become familiar with the configuration and definitions related to the X.25 technology, which this chapter covers. More specifically, if you are given a network design requiring an X.25 WAN connection between any two locations, you will need to know how to configure X.25 at both ends of the WAN link so the sites can exchange data. You should also know how to assign X.121 addresses to a router interface, configure LAPB, and map higher-level addresses to X.25 addresses.

In addition to X.25 WAN configurations and X.121 addresses, this chapter also covers X.25 routing. The chapter presents an in-depth look at the X.25 protocol and explains how packets are addressed and encapsulated using the X.25 standard. You will also learn how to configure a new X.25 connection, troubleshoot an existing X.25 network, verify the proper configuration, and troubleshoot incorrect configurations so data will travel as intended across your WAN link.

The Basics of X.25

T he *X.25 protocol* is a standard protocol that defines a connection between a terminal and a Packet-Switching Network (PSN). A PSN is the switching services provided by your telephone carrier or the carrier providing your access links at the demarcation point into your building. X.25 is one of the most widely used networking protocols for wide area networking due to its serial cable linking abilities.

X.25 has been around for quite some time; it originated in the early 1970s after the success of Telnet and TYMNET PSNs. The networking industry has commonly used the term X.25 to refer to the entire suite of X.25 protocols. The X.25 protocol was designed so that data could be transmitted and received by two alphanumeric terminals through the use of plain old telephone system (POTS) analog phone lines. Thus, when X.25 was enabled, alphanumeric terminals could communicate remotely in order to access applications on servers and mainframes located on both ends of the telephone line.

There was one drawback, however: Modern desktop applications needed to connect two sometimes-dissimilar local area networks (LANs) with a wide area network (WAN). This meant that LAN-to-WAN-to-LAN data communications were necessary. Again, the designers went back and created newer forms of wide area networking technology, such as Integrated Services Digital Network (ISDN) and Frame Relay. These newer WAN protocols complemented or extended the features of the X.25 protocol suite in the network without replacing the need for the protocol.

Because of the way designers have created the X.25 protocol, there are many different Network Layer (Layer 3) protocols (listed below) that can be transmitted across X.25 Virtual Circuits (VCs). In fact, the X.25 protocol acts like a tunnel for datagrams and other Layer 3 packets to cross links within the X.25 Layer 3 packets. X.25 can be used with many Layer 3 protocols, such as the following:

- AppleTalk
- Banyan VINES
- Bridging
- Compressed TCP
- DECnet
- IP
- ISO-CLNS
- Novell IPX
- XNS

The X.25 suite maps to the lower three layers of the Open System Interconnection (OSI) Reference Model, as shown in Figure 7.1.

FIGURE 7.1 How the X.25 protocol suite maps to the lower three layers of the OSI Reference Model

OSI Reference Model

	OSI Reference Model		X.25	
7	Application			
6	Presentation			
5	Session			
4	Transport			
3	Network		X.25	3
2	Data Link		LAPB	2
1	Physical		Physical	1

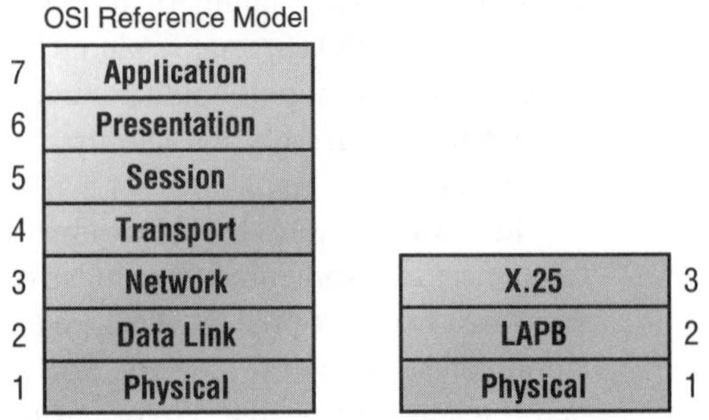

In the rest of this section, we will discuss how X.25 works at the various OSI layers.

X.25 at the Network Layer

At the Network Layer (Layer 3) of the OSI Reference Model, the *Packet Layer Protocol (PLP)* is the X.25 protocol that manages packet exchanges between the virtual circuits. PLP is quite versatile and can be used over Logical-Link Control 2 (LLC2) or Integrated Services Digital Network (ISDN) operating on interfaces running Link Access Procedure on D channel (LAPD).

PLP can operate in five different modes:

Call-setup mode   This mode is used to create a Switched Virtual Circuit (SVC) between two Data Terminal Equipment (DTE) devices. PLP uses the X.121 addressing scheme (discussed later in this section) to create the virtual circuit. In this mode, call setup can be executed on multiple virtual circuits. This allows one virtual circuit to be in call-setup mode while another is in data-transfer mode. This mode is used only when an SVC is being created.

Data-transfer mode   This mode is used for transferring the physical data between two DTE devices through a created virtual circuit. Data-transfer mode handles PLP segmentation and reassembly, and error and flow-control. This mode is executed on a per-virtual-circuit basis for both PVCs and SVCs.

Idle mode   This mode is used when a virtual circuit has been established and data transfer is not occurring. It is executed on a per-virtual-circuit basis on SVCs.

Call-clearing mode   This mode is used to end communication sessions between two DTE devices communicating through an SVC.

Restarting mode   This mode is used to restart a transmission between a DTE device and a Data Communications Equipment (DCE) device. This mode is not executed on a per-virtual-circuit basis. It can affect all the DTE devices with established virtual circuits.

In the following sections, we will look at the PLP packet header and the call- setup packets. This will allow us to get a better look at how the call-setup process works.

X.25 PLP Packet Header

At Layer 3, the X.25 header is made up of three fields. Figure 7.2 shows these different fields and their functions.

FIGURE 7.2   The Layer 3 packet X.25 PLP packet header

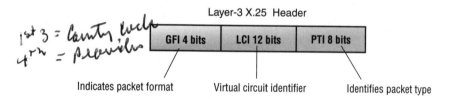

The General Format Identifier (GFI) is a 4-bit field that is used to indicate the general formatting of the packet header. The Logical Channel Identifier (LCI) is a 12-bit field that identifies the virtual circuit information, and the Packet Type Identifier (PTI) is used to identify whether the packet is for DTE or DCE interfaces.

To establish a virtual circuit, the Public Data Network (PDN) connects both logical channels with an independent LCI on both the DTE and DCE interfaces. The PTI field is used to identify 1 of the 17 individual packet types.

X.121 Call Setup Packets and Address Format

The International Telecommunication Union Telecommunication Standardization Sector (ITU-T) is the organization responsible for defining the standard format of X.25 addresses. The standard format is defined as the *X.121 standard*.

In a private X.25 network, each network assigns base addresses that best fit their network configuration. Decimal digits are defined for X.121 addresses in order to allow network protocols to connect across an X.25 link. These statements are used on the router to map the next-hop Network Layer address to an X.121 address. These statements are logically equivalent to the LAN Address Resolution Protocol (ARP) that dynamically maps a Network Layer IP address to a data-link media access control (MAC) address. Maps are required for each protocol since ARP is not supported in an X.25 network. Mapping statements must be manually configured when setting up X.25 on a router.

The router accepts an X.121 base address with anywhere between 1 to 15 numerical digits. In some networks, you will find subscribers that use a sub-address, which is made up of one or more digits after the assigned base address.

The X.121 standard determines that the first four digits of the address specify the Data Network Identification Code (DNIC). The first three of these digits specify the country code. The fourth digit is the provider number assigned by the ITU-T. Countries that require more than 10 provider numbers are assigned multiple country codes. The United States is assigned country codes 310 through 316.

There are 8 to 11 other digits assigned. These digits specify the Network Terminal Number (NTN) assigned by the PSN provider. In your network, you will need to contact your service provider to get your individual DNIC code. Table 7.1 is a sample list of country codes from each zone. A zone corresponds to a continent, as shown in the table.

The complete listing of ITU-T country code assignments can be found on the ITU-T Web site by referring to the information on ITU-T Recommendation X.121. The ITU-T Web site is located at www.itu.org.

TABLE 7.1 A Sample List of Commonly Used DNIC Country Codes for Each Zone

Zone	Example Location	Series	Country Code(s)
Zone 2 (Europe)	Germany	200 Series	262 to 265
Zone 3 (North America)	United States	300 Series	310 to 316
Zone 4 (predominantly Asia)	Japan	400 Series	440 to 443
Zone 5 (Pacific Islands)	Australia	500 Series	505
Zone 6 (Africa)	South Africa	600 Series	655
Zone 7 (South America)	Brazil	700 Series	724

The X.121 addressing fields in the call-setup packets provide source and destination DTE addresses. These are used to establish the virtual circuits for X.25 communication. The address field also specifies the International Data Numbers (IDN) field in the X.121 call-setup packet, as shown in Figure 7.3.

LEC
LOCAL EXCHANGE CARRIER

FIGURE 7.3 The X.121 IDN address format

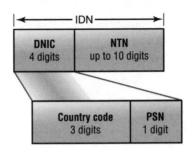

The first four digits of the IDN are referred to as the DNIC. The DNIC is divided into two separate parts: the first part consists of three digits, which specify the country code assigned by the ITU-T, and the last digit specifies the PSN. The network terminal number (NTN) is up to 10 digits long and is used to identify the specific DTE on the PSN.

Fields that make up the X.121 address are only used when an SVC is used. An SVC is a temporary connection used for data transfers, but it is only used during the call setup. When the call has been established, the PSN uses the LCI field to specify the virtual circuit for the remote DTE.

X.25 at Layer 3 uses three individual PLP procedures to create an SVC operation procedure:

1. Call setup

2. Data transfer

3. Call clearing

The procedure used will depend on the virtual circuit type being used. For a Permanent Virtual Circuit (PVC) at Layer 3, X.25 is configured to remain in the data-transfer mode. This is because the circuit has been established as a permanent connection, and the call does not need to be cleared or ended. But if an SVC is used, all three procedures are used.

During data transfer at Layer 3, X.25 can segment and reassemble user data if the packets are too long or exceed the maximum packet size allowable for the circuit. In this case, every data packet is given a sequence number allowing for error and flowcontrol to occur across the DTE and DCE interfaces.

X.25 and LAPB at the Data Link Layer

The Link Access Procedure, Balanced (LAPB), found at the Data Link Layer (Layer 2) of the OSI Reference Model, provides reliability as well as sliding windows in which to send data packets. Because the OSI Data Link and Network Layers provide for good flowcontrol as well as error checking, the need for these functions becomes unnecessary in order to add the extra overhead to some of the protocols in the X.25 protocol suite.

In the past, error rates were much higher than they are in today's POTS analog lines. The use of X.25 began in the 70s, when the use of analog was the most efficient way to build more reliability into the network at the hardware level. With digital and fiber-optic technologies finding their way into the networks of today, the error rates have dropped dramatically. Newer technologies such as Frame Relay have taken advantage of this significant drop in error rates by providing a network protocol that leaves out many of the error controls in exchange for faster delivery.

X.25 was developed in the days when a majority of the end users' data equipment was made up of alphanumeric terminals and data processing on centralized, time-sharing computers. The requirements of packet switching were much less significant than they are in today's networks.

In today's networks the requirements are much more demanding because the networks are much more complex. The desktop PCs demand more bandwidth and the networks demand more speed to move ever increasing amounts of data. With the implementation of new, higher-end applications (which seem to appear almost weekly) and new ways of implementing protocols for WAN delivery, X.25 has added protocols to keep up with the demand (such as those protocols added for ISDN and X.25 over Frame Relay, which add additional packet-switching capabilities).

X.25 uses DTE and DCE to identify the responsibilities for each end of the WAN or remote connections. The movement of Layer 3 data through the internetwork usually involves encapsulation of datagrams inside media-specific frames. When data arrives at the router and is discarded, the router analyzes the datagram and places it inside an LAPB and then forwards the frame.

The opposite is true when an LAPB frame arrives at the router. The router takes the LAPB frame and extracts the datagram from the packet or packets. The router then discards the encapsulated portion of the frame, analyzes the datagram, identifies the frame format as well as the next-hop address, and sends the data out the correct port. The router may reencapsulate the datagram into a frame readable by the outgoing media before forwarding the frame.

Layer 2 (Data Link Layer) X.25 is implemented by LAPB, which allows each side (the DTE and the DCE) to initiate communication with the other. During information transfer, LAPB checks to make sure that the frames arrive at the receiver in the correct sequence and free of errors.

As with other Data Link Layer protocols, LAPB uses three frame formatting types, which can be found in the control field of an LAPB frame:

Information frames (I-Frames) These frames carry upper-layer information and the control information necessary for full-duplex, such as frame sequencing, flowcontrol, error detection, and recovery.

Supervisory frames (S-Frames) These frames provide control information, such as transmission requests, transmission suspensions, status reporting, and acknowledgment information. There is no information field contained in these frames.

Unnumbered frames (U-Frames) These frames are not placed in any sequence. They are used for control purposes, such as error reporting, link setup, and link termination.

Figure 7.4 shows the LAPB frame and fields.

FIGURE 7.4 The LAPB frame and fields

LAPB Frame

Flag 1 byte	Address 1 byte	Control 1 byte	Data variable length	FCS 2 bytes	Flag 1 byte

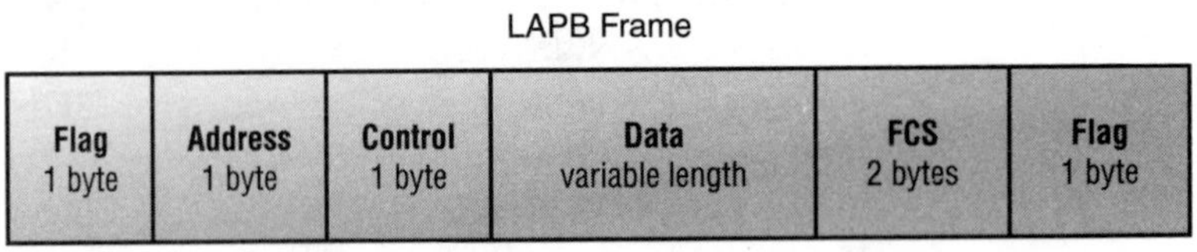

The following lists a description of each field in an LAPB frame:

Flag This field is the delimiter of the LAPB frame. It delimits the beginning and the end of the frame.

Address This field indicates the frame carries a command or a response.

Control This field is used to identify command and response frames. This field also indicates the frame type (I-Frame, S-Frame, or U-Frame).

Data   This field contains upper-layer data. This includes information on the form of PLP packet encapsulation, as well as the size and the format. The maximum length of the field is negotiated between a PSN administrator and the subscriber at subscription time.

Frame Check Sequence (FCS)   This field handles error checking to verify the integrity of the transmitted data.

X.25 at the Physical Layer

X.25 at the Physical Layer (Layer 1) uses the *X.21 bis Physical Layer protocol*, which is roughly equivalent to RS-232-C, now known as the EIA/TIA-232-C. X.21 bis was derived from ITU-T Recommendations V.24 and V.28 and identifies the electrical characteristics of a DTE-to-DCE interface, like the one depicted in Figure 7.5. X.21 bis supports point-to-point connections with modem speeds of up to 19.2Kbps. This protocol also supports full-duplex transmission over four-wire media with a maximum distance of 15 meters between DTE and DCE. Let's take a look at DTE and DCE.

FIGURE 7.5   X.21 DTE and DTE-to-DCE cable (DB-60 to DB-15)

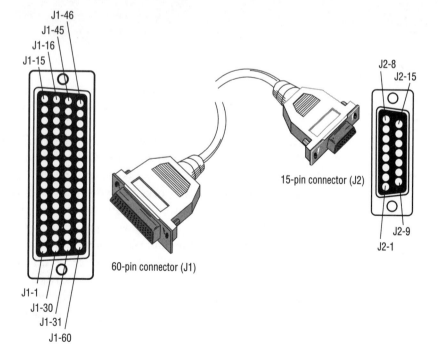

> **NOTE** Using a loopback does not work on an X.21 DTE because a loopback definition is not provided for X.21.

DTE versus DCE

The DTE and the DCE each identify the responsibilities of each demarcation point on both ends of an X.25 link, as shown in Figure 7.6. The X.25 protocol is the protocol that creates the virtual circuits between the X.25 DTE and X.25 DCE.

FIGURE 7.6 The DCE and DTE sides of an X.25 link

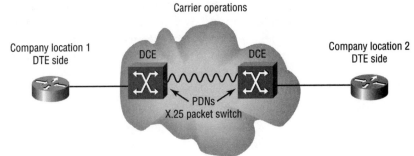

The X.25 DCE is the side of the link on which you will usually find the PDN, which is supplied by the POTS Central Office (CO) switch or concentrator. On the other side of the link is the X.25 DTE side. On the DTE side, you will usually find either the subscriber's router or a packet assembler/disassembler (PAD) or your own router PAD. The way X.25 traffic is carried within the CO cloud of networks depends on the implementation. The CO *cloud* is the maze of networks that your packets must be switched through to get from one destination to another. For example, say you need to get a packet from Sacramento to Denver. You have a Frame Relay link that is using X.25 between you and your phone carrier's office. Once the packet arrives at your local phone carrier's office, it is then routed through many telephone company switches before it reaches its destination in Denver. This maze of network switches is referred to as the cloud, carrier operations (CO), or CO cloud. Sometimes, X.25 is used within the CO cloud, as depicted in Figure 7.7.

FIGURE 7.7   The X.25 CO cloud

The terms DTE and DCE are represented at all three individual layers of the X.25 protocol stack, which was shown in Figure 7.1. The terms can be used to identify individual cables at the Physical Layer or they can be used to identify responsibilities independent of the Physical Layer. At the Physical Layer, they are used to identify a typical plug-gender and clock-source definition as well.

Are you thoroughly confused yet? This concept will be better outlined later in the chapter. What you basically need to know is that the terms DTE and DCE are used to identify physical cables that have a gender type of male or female. Each end can be used to identify a location in the network, and it can also be used to identify other protocols used at different layers of the X.25 protocol stack. As you can see, the X.25 terminology for DTE/DCE differs from layer to layer.

At the X.25 packet-level, DCE typically acts as a boundary function to the PDN within a switch or concentrator. Let's add in another term to make this even more confusing. At the CO, the X.25 switch is sometimes referred to as the Data Switching Equipment (DSE).

Packet Assembler/Disassembler (PAD)

The *PAD* is a protocol standard defined by the ITU-T. The PAD is a device commonly found in many X.25 networks, and it is used to collect data and output it into X.25 packets that can be interpreted by asynchronous or dumb terminals.

A DTE device, such as a dumb terminal, is too simple to interpret X.25 packets, so a PAD is used. When a DTE device is too simple to implement the full X.25 functionality, such as a dumb terminal, a PAD is located on a link between a DTE device and a DCE device. The PAD is then used to perform the buffering, packet disassembly, and packet assembly that the dumb terminal can't perform. Let's take a look at Figure 7.8 and see how this works.

FIGURE 7.8   The PAD process

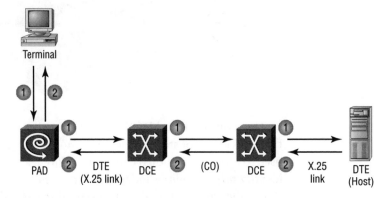

Look at Figure 7.8, and you will see that each exchange has two steps. What takes place in these steps is described below:

1. The PAD works by buffering the data sent to or from a DTE device, assembling the outbound data into packets with an X.25 header, and then forwarding them to the DCE device.

2. When packets arrive at the PAD, the PAD disassembles the packets, removes the X.25 header, and then forwards the data to the DTE.

X.25 Virtual Circuits

An X.25 interface may have a maximum of 4095 virtual circuits (VCs) configured. VCs are used to create a logical connection between two devices in sometimes-foreign networks. They create a reliable communication between the two network devices with a logical, bidirectional path from one DTE device to another across an X.25 network. The virtual circuit passes through any number of devices, including DCE. Multiple virtual circuits can also be multiplexed into a single physical circuit referred to as a *physical connection*. Virtual circuits are demultiplexed at the other side of the link and data is sent to the appropriate destinations.

A PVC has many similarities to a leased line. Both the PSN provider and the subscriber must stipulate and condition the virtual circuit. PVCs do not use a call-setup packet or a call-clearing mode that is apparent to the subscriber. Once a PVC is established, the PVC never terminates and is always present, even when no data traffic occurs across the link.

There are two types of X.25 virtual circuits. There is a *Switched Virtual Circuit (SVC)* and a *Permanent Virtual Circuit (PVC)*. SVCs are temporary connections used for convenient data transfers. The use of these requires that two DTE devices establish, maintain, and terminate a session each time the devices need to communicate. PVCs, on the other hand, are permanently established connections used for frequent and consistent data transfers. PVCs do not require that sessions be established and terminated. Instead, DTEs can begin transferring data whenever necessary because the session is always active.

The basic operation of an X.25 virtual circuit begins when the source DTE device specifies which virtual circuit is to be used (in the packet headers). It then sends the packets to a locally connected DCE device. At this point, the local DCE device examines the packet headers to determine which virtual circuit to use and then sends the packets to the closest PSE in the path of that virtual circuit. PSEs pass the traffic to the next intermediate node in the path, which may be another switch or a remote DCE device.

When the traffic arrives at the remote DCE device, the packet headers are examined and the destination address is determined. The packets are then sent to the destination DTE device. If communication occurs over an SVC and neither device has additional data to send to the other, the virtual circuit is terminated.

VCs are used interchangeably with the terms Virtual Circuit Number (VCN), Logical Channel Number (LCN), and Virtual Channel Identifier (VCI).

X.25 can support any legal configuration of SVCs and PVCs over the same circuit. If you configure a large number of VCs over a serial interface, the result will be a degrading of performance. However, throughput for encapsulating a specific protocol can be improved by using multiple SVCs. Multiple SVCs provide a larger window size for protocols that offer their own higher-layer sequencing. X.25 was originally designed for data sharing between terminal-to-host applications and not host-to-host communications over a WAN link.

With the Cisco IOS 10.2 and later releases, the Cisco router's encapsulation methods have enabled more than one protocol to be transported through an X.25 cloud. Although it appears to be one VC, it is actually more than one VC. Each protocol is given its own individual mapping using the `x25 map` command statement that references the X.121 address to reach the destination.

This router's encapsulation method for multiple protocol capability over a VC is defined in RFC 1356. Basically this says that each individually supported protocol can be mapped to a specific destination host over a WAN link.

WARNING

Routing multiple protocols over a virtual circuit generates very high traffic loads. A better solution is to combine SVCs, as described earlier in this chapter, to maintain a good quality of throughput.

Configuring X.25

When you select X.25 as a WAN protocol, the first thing you must do is set the appropriate interface parameters. To successfully configure an X.25 WAN interface, you must first define the X.25 encapsulation, assign an X.121 address (supplied by the PDN service provider), and then define map statements to associate X.121 addresses with higher-level protocol addresses.

Because X.25 is a flowcontrolled protocol, the flowcontrol parameters must match on both sides of an X.25 link. Mismatches as a result of inconsistent configurations can be a source of trouble in your circuits. The remainder of this chapter will cover all these issues, include troubleshooting steps and commands that will help you to resolve the most common X.25 problems.

Configuring X.25 Encapsulation Types

The first step in configuring your X.25 link parameters is to enter the interface encapsulation mode and assign a higher-layer address. Since using an IP address as the higher-layer protocol is the most common, this is what will be used in the examples in this section.

To enter the interface encapsulation mode, you can use the encapsulation x25 command. This will specify the encapsulation type and it will need to be followed by either dce or dte to be used on the serial interface. The default type is DTE. When the router is configured as an X.25 DTE device, which is typical in most business networking environments, the router is used as an X.25 PDN to transport various protocols. When the router is configured as an X.25 DCE device, the router acts as though it is an X.25 switch.

WARNING If you change the interface configuration on an interface from DTE to DCE or vice versa, all the configurations on the interface will revert to the default interface settings.

The next step is to apply the X.25 address provided by your X.25 PDN. To do this, use the x25 address command followed by the PDN address. This command allows you to define the local router's X.121 address.

Take a look at the configuration commands that have been discussed so far. For this example, assume that you have a 4500 series router with a serial interface. The PDN has supplied you with an address of 316013344323. You will use the serial 0 interface on the switch as your DTE interface connected to your WAN link. First, the configuration mode must be entered for the serial 0 interface using the following command:

```
SeansRTR(config)#int s0
SeansRTR(config-if)#
```

Before you use the encapsulation command, take a look at the following list of available syntaxes:

```
SeansRTR(config-if)#encap ?
```

```
atm-dxi        ATM-DXI encapsulation
frame-relay    Frame Relay networks
hdlc           Serial HDLC synchronous
lapb           LAPB (X.25 Level 2)
ppp            Point-to-Point protocol
smds           Switched Megabit Data Service (SMDS)
x25            X.25
```

By using the encapsulation command as follows, you can assign the serial 0 interface to use X.25 DTE encapsulation:

```
SeansRTR(config-if)#encap x25 dte
SeansRTR(config-if)#
```

Next, you will need to configure the address using the x25 address command. First, take a look at the options available using the x25 command:

```
SeansRTR(config-if)#x25 ?
```

accept-reverse	Accept all reverse charged calls
address	Set interface X.121 address
default	Set protocol for calls with unknown Call User Data
facility	Set explicit facilities for originated calls
hic	Set highest incoming channel
hoc	Set highest outgoing channel
hold-queue	Set VC hold-queue depth
hold-vc-timer	Set time to prevent calls to a failed destination
htc	Set highest two-way channel
idle	Set inactivity time before clearing SVC
ip-precedence	Open one virtual circuit for each IP TOS
ips	Set default maximum input packet size
lic	Set lowest incoming channel
linkrestart	Restart when LAPB resets
loc	Set lowest outgoing channel
ltc	Set lowest two-way channel
map	Map protocol addresses to X.121 address
modulo	Set packet numbering modulus
nvc	Set maximum SVCs simultaneously open to one host per protocol
ops	Set default maximum output packet size
pad-access	Accept only PAD connections from statically mapped

```
    --More--
```

linkrestart	Restart when LAPB resets
loc	Set lowest outgoing channel
ltc	Set lowest two-way channel
map	Map protocol addresses to X.121 address
modulo	Set packet numbering modulus
nvc	Set maximum SVCs simultaneously open to one host per protocol
ops	Set default maximum output packet size
pad-access ·	Accept only PAD connections from statically mapped X25 hosts
pvc	Configure a Permanent Virtual Circuit suppress-called-address Omit destination address in outgoing calls
sup-call-add	Omit source address in outgoing calls
t20	Set DTE Restart Request retransmission timer
t21	Set DTE Call Request retransmission timer
t22	Set DTE Reset Request retransmission timer
t23	Set DTE Clear Request retransmission timer
th	Set packet count acknowledgement threshold
use-source-add	Use local source address for forwarded calls
win	Set default input window (maximum unacknowledged packets)
wout	Set default output window (maximum unacknowledged packets)

Use the following command to assign the address (given to you by your PDN) to the serial 0 interface:

```
SeansRTR(config-if)#x25 address 316013344323
SeansRTR(config-if)#
```

Next assign an IP address and netmask to the interface. Use the IP address 10.1.1.254, as shown below.

```
SeansRTR(config-if)#ip address 10.1.1.254 255.255.255.0
SeansRTR(config-if)#
```

Configuring an SVC

By using the x25 map command, you can provide a static conversion of higher-level addresses to X.25 addresses. This command maps a Network Layer address, such as the IP address of a host, to a peer host's X.121 address. Table 7.2 lists the meaning of the syntaxes of the x25 map command shown below:

```
X25 map protocol address x.121-address [option]
```

IP 200.851.3.3   310 555 1212

TABLE 7.2   The Syntaxes and Meanings for the x25 map Command

Syntax	Meaning
protocol	Selects the protocol type. Supported possible syntaxes are as follows: apollo, appletalk, bridge, clns, compressed tcp, decnet, ip, ipx, vines, and xns.
address	Identifies the protocol address identified by the protocol syntax.
x.121-address	Identifies the X.121 address supplied by the PDN.
option	This is an optional syntax used to customize a connection.

Now, you should use the x25 map command to map the IP address of 10.1.2.1 to the X.121 address of 316020344331, which is the router on the opposite side of our link, as depicted in Figure 7.9. The last syntax of the x25 map command is optional. Take a look at the possible options:

```
SeansRTR(config-if)#x25 map ip 10.1.1.25 316013344323 ?
  accept-reverse  Accepting incoming reverse-charged calls
```

options

broadcast	Send broadcasts to this host
compress	Specify Packet By Packet Compression
cug	Specify a Closed User Group number
idle	Specify VC idle timer
method	Specify encapsulation method
no-incoming	Do not use map for incoming Calls
no-outgoing	Do not use map for outgoing Calls
nudata	Specify user formatted network user ID
nuid	Specify Cisco formatted network user ID
nvc	Set number of virtual circuits for this map
packetsize	Request maximum packet sizes for originated calls
passive	Compress outgoing TCP packets only if incoming TCP packets are compressed
reverse	Use reverse charging on originated calls
rpoa	Specify RPOA
throughput	Request bandwidth in X.25 network
transit-delay	Specify transit delay (msec)
windowsize	Request window sizes for originated calls
<cr>	

FIGURE 7.9 The two sides of our X.25 link

IP address: 10.1.1.254
X.121 address: 316013344323

IP address: 10.1.2.1
X.121 address: 316020344331

You will now use the **broadcast** command because it is the one most commonly used. The broadcast option sends all the broadcasts sent through this interface to the following specified X.121 address:

```
SeansRTR(config-if)#x25 map ip 10.1.2.1 316020344331
broadcast
```

To configure multiple protocol addresses to be able to reach a single location, use the x25 map command with the following syntaxes:

```
Router(config-if)#x25 map protocol address [protocol2
address2]x.121-address [options]
```

This command allows you to communicate with a host across an X.256 link that understands multiple protocols over a single VC. Multiprotocol encapsulations are defined by RFC1356. There is a maximum of nine network protocol addresses that can be associated with one host destination in a single configuration command.

When using multiprotocol encapsulations over an SVC, bridging is not supported.

You can also create a configuration in which multiple circuits are configured to route different encapsulated protocol addresses. To illustrate this, supply an additional router with the IP address of 10.1.3.1 and an X.121 address of 316030121221 to the X.25 cloud, as shown in Figure 7.10.

FIGURE 7.10 An additional router in your configuration

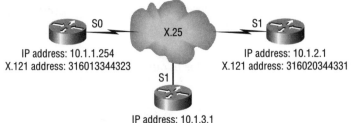

S0   X.25   S1

IP address: 10.1.1.254
X.121 address: 316013344323

IP address: 10.1.2.1
X.121 address: 316020344331

S1

IP address: 10.1.3.1
X.121 address: 316030121221

You will want any packets entering your original router with the destination address or IP address of 10.1.3.5 to be sent over the X.25 link so that they will arrive at the router with the IP address of 10.1.3.1. To do this, you would use the following configuration on your original router:

```
SeansRTR(config-if)#encap x25 dte
SeansRTR(config-if)#x25 address 316013344323
SeansRTR(config-if)#ip address 10.1.1.254 255.255.255.0
```

```
SeansRTR(config-if)#x25 map ip 10.1.2.1 316020344331
broadcast
SeansRTR(config-if)#x25 map ip 10.1.3.5 316030121221
broadcast
```

Configuring a PVC

Since you already configured an SVC by first assigning an encapsulation type, you must assign an encapsulation type using the same command as an SVC. Again, you can use the encapsulation x25 command to specify the encapsulation type followed by either dce or dte.

In addition to an encapsulation type, you must assign the X.25 address provided by your X.25 PDN again. Use the x25 address command followed by the PDN address. This command defines the local router's X.121 address.

At this point, the commands change. To establish an SVC, you used the x25 map command. To establish a PVC, you will use the x25 pvc command. This command will specify how a protocol will reach the intended destination. Table 7.3 looks at the command and meanings of the available syntaxes of the x25 pvc command that is shown below:

```
Router(config-if)#x25 pvc circuit protocol address x.121-
address [options]
```

PVCs are the X.25 equivalent of a leased line and are never disconnected. An address mapping using the x25 address command is not required before using the x25 pvc command.

TABLE 7.3   The Syntaxes and Meanings for the x25 map Command

Syntax	Meaning
circuit	This is the VC channel number, which must be less than the VC numbers assigned to the SVCs.

TABLE 7.3 The Syntaxes and Meanings for the x25 map Command *(continued)*

Syntax	Meaning
protocol	Selects the protocol type. Supported possible syntaxes are as follows: appletalk, bridge, clns, compressed tcp, decnet, ip, ipx, qllc, vines, and xns.
address	This is the protocol address of the host at the other end of the X.25 PVC.
x121-address	Identifies the X.121 address supplied by the PDN.
options	This is an optional syntax used to customize a connection.

Multiple circuits can be established on an interface by creating multiple PVCs on the same interface. Multiple protocols can also be routed on the same PVC using the following command syntaxes for the x25 pvc command:

```
Router(config-if)#x25 pvc circuit protocol address
[protocol2 address2] x.121-address [options]
```

Configuring an X.25 Virtual Circuit Range

In order to make sure that an incoming range of virtual circuits arrives at the opposite end of an X.25 link before a two-way range, use a PVC circuit number that comes before any configured SVC circuit number. The x25 command allows you to configure between 1 and 4095 virtual circuits. Table 7.4 lists the syntax, the description, and the default VC number.

TABLE 7.4 The PVC Command Syntax, Description, and Default VC Number

Syntax	Description	Default VC Number
lic	Low incoming circuit number	(Default 0)
loc	Low outgoing circuit number	(Default 0)

TABLE 7.4 The PVC Command Syntax, Description, and Default VC Number *(continued)*

Syntax	Description	Default VC Number
ltc	Low two-way circuit number	(Default 1)
hic	High incoming circuit number	(Default 0)
htc	High two-way circuit number	(Default 1024)
hoc	High outgoing circuit number	(Default 0)

Remember that a PVC number must come before any configured SVC numbers. Also, X.25 will ignore any events on virtual circuits that are assigned to a VC range. For instance, X.25 will consider any VC number an out-of-range VC and a protocol error. Because of this, a network administrator must specify the VC ranges for an X.25 attachment. It is very important that the X.25 DTE side of the link and the DCE side of the link have identical configurations on the DTE and DCE devices. The valid X.25 virtual circuit commands are listed in Table 7.5.

TABLE 7.5 The Valid X.25 Virtual Circuit Commands for Each Type of Virtual Circuit

Command	Type of VC
x25 pvc circuit-number	PVCs
x25 lic circuit-number or X25 hic circuit-number	SVCs, incoming only
x25 loc circuit-number or X25 hoc circuit-number	SVCs, outgoing
x25 itc circuit-number or X25 htc circuit-number	SVCs, bidirectional

Default Inbound and Outbound Packet Sizes

X.25 allows you to configure the maximum valid inbound or outbound packet size using the x25 ips or x25 ops command. The maximum input and output packet size should match on both sides of the X.25 link, unless you configure the end devices for asymmetric transmissions. Asymmetric transmissions are transmissions that occur at different bandwidths in different directions. Asymmetric Digital Subscriber Line is an excellent example of an asymmetric transmission. The downlink on an ADSL line is about twice as fast as the uplink direction. Should the devices on both sides of the X.25 be configured for different virtual-circuit maximum packet sizes, the link will most likely fail. Because fragmentation is a feature of X.25, the link size is configurable for the most efficient size for your network. When a packet arrives at the DTE device from the local network, the physical network can use larger packet sizes. This packet is broken up into smaller packets for transport over the X.25 link. This process is called fragmentation.

Your PSN provider should provide you with the most efficient packet size to use on your X.25 WAN connection.

In the x25 ips command, the ips syntax enables X.25 to deny packets that are larger than the configured size value. The ops syntax enables X.25 to begin fragmenting packets so that they are the correct configured size before they are sent out of the interface. The default packet size for inbound and outbound packets is 128 bytes, as shown in the example below:

```
SeansRTR(config)#int s0
SeansRTR(config-if)#x25 ops ?
  <16-4096>  Bytes (power of two)

SeansRTR(config-if)#x25 ops  128
SeansRTR(config-if)# x25 ips 128
```

The following packet sizes are valid for the x25 ips or x25 ops command:

- 16 bytes
- 32 bytes
- 64 bytes

- 128 bytes

- 256 bytes

- 512 bytes

- 1024 bytes

- 2048 bytes

- 4096 bytes

Configuring Window Sizes

The x25 win and the x25 wout command allow you to define the default window size so that it is between 1 and 127 for an X.25 interface. The window size represents the number of packets that can be received or sent before an acknowledgment is sent. The default is 2.

In the following configuration example, the x25 win and x25 wout will be set to 127.

```
SeansRTR(config-if)#x25 address 316013344323
SeansRTR(config-if)#x25 ips 1024
SeansRTR(config-if)#x25 ops 1024
SeansRTR(config-if)#x25 win 127
SeansRTR(config-if)#x25 wout 127
```

To use the x25 win 127 or x25 wout 127 commands, you must increase the packet numbering maximum *modulo* (a counter that must always be more than the configured maximum number of window sizes) to one above the maximum window size configured. The x25 modulo command specifies the packet numbering modulo and has two syntaxes, either 8 or 128. Therefore, a modulo of 8 allows VC sizes of up to seven packets, and a modulo of 128 allows the maximum VC window size of up to 127 packets. The default is a modulo of 8, and it is the one that is found in most networks.

Both ends of an X.25 link must be configured with an identical modulo value.

Verifying X.25 Configuration

To verify the configuration of X.25, use the `show interface` command to display the encapsulation type, LAPB information, the interface status, and counter information about an identified interface. The listing below shows an example:

```
SeansRTR>show interface serial0
Serial0 is up, line protocol is up
  Hardware is HD64570
  MTU 1500 bytes, BW 1544 Kbit, DLY 20000 usec, rely 255/
255, load 1/255
  Encapsulation X25, loopback not set
  LAPB DTE, modulo 8, k 7, N1 12056, N2 20
      T1 3000, interface outage (partial T3) 0, T4 0
      State DISCONNECT, VS 0, VR 0, Remote VR 0,
Retransmissions 0
      Queues: U/S frames 0, I frames 0, unack. 0, reTx 0
      IFRAMEs 0/0 RNRs 0/0 REJs 0/0 SABM/Es 0/0 FRMRs 0/0
DISCs 0/0
  X25 DTE, address 316013344323, state R1, modulo 8, timer
0
      Defaults: cisco encapsulation, idle 0, nvc 1
        input/output window sizes 2/2, packet sizes 128/
128
      Timers: T20 180, T21 200, T22 180, T23 180, TH 0
      Channels: Incoming-only none, Two-way 1-1024,
Outgoing-only none
```

X.25 Troubleshooting

This section will cover the primary troubleshooting commands used in troubleshooting X.25 WAN links and the most common troubleshooting issues. The items listed below will be covered in the following sections:

- The `show interface serial` command
- The `debug lapb` command

- The debug x25 events command
- Misconfigured x25 map commands

The *Show Interface Serial* Command

Many times, incorrect cabling or bad router hardware causes a problem with an X.25 link. To identify the problem, you can use the show interface serial command to determine whether the link is down. This command provides important information that is useful for identifying problems in X.25 internetworks. The following fields provide especially important information:

DISC field Identifies the number of disconnects.

FRMR field Identifies the number of protocol frame errors.

REJ field Identifies the number of rejected packets.

RESTART field Identifies the number of restarts.

RNR field Identifies the number of Receiver Not Ready events.

SABM field Identifies the number of set Asynchronous Balance Mode requests.

All but the RESTART fields identify Layer 2 events. Because X.25 requires a stable data link, LAPB Layer 2 problems commonly cause a restart that clears all virtual connections.

Debug Commands

You should exercise caution when using debug commands. It is vital to know this before you begin working with these commands. The main reason behind this is that most debug commands are processor intensive, and therefore, they can cause very serious network problems with degraded performance or losses of connectivity.

As soon as you are finished using a debug command, remember to disable it with its specific no debug command. If you are not sure of the command, use the no debug all command to turn off all debugging.

The debug commands are used only to isolate problems and not to monitor normal network operation. This is because the high processor overhead of debug commands can disrupt router operation. You should use debug commands only when you are looking for specific types of traffic problems and have narrowed your problems to a likely area of causes.

There are multiple ways you can use the **debug** command to verify Layer 2 connectivity problems. If the LAPB state is any other state than CONNECT, use the **debug lapb** command in privileged EXEC mode to look for SABMs being sent and packets being sent in reply to SABMs.

You can also use the **debug lapb** command to determine why X.25 interfaces or LAPB connections are continuously going up and down. This is useful for identifying link problems, as evidenced when the **show interface** command displays a large number of rejects or frame errors over the X.25 link.

You can also attach a serial analyzer to check SABMs.

If you are experiencing unexplained X.25 restarts, examine the underlying LAPB connection for the source of your problems. By using the **debug lapb** command, you will be able to display all traffic for interfaces using LAPB encapsulation.

The no debug lapb and no debug x25 events commands disable the debugging output.

Another helpful privileged EXEC mode **debug** command, if no SABMs are being sent, is the **debug x25 events** command. This **debug** command allows you to view RESTART messages for PVCs or CLEAR REQUESTS with nonzero cause codes for SVCs.

To interpret X.25 cause and diagnostic codes provided in the debug x25 events output, refer to the *Debug Command Reference* found on the Cisco CCO Web site at www.cisco.com.

Misconfigured *x25 map* Commands

To view X.25 mapping problems, use the **show running-config** command in privileged EXEC mode. Look for the **x25 map interface configuration** command entries and make sure that x25 map commands specify the correct address mappings.

To remove an X.25 mapping, use the no x25 map command, including the appropriate network protocol syntaxes, as shown below:

no x25 map *protocol address x121-address*

To reconfigure a new mapping, see the "Configuring an SVC" section above and refer to the x25 map configuration commands.

Summary

In almost every large network, you will find a WAN that connects multiple locations. Although there are many digital lines available that connect the two locations together, one of the most common protocol types that are used to transport your Layer 3 networking protocol data across the WAN link is X.25.

In this chapter, we took an in-depth look at the ways to configure an X.25 WAN connection and how to assign X.121 addresses to routers' DTE and DCE interfaces. Along with the ways to properly configure the links, we covered how to map higher-level addresses to X.25 addresses on the far end of the WAN link.

The last sections covered how to verify the X.25 configuration and some of the common troubleshooting approaches. This material allows an inexperienced person to troubleshoot X.25 and LAPB problems and obtain a clear picture of the current configuration problems.

Now that you have completed this chapter, you should be able to assign an X.121 address to a router interface and map higher-level addresses to X.25 addresses. You should also have a clear picture of X.25 routing as well as the X.121 addresses, which are the focus of questioning on the exam.

Key Terms

Before you take the exam, be certain you are familiar with the following terms:

Packet Layer Protocol (PLP)

PAD

Permanent Virtual Circuit (PVC)

Switched Virtual Circuit (SVC)

X.25 protocol

Commands in This Chapter

Command	Meaning
debug lapb	Provides debug information for the LAPB protocol.
debug x25 events	Provides debugging information on X.25 statistics.
encapsulation x25	Sets the encapsulation method to DTE or DCE.
no debug all	Stops all debugging functions.
no debug x25 events	Stops only X.25 events' debugging functions.
show interface serial	Displays the serial interfaces' configuration and statistics.
show interface	Displays all interfaces' configuration and statistics for X.25.
show running-config	Shows the current IOS configuration.
undebug all	Stops all debugging functions.
x25 address	Assigns an X.25 address to an interface.
x25 hic circuit-number	Sets the highest incoming VC number. Valid number range VC 1–4095.
x25 hoc circuit-number	Sets the highest outgoing-only VC number. Valid number range VC 1–4095.
x25 htc circuit-number	Sets the highest two-way VC number. Valid number range VC 1–4095.
x25 ips	Sets the maximum input packet size. Valid number range VC 1–4095.

`x25 lic circuit-number`	Sets the lowest incoming VC number. Valid VC number range 1–4095.
`x25 loc circuit-number`	Sets the lowest outgoing VC number. Valid VC number range 1–4095.
`x25 ltc circuit-number`	Sets the lowest two-way VC number. Valid number range VC 1–4095.
`x25 map`	Sets the LAN protocols–to–remote host mappings.
`x25 modulo`	Sets the sliding window sequence count to 8 or 128.
`x25 ops`	Sets the output packet size.
`x25 pvc`	Configures PVC encapsulation information.
`x25 win`	Changes the incoming window size.
`x25 wout`	Changes the outgoing window size.

Written Lab

This lab will test your knowledge of the X.25 commands that were learned in this chapter.

1. Write the command that will allow you to configure the X.121 address of 315013323432 to an X.25 interface.

2. Write the command that will allow you to verify the configuration of X.25 on the serial 1 interface.

3. Write the command that will allow you to configure the modulo on an interface to the maximum value.

4. Write the command that will allow you to set the inbound X.25 window size on a WAN interface.

5. Write the command that will allow you to set the inbound packet size to 64 bytes.

6. What command disables debugging of X.25 events?

7. What command would be used to set an interface to use the DTE encapsulation method?

8. Which command allows you to view LAPB debugging information?

9. Write the command that sets the lowest incoming VC number to 2.

10. Which command will allow you to disable all debugging functions?

Hands-on Lab

For this hands-on lab, take a look at Figure 7.11. This figure lists the IP address and the X.121 address assigned to each router. The router interfaces on both ends of the X.25 link must be configured to send traffic to one another as depicted in the figure. The following configurations on each router are only a suggested approach; there are a number of other approaches that can be made.

FIGURE 7.11 Lab configuration diagram

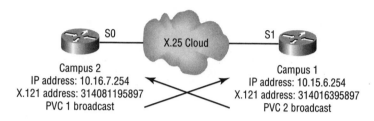

1. Configure Campus Router 1.

```
Campus1(config)#int S1
Campus1 (config-if)#encapsulation x25 dte
Campus1 (config-if)#x25 address 314016395897
Campus1 (config-if)#ip address 10.15.6.254
255.255.255.0
Campus1 (config-if)#x25 pvc 1 ip 10.16.7.254
314081195897 broadcast
```

2. Configure Campus Router 2.

```
Campus2(config)#int s0
Campus2(config-if)#encapsulation x25 dte
Campus2(config-if)#x25 address 314081195897
Campus2(config-if)#ip address 10.16.7.254 255.255.255.0
Branch(config-if)#x25 pvc 1 ip 10.15.6.254 314016395897
broadcast
```

Review Questions

1. Which of the following is not associated with the X.25 protocol suite?

   A. SVCs

   B. PVCs

   C. X.121

   D. PAD

   E. FDDI

2. Which of the following is not identified in the DNIC field of an X.121 call-setup packet?

   A. Sequence number

   B. Country code

   C. Priority number

   D. Packet Switched Network identifier

3. A PVC is configured to remain in what mode after initiation of an X.25 connection?

   A. Call-setup mode

   B. Data-transfer mode

   C. Idle mode

   D. Call-clearing mode

   E. Restarting mode

4. Which of the following ITU-T standards defines the standard format of an X.25 PLP call-setup packet?

 A. V.34

 B. X.21

 C. X.38

 D. X.121

5. NTN stands for which of the following?

 A. Node-to-node

 B. National terminal number

 C. Nation-to-nation

 D. Network-to-network

6. Which of the following Layer 3 WAN protocols is compatible with X.25?

 A. Frame Relay

 B. LAPB

 C. X.21 bis

 D. ISDN

7. Which of the following is not a PLP call-setup mode?

 A. Data-transfer mode

 B. Call-setup mode

 C. Call-transfer mode

 D. Idle mode

8. Which of the following occurs with X.25 if a data packet exceeds the maximum allowable packet size for the virtual circuit?

   A. The packet is segmented.

   B. X.25 terminates the circuit.

   C. The packet is discarded.

   D. The packet is e-mailed.

9. A PTI field identifies which of the following in a PLP packet header?

   A. General formatting of the PLP packet

   B. One of 17 packet types

   C. Whether the packet is destined for a DTE

   D. Whether the packet is destined for a DCE

10. Which of the following modes does PLP use to terminate a virtual circuit?

    A. Call-clearing mode

    B. Stop mode

    C. Call-termination mode

    D. End mode

11. Which LAPB frame is used to supply flowcontrol, frame sequencing, and error detection for full duplex?

    A. I-Frames

    B. S-Frames

    C. U-Frames

    D. D-Frames

12. Which of the following represents an SVC?

A. A connection that is a permanent connection and remains in data transfer mode

B. A connection that is a temporary connection made when data needs to be transferred

C. A connection that never terminates

D. All of the above

13. A PLP packet header does not contain which of the following? (Choose the two best answers.)

A. General Format Identifier

B. Zone Type Identifier

C. Logical Channel Identifier

D. Packet Priority

E. Packet Type Identifier

14. Up to how many packets does the `x25 modulo 128` command allow a VC window size to be?

A. 128

B. 8

C. 127

D. 512

15. In what PLP mode is an SVC connection if a virtual circuit is established but no data is transferred?

A. Stop mode

B. Idle mode

C. Sleep mode

D. Restarting mode

16. Which of the following commands can be used to troubleshoot an X.25 map? (Choose the best two answers.)

    A. `show int serial`

    B. `x25 map`

    C. `show running-config`

    D. `debug x25 events`

17. PLP uses which mode to create an SVC between two DTE devices?

    A. Start mode

    B. Data-transfer mode

    C. Restarting mode

    D. Call-setup mode

18. A GFI identifies which of the following in a PLP packet header?

    A. Whether the packet is destined for a DTE or DCE device

    B. One of 17 packet types

    C. The general formatting of the PLP packet

    D. The packet's priority

19. The PAD is located on an X.25 link between which two required devices?

    A. DTE device

    B. Switch device

    C. DCE device

    D. Router

20. Which of the following Layer 3 protocols can be used with the X.25 protocol?

A. Compressed TCP

B. DECnet

C. IP

D. Novell IPX

E. AppleTalk

F. XNS

G. All of the above

H. None of the above

Answers to Written Lab

1. x25 address 315013323432

2. Show interface s1

3. x25 modulo 128

4. x25 win 127

5. Config t
   Int bri0
   Dialer string 8358662

6. no debug x25 events

7. encapsulation x25 DTE

8. debug lapb

9. x25 lic 2

10. no debug all or undebug all

Answers to Review Questions

1. E. FDDI is a LAN topology and is not part of the X.25 protocol suite or discussed in this chapter.

2. A, C. The DNIC field of an X.121 call-setup packet contains a three-digit country code and a Packet Switched Network identifier, but it does not contain a sequence or a priority number.

3. B. Once a virtual connection is initiated, permanent virtual circuits remain in data-transfer mode.

4. D. The X.121 standard defines the ITU-T standards for an X.25 PLP call-setup packet.

5. B. NTN stands for national terminal number, which is part of the DNIC used to make an SVC connection.

6. A, D. Frame Relay and ISDN are WAN protocols found at Layer 3 that are compatible with X.25. LAPB is compatible with X.25 but is a Layer 2 protocol. X.21 is a protocol used with X.25 but is used at Layer 1.

7. C. Call-transfer mode is not a PLP call-setup mode.

8. A. The packet is segmented and a sequence number is assigned to each packet for error and flowcontrol.

9. B. A PTI field identifies if the packet is one of 17 packet types.

10. A. Call-clearing mode is used to terminate a virtual circuit. The other modes are not used on PLP.

11. A. Information frames are used to supply flowcontrol, frame sequencing, and error detection. Supervisor frames are used to send transmission requests, transmission suspensions, status reporting, and acknowledgments. Unnumbered frames are used to perform error reporting, link setup, and link termination. There is no such thing as a D-Frame.

12. B. Switched virtual connections are temporary connections. Permanent virtual connections remain in data transfer mode.

13. B, C. A Zone Type Identifier and Packet Priority are not found in a PLP packet header.

14. C. There are two syntaxes for the x25 modulo command: 8 and 128. An 8 indicates a window size of up to seven packets, a 128 indicates a window size of up to 127 packets.

15. B. If a switched virtual connection is established but is not transferring data, it is in idle mode.

16. C, D. The show running-config and debug x25 events commands are used to troubleshoot an X.25 map.

17. D. Call-setup mode is used to create an SVC between two DTE devices.

18. C. The LCI identifies whether the packet is destined for a DTE or DCE device. The PTI identifies one of 17 packet types, and the GFI identifies the general formatting of the PLP packet.

19. A, C. A PAD is located between a DTE device and a DCE device. A PAD is used to translate X.25 packets for terminals that are too simple to interpret X.25 packets.

20. G. All the above listed protocols in addition to bridging, Banyan VINES, and ISO-CLNS can be used with X.25 at the Network Layer.

Chapter

8

Frame Relay

THE CCNP REMOTE ACCESS EXAM TOPICS COVERED IN THIS CHAPTER INCLUDE THE FOLLOWING:

- ✓ Understanding and configuring Virtual Circuits (VCs)
- ✓ Configuring Data Link Connection Identifiers (DLCIs)
- ✓ Learning the three Local Management Interface (LMI) types
- ✓ Configuring Frame Relay
- ✓ Discussing and configuring Frame Relay congestion control
- ✓ Configuring subinterfaces
- ✓ Verifying Frame Relay
- ✓ Frame Relay switching
- ✓ Understanding the Committed Information Rate
- ✓ Configuring Frame Relay traffic shaping

he use of *packet switching* protocols has become the most popular method for moving traffic across a wide area network (WAN). One particular packet switching protocol, Frame Relay, has become the dominant player in the packet switching market. Other methods of passing data between routers across the WAN include dedicated lines, time division multiplexing, ATM, ISDN, DSL, and others.

As networks expand, you should pay particular attention to what is happening with DSL, but for right now, DSL still has too many distance limitations to replace Frame Relay completely anytime soon. However, since DSL is so much cheaper and faster than Frame Relay, it could eventually replace Frame Relay and ISDN as the dominant player in the WAN markets.

Understanding the theory and function of Frame Relay is important for numerous reasons. Not only is it heavily tested on Cisco's Remote Access exam, but when you get a Cisco-related job, you will probably see quite a few networks that depend on Frame Relay. Mastery of the information covered in this chapter should allow you to get an in-depth understanding of how and why you would implement Frame Relay on your internetwork.

What Is Frame Relay?

*F**rame Relay* is a telecommunication service designed for cost-efficient data transmission across the WAN. Frame Relay puts data in a variable-size unit called a *frame* and leaves any necessary error correction up to the endpoints. This provides for a high-speed, low-overhead, efficient network.

Frame Relay is a Layer 2 (Data Link Layer) connection-oriented protocol that creates virtual circuits, usually Permanent Virtual Circuits (PVCs), between two routers through a Frame Relay switch. A Frame Relay *bearer service* was defined as a network service within the framework of ISDN. It was designed to be more efficient than X.25. It was successful in this quest because it had a low overhead and required less error checking than X.25. It was also designed to take advantage of the full primary rate bandwidth.

The major difference between Frame Relay and traditional ISDN was that the control information needed to keep the link synchronized would not be a separate channel, like ISDN, but instead, it would be included with the data in this Layer 2 VC service. This single stream of data would provide for flow control, congestion control, and frame routing.

NOTE You should understand that the error and congestion control only works at the Data Link Layer and that Frame Relay also relies on upper layer protocols and applications for error correction.

A Brief History of Frame Relay

Currently, Frame Relay is the most prevalent type of packet switching used in North America; however, Frame Relay's origin is very humble. Initially, Frame Relay was not even a standard unto itself; instead, it was an extension of the Integrated Services Digital Network (ISDN) standard. The International Telecommunication Union, or ITU-T, (formerly known as the *Comité Consultatif International Télègraphique et Télèphonique*, or CCITT) was the first to define the Frame Relay standard.

Many companies that saw the value of this technology quickly adopted the ITU-T standard for Frame Relay. After these companies showed interest, ITU-T and other organizations proceeded to develop the standard, but very slowly. Several corporations saw a need for a more rapid development and implementation of a Frame Relay standard. These companies, including Digital Equipment Corporation (DEC), Northern Telecom (Nortel), Cisco, and Stratacom, bound together to form the *Group of Four*. This group began developing Frame Relay technology more quickly, which allowed Frame Relay to work on disparate routers. In September 1990, the Group of Four published *Frame Relay Specifications with Extensions*. This group eventually became what is currently known as the *Frame Relay Forum*.

Frame Relay Virtual Circuits

As mentioned earlier, Frame Relay is a Layer 2 (Data Link Layer) connection-oriented protocol. Once a connection has been established, end devices may transmit data across the network. This Layer 2 connection across the packet-switched network is called a *virtual circuit*.

The end devices (in this case, routers) will act as *data terminal equipment (DTE)* and the Frame Relay switch will be the *data circuit-terminating equipment (DCE)*. The most important difference between the two is that the DCE device is responsible for the clocking of the line. From the point of view of the router, the virtual circuit is transparent. Even though the circuit may traverse a large number of switches en route to its destination, the router simply sees its connection to the local Frame Relay switch. Figure 8.1 shows how routers see the Frame Relay network. In the figure, notice that Frame Relay is configured between the routers and the switching office.

FIGURE 8.1 Frame Relay Operation

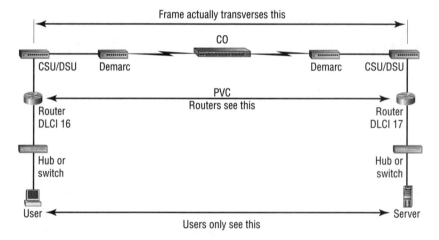

There are two ways for Frame Relay to establish this connectivity. Either you can set up a circuit that is enabled only when you need it using a Switched Virtual Circuit (SVC), or you can set up a dedicated circuit between you and your provider using a Permanent Virtual Circuit (PVC). Each of these will be discussed in more detail in the following sections.

[handwritten: provide unique address]

Switched Virtual Circuits

Switched Virtual Circuits provide an economical way to connect to a Frame Relay network. An SVC is a type of circuit that is brought up only when there is data to send. Because of this, these circuits provide temporary connectivity to the network on an as-needed basis. Switched virtual circuits are used with many technologies, like your standard telephone call.

It is rare to find a Frame Relay SVC connection. Indeed, you may never see one. Typically, PVCs are the only connections used with Frame Relay, although Cisco routers do support Frame Relay with SVCs.

Because they are rarely used, SVCs are not covered further in this book or on the Remote Access exam.

Permanent Virtual Circuits

[handwritten: DLCI]   *[handwritten: PNNI almost like anpt]*

Permanent Virtual Circuits (PVCs) are dedicated lines that are up and running 100 percent of the time (well, at least in theory!). Unlike an SVC, a PVC does not require the call establishment and call tear-down phases. However, when the circuit initially comes up, there are some parameter negotiations that do pass over the wire; these communications should occur only when the dedicated circuit goes down.

The two phases for PVCs are as follows:

Data exchange   Data is transmitted between the two devices. The end devices can transmit data as needed, and they don't need to wait for call to be established to do so. The data exchange can happen at any time since the line is permanent and always available.

Idle   The circuit is still active, but data is not being transmitted. The idle time can be indefinite: the circuits will not time out. The idle time keeps the VC up and the line from timing out when no data is present.

PVCs have gained popularity as the price for dedicated lines has decreased. They are the types of links we will configure later in this chapter.

[handwritten: ATM - NSAPe unique address, SPVC]

[handwritten: Rual PVP PVC PNNI SPVC SPVP example]

Data Link Connection Identifier (DLCI)

Frame Relay provides statistical time-division multiplexing (Stat-TDM). Time-division multiplexing (TDM) is like going to Disneyland. It's true. Remember how you have to stand in line to get into Space Mountain? Well, once you get to the loading area, you are placed in a section with rails that separate you from the other passengers. You can then only get into the one car that is in front of you and only when it is empty. Basically, think of the holding area as the interface buffers of a router; the cars would then be the timeslots on the circuit. When a timeslot drives up, you can get in, but not before, and not if someone is already in that slot.

Now, Stat-TDM, an improvement over straight TDM, allows you to jump into a different line if it is not in use and get into any car. This is a first-come, first-served technology. Stat-TDM is used with Frame Relay to allow multiple logical data connections (virtual circuits) over a single physical link. Basically, these circuits give timeslots to first-come, first-served and priority-based frames over the physical link. Going back to our analogy, you can think of Frame Relay as the ability to send multiple cars through space on one train, each car holding a different person.

So, how is each person (data) identified in the car (timeslot)? How does the frame switch know where to send each frame? The answer to this is something called a *data link connection identifier (DLCI)*. Since Frame Relay is based on virtual circuits instead of physical ones, DLCIs are used to identify a virtual circuit and tie it to a physical circuit. This means each frame can be identified as it traverses the Frame Relay switch and is then sent to the routers at the remote ends.

DLCIs are considered only locally significant, which means that they identify a particular circuit between the router and the Frame Relay switch, and they might not be unique to the internetwork. The provider is responsible for assigning DLCIs and their significance to the network.

DLCIs identify the logical virtual circuit between the CPE and the Frame Relay switch, and the switch then maps the DLCIs between each pair of routers in order to create the PVC. The Frame Relay switch keeps a mapping table of DLCI numbers to outgoing ports; it uses this table to forward frames out ports on the switch. (More information about mapping will follow in the next section.)

When configuring your Cisco router to participate in a Frame Relay network, you must configure a DLCI number for each connection. The switch provider supplies the DLCI numbers for your router. If a DLCI is not defined on the link, the switch will discard the frame.

Figure 8.2 shows an example of how DLCIs are assigned to offices in Chicago and Miami. The Chicago office will communicate through the Frame Relay switch to Miami using DLCI 17. Miami will communicate to Chicago using DLCI 16.

FIGURE 8.2   Frame Relay PVC configuration

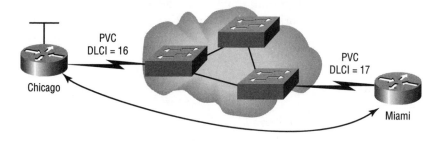

Some providers assign a DLCI in such a way that it appears that the DLCI is globally significant. For example, all circuits that terminate in Miami could be assigned the local DLCI 17 at each site. But remember that even though all of these DCLIs have the same number, they are not the same because DLCIs are typically only locally significant.

DCLI Mapping

There needs to be a way to link the Layer 2 identifiers (DLCI) to Layer 3 (network) addresses. *Mapping* provides a mechanism to map one or many network addresses to a DLCI. Remember that Frame Relay only works at the Data Link Layer (Layer 2 of the OSI model), and it does not understand IP addressing. In fact, to communicate via IP (since it could just as easily be IPX and AppleTalk instead of IP), you need to convert the destination IP address to a destination DLCI (PVC) number. The frame switch only uses DLCI numbers to communicate, not IP addresses.

Mappings can be done either statically by an administrator, or dynamically via the router. If you are trying to map a static Network Layer address to a

DLCI number, you use the `frame-relay map` command. You would create static mappings when the remote router does not support dynamic addressing, or when you are using OSPF in some network configurations, or maybe even if you want to control broadcasts over your Frame Relay network.

To explain how to use static mappings, we'll use Figure 8.3. Figure 8.3 shows a corporate office in Chicago connected to two other sites, one in Miami and one in New York. The IP address of the serial interface in New York is 172.16.1.2/24 and the Miami serial interface is 172.16.1.3/24. It is important to note that the Miami location is a Cisco router, and the New York location is a non-Cisco router. A static mapping would have to be used in order for different Frame Relay encapsulation methods to run under the same physical serial interface.

FIGURE 8.3   Configuring Frame Relay Static Mappings

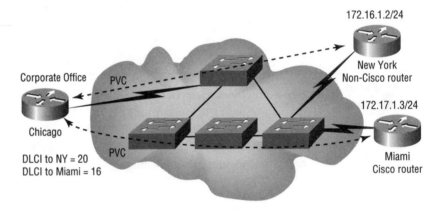

The following router output shows an example of how you would create static Frame Relay mappings on the Chicago router.

```
Router(config-if)#frame-relay map ip 172.16.1.2 20
broadcast ietf
Router(config-if)#frame-relay map ip 172.16.1.3 16
broadcast
```

The `frame-relay` map command maps the IP address of the remote location to a configured PVC. The first map statement tells the Chicago router that if it has an IP packet with a destination IP address of 172.16.1.2, it should use PVC 20 to get there. Also, since the New York office is not a

Cisco router (can you imagine that?), it should use the standard Internet Engineering Task Force (IETF) encapsulation method. We'll talk about encapsulation methods with Frame Relay in a minute.

Since Miami is a Cisco router, no encapsulation is necessary because Cisco is the default encapsulation. The broadcast statement at the end of each line specifies that broadcasts should be forwarded over the PVC since they are not forwarded by default. The `frame-relay map` command supports many protocols including the following: IP, CLNS, DECnet, XNS, and Vines.

Dynamic addressing is turned on by default. It then automatically maps Network Layer addresses to DLCI addresses rather well. *Inverse ARP (IARP)* can automatically map a DLCI to a network address (IP, IPX, etc.) without any user configuration. It provides Network Layer to DCLI number translation and creates a mapping table. This table is used by the router to route outgoing traffic. No map configuration is necessary for this to work.

Frame Relay Local Management Interface (LMI)

In 1990, the Group of Four developed extensions to the Frame Relay standard to ease the management and configuration burden. One of these extensions was the *Local Management Interface (LMI)*. LMI provides for virtual circuit status messages, multicasting, and IARP.

Cisco routers support three versions of the LMI standard: Cisco, ANSI, and ITU-T (q933a). Autosense, the automatic detection of the LMI type, was introduced in IOS version 11.2. Autosense determines the LMI type by rapidly trying them in order: ANSI, ITU-T (q933a), and then Cisco. If it cannot determine the LMI type within 60 seconds, it will terminate the autosense process and revert to the Cisco LMI type.

Once LMI is established between the router and the switch, the next stage is DLCI determination and IARP. The router will query the switch, asking what the DLCI is for this circuit. The router will configure itself with that DLCI and query the switch to determine the status of the circuit.

This query is the first stage of IARP. The query that is sent includes the local router's network information. The remote router will record the network information and reply in kind. The local router will map the DLCI it learned about from static or dynamic addressing to other network address it just discovered from queries.

When an IARP is made, the router updates its map table with one of three possible LMI connection states:

Active This indicates that the connection is active and that the routers can exchange data through the PVC.

Inactive This indicates that the local connection to the Frame Relay switch is working, but the remote route is not communicating to the Frame Relay switch.

Deleted This indicates that no keepalive (LMI) information from the switch to the router is being received.

Figure 8.4 shows that the Chicago office PVC to Miami is inactive because the Miami office is not receiving keepalives from the Frame Relay switch.

FIGURE 8.4 LMI Connection states

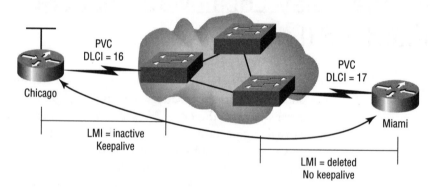

This inactive state does not affect the other connections (PVCs) that Chicago may have to other locations.

Configuring Frame Relay

The first step in configuring Frame Relay is to select the interface and then enable the Frame Relay encapsulation on the serial interface. You do this with the `encapsulation frame-relay` command. As you will notice in the router configuration commands below, there are two options: Cisco and IETF.

```
Router#config t
Router(config)#interface serial 0
Router(config-if)#encapsulation frame-relay [cisco or ietf]
```

Cisco is the default encapsulation, which means that you have another Cisco router on the remote end with which your router will communicate. You will use the IETF encapsulation when communicating with a remote router that is not a Cisco device.

Once you configure the encapsulation to the serial interface, you then need to add the Network Layer address, DLCI number, and LMI type. Cisco's ability to autosense the LMI type (when you are using the LMI configuration along with IARP) has greatly simplified configuration. The following router configuration shows the process of specifying the IP address and DLCI number:

```
Router(config-if)#ip address 172.16.10.1 255.255.255.0
Router(config-if)#frame-relay interface-dlci 16
Router(config-if)#no shutdown
```

Frame Relay Congestion Control

Frame Relay is optimized for speed and contains little error or congestion control. Ideally, users can send as much data as they want across the network without interference. However, because user requests for bandwidth always outstrip the network's ability to provide bandwidth, a mechanism is needed to handle congestion in the frame switch.

In this section, you will learn about the factors that impact network performance, as well as methods for handling Frame Relay congestion. The two primary methods of congestion handling involve using Frame Relay switches and routers.

Factors Affecting Performance

Network performance at the router level is affected by three primary factors:

- Access rate

- Committed Information Rate (CIR)
- Bursting

Each of these has an effect on Frame Relay.

Access Rate

Access rate is the maximum speed at which data can be transferred to the Frame Relay network. This number denotes the actual line speed of the connection to the provider. In a dedicated circuit, you would consider this to be the actual data rate. However, in a Frame Relay network, this is considered the maximum data rate. Oversubscription of the access rate can cause packets to be dropped.

Committed Information Rate (CIR)

Committed Information Rate (CIR) is the rate at which the provider guarantees to deliver network traffic. The CIR is always less than or equal to the access rate. The CIR is advertised in Kbps, but it is actually averaged over a specified time period, referred to as committed rate measurement interface (T_c). This is what the cost of the Frame Relay line is normally based upon.

Bursting

Bursting is one of the features that has made Frame Relay so very popular. Bursting allows a user to transmit data faster than the CIR for a short period of time. Figure 8.5 shows the difference between the CIR and the access rate, and how the burst traffic rate can increase beyond the CIR. This bursting ability is controlled by the network, and it usually does not incur any additional fees on the user. There is a catch, though. Some burst traffic has the *Discard Eligibility (DE) bit* turned on, indicating excess traffic. If a Frame Relay switch becomes congested, traffic with the DE bit set (burst traffic) is the first to be dropped.

FIGURE 8.5 Frame Relay Rates

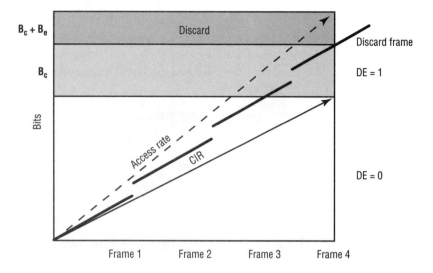

In Figure 8.5, you will see the following symbols. Committed burst size (B_c) and excess burst size (B_e) are the two types of burst sizes. Each of these sizes is measured over a specific time interval called the committed rate measurement interval (T_c). B_c is the maximum amount of data that the network can guarantee will be delivered during the time T_c. B_e is the amount of traffic by which the user may exceed the committed burst size.

For example, take a user who buys a Frame Relay circuit with the following characteristics:

- 1544Kbps access rate

- 256Kbps committed information rate

- Four-second committed time interval

The user is guaranteed a CIR of 256Kbps over a four-second period. The user could transmit 256Kbps for four seconds, and the network would ensure delivery. The user could alternately send 1024Kbps for one second, representing the committed burst. However, for the remaining three seconds, there would be no guarantee of delivery for the excess burst traffic.

Congestion Handling by Frame Relay Switches

A Frame Relay switch has a simple job: it forwards all the data that it can. If there is more data than bandwidth, the switch will first drop the data with the DE bit set, and then it will drop committed data if needed. In addition, the Frame Relay switch will also send out messages that congestion is occurring.

Backward Explicit Congestion Notification (BECN) and *Forward Explicit Congestion Notification (FECN)* are the primary notification mechanisms used for handling congestion on the Frame Relay switching internetwork. BECNs and FECNs both send notices that congestion is occurring. A BECN is transmitted in the direction from which the traffic came, and a FECN is transmitted in the direction in which the traffic is going.

Only Frame Relay switches send BECN and FECN messages.

The end devices receive notices indicating that they should reduce the amount of traffic that they are sending. A Frame Relay switch does not enforce the reduction; it simply notifies the end devices. It is the responsibility of the end devices to reduce the traffic.

The congestion mechanisms are important to understand because congestion occurs frequently on Frame Relay networks. As providers attempt to maximize the use of their lines, they sell more bandwidth than they can actually provide. This is called *oversubscription.* Oversubscription is a growing trend, so we must be aware of the implications and effects of the resulting congestion.

Some providers will attempt to sell you a zero CIR. Although inexpensive, you have no guarantee that mission-critical data (or any data, for that matter!) will get through.

Congestion Handling by Routers

The router can also play a part in determining which traffic is more or less important on the Frame Relay network. Discard Eligibility list (DE-list) and Discard Eligibility group (DE-group) give the router the ability to set the discard eligibility bit on a frame. Consider a company that has noticed an increased amount of dropped frames on the Frame Relay network. They have determined that the primary cause has been an increase in the amount of AppleTalk traffic across the Frame Relay network. The additional traffic has impaired the performance of mission-critical traffic.

To have the router turn on the DE bit for AppleTalk traffic, which will drop the non-critical AppleTalk traffic before any other traffic, use the `frame-relay de-list` command. Here is an example of how to configure a router to do this:

```
RouterA#config t
RouterA(config)#frame-relay de-list 1 protocol appletalk
Router(config)#int s0
RouterA(config-if)#frame-relay de-group 1 100
```

In the above lines of code, the `frame-relay de-list` command used a list number of 1 and a protocol of AppleTalk. The list number of 1 is then applied to the interface connected to the Frame Relay network with the `frame-relay de-group` command.

The modified router configuration looks like this:

```
RouterA#show running-config
Building configuration...

Current configuration:
!
version 11.2
!
!
frame-relay de-list 1 protocol appletalk
!
interface Serial0
 ip address 192.168.1.1 255.255.255.0
 encapsulation frame-relay
 frame-relay de-group 1 100
 frame-relay map ip 192.168.1.2 100 broadcast
!
end
RouterA#
```

The Frame Relay DE list will match AppleTalk frames. The `frame-relay de-group` command binds the list to the interface. In the event of congestion, these two packet types are much more likely to be dropped than mission-critical traffic. The 100 at the end of the `de-group` command specifies the use of DLCI 100.

Point-to-Point and Multipoint Interfaces

MBMA

There are times when it is useful to have a multipoint network behave as if each connection were a point-to-point connection. The network example in Figure 8.6 has two connections from one location (multipoint); this type of setup can lead to network problems if not thoroughly understood. The primary reason for the problems experienced with this multipoint configuration is the way it handles routing updates.

In distance-vector routing there is a property known as *split horizon*. This feature of the routing protocol states that it is never useful to send information back out on the interface through which is was learned. Or, simply put, "Don't tell me what I told you." This is used to stop possible routing loop problems. Consider the split-horizon implication of Figure 8.6:

FIGURE 8.6 Split-horizon issues with Frame Relay

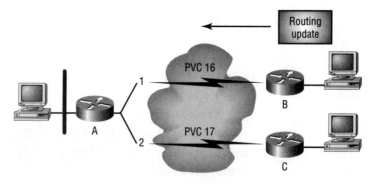

In this figure, Router B would send a routing update to Router A telling about its directly connected networks. Router A would receive the information on its serial 0 interface and modify the routing table on Router A. Router A would not send the information back out serial 0 because of split-horizon. Because the information could not be sent back out, Router C would never learn of Router B's network table entries, and therefore, the networks would be unreachable since Router C would not have heard of Router B's directly connected networks.

The problem in Figure 8.6 is that there is only one physical interface and two virtual circuits. The solution is to create a logical interface for each circuit, which automatically solves the split-horizon issues. A *subinterface* is a logical interface within the router that is mapped to a particular DLCI. When you set up a subinterface, the interface previously configured for multipoint will now appear as two point-to-point interfaces to the router. This would change the previous example, as shown in Figure 8.7.

FIGURE 8.7 Split-horizon issues with subinterfaces

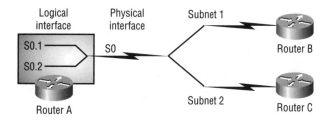

In this figure, Router A learns of Router B's networks on the Serial 0.1 subinterface. Without violating the split-horizon rule, Router A can send all the network information out on subinterface Serial 0.2 to Router C.

To configure a subinterface on an interface, use the `interface type.subinterface number` command. To configure Router A with a subinterface, the router commands would be as shown below. Both types of subinterfaces that can be configured appear in this code: point-to-point and multipoint. Point-to-point is used when each PVC is a separate subnet. Multipoint is used when all PVCs use the same subnet.

Also notice in the following configuration that you can use any subinterface number, but for administration purposes, the DLCI number can be used. The subinterface number is only locally significant.

```
Router(config)#int s0.?
  <0-4294967295>  Serial interface number
Router(config)#int s0.16 ?
  multipoint      Treat as a multipoint link
  point-to-point  Treat as a point-to-point link
```

```
Router(config)#int s0.16 point-to-point
Router(config-subif)#ip address 192.168.1.1 255.255.255.0
Router(config-subif)#frame-relay interface-dlci 16
Router(config-subif)#exit
Router(config)#int s0.17 point-to-point
Router(config-subif)#ip address 192.168.2.2 255.255.255.0
Router(config-subif)#frame-relay interface-dlci 17
```

The configuration of Router A will now look like this:

```
RouterA#show running-config
Building configuration...
Current configuration:
!
version 11.3
!
interface Serial0
 no ip address
 encapsulation frame-relay
!
interface Serial0.1 point-to-point
 ip address 192.168.1.1 255.255.255.0
 frame-relay interface-dlci 16
!
interface Serial0.2 point-to-point
 ip address 192.168.2.2 255.255.255.0
 frame-relay interface-dlci 17
!
end
RouterA#
```

This configuration specifies which DLCI is associated with which subinterface. This is necessary because LMI has no way of determining which particular DLCI should be associated with a subinterface. If you don't specify which DLCI goes with which subinterface, the two subinterfaces will be treated as if they were physical interfaces by the routing protocol.

Many people find the subinterface configuration easier and less prone to routing errors than using a multipoint configuration.

Verifying Frame Relay

It is just as important to be able to verify Frame Relay as it is to be able to understand how to configure it. In this section, you will learn about the various commands used to verify Frame Relay. These include the following:

- show interface
- show frame-relay pvc
- show frame-relay map
- clear frame-relay-inarp
- show frame-relay lmi
- debug frame-relay lmi

The *show interface* Command

The show interface command can be used with interface parameters, for example, show interface serial 0. This provides information pertaining to just serial 0. By itself, the show interface command provides information about all interfaces.

The show interface command displays information regarding the encapsulation, Layer 1 and Layer 2 status, and the LMI DLCI. Below, the show interface serial 0 command is used. Notice the encapsulation is Frame Relay. The LMI information is shown as well.

```
Router#show interface serial0
Serial0 is up, line protocol is up
  Hardware is HD64570
  MTU 1500 bytes, BW 1544 Kbit,DLY 20000 usec,rely 255/
255,load 1/255
```

```
      Encapsulation FRAME-RELAY,loopback not set,keepalive
set(10 sec)
      LMI enq sent  0, LMI stat recvd 0, LMI upd recvd 0, DTE
LMI down
      LMI enq recvd 0, LMI stat sent  0, LMI upd sent  0
      LMI DLCI 1023  LMI type is CISCO  frame relay DTE
      FR SVC disabled, LAPF state down
      Broadcast queue 0/64, broadcasts sent/dropped 0/0,
interface broadcasts 0
      Last input never, output never, output hang never
      Last clearing of "show interface" counters never
      Queueing strategy: fifo
      Output queue 0/40, 0 drops; input queue 0/75, 0 drops
      5 minute input rate 0 bits/sec, 0 packets/sec
      5 minute output rate 0 bits/sec, 0 packets/sec
         0 packets input, 0 bytes, 0 no buffer
         Received 0 broadcasts, 0 runts, 0 giants, 0 throttles
         0 input errors, 0 CRC, 0 frame, 0 overrun, 0 ignored,
0 abort
         0 packets output, 0 bytes, 0 underruns
         0 output errors, 0 collisions, 19 interface resets
         0 output buffer failures, 0 output buffers swapped out
         0 carrier transitions
         DCD=down  DSR=down  DTR=down  RTS=down  CTS=down
Router#
```

Notice the LMI information is shown, as well as the LMI type, which is Cisco by default. As you can see, this output shows both errors for the interface as well as when the interface counters were last cleared.

The *show frame-relay pvc* Command

The show frame-relay pvc command displays the status of each configured connection as well as traffic statistics. As you'll notice in the router output below, if you enter the command show frame-relay pvc, you'll see all the PVCs that are configured on your router and their status. You can also use a specific PVC number or parameters at the end of the command to see only that particular PVC information.

```
Router_A#show frame-relay pvc

PVC Statistics for interface Serial0 (Frame Relay DTE)

DLCI = 160, DLCI USAGE = LOCAL, PVC STATUS = ACTIVE,
INTERFACE = Serial0

   input pkts 7      output pkts 13      in bytes 2252
   out bytes 1886    dropped pkts 0      in FECN pkts 0
   in BECN pkts 0    out FECN pkts 0     out BECN pkts 0
   in DE pkts 0      out DE pkts 0
   out bcast pkts 8 out bcast bytes 1366
   pvc create time 00:06:54, last time pvc status changed
00:03:17

DLCI = 17, DLCI USAGE = LOCAL, PVC STATUS = ACTIVE,
INTERFACE = Serial0

   input pkts 1      output pkts 7       in bytes 30
   out bytes 832     dropped pkts 0      in FECN pkts 0
   in BECN pkts 0    out FECN pkts 0     out BECN pkts 0
   in DE pkts 0      out DE pkts 0
   out bcast pkts 7 out bcast bytes 832
   pvc create time 00:01:59, last time pvc status changed
00:00:49
Router_A#
```

As you can see, this command also shows you the number of BECN and FECN packets received on the router.

The *show frame-relay map* Command

You can see the current map entries and information about the connections with the show frame-relay map command. This will show your Network

Layer to DLCI mappings the router knows about. An example of this is given here:

```
Router_A#show frame-relay map
Serial0 (up): ip 172.16.1.2 dlci 500(0x64,0x1840),
dynamic,
               broadcast,, status defined, active
Router_A#
```

LMI used IARP to determine the address of the remote router and created this dynamic mapping.

If you wanted to clear out the Network Layer to DLCI mappings on a router, you can use the command clear frame-relay-inarp, which clears dynamically created maps on the router.

The *show frame-relay lmi* Command

The show frame-relay lmi command shows you the LMI statistics for an interface. An example is provided here:

```
Router#sh frame lmi
LMI Statistics for interface Serial0 (Frame Relay DTE) LMI
TYPE = CISCO
  Invalid Unnumbered info 0              Invalid Prot Disc
0
  Invalid dummy Call Ref 0              Invalid Msg Type 0
  Invalid Status Message 0              Invalid Lock Shift
0
  Invalid Information ID 0              Invalid Report IE
Len 0
  Invalid Report Request 0              Invalid Keep IE
Len 0
  Num Status Enq. Sent 109087          Num Status msgs
Rcvd 109087
  Num Update Status Rcvd 0              Num Status
Timeouts 0
Router#
```

The important statistic to notice is the number of enquiries sent and received. This is the number of status messages sent and received between routers. This allows you to see if data is passing between the two routers.

The *debug frame-relay lmi* Command

The debug frame-relay lmi command is used to help you troubleshoot and verify Frame Relay connections. As you'll see in the router output below, the (out) parameter is an LMI status inquiry sent out from the router, and the (in) parameter is a replay from the Frame Relay switch:

```
Router#debug frame-relay lmi
Serial0(in): Status, myseq 128
RT IE 1, length 1, type 0
KA IE 3, length 2, yourseq 128, myseq 128
PVC IE 0x7 , length 0x6 , dlci 16, status 0x2 , bw 0
Serial3/1(out): StEnq, myseq 128, yourseen 214, DTE up
datagramstart = 0x1959DF4, datagramsize = 13
FR encap = 0xFCF10309
00 75 01 01 01 03 02 C6 E5

Serial0(in): Status, myseq 129
RT IE 1, length 1, type 1
KA IE 3, length 2, yourseq 129, myseq 129
Serial3/1(out): StEnq, myseq 130, yourseen 129, DTE up
datagramstart = 0x1959DF4, datagramsize = 13
FR encap = 0xFCF10309
00 74 01 01 01 03 02 C9 E3
```

The type 0 is a LMI keepalive from the router to the Frame Relay switch every 10 seconds. This tells the router that the switch is still active. The type 1 is an IARP exchanged between routers every 60 seconds.

The DLCI 16, status 0x2 means the DLCI is active. However, you could receive a 0x0, which means the DLCI is not communicating to the remote router. If you receive a 0x4, it means the DLCI was deleted and the router is not communicating with the Frame Relay switch.

Frame Relay Switching

Routers are typically edge devices that connect your LANs to the Frame Relay network. However, you can use a router as part of the Frame Relay cloud or you can use it to create your own Frame Relay network. *Frame Relay switching* is the action of forwarding of Frame Relay frames based upon their DLCI assignments. We have seen how to configure a Frame Relay DTE device; now, we will look at how to configure a Frame Relay DCE switch. Routers are DTE devices by default; however, by changing an interface to a DCE, you can provide switching of frames.

Compare Figure 8.8 with Figure 8.9. Both of these diagrams represent the same network. In the Figure 8.8, you see the Frame Relay cloud without any detail. This is the normal way that you should think about the frame cloud. It is typically not your concern what happens within the Frame Relay network. Figure 8.9 shows that this particular Frame Relay cloud is a single router configured as a switch.

FIGURE 8.8 Logical Frame Relay Network

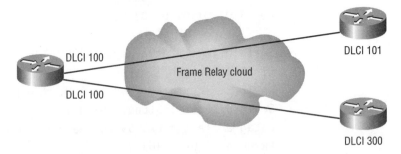

FIGURE 8.9 Physical Frame Relay Network

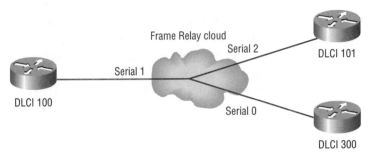

Frame Relay Switching Commands

The command used to enable Frame Relay switching on a Cisco router is as follows:

```
frame-relay switching
```

This command must come before any of the other Frame Relay switching–related commands can be executed, or these commands won't be allowed. When Frame Relay encapsulation is enabled on an interface, it defaults to DTE. For a serial connection to function, you must have a DTE at one end and a DCE at the other. You first configure the router with the following command:

```
frame-relay intf-type dce
```

The next step in the configuration process is to create the proper DLCI forwarding rules. These rules dictate that when a frame enters a particular interface on a certain DLCI, it will be forwarded to another interface and DLCI. Let's look at such an example on interface serial 1:

```
frame-relay route 100 interface Serial2 101
```

This command states that any frame received on interface serial 1, DLCI 100, shall be forward to interface serial 2, DLCI 101. You can view all the frame routing information with the show frame-relay route command. The router output below shows the configuration of Router A:

```
Router_A#show frame-relay route
Input Intf    Input Dlci    Output Intf    Output Dlci    Status
Serial0       300           Serial1        200            active
Serial1       100           Serial2        101            active
Serial1       200           Serial0        300            active
Serial2       101           Serial1        100            active
Router_A#
```

The configuration of a router as a Frame Relay switch can be useful for a lab environment or even part of a production network.

Now, let's look at the configuration of the Frame Relay switch:

```
Router_A#show running-config
Building configuration...
Current configuration:
!
```

```
version 11.2
!
frame-relay switching
!
interface Serial0
 no ip address
 encapsulation frame-relay
 clockrate 56000
 frame-relay intf-type dce
 frame-relay route 300 interface Serial1 200
!
interface Serial1
 no ip address
 encapsulation frame-relay
 clockrate 56000
 cdp enable
 frame-relay intf-type dce
 frame-relay route 100 interface Serial2 101
 frame-relay route 200 interface Serial0 300
!
interface Serial2
 no ip address
 encapsulation frame-relay
 clockrate 56000
 frame-relay intf-type dce
 frame-relay route 101 interface Serial1 100
!
end
Router_A#
```

Notice the global command frame-relay switching is at the top of the configuration. Also notice that both interfaces are configured with frame-relay intf-type dce commands. On the serial interfaces, you'll also see that the clock rate command is used to provide clocking for the line. This may, or may not, be needed. It is based on the type of network you are using.

Frame Relay Traffic Shaping

Traffic shaping on Frame Relay provides different capabilities, and since this information may be covered on the exam, it is important that you can describe each one. On production networks, this can help you understand whether switch problems are occurring.

The list below outlines the different traffic shaping techniques with Frame Relay.

- To control the access rate transmitted on a Cisco router, you can configure a peak rate to limit outbound traffic to either the CIR or Excess Information Rate (EIR).

- You can configure BECN to support a per-VC basis, which will allow the router to then monitor BECNs and throttle traffic based on BECN-designated packets.

- Queuing can be used for support at the VC level. Priority, Custom, and Weighted Fair Queuing can be used. This gives you more control over traffic flow on individual VCs.

It is also important to understand when you would use traffic shaping with Frame Relay. The list below explains this:

- You would use traffic shaping when the corporate office you are trying to set up a connection for has a higher speed line (for example a T1), and its remote branches have slower lines (for example 56K). On a VC, this connection would cause bottlenecks, and it would results in poor response times for time-sensitive traffic like SNA and Telnet. This can cause packet drop. By using traffic shaping at the corporate office, you can improve response between VCs.

- Traffic shaping is also helpful on a router with many subinterfaces. Since these subinterfaces will use traffic as fast as the physical link allows, you can use rate enforcement on the interface to match the CIR of the line. This means you can preallocate bandwidth to the VC.

- Traffic shaping can be used to throttle back transmission on a frame network that is constantly congested. This can help prevent packet loss. This is done on a VC basis.

- Traffic shaping is used effectively if you have multiple Network Layer protocols and want to queue each protocol to allocate bandwidth effectively. Since IOS version 11.2, queuing can be performed at the VC level.

In the following section you will learn more information about how to configure traffic shaping.

Configuring Traffic Shaping

To configure traffic shaping, you must first enter map class configuration mode so you can define a map class. You enter the map class with the global configuration command `map-class frame-relay [name]`. The name parameter is the name you apply to the VC where you want traffic shaping performed. The command would look like the following:

```
RouterA#config t
RouterA(config)#map-class frame-relay todd
RouterA(config-map-class)#
```

Notice that the `map-class frame-relay todd` command changed the prompt to `config-map-class`. This will not allow you to configure the parameters for your map class.

The map class is used to define the average and peak rates allowed in each VC associated with the map class. The map class also allows you to specify that the router dynamically fluctuates the rate at which it sends a packet, depending on the BECNs received. It also allows you to configure queuing on a VC basis.

To define the average and peak rate for links that are faster than the receiving link can handle, use the following command:

```
RouterA(config-map-class)#frame relay traffic-rate average
[peak]
```

The average parameter sets the average rate in bits per second, which is your CIR. The Peak is the CIR, which is equivalent to $CIR+B_e/T_c=CIR(1+B_e/B_c)=CIR+EIR$. The peak parameter is optional. An example of a line would be

```
RouterA(config-map-class)#frame relay traffic-rate 9600
18000
```

To specify that the router should dynamically fluctuate the rate at which it is sending packets depending on the number of BECNs received, use the following command:

```
RouterA(config-map-class)#Frame-relay adaptive-shaping
becn
```

To set bandwidth usage for protocols, you can configure traffic shaping to use queuing on a VC basis. To perform this function, use the following commands:

```
RouterA(config-map-class)#frame-relay custom-queue-list
number
RouterA(config-map-class)#frame-relay priority-group
number
```

You can use either command, depending on the type of queuing you are using. The number parameter at the end of the command is the queue list number.

Once the map class parameters are completed, you then need to configure the traffic shaping on the interface you want. The following commands are used to configure the map class parameters to an interface and then to an individual VC.

```
RouterA#config t
RouterA(config)#int s0
RouterA(config-if)#frame-relay traffic-shaping
RouterA(config-if)#int s0.16 point-to-point
RouterA(config-if)#frame-relay class todd
```

You first must enable traffic shaping on the interface with the frame-relay traffic-shaping command. You can then go to the interface or subinterface and assign the map class with the frame-relay class *name* command. The example above use the name todd since that is the name of the map class defined in the example earlier.

Once you have completed the configuration, use the show running-config and the show frame-relay pvc commands to verify the configuration.

Summary

In this chapter, you have learned about the theory and function of Frame Relay network, including the following:

- Frame Relay versus other technologies
- Frame Relay history and terminology
- Frame Relay congestion control
- Frame Relay point-to-point and multipoint
- Frame Relay switching

Frame Relay is one of the most popular WAN protocols in the world. The technologies will become even more critical as corporations stretch their networks globally and the Internet become more pervasive.

In order to become a successful CCNP you need to understand the Frame Relay protocol. Because this technology makes up the majority of the world's non-dedicated circuits, its importance cannot be underestimated.

Key Terms

Before you take the exam, be certain you are familiar with the following terms:

access rate

Backward Explicit Congestion Notification (BECN)

bearer service

bursting

Committed Information Rate (CIR)

data circuit-terminating equipment (DCE)

data terminal equipment (DTE)

Discard Eligibility (DE) bit

data link connection identifier(DLCI)

Forward Explicit Congestion Notification (FECN)

frame

Frame Relay

Frame Relay switching

Group of Four

Inverse ARP (IARP)

Local Management Interface (LMI)

packet switching

Permanent Virtual Circuit (PVC)

split horizon

Switched Virtual Circuit (SVC)

traffic shaping

virtual circuit

Commands in This Chapter

Command	Meaning
`clear frame-relay-inarp`	Deletes the dynamically assigned PVC to Network Layer addresses
`encapsulation frame-relay`	Sets an interface to use Frame Relay
`frame-relay adaptive-shaping becn`	Sets bandwidth usage for protocols
`frame-relay class name`	Assigns the map-class to a VC
`frame-relay custom-queue-list`	Creates a queue list to be applied to a VC
`frame-relay de-group`	Assigns the DE-list to an interface
`frame-relay de-list`	Creates a list of protocols or applications that will be set with the DE bit on

`frame-relay interface-dlci`	Sets a DLCI number on an interface
`frame-relay intf-type dce`	Sets an interface as a DCE Frame Relay switch
`frame-relay map`	Creates a static PVC to Network Layer mapping
`frame-relay priority-group`	Creates a queue list to be applied to a VC
`frame-relay route`	Creates static maps on a Frame Relay switch
`frame-relay switching`	Turns your router into a Frame Relay switch
`frame-relay traffic-rate`	Changes the traffic rates on a Cisco router Frame Relay interface
`frame-relay traffic-shaping`	Aligns the map-class to an interface
`int s0.16 point-to-point`	Creates a point-to-point subinterface
`map-class frame-relay`	Creates a map-class on a Cisco router to perform traffic shaping
`show frame-relay lmi`	Shows the LMI information on the router
`show frame-relay map`	Shows the dynamic and static mappings of DLCI to Network Layer addresses
`show frame-relay pvc`	Shows the configured PVC on the router
`show frame-relay route`	Shows the routes configured on the Frame Relay switch
`show interface`	Displays the line, encapsulation DLCI, and LMI information of an interface

Written Lab

In this lab, you will write in the answers to the following questions.

1. Write the command to see the encapsulation method on serial 0 of a Cisco router.

2. Write the command to configure s0 to Frame Relay encapsulation.

3. Write the command to configure a point-to-point subinterface number of 16 on serial 0.

4. Write the command to add the LMI type of ANSI to the subinterface 16.

5. Write the commands to configure the DLCI numbers for subinterface 16. Use PVC number 16.

6. Write the commands to configure the IPX protocol to be the first packets discarded in the frame switch if congestion occurs. Assign this to the subinterface 16.

7. Write the command to make your router a Frame Relay switch.

8. Write the command to see the line, encapsulation, DLCI, and LMI information of the serial interface.

9. Write the two commands that will show you all the configured PVCs on your router.

10. Write the command that will show you the Network Layer protocol to PVC mappings.

11. Write the command to create a map class.

12. Write the command to define the average and peak rate for links that are faster than the receiving link can handle.

13. Write the command that specifies that the router should dynamically fluctuate the rate at which it is sending packets depending on the number of BECNs received.

14. Write the command that will set the bandwidth usage for protocols on a VC basis.

15. Write the command to configure traffic shaping on an interface.

16. Write the command to configure the map class parameters to an individual VC.

Hands-on Labs

In this section, you will perform two labs. These labs both require a minimum of three 2501 routers. Figure 8.10 will provide you with a visual network layout for labs 8.1 and 8.2.

FIGURE 8.10 Frame Relay lab

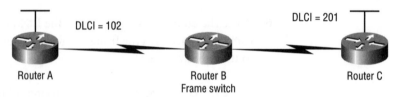

DLCI = 102

DLCI = 201

Router A

Router B
Frame switch

Router C

Lab 8.1: Configuring Frame Relay with Subinterfaces

1. Set the hostname, `frame-relay switching` command, and the encapsulation of each serial interface on the Frame Relay switch.

```
Router#config t
Router(config)#hostname RouterB
RouterB(config)#frame-relay switching
RouterB(config)#int s0
RouterB(config-if)#encapsulation frame-relay
RouterB(config-if)#int s1
RouterB(config-if)#encapsulation frame-relay
```

2. Configure the Frame Relay mappings on each interface. You do not have to have IP addresses on these interfaces because they are only switching one interface to another with Frame Relay frames.

```
RouterB(config-if)#int s0
RouterB(config-if)#frame-relay route 102 interface
Serial1 201
RouterB(config-if)#frame intf-type dce
RouterB(config-if)#int s1
RouterB(config-if)#frame-relay route 201 interface
Serial0 102
RouterB(config-if)#frame intf-type dce
```

This is not as hard as it looks. The frame-relay route command just says that if you receive frames from PVC 102, send them out int s1 using PVC 201. The second mapping on serial 1 is just the opposite. Anything that comes in int s1 is routed out serial 0 using PVC 102.

3. Configure your Router A with a point-to-point subinterface.

```
Router#config t
Router(config)#hostname RouterA
RouterA(config)#int s0
RouterA(config-if)#encapsulation frame-relay
RouterA(config-if)#clock rate 64000
RouterA(config-if)#int s0.102 point-to-point
RouterA(config-if)#ip address 172.16.10.1 255.255.255.0
RouterC(config-if)#ipx network 10
RouterA(config-if)#frame-relay interface-dlci 102
```

4. Configure Router C with a point-to-point subinterface.

```
Router#config t
Router(config)#hostname RouterC
RouterC(config)#int s0
RouterC(config-if)#encapsulation frame-relay
RouterC(config-if)#clock rate 64000
RouterC(config-if)#int s0.201 point-to-point
RouterC(config-if)#ip address 172.16.10.2 255.255.255.0
RouterC(config-if)#ipx network 10
RouterC(config-if)#frame-relay interface-dlci 201
```

5. Verify your configurations with the following commands:

```
RouterA>sho frame ?
  ip     show frame relay IP statistics
  lmi    show frame relay lmi statistics
  map    Frame-Relay map table
  pvc    show frame relay pvc statistics
  route  show frame relay route
  traffic Frame-Relay protocol statistics
```

6. Use Ping and Telnet to verify connectivity.

Lab 8.2: Frame Relay Traffic Shaping

1. Create a map class named lab2.

```
RouterA#config t
RouterA(config)#map-class frame-relay lab2
RouterA(config-map-class)#
```

2. Define the average and peak rates for Router A's serial 0 subinterface. Since the subinterface is the only link, we'll set the CIR to 56K and the EIR to a full T1.

```
Router(config-map-class)#frame-relay traffic-rate ?
  <600-45000000>  Committed Information Rate (CIR)
Router(config-map-class)#frame-relay traffic-rate 56000
?
  <0-45000000>  Peak rate (CIR + EIR)
  <cr>
Router(config-map-class)#frame-relay traffic-rate 56000
1544000
Router(config-map-class)#
```

3. Tell Router A to dynamically fluctuate the rate at which it is sending packets depending on the number of BECNs received.

```
RouterA(config-map-class)#Frame-relay adaptive-shaping
becn
```

4. Assign priority queue 1 to be used with the map class.

   RouterA(config-map-class)#**frame-relay custom-queue-list
   number**

5. Assign the map class serial 0.

   RouterA#**config t**
   RouterA(config)#**int s0**
   RouterA(config-if)#**frame-relay traffic-shaping**

6. Assign the map class to the subinterface.

   RouterA(config-if)#**int s0.102 point-to-point**
   RouterA(config-if)#**frame-relay class todd**

7. Use the show running-config and the show frame-relay pvc
   commands to verify your configuration.

Review Questions

1. Which two Frame Relay encapsulation types are supported on Cisco routers?

    A. ANSI

    B. q933a

    C. Cisco

    D. IETF

    E. Shiva

2. Which three Frame Relay LMI types are supported on Cisco routers?

    A. ANSI

    B. q933a

    C. Cisco

    D. IETF

    E. Shiva

3. Your site has a T1 connection to the WAN. The streaming video application you are using periodically requires 100 percent utilization of the T1. Which technology would be best for this application in order to ensure that no video frames are lost?

    A. Frame Relay

    B. X.25

    C. Dedicated circuit

    D. TDM circuit

    E. Not possible

4. Your site has a 256Kbps satellite link to the WAN. The circuit will be used by a variety of applications. The main concern is speed of delivery and cost. It is acceptable for some frames to be delayed and even retransmitted. Which technology would best suit this environment?

A. Frame Relay

B. X.25

C. Dedicated circuit

D. TDM circuit

E. Not possible

5. A provider can sell more bandwidth than the actual Frame Relay network can supply. What is this called?

A. Illegal

B. Zero-sum multiplexing

C. Frame stealing

D. Oversubscription

E. XOT

6. Frame Relay was first intended to work with what other protocols?

A. SNA

B. LAT

C. TCP/IP

D. X.25

E. ISDN

7. What are the types of VCs used with Frame Relay? (Choose all that apply.)

A. DLCI

B. PVC

C. Switched VC

D. LMI

8. What is used to identify the PVC in a Frame network?

   A. LMI

   B. BECN

   C. DLCI

   D. FECN

9. Your Frame Relay circuit is installed on a full T1 (1544Kbps). You were told that you would be guaranteed 256Kbps on the circuit. What is your access rate?

   A. Depends on the burst rate

   B. 256Kbps

   C. 512Kbps

   D. 1544Kbps

   E. Not possible to determine from information

10. You have a CIR of 256K and you are told your committed rate measurement interval is 10 seconds. What is your burst-committed rate?

   A. 256Kbps

   B. 2560Kbps

   C. 1544Kbps

   D. 15440Kbps

   E. 10

11. Which of the following is a feature of LMI?

   A. Status inquiry

   B. BECN

   C. FECN

   D. Inverse ARP

   E. DE

12. Your central site has a single serial connection to the Frame Relay cloud. You have five virtual circuits from your central site to the remote site. Your remote sites are not receiving routing updates. You suspect a problem with split-horizon. What would be a typical solution?

A. Static routes

B. Subinterfaces

C. Disable split-horizon

D. Route filtering

E. Modify administrative distance

13. You wish to configure your router so that it forwards frames based on their DLCI. What is this known as?

A. IP routing

B. Frame routing

C. Impossible

D. Frame switching

E. Frame tagging

14. For which of the following OSI layers is Frame Relay defined?

A. Physical

B. Data Link

C. Network

D. Transport

E. Session

15. What is used to tell a transmitting router to slow down because the frame switch is congested?

A. DLCI

B. BECN

C. FECN

D. LMI

16. What is used to tell a receiving router that the path the frame just traversed is congested?

A. DLCI

B. BECN

C. FECN

D. LMI

17. If you wanted to create a map class named bob, what is the command you need to use?

A. RouterA# **frame-relay map-class bob**

B. RouterA(config-if)# **frame-relay map-class bob**

C. RouterA(config-if)#**map-class frame-relay todd**

D. RouterA(config)#**map-class frame-relay todd**

18. What command allows traffic shaping on a Cisco Frame Relay link?

A. RouterA(config-if)#**frame-relay class name**

B. RouterA(config)#**frame-relay class name**

C. RouterA(config)#**frame-relay traffic-shaping**

D. RouterA(config-if)#**frame-relay traffic-shaping**

19. Once an interface is configured to allow traffic shaping, what command places the map class on the actual VC?

A. RouterA(config-if)#**frame-relay class name**

B. RouterA(config)#**frame-relay class name**

C. RouterA(config)#**frame-relay traffic-shaping**

D. RouterA(config-if)#**frame-relay traffic-shaping**

20. What is the solution of multipoint links and split-horizon protocols?

A. Frame Relay

B. ATM

C. ISDN

D. PPP

E. Subinterfaces

Answers to Written Lab

1. show int s0

2. Config t
   Int s0
   Encapsulation frame-relay

3. Config t
   Int s0.16 point-to-point

4. Config t
   int s0.16 point-to-point
   frame-realy lmi-type ansi

5. Config t
   Int s0.16 point-to-point
   Frame-relay interface-dlci 16

6. config t
   frame-relay de-list 1 protocol ipx
   int s0.16 point-to-point
   frame-relay de-group 1 100

7. Config t
   Frame-relay switching

8. Show interface

9. Show frame-relay pvc
   Show running-config

10. Show frame-relay map

11. map-class frame-relay *name*

12. frame relay traffic-rate *average* [peak]

13. Frame-relay adaptive-shaping becn

14. frame-relay custom-queue-list *number*
    frame-relay priority-group *number*

15. config t
    int s0
    frame-relay traffic-shaping

16. int s0.16 point-to-point
    frame-relay class *name*

Answers to Review Questions

1. C and D. Cisco is the default Frame Relay encapsulation type. Internet Engineering Task Force (IETF) is used to communicate between dissimilar routers.

2. A, B & C. The three LMI types supported are ANSI, q933a, and Cisco. Cisco is the default LMI type.

3. C. Although it may be possible to get Frame Relay to deliver the video, the best way to guarantee 100 percent of the bandwidth, with no drops, is a dedicated circuit.

4. A. When cost is a concern, packet switching technology is the solution. Both X.25 and Frame Relay are inexpensive, but Frame Relay is faster.

5. D. Oversubscription is what happens when the combined committed information rate exceeds the backbone capabilities.

6. E. Frame Relay was first flushed out in an ISDN RFC.

7. B, C. The two types of VC's used with Frame Relay are permanent virtual circuits and switched virtual circuits. Permanent virtual circuits are most frequently used.

8. C. The PVCs in a frame cloud are identified by the DLCI address.

9. D. Access rate is the actual line speed.

10. B. The burst-committed rate is the CIR multiplied by the measurement interval. In this case, it is 256Kbps multiplied by 10 seconds.

11. A and D. Local management interface provides for both status inquiry and inverse ARP. Inverse ARP provides a mechanism to map DLCIs to IP addresses.

12. A, B, and C. Most IP routing protocols support disabling split-horizon; however, IPX RIP and Apple RTMP do not. Static routes are a popular, but choosing them is an inflexible solution. Subinterfaces are the most popular and the best solution.

13. D. Cisco routers can be configured as Frame Relay switches.

14. B. Frame Relay is only defined at the Data Link Layer of the OSI model.

15. B. Backward Explicit Congestion Notification (BECN) is used to tell a transmitting router to slow down its transfer rate.

16. C. Forward Explicit Congestion Notification (FECN) is used to tell a receiving router that the frame switch is congested.

17. D. To create a map class, use the `map-class frame-relay name` command.

18. D. The interface command `frame-relay traffic-shaping` is used to enable an interface to accept map class parameters.

19. A. The command `frame-relay class name` sets the map class on a VC. The `frame-relay traffic-shaping` command must first be enabled on the interface.

20. E. Subinterfaces will automatically fix spit-horizon issues associated with routing protocols.

Chapter

9

Queuing and Compression

THE CCNP REMOTE ACCESS EXAM TOPICS COVERED IN THIS CHAPTER INCLUDE THE FOLLOWING:

- ✓ Defining and explaining queuing techniques
- ✓ Configuring queuing and verifying the configuration
- ✓ Explaining the differences between the Cisco queuing options
- ✓ Explaining the reasons for using compression
- ✓ Explaining the different compression methods used with Cisco routers
- ✓ Configuring and verifying the various compression methods

This chapter will teach you how to use both queuing and compression to help maintain a healthy network, which is important because user data consists of many different types of data packets roaming the internetwork, hungering for and consuming bandwidth.

As a network administrator, you can help save precious bandwidth on WAN links, the largest bottlenecks in today's networks. With Gigabit Ethernet running the core backbones and 10-gigabit Ethernet networks just around the corner, a 1.544Mbps T-1 link is painfully slow. By implementing both queuing and compression techniques, you can help save bandwidth and get the most for your money from the WAN.

In addition, this chapter will teach you the three queuing techniques available on the Cisco router. These techniques are weighted fair queuing, priority queuing, and custom queuing. You will learn when to use each type of queuing, as well as how to configure each type of queuing on your router.

Finally, this chapter will provide the information you need to both understand the different types of compression on Cisco routers and configure each type. The types of compression covered in this chapter include header, payload, and link compression techniques.

Queuing

When a packet arrives on a router's interface, a protocol-dependent switching process handles it. The router then switches the traffic to the outgoing interface buffer. An example of a protocol-dependent switching process is first-in, first-out (FIFO), which is the original algorithm for packet transmission. FIFO was the default for all routers until weighted fair queuing (WFQ) was developed. The problem with FIFO is that transmission occurs in the same order as messages are received. If an end user required traffic to be reordered, the department or company needed to establish a queuing policy other than FIFO queuing.

Cisco IOS software offers three queuing options as an alternative to FIFO queuing:

Weighted fair queuing (WFQ) Prioritizes interactive traffic over file transfers to ensure satisfactory response time for common user applications.

Priority queuing Ensures timely delivery of a specific protocol or type of traffic that is transmitted before all others.

Custom queuing Establishes bandwidth allocations for each different type of traffic.

We will discuss these three queuing options in detail throughout this chapter.

Traffic Prioritization

Packet prioritization has become more important in the network because many different types of data traffic need to share a data path through the network, often congesting WAN links. If the WAN link is not congested, you don't need to implement traffic prioritization, although it might be appropriate to add more bandwidth in certain situations.

Prioritization of traffic will be required on your network if you have, for example, a mixture of file transfer, transaction-based, and desktop video conferencing. Prioritization is most effective on WAN links where the combination of bursty traffic and relatively lower data rates can cause temporary congestion. This is typically only necessary on WAN links slower than T-1/E-1. However, prioritization can also be used across OC (Optical Carrier)-12 and OC-48 links, because at times tests can be run to saturate these links, but you may still want voice and video to have a priority.

Queuing Policy

Queuing policies help network managers provide users with a high level of service across a WAN link, as well as control WAN costs. Typically, the corporate goal is to deploy and maintain a single enterprise network even

[handwritten margin notes]

though the network supports disparate applications, organizations, technologies, and user expectations. Consequently, network managers are concerned about providing all users with an appropriate level of service while continuing to support mission-critical applications and having the ability to integrate new technologies at the same time. Figure 9.1 shows a serial interface that is congested and needs queuing implemented. It is important to remember that you need to implement queuing only on interfaces that experience congestion.

FIGURE 9.1 Queuing policy

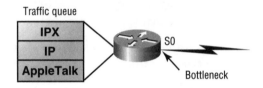

The network administrator should understand the delicate balance between meeting the business requirements of users and controlling WAN costs. Queuing allows network administrators to effectively manage network resources.

IOS Queuing Options

If your serial links are not congested, you do not need to implement queuing. However, if the load exceeds the transmission rate for small periods of time, then you can use a Cisco IOS queuing option to help the congestion on a serial link.

To effectively configure queuing on a serial link, you must understand the different types of queuing available. If you choose the wrong type of queuing, you can actually harm the link instead of helping it. Also, this is not a one-time analysis of traffic patterns. You must constantly repeat your analysis of your serial link congestion to make sure you have implemented the queuing strategy correctly.

Figure 9.2 shows the different queuing options available from Cisco.

FIGURE 9.2 Queuing options

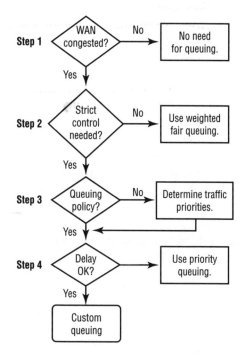

The list below describes the analysis you should take when deciding on a queuing policy:

1. Determine whether the WAN is congested.

2. Decide whether strict control over traffic prioritization is necessary and whether automatic configuration is acceptable.

3. Establish a queuing policy.

4. Determine whether any of the traffic types you identified in your traffic pattern analysis can tolerate a delay.

Weighted Fair Queuing

Weighted fair queuing (WFQ) provides equal amounts of bandwidth to each conversation that traverses the interface using a process that refers to the timestamp found on the last bit of a packet as it enters the queue.

Assigning Priorities

WFQ assigns a high priority to all low-volume traffic. Figure 9.3 demonstrates how the timing mechanism for priority assignment occurs. The algorithm determines which frames belong to either a high-volume or low-volume conversation and forwards out the low-volume packets from the queue first. Through this timing convention, remaining packets can be assigned an exiting priority.

In Figure 9.3, packets are labeled A through F. As depicted in the diagram, Packet A will be forwarded out first because it's part of a low-volume conversation, even though the last bit of session B will arrive before the last bit of the packets associated with Packet A did. The remaining packets are divided between the two high-traffic conversations, with their timestamps determining the order in which they will exit the queue.

FIGURE 9.3 Priority assignment using WFQ

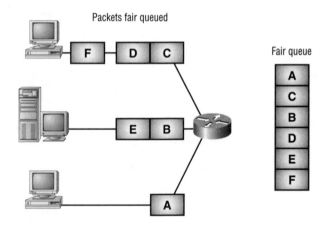

• Conversations are assigned a channel.

• Sorts the queue by order of the last bit crossing its channel

Assigning Conversations

We've discussed how priority is assigned to a packet or conversation, but it's also important to understand the type of information the processor needs to associate a group of packets with an established conversation.

The most common elements used to establish a conversation are as follows:

- Source and destination IP addresses
- MAC addresses
- Port numbers
- Type of service
- DLCI number assigned to an interface

If a router has two active conversations, one a large FTP transfer and the other an HTTP session, the router, using some or all of the above factors to determine which conversation a packet belongs to, allocates equal amounts of bandwidth for the conversations. Each of the two conversations receives half of the available bandwidth.

Configuring Weighted Fair Queuing

You're now ready to learn how to configure WFQ. For all interfaces having a line speed equal to or lower than 2.048Mbps (E-1 speed), WFQ is on by default. Here's an example of how WFQ is configured on an interface. You can use this command to alter the default settings:

```
Router_C#conf t
Enter configuration commands, one per line. End with CNTL/Z.
Router_C(config)#int s0
Router_C(config-if)#fair-queue 96
Router_C(config-if)#^Z
Router_C#
```

To understand what was done, let's look at the syntax of the command:

```
fair-queue {congestive-discard-threshold [dynamic-queues
[reservable-queues]]}
```

Congestive-discard-threshold Is a value from 1 to 512 that specifies the number of conversations that can exist within the queue. Once this number is exceeded, the following conversations won't be allocated their equal amount of bandwidth. Without a place in the queue, new conversations will be dropped. The default value is 64.

Dynamic-queues   Are exactly that—queues established dynamically to handle conversations that don't have special requirements. The valid values for this option are 16, 32, 64, 128, 256, 512, 1024, 2048, and 4096, with the default value being 256.

Reservable-queues   Define the number of queues established to handle conversations. The available range is from zero to 1000, with the default being zero. These queues are for interfaces that use RSVP (Resource Reservation Protocol).

Verifying Weighted Fair Queuing

Now that WFQ is configured on our router's serial 0 interface, let's see what it's doing. To verify the configuration and operation of the queuing system, we can issue the following two commands:

```
show queueing [fair | priority | custom]
show queue [interface-type interface-number]
```

When you use the show commands, note that *queuing* is misspelled. It has that extra "e."

Results from these commands on Router C can be seen below. Since WFQ is the only type of queuing that's been enabled on this router, it wasn't necessary to issue the optional commands of `fair`, `custom`, or `priority`.

```
Router_C#show queueing
Current fair queue configuration:

    Interface  Discard      Dynamic       Reserved
               threshold    queue count   queue count
    Serial0       96          256            0
    Serial1       64          256            0

Current priority queue configuration:
Current custom queue configuration:
Current RED queue configuration:
Router_C#
```

This command shows us that WFQ is enabled on both serial interfaces and that the discard threshold for serial 0 was changed from 64 to 96. There's a maximum of 256 dynamic queues for both interfaces—the default value. The lines following the interface information are empty because their corresponding queuing algorithms haven't been configured yet.

The next command displays more detailed information pertaining to the specified interface:

```
Router_C#show queue serial0
 Input queue: 0/75/0 (size/max/drops); Total output drops: 0
 Queueing strategy: weighted fair
 Output queue: 0/1000/96/0 (size/max total/threshold/
 drops)
    Conversations 0/1/256 (active/max active/max total)
    Reserved Conversations 0/0 (allocated/max allocated)
```

The input queue information is explained, as is the size of the queue, the maximum size of the queue, and the number of conversations that have been dropped. The algorithm is defined as WFQ. The output queue (usually the one with the most activity) defines the size, maximum number of output queues, number of conversations per queue, and number of conversations dropped. The number of conversations represents the number of conversations in the queue, and active describes the number of active conversations in it. The max active keeps a record of the maximum number of active conversations, and finally, max total gives the number of all conversations within the queue. Reserved queues are also displayed by issuing the following command:

```
show queue serial0
```

Priority Queuing

Priority queuing occurs on a packet basis instead of a session basis and is ideal in network environments that carry time-sensitive applications or protocols. When congestion occurs on low-speed interfaces, priority queuing guarantees that traffic assigned a high priority will be sent first. In turn, if the queue for high-priority traffic is always full, monopolizing bandwidth, packets in the other queues will be delayed or dropped.

Assigning Priorities

The header information that priority queuing uses consists of either the TCP port or the protocol being used to transport the data. When a packet enters the router, it's compared against a list that will assign a priority to it and forward it to the corresponding queue.

Priority queuing can assign a packet four different priorities: high, medium, normal, and low, with a separate dispatching algorithm to manage the traffic in all four. Figure 9.4 shows how these queues are serviced—you can see that the algorithm starts with the high-priority queue processing all the data there. When that queue is empty, the dispatching algorithm moves down to the medium-priority queue, and so on down the priority chain, performing a cascade check of each queue before moving on. So if the algorithm finds packets in a higher-priority queue, it will process them first before moving on. This is where problems can develop; traffic in the lower queues could be totally neglected in favor of the higher ones if they're continually busy with the arrival of new packets.

FIGURE 9.4 Using priority queuing

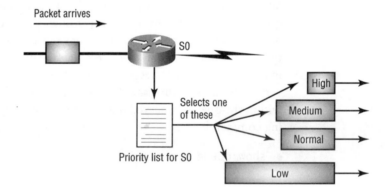

Configuring Priority Queuing

Implementing priority queuing on an interface requires three steps:

1. Create a priority list that the processor will use to determine packet priority.

2. Adjust the size of the queues if desired.

3. Apply the priority list to the desired interfaces.

Let's go over how to build a priority list. Start by using the following command:

```
priority-list list-number {[protocol protocol-name] |
[interface interface-type] (high | medium | normal | low)
| default | queue-limit]} queue-keyword
```

List-number identifies the list, and its valid values are 1 through 16. The protocol option directs the list to assign priorities based on the protocol, and protocol-name defines which protocol to match. With the interface option, the physical interface is listed, along with the type of queue that pertains to it. Next, after specifying the protocol or interface, the type of queue needs to be defined—high, medium, normal, or low.

The same priority-list command can be used to configure a default queue for traffic that doesn't match the priority list and that you do not want placed in the normal queue.

Queue-limit is used to create the size limits of the queue. The configuration of the queue size must be handled carefully, because if a packet is forwarded to the appropriate queue but the queue is full, the packet will be discarded—even if bandwidth is available. This means that enabling priority queuing on an interface can be useless (even destructive) if queues aren't accurately configured to respond to actual network needs. It's important to make the queues large enough to accommodate congestion so that the influx of packets can be accepted and stored until they can be forwarded.

Queue-keyword allows packets to be compared by their byte count, existing access list, protocol port number, or name and fragmentation.

The above commands create the priority list, which you can then apply to an interface with the following command:

```
priority-group list
```

List is the priority list number from 1 to 16. Once the list is applied to the interface, it is implicitly applied outbound. All packets will be checked against the priority list before entering their corresponding queue. The ones that don't match will be placed in the default queue. Here's an example:

```
Router_C#conf t
Enter configuration commands, one per line. End with CNTL/Z.
Router_C(config)#priority-list 1 protocol ip high gt 1500
Router_C(config)#priority-list 1 protocol ip low lt 256
```

```
Router_C(config)#priority-list 1 protocol ip normal
Router_C(config)#priority-list 1 interface serial 1 normal
Router_C(config)#priority-list 1 interface ethernet 0 high
Router_C(config)#priority-list 1 default normal
Router_C(config)#priority-list 1 queue-limit 40 80 120 160
Router_C(config)#interface serial 0
Router_C(config-if)#priority-group 1
Router_C(config-if)#^Z
Router_C#
```

apply →

The first line of the priority list assigns high priority to all IP traffic with a packet size greater than 1500, and the second line assigns low priority to IP traffic with a packet size lower than 256. The next line assigns all remaining IP traffic to the normal queue. The following line (line 4) assigns all incoming traffic on serial 1 to the normal queue also. All incoming traffic on ethernet 0 is assigned a high priority, and any remaining traffic will be assigned normal priority. The size of all the queues is defined by the `queue-limit`, and their numbers follow the order of their high, medium, normal, and low queue sizes.

Below is an example of what the interface configuration looks like. The priority list has been assigned to the interface with the `priority-group` command. You can see the final form of the applied priority list following the interface configuration.

```
!
interface Serial0
 ip address 172.16.40.6 255.255.255.252
 priority-group 1
!
priority-list 1 protocol ip high gt 1500
priority-list 1 protocol ip low lt 256
priority-list 1 protocol ip normal
priority-list 1 interface Serial1 normal
priority-list 1 interface Ethernet0 high
priority-list 1 queue-limit 40 80 120 180
```

Verifying Priority Queuing

To make sure the queuing configuration is working and configured properly, you can use the same command used to verify WFQ with the added option for priority queuing.

The following information summarizes the above priority list:

```
Router_C#show queueing priority
Current priority queue configuration:

List  Queue  Args
1    high   protocol ip      gt 1500
1    low    protocol ip      lt 256
1    normal protocol ip
1    normal interface Serial1
1    high   interface Ethernet0
1    high   limit 40
1    medium limit 80
1    normal limit 120
1    low    limit 160
Router_C#
```

Custom Queuing

Custom queuing functions on the concept of sharing bandwidth among traffic types. Instead of assigning a priority classification to a specific traffic or packet type, custom queuing forwards traffic in the different queues by referencing FIFO. Custom queuing offers the ability to customize the amount of actual bandwidth a specified traffic type uses.

While remaining within the limits of the physical line's capacity, virtual pipes are configured through the custom queuing option. Varying amounts of the total bandwidth are reserved for various specific traffic types, and if the bandwidth isn't being fully utilized by its assigned traffic type, other types can access it. The configured limits go into effect during high levels of utilization or when congestion on the line causes different traffic types to compete for bandwidth.

Figure 9.5 shows each queue being processed, one after the other. Once this begins, the algorithm checks the first queue, processes the data within it, then moves to the next—if it comes across an empty one, it will simply move on without hesitating. Each queue's *byte-count* specifies the amount of data that will be forwarded, which directs the algorithm to move to the next queue once it's been attained. Custom queuing permits a maximum of 16 configurable queues.

FIGURE 9.5 Custom queuing algorithm

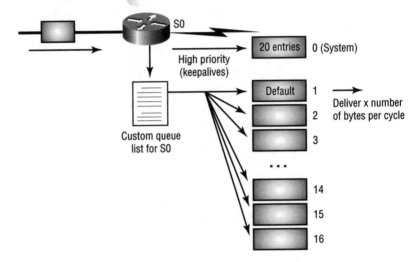

Figure 9.6 shows how the bandwidth allocation via custom queuing looks relative to the physical connection. Using the frame size of the protocols and configuring the byte-count for each different queue configures bandwidth allocations.

FIGURE 9.6 Bandwidth allocation using custom queuing

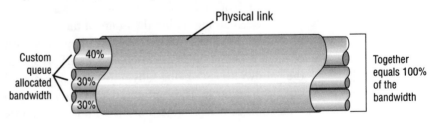

Configuring Custom Queuing

Configuring custom queuing is similar to configuring priority queuing, but instead of completing three tasks, you must complete five. As with priority queuing, you have to configure a list to separate types of incoming traffic into their desired queues. After that, you must configure a default queue for the traffic unassigned to any of the other queues. Once your specific and default queues are defined, you can adjust the capacity or size of each queue or just stick with the default settings.

When that's complete, specify the transfer rate, or byte-count, for each queue. This is important—the byte-count determines the percentage of bandwidth reserved for a specified queue. After these parameters are set, apply them to an interface.

The commands used to configure the queuing list, default queue, queue size, and transmit rate follow. Here's the command syntax:

```
queue-list list-number {default | interface [interface-
type interface-number] | lowest-custom | protocol
[protocol-name] | queue [queue-number byte-count | limit ]
| stun } queue-number queue-keyword keyword-value
```

The syntax may be presented in many different ways to configure the desired command. *List-number* is a value from 1 to 16 and associates the list with the given number. The following are available options:

Default   Designates a custom queue for packets that didn't match the queue-list.

Interface   Assigns priorities for incoming packets on the specified physical interface.

Lowest-custom   Specifies the lowest queue number considered a custom queue.

Protocol   Indicates that the packets are to be sorted by protocol.

Queue   Allows for specific queue parameters to be configured.

Stun   Establishes queuing priority for STUN packets.

When the interface option is specified, you must supply the *interface-type* and *interface-number* as well. *Interface-type* is the type of physical interface, and *interface-number* is the interface's physical port.

The protocol option also requires additional information. Obviously, the *protocol-name* must be specified. In Table 9.1, we list the available protocol names. After supplying the *queue-number*, you may supply the *keyword-value* to refine the protocols and port numbers used for filtering.

TABLE 9.1 Available Protocol Names

Protocol Name	Description
aarp	AppleTalk ARP
appletalk	AppleTalk
arp	IP ARP
bridge	Bridging
cdp	Cisco Discovery Protocol
compressedtcp	Compressed TCP
decnet	DECnet
decnet_node	DECnet Node
decnet_router-l1	DECnet Router L1
decnet_router-l2	DECnet Router L2
ip	IP
llc2	Llc2
pad	PAD links
snapshot	Snapshot routing support
ipx	Novell IPX

Table 9.2 lists the available keyword values.

TABLE 9.2 Available Keyword Values

Keyword Value	Description
fragments	Prioritize IP fragments
gt	Greater than specified value
list	Access list
lt	Less than specified value
tcp	TCP packets
udp	UDP packets

To define the parameter of the custom queues, you use the queue option. After specifying the *queue-number*, you're given two different parameters to configure:

Limit Allows you to change the queue size.

Byte-count Specifies the rate at which the queues will be emptied.

Configuring Byte-Count

Configure the byte-count queues carefully, because if the setting is too high, the algorithm will take a longer time than necessary to move from one queue to the next. This is not a problem while the processor empties the queue, but if it takes the processor too long to get back to the queue, the queue could fill up and start dropping packets.

This is why it's important to understand how to configure the bandwidth percentage relationship using the byte-count command. Since frame sizes vary from protocol to protocol, you'll need to know the exact frame sizes of the protocols transiting the custom queued interface to define the byte-count efficiently. You do this using simple math.

Suppose you have a router that uses IP, IPX, and SNA as its protocols. Let's arbitrarily assign frame sizes, realizing that the values aren't the real ones. We'll assign a frame size of 800 bytes to IP, 1000 bytes to IPX, and

1500 bytes to SNA. You calculate a simple ratio by taking the highest frame value and dividing it by the frame size of each protocol:

IP = 1500/800 = 1.875
IPX = 1500/1000 = 1.5
SNA = 1500/1500 = 1.0

These values equal your frame size ratios. To assign correct bandwidth percentages, multiply each ratio by the bandwidth percentage you want to assign to that protocol. For example, let's assign 40 percent to IP, 30 percent to IPX, and 30 percent to SNA.

IP = 1.875 (0.4) = 0.75
IPX = 1.5 (0.3) = 0.45
SNA = 1 (0.3) = 0.35

These values now need to be normalized by dividing the results by the smallest value.

IP = 0.75/0.3 = 2.5
IPX = 0.45/0.3 = 1.5
SNA = 0.3/0.3 = 1

Custom queuing will send only complete frames, so because the ratios are fractions, you must round them up to the nearest integer values that maintain the same ratio. To arrive at the nearest integer value, multiply the original ratios by a common number that will cause the ratios to become integers. In this case, you can multiply everything by two and get the resulting ratio of 5:3:2. What does this mean? Well, five frames of IP, three frames of IPX, and two frames of SNA will be sent. Because of the protocols' varying frame size, the bandwidth percentage works out just the way we calculated.

IP = 5 frames × 800 bytes = 4000 bytes
IPX = 3 frames × 1000 bytes = 3000 bytes
SNA = 2 frames × 1500 bytes = 3000 bytes

Total bandwidth is 10,000 bytes. Percentages are verified by dividing the protocol rate by the total. After doing the math, we verify that IP = 40 percent, IPX = 30 percent, and SNA = 30 percent.

Now that the byte-count is calculated (4000, 3000, and 3000), you can apply the results in the `queue-list` command. The custom queuing algorithm will forward 4000 bytes worth of IP packets, move to the IPX queue and forward 3000 bytes, and then go to the SNA queue and forward 3000 bytes.

Check out this example of how to configure and apply custom queuing lists:

```
Router_B#conf t
Enter configuration commands, one per line. End with CNTL/Z.
Router_B(config)#queue-list 1 interface Ethernet0 1
Router_B(config)#queue-list 1 protocol ip 2 tcp 23
Router_B(config)#queue-list 1 protocol ip 3 tcp 80
Router_B(config)#queue-list 1 protocol ip 4 udp snmp
Router_B(config)#queue-list 1 protocol ip 5
Router_B(config)#queue-list 1 default 6
Router_B(config)#queue-list 1 queue 1 limit 40
Router_B(config)#queue-list 1 queue 5 byte-count 4000
Router_B(config)#queue-list 1 queue 4 byte-count 500
Router_B(config)#queue-list 1 queue 3 byte-count 4000
Router_B(config)#queue-list 1 queue 2 byte-count 1000
Router_B(config)#int serial0
Router_B(config-if)#custom-queue-list 1
Router_B(config-if)#^Z
Router_B#
```

(handwritten margin notes: "Q LIST"; "for all other IP traffic"; "apply")

After analyzing the list, you can see that six different queues were configured. The first one was configured to handle incoming traffic from interface ethernet 0, and the second is reserved for Telnet traffic. Queue number 3 is for WWW traffic, and the fourth is configured to handle SNMP traffic. The fifth queue will deal with all other IP traffic, and queue 6 is the default queue where all unspecified traffic will go. A limit of 40 packets was placed on queue 1, and the byte-count was changed from the default value of 1500 for queues 2, 3, 4, and 5. Finally, after the list was written, it was applied to interface serial 0.

Here is what the configuration looks like:

```
!
interface Serial0
 no ip address
 shutdown
 custom-queue-list 1
!
```

```
queue-list 1 protocol ip 2 tcp telnet
queue-list 1 protocol ip 3 tcp www
queue-list 1 protocol ip 4 udp snmp
queue-list 1 protocol ip 5
queue-list 1 default 6
queue-list 1 interface Ethernet0 1
queue-list 1 queue 1 limit 40
queue-list 1 queue 2 byte-count 1000
queue-list 1 queue 3 byte-count 4000
queue-list 1 queue 4 byte-count 500
queue-list 1 queue 5 byte-count 4000
```

As with the other queuing algorithms, you need to verify both the configuration and the status of custom queuing. Issuing the same command as before, except this time substituting custom for priority, produces this output:

```
Router_B#show queueing custom
Current custom queue configuration:

List  Queue Args
1    6    default
1    1    interface Ethernet0
1    2    protocol ip     tcp port telnet
1    3    protocol ip     tcp port www
1    4    protocol ip     udp port snmp
1    5    protocol ip
1    1    limit 40
1    2    byte-count 1000
1    3    byte-count 4000
1    4    byte-count 500
1    5    byte-count 4000
Router_B#
```

This output information gives you a breakdown of the custom queue list, detailing queue assignments and any limits or byte-counts assigned to the queue.

Compression

The Cisco IOS provides congestion control on WAN links by adding compression on serial links. This can ease the WAN bandwidth bottleneck problems. Besides using the different queuing methods we discussed earlier in this chapter, one of the more effective methods of WAN optimization is compression on the data traveling across the WAN link.

Software compression can significantly affect router CPU performance, and the Cisco rule of thumb is that the router's CPU load must not exceed 65 percent when running software compression. If it does, you'd be better off disabling any compression method.

Cisco equipment supports the following types of data compression:

- Header compression

- Payload compression

- Link compression

- Microsoft Point-to-Point Compression (MPPC)

- Other compression considerations

By default, Cisco routers transmit data across serial links in an uncompressed format, but by using Cisco serial compression techniques, you can make more efficient use of your available bandwidth. It's true that any compression method will cause overhead on the router's CPU, but the benefits of compression on slower links can outweigh that disadvantage.

Figure 9.7 shows the three types of compression used in a Cisco internetworking environment.

FIGURE 9.7 Cisco serial compression methods

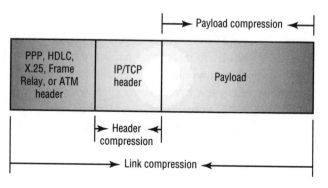

The compression methods are discussed below:

TCP header compression   Cisco uses the Van Jacobson algorithm to compress the headers of IP packets before sending them out onto WAN links. This method leaves the data intact, compressing only the header information, and can be used for applications (e.g., Telnet) and HDLC or X.25 encapsulation. However, it doesn't allow for protocol independence.

Payload compression   This approach compresses the data but leaves the header intact. Because the packet's header isn't changed, it can be switched through a network. So this method is the one generally used for switching services such as X.25, SMDS, Frame Relay, and ATM.

Link compression   This method is a combination of both header and payload compression, and for you to be able to use it, the data must be encapsulated in either PPP or LAPB. Link compression allows for protocol independence.

Microsoft Point-to-Point Compression (MPPC) protocol   This is defined in RFC 2118 and allows Cisco routers to exchange compressed data with Microsoft clients. You would configure MPPC when exchanging data with a host using MPPC across a WAN link. The MPPC is not discussed further in this section.

The Cisco compression methods are discussed in more detail in the following sections.

TCP Header Compression

TCP header compression is defined in RFC 1144 and only compresses the header, not the data. TCP header compression lowers the overhead generated by the disproportionately large TCP/IP headers as they are transmitted across the WAN.

It is important to realize that the Layer 2 header is not touched, and only the TCP header at Layers 3 and 4 is compressed. This allows the Layer 2 header to direct that packet across a WAN link.

You would use the header compression on a network with small packets and a few bytes of data such as Telnet. Cisco's header compression supports X.25, Frame Relay, and dial-on-demand WAN link protocols. Because of processing overhead, header compression is generally used at lower speeds, such as 64Kbps links.

TCP header compression is achieved using the `ip tcp header-compression` command:

```
Router(config)#int s0
Router(config-if)#ip tcp ?
  compression-connections  Maximum number of compressed
connections
  header-compression       Enable TCP header compression
Router(config-if)#ip tcp header-compression ?
  passive  Compress only for destinations which send
compressed headers
  <cr>
```

The `passive` argument is optional and used to add restrictions to outbound TCP traffic. If you don't include the `passive` argument, all TCP traffic will be compressed. If you do use it, outgoing TCP traffic will be compressed only if the data received on the same interface are compressed.

Payload Compression

Payload compression, also known as per–virtual circuit compression, only compresses the payload, or data portion of the packet. The header of the packet is not touched.

You use payload compression when an application will be going over point-to-point lines. If you were to use link compression, which compresses both the header and data fields, the header may not be readable at a particular hop.

Because the header is not touched, the packets can be switched through a WAN packet network. Payload compression is appropriate for virtual network services such as X.25, SMDS, Frame Relay, and ATM. It uses the same Stac compression method discussed in the following section, "Link Compression."

Link Compression

Link compression, also known as per-interface compression, compresses both the header and payload section of a data stream. Link compression is protocol independent, unlike header compression, which was previously discussed.

The link compression algorithm uses Stac or Predictor to compress the traffic in another link layer such as PPP or LAPB, ensuring error correction and packet sequencing. Cisco HDLC uses Stac compression only.

Predictor   Use this approach to solve bottleneck problems caused by a heavy load on the router. The Predictor algorithm learns data patterns and "predicts" the next character by using an index to loop up a sequence in a compression dictionary. This is sometimes referred to as *lossless* because no data are lost during the compression and decompression process.

Stac   Opt for this method when bottlenecks are related to bandwidth issues. It searches the input data stream for redundant strings and replaces them with a token that is shorter than the original redundant data string.

If the data flow transverses across a point-to-point connection, use link compression. In a link compression environment, the complete packet is compressed and the switching information in the header is not available for WAN switching networks. Thus, the best applications for link compression are point-to-point environments with a limited hop path. Typical examples are leased lines or ISDN.

In the following example, we turned on LAPB encapsulation with Predictor compression and set the maximum transmission unit (MTU) and the LAPB N1 parameters:

```
Router#config t
Enter configuration commands, one per line.  End with
CNTL/Z.
Router(config)#int s0
Router(config-if)#encap lapb
Router(config-if)#compress ?
predictor  predictor compression type
stac       stac compression algorithm
Router(config-if)#compress predictor
Router(config-if)#mtu 1510
Router(config-if)#lapb n1 1296
```

The LAPB N1 represents the number of bits in an LAPB frame, which holds an X.25 packet. It is set to eight times the MTU size, plus any overhead when using LAPB over leased lines. For instance, the N1 is specified at 1280 (1510×8) plus 16 bits for protocol overhead. The LAPB N1 parameter can cause major problems if it's not configured correctly and most often should be left at its default value. Even so, it can be really valuable if you need to set the MTU size.

Compression Considerations

Keep a few compression considerations in mind when selecting and implementing a compression method:

Modem compression   Modems can compress data up to four times. There are different types of modem compression techniques, so make sure you understand that the different specifications are not compatible. However, the modems at both ends of the connection will try to negotiate the standard to use. If compression is being done at the modem, do not configure the router to run compression.

Encrypted data   Compression happens at the Data Link Layer (Layer 2), and encryption functions at the Network Layer (Layer 3). After the application encrypts the data, the data is then sent to the router, which provides compression. The problem is that encrypted data does not have repetitive patterns, so the data will not compress. So, if data is encrypted, do not compress it using a Layer 2 compression algorithm.

CPU cycles versus memory   The amount of memory that a router must have varies according to the protocol being compressed, the compression algorithm, and the number of configured interfaces on the router. Memory requirements will be higher for Predictor than for Stac, and payload will use more memory than link compression, but link compression uses more CPU cycles.

Summary

This chapter introduced you to the three main types of queuing:

- Weighted fair
- Priority
- Custom

Each algorithm has a distinct way of processing the queues it uses. Because of these differences, queuing can be adapted to individual network needs. Bandwidth management is a cost-effective way of dealing with network congestion.

This chapter also discussed the significant differences between each queuing algorithm:

Weighted fair queuing   Shares equally with all traffic but gives low-volume traffic higher priority. Instead of assigning priorities to each packet, this algorithm tracks the session a packet belongs to. There is no queue list to configure or apply to the interface.

Priority queuing   Is a stringent algorithm that can cause one type of traffic to monopolize available bandwidth, because high-priority packets in the queue will always be processed first. Other traffic is processed only when there's available bandwidth left over from high-priority traffic. It gives you four queues.

Custom queuing   Is an equitable, controllable algorithm allowing an administrator to configure the amount of bandwidth reserved for specified traffic types. All traffic will be processed in turn. Custom queuing allows for the configuration of 16 queues.

The compression methods we discussed in this chapter are as follows:

TCP header compression   This method leaves the data intact, compressing only the header information, and can be used for applications (e.g., Telnet) and HDLC or X.25 encapsulation.

Payload compression   This approach compresses the data but leaves the header intact.

Link compression   This method is a combination of both header and payload compression.

Microsoft Point-to-Point Compression (MPPC) protocol   This is defined in RFC 2118 and allows Cisco routers to exchange compressed data with Microsoft clients.

Key Terms

compression

custom queuing

link compression

payload compression

Predictor

priority queuing

queuing

Stac

TCP header compression

weighted fair queuing

Commands in This Chapter

Command	Meaning
`compress predictor`	Turns on predictor compression
`custom-queue-list`	Assigns a custom queue to an interface
`fair-queue`	Enables or disables fair-queuing on a routing interface
`ip tcp header-compression`	Turns on header compression
`priority-group`	Assigns a priority queue to an interface
`priority-list`	Creates a priority queue list
`queue-list`	Creates a custom queue list
`show queue`	Displays more detailed information about queuing on an interface
`show queueing`	Displays the current queuing configuration

Written Lab

In this section, write the answer to the following questions:

1. What command would you use to view the custom queues configured on your router?

2. What type of compression leaves the data intact, compressing only the header information?

3. What command do you use to see queue information related only to serial 0?

4. How do you change the amount of conversations available with WFQ from the default of 64 to 96?

5. What type of compression compresses both the header and payload section of a data stream and is also called per-interface compression?

6. What priority queue command takes all packets received on ethernet 0 and places them in a high queue?

7. What type of compression only compresses the data portion of the packet?

8. What command would you use to assign a custom queue for Telnet to queue 2?

9. What type of queuing function is based on the concept of sharing bandwidth among traffic types?

10. How do you assign a high priority list to all IP traffic with a packet size greater than 1500?

Hands-on Lab

Use the network diagram in Figure 9.8 to complete the tasks in this lab.

FIGURE 9.8   Network diagram for lab

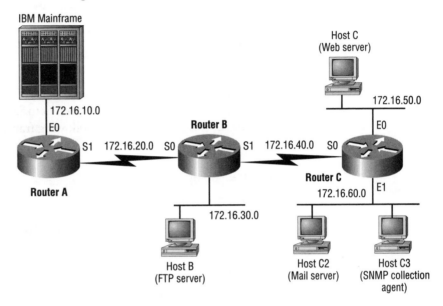

1. Configure the queuing algorithm that will give the SNA traffic from the IBM mainframe the highest priority across the 172.16.20.0 network. Apply queuing to the appropriate router and interface. Here is how you would perform this on Router A:

```
config t
priority-list 1 int e0 high
int s1
priority-group 1
```

2. Configure the queuing algorithm that will allow all traffic to be processed yet will give precedence to WWW traffic over file transfer sessions. Apply the queuing to the appropriate router and interface(s). Here is how you would configure this on Router B:

```
config t
int s0
fair-queue
int s1
fair-queue
```

3. Configure the correct queuing algorithm that will allocate 50 percent of the bandwidth to WWW traffic, 25 percent to SMTP, and 25 percent to SNMP. For this example, use the following frame size information:

WWW = 500 bytes

SMTP = 300 bytes

SNMP = 200 bytes

Here is how you would configure this on Router C:

```
Config t
Queue-list 1 protocol ip 1 tcp www
Queue-list 1 protocol ip 2 tcp smtp
Queue-list 1 protocol ip 3 udp snmp
Queue-list 1 queue 1 byte-count 2400
Queue-list 1 queue 2 byte-count 1200
Queue-list 1 queue 3 byte-count 1200
Int s0
Custom-queue-list 1
```

4. Show the details of all the queuing that was configured in the above tasks.

On Router A, use the following command:

```
Show queueing priority
```

On Router B, use the following commands:

```
Show queueing fair
Show queue serial 0
Show queue serial 1
```

On Router C, use the following command:

```
Show queueing custom
```

Review Questions

1. What is the correct syntax for implementing weighted fair queuing?

   A. `weighted-fair queue`

   B. `fair-queue`

   C. `queue-fair`

   D. None of the above

2. To which type of traffic does weighted fair queuing assign the highest priority?

   A. SNA

   B. IPX

   C. High volume

   D. Low volume

3. When should weighted fair queuing be used?

   A. To provide priority to interactive traffic

   B. To provide priority to file transfers

   C. To allow all traffic to be forwarded

   D. A and C

   E. A and B

4. Where is the most effective place to implement queuing?

   A. High-speed LAN links

   B. T-1/E-1 links only

   C. Any WAN link whose capacity is 2Mbps or slower

   D. All interfaces

5. When should priority queuing be used?

    A. When traffic has a hierarchical order of importance

    B. When delay doesn't matter

    C. When all traffic must be forwarded

    D. None of the above

6. Which one of the following steps is *not* part of configuring priority queuing?

    A. Configuring a default queue

    B. Configuring a priority list

    C. Configuring the queue transfer rate

    D. Assigning the priority list to an interface

7. How many queues are defined by priority queuing?

    A. 1–16

    B. No limit

    C. 4

    D. 1–10

8. When should custom queuing be used?

    A. When traffic has a hierarchical order of importance

    B. To overcome the possible problem that is introduced with priority queuing

    C. When trying to provide bandwidth-sharing for all traffic

    D. When delay is not important

9. Which step is *not* part of configuring custom queuing?

   A. Defining the custom queuing filter

   B. Assigning a default queue

   C. Configuring the transfer rate per queue

   D. Assigning a priority queue list to the interface

10. What is accomplished by configuring the byte-count for a queue?

    A. Allocating a percentage of the total bandwidth to defined queues

    B. Setting the size of the queue

    C. Setting the amount of data that will be processed before moving to the next queue

    D. A and C

11. Which of the following options best describes weighted fair queuing?

    A. Queues based on the source and destination of packets

    B. Shares bandwidth among all traffic types, giving priority to low-volume traffic

    C. Shares bandwidth among high-priority traffic only

    D. Queues using FIFO

12. Which option best describes priority queuing?

    A. Processes all queues in a round-robin fashion

    B. Queues based on the destination address of the packet

    C. Queues based on the traffic type; processes all queues equally

    D. Queues based on the traffic type; will always process the highest-priority traffic first

13. Which option best describes custom queuing?

    A. Queues based on traffic type; processes all queues equally

    B. Queues based on traffic type; always processes the high-priority traffic first

    C. Queues based on bandwidth allocation

    D. Processes packets based on the source address

14. What is accomplished by the following configuration?

```
Router_C(config)#priority-list 1 protocol ip low lt 256
Router_C(config)#interface serial 0
Router_C(config-if)#priority-group 1
Router_C(config-if)#^Z
Router_C#
```

    A. IP is held to a packet size of less than 256.

    B. Priority list 1 is applied to serial interface 0 and permits packet sizes less than 256.

    C. IP packets with sizes less than 256 are assigned to the low-priority queue, and the list is applied to serial interface 0.

    D. IP packets with sizes less than 256 are assigned a low priority, and the list is applied to serial interface 0.

15. Which of the following is *not* used to establish a conversation for weighted fair queuing?

    A. Source address

    B. Destination address

    C. Packet size

    D. Port number

16. Why is queue size important when configuring queuing?

    A. If the queue is full, the packet will be discarded.

    B. If the queue is full, the interface will become congested.

    C. If the queue is full, the algorithm halts and allows FIFO queuing.

    D. None of the above.

17. Which of the following commands should be used to assign all traffic from serial interface 1 to queue 1?

    A. Router_B(config-int)#**queue 1**

    B. Router_B(config)#**priority-list 1 interface Serial 1 1**

    C. Router_B(config)#**queue-list 1 interface Serial1 1**

    D. Router_B(config-int)#**queue-list 1 queue-number 1**

18. How many separate priority lists may be written for priority queuing?

    A. 4

    B. 8

    C. 12

    D. 16

19. Which algorithm does custom queuing use within each defined queue to forward packets?

    A. Priority

    B. Weighted fair

    C. FIFO

    D. None of the above

20. When should the default byte-count for custom queuing be changed?

   A. When available bandwidth needs to be allocated as a percentage of the total bandwidth.

   B. When the application uses larger packet sizes.

   C. It should never be changed from the default setting.

   D. To utilize all available bandwidth.

Answers to Written Lab

1. show queueing custom

2. Header compression

3. show queue serial0

4. fair-queue 96

5. Link compression

6. priority-list 1 interface ethernet 0 high

7. Payload

8. queue-list 1 protocol ip 2 tcp 23

9. Custom queuing

10. priority-list 1 protocol ip high gt 1500

Answers to Review Questions

1. B. From a serial interface, use the command `fair-queue` to change the defaults of weighted fair queuing (WFQ).

2. D. Low volume has priority in a WFQ environment. This stops a large file transfer from hogging the line.

3. A. WFQ is used to allow low-priority interactive traffic to share the link with file transfers.

4. C. Typically, queuing should be implemented on slow serial links that experience only temporary congestion. Queuing will not help any link faster than T-1/E-1.

5. A. Priority queuing is used when you have a hierarchical order of importance that you want to implement on your serial link.

6. C. You do not configure the queue transfer rate with priority queuing.

7. C. When you initiate priority queuing, you define four different queues.

8. B. When priority queuing does not meet an application congestion issue, then custom queuing should be used.

9. D. A priority queue list has nothing to do with custom queuing.

10. D. By configuring the byte-count for a queue, you allocate a percentage of the bandwidth to individual queues and set the amount of data that is processed for each queue.

11. B. WFQ was designed to stop large file transfers from hogging the bandwidth of a serial link.

12. D. The highest-priority queues, based on the different types of traffic, will always be processed first.

13. A. Unlike priority queuing, custom queuing processes all queues equally. However, the administrator bases the queues on traffic types.

14. C. A priority queue list was created and assigned to serial 0, which assigns any packet smaller than 256 bytes to a low-priority queue.

15. C. Source and destination address, as well as port number, are used to establish a conversation for WFQ.

16. A. Size is always important, even in queuing. If the queue becomes full, then the packets will be discarded.

17. C. To assign packets received on an interface to a priority queue, use the `queue-list [#] [int] [queue]` command.

18. D. You may have up to 16 priority lists configured on a router.

19. C. Custom queuing uses a first-in, first-out queuing algorithm within each queue.

20. A. You should change the byte-count with custom queuing when you need to allocate a percentage of the bandwidth.

Chapter 10

Network Address Translation (NAT) and Port Address Translation (PAT)

THE CCNP REMOTE ACCESS EXAM TOPICS COVERED IN THIS CHAPTER INCLUDE THE FOLLOWING:

- ✓ Configuring static NAT
- ✓ Configuring dynamic NAT
- ✓ Configuring inside global address overloading
- ✓ Configuring TCP load distribution
- ✓ Configuring translation of overlapping addresses
- ✓ Verifying NAT's configuration
- ✓ Clearing NAT translation entries
- ✓ Configuring and troubleshooting NAT
- ✓ Configuring and troubleshooting PAT
- ✓ Verifying a PAT configuration

As the Internet grows and individuals increasingly need more than one IP address to use for Internet access on their home and office PCs, on their phones (voice over IP), in their office's network printers, and in many other network devices, the number of available IP addresses is diminishing. To add insult to injury, the early designers of TCP/IP—back when the project was being created by the Advanced Research Projects Agency (ARPA)—never anticipated the explosion of users from private industry that has occurred.

ARPA's goal was to design a protocol that could connect all the United States defense department's major data systems together and allow them to talk to one another. The ARPA designers created not only a protocol that would allow all the defense department's data systems to communicate with each other but one that the entire world now relies on to communicate over the Internet.

Unfortunately, because of the unexpected popularity of this protocol, the distribution of IP addresses was inadequately planned. As a result, many IP addresses are unusable and many are placed in networks that will never use all the addresses assigned to them. For example, every organization with a Class A network, which provides 16,777,214 addresses per Class A assignment, could never use more than half those (except maybe the United States Department of Defense). (It is rumored that Hewlett Packard found a way to max out the IP addresses on a Class A address, but I am not sure whether that is true.) However, because these organizations got in the door early and have a Class A address, they have the option to use any of the ones they choose. Those that aren't used are wasted.

All the Class A and Class B addresses are already assigned to organizations. If a new organization needs more than one Class C address range, which provides only 255 addresses, they must get another Class C address range. IP version 6 and the World Wide Web 2 (Internet-2), ways of communicating over the WAN and Internet using registered Internet IP addresses that number far fewer than the local network's interfaces, will eventually alleviate IP addressing problems. These solutions are currently being beta tested.

This chapter introduces you to Network Address Translation (NAT) and Port Address Translation (PAT). Cisco routers and internal route processors use these two protocols, so a limited number of Internet-registered IP addresses allow a larger number of interfaces using nonregistered IP addresses to access another outside network, such as the Internet. As you progress through the chapter, you will learn the differences between NAT and PAT, as well as their operational boundaries, how to configure them, and how to troubleshoot problems associated with these two protocols.

Understanding Network Address Translation (NAT)

Before exploring the details of Network Address Translation (NAT) operations, configuration, and troubleshooting, it is important to thoroughly understand what it is, the terminology associated with it, its advantages and disadvantages, and the traffic types it supports. NAT is a protocol that gives you the ability to map an inside IP address used in the local network environment to the outside network environment and vice versa. There are many reasons for using NAT in your network environment. Some of the benefits you will receive from NAT include the following:

- Enabling a private IP network to use nonregistered IP addresses to access an outside network such as the Internet

- Providing the ability to reuse assigned IP addresses that are already in use on the Internet

- Providing Internet connectivity in networks where there are not enough Internet-registered individual IP addresses

- Appropriately translating the addresses in two merged intranets such as two merged companies

- Translating internal IP addresses assigned by old Internet Service Providers (ISPs) to a new ISP's newly assigned addresses without manually configuring the local network interfaces

NAT Terminology

Before continuing with this chapter, you should be familiar with the following Cisco terms:

Inside network   This is the set of network addresses that is subject to translation. The IP addresses used within the network are invalid on an outside network, such as the Internet or the network's ISP. Often, the IP addresses used in the inside network are obsolete, or an IP address is allocated in RFC 1918, which reserves certain IP addresses for specific use.

Outside network   This is a network that is not affiliated or owned by the inside network organization. This can be the network of another company when two companies merge but typically is the network of an Internet Service Provider (ISP). The addresses used on this network are legally registered IP addresses.

The merging of two corporate Internets, as sometimes happens with corporate mergers using NAT, is referred to as "stacked NATs."

Inside local IP address   This is the IP address assigned to an interface in the inside network. This address is illegal to use on the Internet or can be an address defined by RFC 1918 as unusable on the Internet. In both cases this address is not globally routable. If the address is globally routable, it may be assigned to another organization and cannot be used on the Internet.

Inside global IP address   This is the IP address of the inside host after it has been translated by NAT and as it appears to outside network interfaces. This address is usable on the outside network or the Internet.

Simple translation entry   This is an entry in the NAT table when the NAT router matches an illegal inside–IP address to a globally routable IP address that is legally registered for Internet use.

> **Extended translation entry**   This is an entry into the NAT table that maps an IP address and port pair to an inside IP address.

How NAT Works

NAT is configured on the router or route processor closest to the border of a stub domain, between the inside network (local network) and the outside network (public network such as an ISP or the Internet). (The outside network can also be another company, such as when two networks merge after an acquisition.) This is shown in Figure 10.1. Notice that the router separates the inside and outside network. NAT translates the internal local addresses into globally unique IP addresses, allowing data to flow into the outside network.

FIGURE 10.1   The NAT router on the border of an inside network and an outside network such as the Internet.

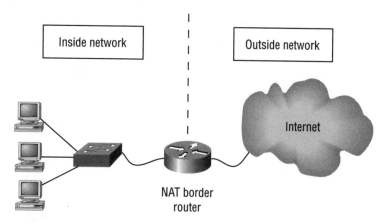

NAT takes advantage of the fact that there are relatively few network users using the outside network at any given time. NAT does this by using process switching to change the source address on the outbound packets, directing them back to the appropriate router. This allows for fewer IP addresses to be used than the number of hosts in the inside network. Before the implementation of NAT on all Cisco enterprise routers, the only way to implement these features was to use pass-through firewall gateways.

NAT was implemented in Cisco's IOS release 11.2 and spelled out in the RFC 1631 standard.

The Advantages of NAT

There are many advantages to using NAT. In this section, you will learn about some of the more important benefits. If your internal addresses must change because you have changed your ISP or have merged with another company, you can use NAT to translate the addresses from one network to the other.

- NAT allows you to incrementally increase or decrease registered IP addresses without changes to hosts, switches, or routers within the network. (The exception to this is the NAT border routers that connect the inside and outside networks.)

- NAT can be used either statically or dynamically:

  - Static translation occurs when you manually configure an address table with IP addresses. A specific address on the inside of the network uses an IP address, manually configured by the network administrator, to access the outside network.

  - Dynamic mappings allow the administrator to configure one or more pools of registered IP addresses on the NAT border router. The addresses in the pools can be used by nodes on the inside network to access nodes on the outside network. This allows for multiple internal hosts to utilize a single IP address.

- NAT shares packet processing among routers using the Transmission Control Protocol (TCP) load distribution feature. NAT load distribution can be accomplished by using one individual external address mapped to an internal router address. This round-robin approach is used between multiple routers distributing incoming connections across the routers. Each individual connection can be configured to use one individual router.

There is no limit to the number of NAT sessions that can be used on a router or route processor. The limit is placed on the amount of DRAM the router contains. The DRAM must store the configurable NAT pools and handle each translation. Each NAT translation uses approximately 160 bytes, which translates into about 1.6MB for 10,000 translations. This is far more than the average router needs to provide.

The Disadvantages of NAT

Now that you have learned about the advantages of using NAT, you should look at the disadvantages as well. The following is a list of some of the disadvantages of using NAT compared to using individually configured, registered IP addresses on each network host:

- NAT increases latency (delay). Delays are introduced in the switching paths due to the sheer number of translations of each IP address contained in the packet headers. The router's CPU must be used to process every packet to decide whether the router needs to translate and change the IP header.

- NAT hides end-to-end IP addresses that render some applications unusable. Some applications that require the use of physical addresses instead of a qualified domain name will not reach destinations when NAT translates the IP addresses across the NAT border router.

- Since NAT changes the IP address, there is a loss of IP end-to-end traceability. The multiple-packet address changes confuse IP tracing utilities. This provides one advantage from a security standpoint: it eliminates some of a hacker's ability to identify a packet's source.

NAT Traffic Types

NAT supports many traffic types. The CCNP exam includes questions on both the supported and unsupported types. Let's take a look at these types in the following two sections.

Supported Traffic Types

NAT supports the following traffic types:

- TCP traffic that does not carry source and destination addresses in an application stream

- UDP traffic that does not carry source and destination addresses in an application stream

- Hypertext Transfer Protocol (HTTP)

- Trivial File Transfer Protocol (TFTP)

- File Transfer Protocol (FTP)

- Archie, which provides lists of anonymous FTP archives

- Finger, a software tool for determining whether a person has an account at a particular Internet site

- Network Time Protocol (NTP)

- Network File System (NFS)

- rlogin, rsh, rcp (TCP, Telnet, and UNIX entities to ensure the reliable delivery of data)

- Internet Control Message Protocol (ICMP)

- NetBIOS over TCP (datagram and name service only)

- Progressive Networks RealAudio

- White Pines CuSeeMe

- Xing Technologies StreamWorks

- DNS "A" and "PTR" queries

- H.323 (versions 12.0(1)/12.0(1)T or later)

- NetMeeting (versions 12.0(1)/12.0(1)T or later)

- VDOLive (versions 11.3(4)/11.3(4)T or later)

- Vxtreme (11.3(4)/11.3(4)T or later)

- Telnet

- Domain Name Service (DNS)

Unsupported Traffic Types

NAT does not support some traffic types, including the following:

- IP Multicast
- Routing table updates
- DNS zone transfers
- BOOTP
- Talk
- Ntalk
- Simple Network Management Protocol (SNMP)
- Netshow

NAT Operations

Understanding how NAT functions when the protocol is configured for each individual configuration will aid you in your configuration decisions. In this section we will cover NAT's operations when NAT is configured to provide the following functions:

- Translating inside local addresses
- Overloading inside global addresses
- Using TCP load distribution
- Overlapping networks

Translating Inside Local Addresses

NAT operates on a router and usually connects two networks. NAT translates the local non-unique (illegal to use on the Internet) IP addresses into legal, registered Internet IP addresses before placing packets from the local network to the Internet or other outside network. To do this, NAT uses a six-step process, as shown in Figure 10.2.

FIGURE 10.2 The process of translating inside local addresses

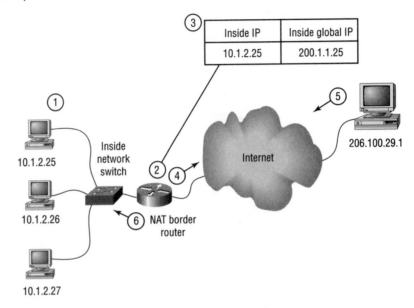

The six-step process, as Figure 10.2 shows, is as follows:

1. User 10.1.2.25 sends a packet and attempts to open a connection to 206.100.29.1.

2. When the first packet arrives at the NAT border router, the router then checks to see if there is an entry for the source address that matches an outside address in the NAT table.

3. If a match is found in the NAT table, it continues to step 4. If a match is not found, the NAT router uses what is called a simple entry from its pool of legal Internet addresses. A simple entry occurs when the NAT router matches an illegal Internal IP address (such as the one we are using) to a registered legal Internet usable IP address. In this example, the NAT router will match the address of 10.1.2.25 to 200.1.1.25.

4. The NAT border router then replaces the local illegal address of 10.1.2.25 (listed as the packet's source address) with 200.1.1.25. This makes the destination host believe that the sending interface's IP address is 200.1.1.25.

5. When the host on the Internet using the IP address 206.100.29.1 replies, it lists the NAT router–assigned IP address of 200.1.1.25 as the destination address.

6. When the NAT border router receives the reply from 206.100.29.1 with the packet destined for 200.1.1.25, the NAT border router then checks its NAT table again. The NAT table shows that the internal address of 10.1.2.25 should receive the packet destined for 200.1.1.25 and replaces the destination address with the internal interface's IP address.

Steps 2 through 6 are repeated for each individual packet.

Overloading Inside Global Addresses

You can conserve addresses in the inside global address pool by allowing the router to use one global address for many local addresses. When NAT overloading is enabled, the router maintains higher-level protocol information in the NAT table for TCP and UDP port numbers to translate the global address back to the correct inside local address. When multiple local addresses map to one global address, NAT uses the TCP or UDP port number of each inside host to make unique, distinguishable inside network addresses.

Figure 10.3 shows the NAT operation when one inside global address represents multiple inside local addresses. The TCP port number is the portion of the network address that differentiates between the other addresses on the network.

FIGURE 10.3   NAT overloading inside global addresses

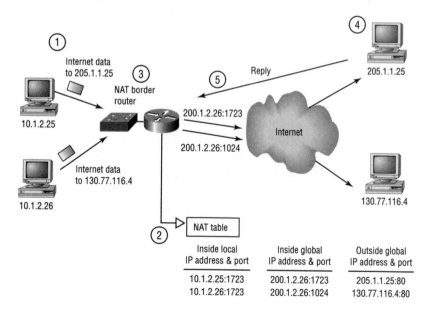

When the router processes multiple nonroutable inside IP addresses to one globally routable outside IP address, it performs the following steps to overload inside global addresses:

1. The user at the inside address of 10.1.2.25 opens a connection to a host on 205.1.1.25.

2. The first packet the NAT border router receives from the host at 10.1.2.25 causes the router to check its NAT table. Since no translation entry exists, the router determines that address 10.1.2.25 must be translated and configures a translation to the inside global address of 200.1.2.25. If overloading is enabled, and another translation is active, the router reuses the global address from that translation and saves enough information to translate back. This type of entry is called an extended entry.

3. The router replaces the inside local source address 10.1.2.25 with the selected globally routable address and a unique port number and forwards the packet. In this example the source address is now shown as 200.1.2.26:1723 in the NAT table.

4. The host at 205.1.1.25 receives the packet and responds to the host at 10.1.2.25 by using the inside global IP address in the source address field of the packet received (200.1.2.26).

5. The NAT border router will receive the packet from 205.1.1.25. It then performs a NAT table lookup, using the protocol, inside global address, and port, with the outside address and outside port address translating the address back to the current destination address of 10.1.2.25. The NAT border router then forwards the packet to the host using the IP address of 10.1.2.25 on the inside network.

Steps 2 through 5 are continued for all subsequent communications until the connection is closed.

Both the host at IP address 205.1.1.25 and the host at 130.77.116.4 think they are talking to a single host at address 200.1.2.26. They are actually talking to different hosts, with the port number being the differentiator that the NAT border router uses to forward the packets to the correct host. In fact, the port addressing scheme you use could allow about 4000 different hosts to share the same inside global IP address by using the many available TCP and UDP port numbers.

Using TCP Load Distribution

TCP load distribution is a dynamic form of destination IP address translation that can be configured for certain outside network traffic to a valid inside network IP traffic destined for more than one node. After a mapping scheme is created, destination IP addresses matching an access list are replaced with an address from a rotary pool on a round-robin basis.

When a new connection is established from the outside network to the inside network, all non-TCP traffic will be passed without being translated, unless another translation type is applied to the interfaces. Figure 10.4 demonstrates TCP load distribution, which is explained in further detail below.

FIGURE 10.4   TCP load distribution steps

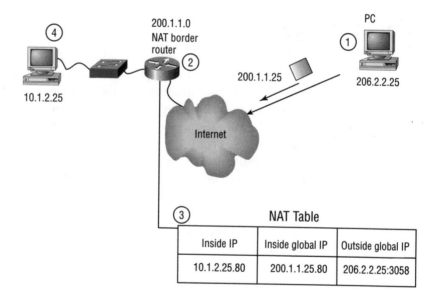

Let's look at the process NAT uses to map one virtual host to several real hosts:

1. In Figure 10.4, the PC using global IP address 200.1.1.25 opens a TCP connection to a virtual host at 10.1.2.25.

2. The NAT border router receives this new connection request and creates a new translation, which allocates the next real host of 10.1.2.25 for the inside local IP address and adds this information to the NAT table.

3. The NAT border router then replaces the destination address with the selected real host IP address and then forwards the packet.

4. The real host at IP address 10.1.2.25 receives the packet and responds to the NAT border router.

5. The NAT border router receives the packet and performs another NAT table lookup using the inside local IP address and port number and the outside IP address and port number as the key. The NAT border router then translates the source address to the virtual host's address and forwards the packet.

6. The next connection request causes the NAT border router to allocate 10.1.2.26 for the inside local address.

Overlapping Networks

Let's say your network uses an IP addressing scheme that is valid and globally usable. But say another company is using it or you are no longer authorized to use it. Now imagine your ISP thinks it has you locked in because it is providing your IP address scheme, and suddenly it doubles your prices. Rather than pay the higher prices, you shop for a new ISP with a different IP address range.

You finally find this terrific new ISP that is going to supply you with terrific Internet speeds at a third of the cost of your other ISP. Unfortunately, it is also going to supply you with a terrific new IP address scheme that you must apply to your network. Even in a mid-size network, you would spend many hours changing your IP address scheme—and waiting for this would impact the users tremendously. The solution is to implement a *NAT overlapping address translation*.

In this section you will learn how to translate IP addresses that are not legally usable on an outside network such as the Internet and how to translate them to the new officially assigned IP addresses from your ISP. We only cover the steps NAT uses to translate overlapping addresses. We will cover configuring overlapping address translation later in this chapter.

The following steps are used when translating overlapping addresses:

1. The host on the inside network tries to open a connection to a host on the outside network by using a fully qualified domain name, requesting a name-to-address lookup from an Internet Domain Name Server (DNS).

2. The NAT border router intercepts the Internet DNS's reply and begins the translation process with the returned address if there is an overlapping address that is residing illegally in the inside network.

3. To translate the return address, the NAT border router creates a simple translation entry that maps the overlapping illegal inside address to an address from a pool of addresses legally usable on the outside network.

4. The NAT border router replaces the source address with the new inside global address, replaces the destination address with the outside global address, and forwards the packet.

5. The host on the outside network receives the packet and continues the conversation.

6. For each packet sent between the inside and outside host, the router will perform a NAT table lookup, replace the destination address with the inside local address, and replace the source address with the outside local address.

Configuring NAT

In this section you will learn to configure NAT for the following situations:

- Static NAT
- Dynamic NAT
- Inside global address overloading
- TCP load distribution
- Translation of overlapping addresses
- Verifying NAT's configuration
- Troubleshooting NAT
- Clearing NAT translation entries

Configuring Static NAT

In this section you will learn how to configure static NAT, which maps an illegal inside IP address to a legal global IP address so that the data can be sent through the Internet. Before trying to configure static NAT, IP routing should be enabled on your router, and the appropriate IP addresses and subnet masks should be configured on each interface. We will start the configuration process in global configuration mode, assuming that we have only one interface on the router connected to our inside network. In this example, the PC using the illegal inside IP address of 10.1.2.25 needs to access data on the Internet. When the NAT border router receives a packet going to the outside network from the IP address of 10.1.2.25, we will configure it to translate the source address to a legally usable address of 200.1.1.25. Do this by using the following command:

BorderRouter (config)# **ip nat inside source static 10.1.2.25 200.1.1.25**

To enable NAT, you must first select the interface that connects your inside network to the router or internal route processor. There is at least one interface on the router connected to the inside network and at least one interface connected to the outside interface. You need to identify each and enable NAT on both with different commands. In this example, the router's inside network interface is ethernet 0 and the outside interface is serial 0. To enable static NAT on ethernet 0, use the following steps from global configuration mode:

1. Enter the interface configuration mode, enable NAT, and identify if you would like NAT to translate inside or outside addresses. In this example, we will have NAT translate inside addresses to outside addresses.

   BorderRouter (config)# **interface e0**
   BorderRouter (config-if)# **ip nat inside**
   BorderRouter (config-if)

2. Next you will need to enable NAT on serial 0 and identify that serial 0 is the interface connected to our outside network. From global configuration mode, use the following commands:

   BorderRouter (config)# **interface s0**
   BorderRouter (config-if)# **ip nat outside**
   BorderRouter (config-if)#

3. You should see the following when displaying the router configuration. The IP addresses of 10.1.2.254 and 200.1.1.1 are the IP addresses configured on the physical interfaces on the router.

```
!
interface Ethenet0
  ip address 10.1.2.254 255.255.0.0
  ip nat inside
!
interface Ethenet0
  ip address 200.1.1.1 255.255.0.0
  ip nat outside
```

Configuring Dynamic NAT, Inside Global Address Overloading, and TCP Load Distribution

In this section we will explain how to configure dynamic NAT, which maps an illegal inside IP address to any one legally registered, globally routable IP address from an identified pool of addresses. Before trying to configure dynamic NAT, you should enable IP routing on your router and configure the appropriate IP addresses and subnet masks on each interface.

Again, we will start the configuration process in global configuration mode, assuming we have only one interface on the router connected to our inside network. In our example, a PC using the illegal inside IP address of 10.1.2.25 needs to access data on the Internet. When the NAT border router receives a packet going to the outside network from IP address 10.1.2.25, the NAT border router will choose an available globally routable IP address from the address pool to translate the source address to a legally usable address of 200.1.1.26. We do this by using the following steps:

1. NAT translations from the inside network to the outside network take place after routing. Therefore, any access lists or policy routing will have been applied before the translation occurs. You will want to create an access list and apply it to the inside access list for the IP addresses your local addresses are using. In this example, we have a rather large network using the 10.1.0.0 IP address series, so using the

following command, we will create a standard IP access list that contains a wildcard for the last two octets:

BorderRouter(config)# **access-list 2 permit 10.1.0.0**
0.0.255.255

2. Now that we know an access list for our packets coming from 10.1.2.25 will clear policy routing when we apply the access list, we need to define the actual pool of addresses that are routable on the Internet. This would be the legal IP addresses our ISP gave us to use. We may have only been given 100 addresses for our 1000 PCs and servers in the network, but since all our PCs aren't on the Internet at any given time, this may be enough. If it isn't, we need to use another solution, such as configuring inside global address overloading. Before we begin configuring our pool of addresses, we need to decide on a name. In this case, we will call our address pool "InternetIPPool." To define the 100 IP addresses our ISP gave us (200.1.1.1 to 200.1.1.100 with the subnet mask 255.255.255.0), use the following command:

BorderRouter(config)# **ip nat pool InternetIPPool**
200.1.1.1 200.1.1.100 netmask 255.255.255.0

The command ip nat pool has two other options you can use. Instead of using the netmask syntax, you can use the prefix-length command followed by the number of bits in the mask, which indicate how many are ones. In this case, 24 would indicate our netmask. You can also use the syntax type rotary after the netmask to enable TCP load distribution. This indicates that the IP addresses in the pool are real inside hosts that can be used for TCP load distribution.

3. At this point we need to map the access list 2 we created in step 1 with the IP NAT pool "InternetIPPool" we created in step 2. To do this we will use the following command:

BorderRouter(config)# **ip nat inside source list 2 pool**
InternetIPPool

To configure inside global address overloading to use individual TCP ports, allowing an IP address to be used more than once, add the syntax `overload` after the NAT pool name.

4. To enable NAT, you must first select the interface that connects your inside network to the router or internal route processor. To enable NAT on ethernet 0, use the following commands from global configuration mode:

```
BorderRouter (config)# interface e0
BorderRouter (config-if)# ip nat inside
BorderRouter (config-if)
```

5. Next you will need to enable NAT on the serial 0 connected to our outside network. From global configuration mode, use the following commands:

```
BorderRouter (config)# interface s0
BorderRouter (config-if)# ip nat outside
BorderRouter (config-if)#
```

Configuring NAT to Perform Overlapping Address Translation

Configuring NAT to perform overlapping address translation is similar to dynamic NAT configuration. The difference is you must identify and apply a pool of addresses for the NAT border router interface connecting to the inside network interface, as well as a pool to allow for connection to the outside network.

NAT will start the configuration process in global configuration mode. The pool of addresses used in the inside network is 10.1.2.1 to 10.1.2.254. On the outside interface, we will configure a smaller pool of addresses that are globally routable on the Internet, assuming not all our 100 PCs will need to access the outside network at the same time. The pool of addresses we will configure will be 200.1.1.1 to 200.1.1.50. It is assumed that the NAT border router interfaces are configured with IP routing and the proper IP addresses. Again we will assume that our inside network is connected to the ethernet 0 interface on the router, and the serial 0 interface connects our NAT border router to the outside network. To configure NAT to perform overlapping address translation, complete the following steps:

1. Define the standard IP access list for the inside network, as discussed in the previous configuration section on dynamic NAT. The access list needs to be configured to allow data traffic from any address from the inside network that needs to be translated by NAT.

   ```
   BorderRouter(config)# access-list 2 permit 10.1.2.0
   0.0.0.255
   ```

2. Define an IP NAT pool for the inside network addresses. The pool name will be called "insidepool" and the range of addresses is 10.1.2.1 to 10.1.2.100. The final syntax indicates the number of bits for the subnet mask. You can also use the command `netmask 255.255.255.0` as shown in step 3, which also identifies a 24-bit netmask. The pool does not include address 10.1.2.254 because that is the NAT border router's inside interface address.

   ```
   BorderRouter(config)# ip nat pool insidepool 10.1.2.1
   10.1.2.253 prefix-length 24
   ```

3. Define an IP NAT pool for the outside network addresses. The pool name will be called "outsidepool" and the range of addresses is 200.1.1.1 to 200.1.1.50.

   ```
   BorderRouter(config)# ip nat pool outsidepool 200.1.1.1
   200.1.1.50 netmask 255.255.255.0
   ```

4. Map your created access list to the inside interface with the following command:

   ```
   BorderRouter(config)# ip nat inside source list 2 pool
   insidepool
   ```

NOTE Again you can use the overload command after the NAT pool name.

5. Map your created access list to the outside interface with the following command:

```
BorderRouter(config)# ip nat outside source list 2 pool
outsidepool
```

6. To enable NAT you must first select the interface that connects your inside network to the router. To enable NAT on ethernet 0, use the following commands from global configuration mode:

```
BorderRouter (config)# interface e0
BorderRouter (config-if)# ip nat inside
BorderRouter (config-if)
```

7. Next you will need to enable NAT on the serial 0 connected to our outside network. From global configuration mode, use the following commands:

```
BorderRouter (config)# interface s0
BorderRouter (config-if)# ip nat outside
BorderRouter (config-if)#
```

You should see the following when displaying the router configuration:

```
ip nat pool outsidepool 200.1.1.1 200.1.1.50 netmask
255.255.255.0
ip nat pool inside 10.1.2.1 10.1.2.253 prefix-length 24
ip nat outside source list 2 pool outsidepool
ip nat inside source list 2 pool inside pool
!
interface Serial0
 ip address 200.1.1.51 255.255.255.0
 ip nat outside
!
interface Ethernet0
 ip address 10.1.2.254 255.255.255.0
 ip nat inside
!
access-list 2 permit 10.1.2.0 0.0.0.255
```

Verifying NAT Configuration

To aid in verifying the configuration of NAT, you can use two specific commands. The show ip nat translation command shows the translations in the NAT table as in the following simple example:

```
BorderRouter(config)# show ip nat translation
Pro Inside global Inside local Outside local Outside
global
--- 200.1.1.25    10.1.1.25    ---         ---
--- 200.1.1.26    10.1.1.26    ---         ---
```

The show ip nat translation verbose command displays other NAT table information, such as the time left for the entries in the NAT table to expire, as shown below:

```
BorderRouter(config)# show ip nat translation verbose
Pro Inside global Inside local Outside local Outside
global
--- 200.1.1.25    10.1.1.25    ---         ---
    create 00:05:01, use 00:00:00, left 23:12:40, flags: none
```

The show ip nat statistics command displays some configuration information, statistics for translations, and entry information in the NAT table as shown below:

```
BorderRouter(config)# show ip nat statistics
Total active translations:2(0 static, 2 dynamic,0
extended)
Outside interfaces: Loopback 0, Serial1
Inside interface: Serial0
Hits: 243 Misses: 2
Expired translations: 0
Dynamic mappings:
-- Inside Source
access-list 2 pool insidepool refcount 1
  pool insidepool: netmask 255.255.255.0
    start 200.1.1.1 end 200.1.1.4
      type generic,total address 5,allocated 2 (50%),misses 0
```

Troubleshooting NAT

Using the debug ip nat feature can aid you when troubleshooting NAT problems. In the following output you will notice the source address of 10.1.2.5 is sending a packet to the destination address of 206.1.2.5. An "->" indicates that a packet's source address was translated. An "*" indicates that a packet is traveling through the *fast path*. A packet in a conversation with another node will always travel a process-switched *slow path*. Any other packets used will go through the fast path if there is a cache entry for the source and destination address.

Here is the output from the described scenario:

```
Router#debug ip nat
NAT: s=10.1.2.5->200.1.2.25, d=206.1.2.5 [0]
NAT: s=206.1.2.5, d=200.1.2.25->10.1.2.5 [0]
NAT: s=10.1.2.5->200.1.2.25, d=206.1.2.5 [1]
NAT: s=10.1.2.5->200.1.2.25, d=206.1.2.5 [2]
NAT: s=10.1.2.5->200.1.2.25, d=206.1.2.5 [3]
NAT*: s=206.1.2.5, d=200.1.2.25->10.1.2.5 [1]
NAT: s=206.1.2.5, d=200.1.2.25->10.1.2.5 [1]
NAT: s=10.1.2.5->200.1.2.25, d=206.1.2.5 [4]
NAT: s=10.1.2.5->200.1.2.25, d=206.1.2.5 [5]
NAT: s=10.1.2.5->200.1.2.25, d=206.1.2.5 [6]
NAT*: s=206.1.2.5, d=200.1.2.25->10.1.2.5 [2]
```

Two syntaxes can be used in conjunction with the debug ip nat command: list and detailed. The value in brackets is the IP identification number. This information enables you to correlate with other packet traces from sniffers used for troubleshooting in the network. (Sniffers are small devices that can be used to look at the traffic flowing through the network.)

Clearing NAT Translation Entries

Occasionally, NAT is properly configured but translations are not occurring. Most of the time, clearing the NAT translations resolves the issue. Table 10.1 shows the available commands for clearing the NAT table.

TABLE 10.1 The Commands Available to Clear the NAT Table

Command	Meaning
clear ip nat translation	Clears all NAT table entries
clear ip nat translation inside *global-ip local-ip* [outside *local-ip global-ip*]	Clears all inside NAT-table simple translation entries
clear ip nat translation outside *local-ip global-ip*	Clears all outside NAT-table simple translation entries
clear ip nat translation protocol inside global-ip global-port local-ip local-port [outside local-ip local-port global-ip global-port]	Clears all NAT-table extended entries

Port Address Translation (PAT)

If you wish to enable address translation on the 700 series router, you use *Port Address Translation (PAT)*. PAT is a subset of NAT and is the only address translation feature on the Cisco 700 series of routers. PAT uses TCP ports to allow an entire network to use only one globally routable IP address in the network.

The Cisco 700 series routers with release 4 software and higher support PAT, which enables local hosts on an inside IP network to communicate to an outside IP network such as the Internet. Traffic designated for an outside IP address on the other side of a border router will have its source IP address translated before the packet is forwarded to the outside network. IP packets returning to the inside network will have their IP addresses translated back to the IP addresses the destination interface is using on the inside network.

PAT conserves network addresses by enabling a single IP address to be assigned to an entire LAN. All WAN traffic is mapped to a single address, which is the ISDN-side IP address of the Cisco 700 series router. Since all the traffic on the outside network appears to come from the Cisco 700, the inside network appears invisible to the outside network or Internet.

You should configure a static address if users need to access a specific remote server on the inside network. PAT will allow packets with a specific well-known port number to get through, such as File Transfer Protocol (FTP) or Telnet.

Disadvantages to PAT

Using PAT has some disadvantages because it takes away end-to-end IP translation. These disadvantages are listed as follows:

- You cannot use Ping from an outside host to a host in the private network.

- Telnet from an outside host to an inside host is not forwarded unless the Telnet port handler is configured.

- Only one FTP server and one Telnet server are supported on the inside network.

- Packets destined for the router itself and not an inside network address such as DHCP, SNMP, PING, or TFTP are not rejected or filtered by PAT.

- If more than 12 PCs try to boot up simultaneously on the inside, one or more may get an error message about not being able to access the server.

- PAT entries are allocated and limited to 400 entries for the inside machines to share. If TCP connections are set up and TCP timeouts are set to keep alive, no more than 400 machines can get to the outside world at any one time.

- The Cisco 700 series router with PAT enabled does not handle any fragmented FTP packets.

- Some well-known ports cannot have port handlers defined. They include the following:

    - DHCP client ports used by the router for getting DHCP server responses

    - WINS NetBIOS ports used by the inside network clients operating Windows 95 PCs to get WINS information

Configuring PAT

The PAT feature enables local hosts with designated private IP addresses to communicate with the outside world. Basically, the router translates the source address of the IP header into a global, unique IP address before the packet is forwarded to the outside world. Likewise, IP packets on the return path go through address translations to the designated private IP addresses.

When PAT is enabled, RIP packet transmission is automatically disabled to prevent leaking private IP addresses to the outside network.

The two commands that you need to enable PAT are

set ip pat on This feature enables NAT and must be configured before the set ip pat port command can be used.

set ip pat porthandler The port handler translates a public TCP or UDP port to a private IP address. When a packet is received from the outside, PAT compares the port number with an internally configured port-handler list of up to 15 entries. If a port handler is defined for this port, it routes the packet to the appropriate port handler (IP address). If a default port handler is defined, it routes the packet there. The possible syntaxes are as follows:

default Enables the port handler for all ports' default handlers, except ports specifically assigned a handler.

telnet Enables the port handler for Telnet protocol port 23.

ftp Enables the port handler for File Transport Protocol (FTP) and uses protocol port 21.

smtp Enables the port handler for Simple Mail Transfer Protocol (SMTP) and uses protocol port 25.

wins Enables the port handler for NetBIOS session service on port 139.

http World Wide Web–HTTP and secure-HTTP port 80 or 443.

off Disables the port handler.

All syntaxes are followed by the appropriate IP address.

The following configuration enables IP unnumbered across the WAN, Dynamic Host Configuration Protocol (DHCP) server functionality, and PAT on the Cisco 765 router. It sets the IP address on the router to 10.1.2.1 and then creates a username, "user1." The following lists the entire configuration on a 765 router. The bold commands are those discussed in the previous sections.

```
>cd Internal
Internal>set IP 10.1.2.1
>set system 765
>765>set user user1
>765:user1>set ip pat on
765:user1>cd
765>set ppp authentication chap
765>set ppp secret client
765>set dhcp server
765>set dhcp dns primary 200.1.1.48
765>set dhcp wins primary 200.1.1.49
765>set dhcp domain mydomain
765>set ip pat port http 10.1.2.21
765>set user user1
765:user1> set bridging off
765:user1> set ip routing on
765:user1> set ip route destination 0.0.0.0 gateway
0.0.0.0
765:user1> set number 5555555
765:user1> set ppp secret host
765:user1> set active
```

Monitoring PAT

To monitor PAT and view the configuration settings, use the show ip pat command. When monitoring PAT you can view the number of packets dropped, the timeouts, and the service or IP address using each individual

TCP port. When you configure a Cisco 765 with the configuration shown in the previous section, you should see output similar to the following example using the show ip pat command:

```
765:user1>show ip pat
Dropped - icmp 0, udp 0, tcp 0, map 0, frag 0
Timeout - udp 5 minutes, tcp 30 minutes
Port handlers [no default]:


Port      Handler        Service
------------------------------------------
21        Router         FTP
23        Router         TELNET
67        Router         DHCP Server
68        Router         DHCP Client
69        Router         TFTP
80        10.1.2.21      HTTP
161       Router         SNMP
162       Router         SNMP-TRAP
520       Router         RIP
```

Summary

Throughout this chapter we learned how to overcome IP address problems by using NAT and PAT. As the Internet grows and individuals often need more than one IP address, the number of available IP addresses is diminishing. This is one of the main reasons for the implementation of NAT and PAT.

These two protocols, which allow for specifically defined address translations, allow for some other interesting uses as well. For instance, NAT and PAT enable private IP networks to use nonregistered IP addresses to access outside networks such as the Internet. They also provide the ability to reuse assigned IP addresses already in use on the Internet. In addition, they appropriately translate the addresses in two merged intranets, such as those of two merged companies. Finally, NAT and PAT translate internal IP addresses assigned by an old Internet Service Provider (ISP) to a new ISP's newly assigned addresses without manual configuration of the local network interfaces.

As we progressed through the chapter, you learned about NAT's and PAT's operational boundaries, NAT and PAT terminology, how to configure NAT and PAT, and how to troubleshoot problems associated with these two protocols.

Key Terms

Before you take the exam, be certain you are familiar with the following terms:

- border router

- NAT

- PAT

Commands in This Chapter

Command	Meaning
`access-list`	Configures a standard IP access list for the inside network
`clear ip nat translation`	Clears all NAT-table entries
`clear ip nat translation inside`	Clears all inside NAT-table simple translation entries
`clear ip nat translation outside`	Clears all outside NAT-table simple translation entries
`debug ip nat`	Displays IP NAT debugging information
`ip nat inside`	Enables NAT on the inside NAT interface
`ip nat inside source list`	Maps an access list to the IP NAT pool

`ip nat inside source static`	Configures the static NAT IP addresses to be used for translation
`ip nat outside`	Enables NAT on the outside NAT interface
`ip nat pool`	Configures an IP pool of addresses for the inside network
`set ip pat on`	Enables PAT on Cisco 700 series routers
`set ip pat port`	Allows all PAT services on Cisco 700 series routers
`show ip nat statistics`	Shows NAT statistics
`show ip pat`	Displays PAT monitoring information
`show nat translations`	Shows NAT translations in the NAT table

Written Lab

Write the command or commands for the following questions.

1. Which command enables PAT on a 700 series router?

2. Which command displays IP NAT debugging information?

3. Which command enables IP NAT on an interface connected to an outside network?

4. Which command will allow you to view NAT statistics?

5. Which command allows you to view the current NAT translation table information?

6. Which command allows you to view the current PAT monitoring information?

7. Which command disables IP NAT debugging?

8. Which command deletes all NAT table entries?

9. Which command enables IP PAT on a Cisco 700 series?

10. Access lists are created with what command?

Hands-on Lab

In this hands-on lab, you will configure NAT on a router using another router to loop your packets back. This step-by-step lab exercise allows you to configure a simulated NAT environment using two IOS-based routers.

You will configure an inside PC with the nonroutable inside IP address of 10.1.2.200 to have a static outside address of 200.1.1.200. To do this, complete the following steps:

1. Enter global configuration mode on the branch office router and configure the router with the following information to create a static mapping of the outside IP address to the inside IP address:

   `ip nat inside source static 200.1.1.200 10.1.2.200`

2. Enter interface configuration mode for the inside interface. In our example we will use ethernet 0 as the inside interface. To do this, use the following command:

   `Interface e0`

3. Next we need to simulate our inside network. Enter loopback 1 configuration mode with the following command:

   `interface loopback 1`

4. Configure the IP address of the loopback 1 interface with the following command:

   `ip address 200.1.1.200 255.255.255.0`

5. Enable NAT on the inside interface with the following command:

   `ip nat inside`

6. Enter the configuration mode for the outside interface. In our example we will use the serial 0 interface as our outside network interface using the following command:

   `interface serial 0`

7. Enable NAT on the outside interface with the following command:

   `ip nat outside`

8. Exit interface configuration mode.

9. On another router connected to the outside interface serial 0, create a static IP route that will route our packets back to the router we just configured. To do this, use the following command:

ip route 10.1.1.1 255.255.255.255 10.1.2.200

This will allow any packets, such as those created with a Ping, to route back to the interface on the originally configured router simulating your NAT environment. You can enable debug on the originally created router to view the processing of the packets. To do this, use the debug ip nat command.

Review Questions

1. Which of the following NAT table entries indicates a static inside IP address to globally routable address translation?

   A. Simple translation entry

   B. Extended translation entry

   C. Global translation entry

   D. Inside translation entry

2. Which of the following best describes an inside network?

   A. The network of another company

   B. The set of networks that are subject to IP translation

   C. The side of the network using global addresses

   D. The Internet

3. NAT cannot perform which of the following?

   A. Enable a private network using unregistered IP addresses to access another outside network.

   B. Provide the ability to reuse addresses already in use on the Internet.

   C. Replace the functions provided by a DHCP server.

   D. Provide IP address translation for merged internetworks.

4. A Class A IP address scheme can provide a maximum of how many individual hosts with unique IP addresses on the inside network?

   A. 254

   B. 16,777,214

   C. 255

   D. None of the above

5. Which of the following is a problem that NAT and PAT are designed to address?

    A. Assigning a DHCP address

    B. Assigning an IP address to a border router

    C. Translating nonroutable IP addresses to legal routable addresses

    D. Resolving IP addresses to fully qualified domain names

6. Which of the following describes the router that should be configured with NAT? (Choose the two best answers.)

    A. A spoke router on a hub-and-spoke network

    B. The router that is the demarcation point between the inside network and the outside network

    C. The local bridging router between two subnets

    D. The router closest to the border of a stub domain

7. Which of the following types of NAT configurations would you implement if you were mapping all your inside IP addresses to one globally routable address?

    A. TCP load distribution

    B. Static NAT

    C. One-on-one mapping

    D. Overloading

8. Which of the following traffic types is not supported by NAT?

    A. File Transfer Protocol (FTP)

    B. Network Time Protocol (NTP)

    C. Telnet

    D. IP multicast

    E. Internet Control Message Protocol (ICMP)

    F. Trivial File Transfer Protocol (TFTP)

    G. All of the above

9. Approximately how much DRAM on the NAT border router is used during each NAT translation?

   A. 160 bytes

   B. 100KB

   C. 1MB

   D. 64KB

10. Enabling which syntax used with the `set ip porthandler` command configures all well-known TCP ports except for the ports specifically assigned?

    A. `all`

    B. `enable`

    C. Do not use a syntax

    D. `default`

11. In which of the following router configuration modes should you use the command `ip nat inside source static 10.2.2.2.6 200.4.4.7`?

    A. Global configuration mode

    B. Interface configuration mode

    C. User EXEC mode

    D. Any of the above

12. The command `ip nat inside static 10.1.3.2 200.4.2.5` is an example of which type of NAT translation?

    A. Static NAT

    B. Dynamic NAT

    C. Overlapping NAT

    D. Port mapping

13. Which of the following commands can be used to verify the NAT configuration? (Choose the two best answers.)

A. `show ip nat statistics`

B. `show ip nat configuration`

C. `show ip nat all`

D. `show ip nat translation`

14. Which of the following protocols can be enabled on a Cisco 765 router? (Choose all that apply.)

A. NAT only

B. PAT only

C. Both NAT and PAT

D. None of the above

15. NAT is used to translate which types of protocol addresses?

A. IP

B. IPX

C. AppleTalk

D. IP and IPX

16. Which of the following commands can be used to monitor PAT?

A. `show ip pat`

B. `show ip pat statistics verbose`

C. `show ip pat all`

D. `show ip pat configuration`

17. Which of the following defines the NAT protocol?

    A. RFC 1911

    B. IEEE 802.11

    C. RFC 1631

    D. ANSI X311

18. When looking at a routing table, what does the S mean?

    A. Dynamically connected

    B. Directly connected

    C. Statically connected

    D. Sending packets

19. Which of the following traffic types is supported by NAT?

    A. Routing table updates

    B. BOOTP

    C. IP multicast

    D. DNS zone transfers

    E. None of the above

20. Which of the following is not a disadvantage of using NAT?

    A. Delay in switching paths.

    B. All IP address translation pools can be changed only on the NAT border router.

    C. Hidden end-to-end IP addresses from applications.

    D. Loss of traceability.

    E. None of the above.

Answers to Written Lab

1. `set ip pat on`

2. `debug ip nat`

3. `ip nat outside`

4. `show ip nat statistics`

5. `show ip nat translations`

6. `show ip pat`

7. `no debug ip nat`

8. `clear ip nat translation`

9. `set ip pat on`

10. `access-list`

Answers to Review Questions

1. A. The single translation entry indicates a static inside IP address to a globally routable IP address translation.

2. B. The inside network is a network where addresses need to be translated to enter another outside network such as the Internet.

3. C. NAT will support certain DHCP server traffic but does not replace any functions of a DHCP server.

4. B. A properly subnetted Class A network can provide up to 16,777,214 unique IP addresses for individual hosts.

5. C. NAT and PAT provide functions that allow a nonroutable IP address to be translated into a routable IP address. Some of NAT's and PAT's functions allow for fewer routable addresses than there are nonroutable addresses.

6. B, D. The router closest to the edge of the network that separates the inside network and the outside network is the router that should be configured with NAT or PAT.

7. D. By enabling NAT overloading, you can map more than one inside IP address to a single IP address by using port information as a differentiator.

8. D. IP multicast is the only traffic type listed that is not supported by NAT.

9. A. The NAT border router uses about 160 bytes per translation. This means that about 10,000 translations, which is far more than the average router should need to translate, will use about 1.6MB of DRAM.

10. D. The `set ip porthandler default` command configures all well-known TCP ports except for the ports specifically assigned a handler.

11. A. IP NAT configuration additions and change commands are config-
    ured in the global configuration mode. The `ip nat inside` or `ip nat
    outside` commands enable NAT on the interface they are applied on
    the router.

12. A. The `ip nat inside static 10.1.3.2 200.4.2.5` command is
    an example of a manually configured static NAT table entry.

13. A, D. The three commands that can be used to verify the NAT config-
    uration are `show ip nat translation`, `show ip nat translation
    verbose`, and `show ip nat statistics`.

14. B. The Cisco IOS for the 765 uses a SET/CLEAR command set typically
    found in switches and does not support NAT. PAT is the only address
    translation protocol supported by the Cisco 700 series of routers.

15. A. NAT only translates IP addresses and uses TCP and UDP ports to
    create unique IP addresses. It does not support IPX or AppleTalk.

16. A. The command `show ip pat` shows the statistical and configuration
    information for PAT.

17. C. The NAT protocol is defined in the Internet standard Request For
    Comments 1631 document, titled "The IP Network Address Transla-
    tor (NAT)."

18. C. Statically connected routes are identified in the routing table with an S.

19. E. None of the above traffic types is supported by NAT.

20. B. The ability to change the global IP address pool on only the NAT
    border router is a great feature, not a disadvantage. This allows for the
    address pool to be changed without any manual configuration of any
    other host on the inside network.

Chapter 11

Centralized Security in Remote Access Networks

THE CCNP REMOTE ACCESS EXAM TOPICS COVERED IN THIS CHAPTER INCLUDE THE FOLLOWING:

- ✓ Identification of centralized security concepts, including authentication, authorization, and accounting

- ✓ Configuration of authentication, authorization, and accounting

- ✓ Using the protocols of AAA—TACACS+, and RADIUS

- ✓ Using CiscoSecure in AAA installations

he primary concepts of remote access are the concept of access itself, the granting of permission to the correct party, and a method for confirming this access in order to verify the proper access controls.

These three concepts are known as *authentication, authorization, and accounting (AAA)*. AAA is Cisco's way of explaining the access control components and processes, and it is the topic of this chapter.

This book has covered many of the fundamental elements of authentication and authorization—particularly in the context of CHAP, or the Challenge Handshake Authentication Protocol (see Chapter 3). This chapter will explore these concepts further, but the discussion will be more focused on the theoretical concepts of security and Cisco's preferred implementation of each of these concepts. AAA services are essential in order to provide centralized access control services, which will be recurrent themes in this chapter and most Cisco security implementations.

Security Terminology

Many of the terms presented in the other chapters of this book are familiar or easily interpreted from the context. This chapter's terms differ slightly because they may not be familiar to all readers. Treat this list as a high-level introduction to these security components, but realize that more detail will be provided throughout the chapter.

Authentication The *authentication* function answers the fundamental question: who is the user? By performing this function, you can ensure that unwanted intruders can be denied access to the network while other users may be permitted. The user's identity may then be used to determine access permissions and to provide an audit trail of activity.

Authorization   The *authorization* function often works in concert with authentication. It provides a means for defining which network services will be available to the authenticated user.

Accounting   *Accounting* is an optional function in AAA; however, it is responsible for the auditing process, which can greatly augment the security of the network. Accounting can also log the activities of the user, including the time that they start and stop their connection.

RADIUS   *Remote Access Dial-in User Service (RADIUS)* is a protocol that is used to communicate between the remote access device and an authentication server. Sometimes an authentication server running RADIUS will be called a RADIUS server.

TACACS+   *Enhanced Terminal Access Controller Access Control System (TACACS+).* This protocol is similar to RADIUS. Sometimes the server is called a T-plus or T+ server.

Security server   A *security server* runs the protocol, TACACS+ or RADIUS, which is used to provide AAA services. It should be secured and redundant—especially if it provides business-critical access control. CiscoSecure is Cisco's version of this type of server, and is available on NT and Unix.

Cisco Access Control Solutions

Consider your home or apartment for a moment. It contains all of your property, and theoretically, it is a private space for you and your family. Most likely, the door has a lock of some kind that restricts entry, and, with the use of a key, only you and other authorized persons will be able to enter.

In this example, the door is very much like the remote access device in the network. It provides a gateway between the outside world and the home—in this case, the corporate network. The electronic door also has a key of sorts—frequently a username and password. *Access control* defines the manner in which these metaphorical keys are allocated and used; also, it defines what may be done by each person who enters the system.

Cisco access control solutions are used to implement the security policies of the network—specifically the remote access connectivity. These solutions are targeted for a wide variety of platforms and functions. You will find Cisco access solutions for several platforms, including Windows NT and Unix. Consider the following components used in remote access:

Clients In Cisco access control, a client is typically a remote dial-in connection, like the one that would be found on an asynchronous or an ISDN connection. Such clients can use different forms of security and authentication, including CHAP and PAP (discussed in Chapter 3), or they can use remote client software, such as CiscoRemote. In addition, hardware-based tokens may be used to augment security—the tokens do this by calculating the proper response to a one-time challenge from the access server.

RADIUS and token-based authentication usually require the use of PAP.

Access servers Clients connect to *access servers*, which provide the far end of a connection as viewed from the remote user's perspective. Stated another way, the access server is the front door to the network for remote users. The Cisco IOS and other software, including CBOS (Cisco Broadband Operating System), can provide varying degrees of security, including dialer profiles, access control lists (ACLs), and encryption.

To communicate between security servers and access servers, new protocols were developed, including TACACS+, RADIUS, and Kerberos.

Security servers Security servers provide a centralized means of controlling policy and storing account information. This can greatly simplify administration—similar to the way DNS eases name-to-address resolution. Recall that before DNS, each workstation was populated with a hosts file, which had to be modified for each change. DNS servers allowed hosts to query a single server for the resolution. Security servers operate in the same manner—rather than storing usernames and passwords on each router, they can be stored on the server and queried by the network device when needed. Cisco's security server offering is called CiscoSecure, and it operates on Unix and NT platforms. CiscoSecure is discussed in the following section.

Protocols for centralized authentication CHAP and PAP were designed for use on serial connections, making them unsuitable for Ethernet and other LAN technologies.

Readers should note that a newer implementation of PPP—PPP over Ethernet—is available. This protocol provides CHAP and PAP services over Ethernet media. At present, this type of installation is being used by some DSL service providers to augment security; however, few corporate networks have implemented the protocol.

CiscoSecure

The CiscoSecure product is Cisco's security server solution. The product incorporates many different services, including TACACS+ and RADIUS servers, as well as logging functionality.

CiscoSecure uses Web-based interfaces and Java to provide multiple administrators with access to the server. Though the product supports both Internet Explorer and Netscape, it ships with a Netscape Fastrack server, and some administrators find it to be more reliable with the Netscape client. CiscoSecure also relies on a relational database to manage accounts and store information—currently it supports the Oracle and Sybase platforms.

For enhanced security, administrators may choose to use *one-time challenge tokens*. These tokens provide for the use of a different password for each login—a tactic that prevents session reply and other techniques that would otherwise compromise security. Token cards from CRYPTOCard, Enigma Logic, Inc., and Security Dynamics Technologies are supported with CiscoSecure.

Authentication, Authorization, and Accounting

Regarded as distinct elements, authentication, authorization, and accounting (AAA) all work cooperatively to establish and enforce a security

CiscoSecure's Response to Brute Force and Denial of Service Attacks

The CiscoSecure product, like other such products, has the ability to disable accounts automatically in response to brute force attacks. This is accomplished with the concept of *intruder detection*, where the software assumes that the party is an intruder after a certain number of failed logins. A *brute force attack* is one in which the attacker bombards the system with login attempts. Ultimately, such an attack can lead to access—especially when passwords and account information are relatively simple. By detecting such an attack, products can disable the account before it is compromised. Frequently, such logic is limited to the number of attempts per unit time, however. For example, a brute force rule might allow five bad login attempts per hour before locking the account for a day, or it may detect three bad passwords and then lock the account until the administrator releases it.

Unfortunately, most solutions to brute force attacks lead to another type of attack—denial-of-service. A *denial-of-service attack* usually does not lead to the access of private information, rather, as the name suggests, it prevents legitimate users from obtaining that data. As a result, administrators must balance the impact of brute-force compromises against the potential of blocking access as a result of this protection. As with most products, CiscoSecure and others, the responsibility to balance access control with access is placed on the administrator.

model. This model is the result of a *security policy*, which should define an overall set of standards that will be used by the organization. This may include definitions of access rights that will be assigned to different groups and the protocols that will be used for various functions. For example, one policy statement may include that TACACS+ is the sole protocol used and that SSH, a secure tool used for administration, is preferred to Telnet.

It is important to understand how authentication, authorization, and accounting work together to promote and support a security model. In this section, you will learn about how AAA works, as well as how AAA functions in Cisco's router access modes. AAA services are the basic tenet of Cisco remote access solutions, and, while their presentation has been left to the end of the book, readers should find that the physical and network layers augment these concepts well. This would include physical security, the use of access lists, static or authenticated IP routing, and other security techniques.

How AAA Works

It is important to remember that AAA is simply a grouping of three different security functions—authentication, authorization, and accounting. Most texts examine each component as an isolated process, and, while this is perhaps more accurate, here they have been placed into a three-step process to better communicate the interactions between each service. For example, it is perfectly valid to use only authentication and authorization while omitting accounting, but if you do so, administrators will lose the auditing benefits that are provided by the auditing service.

Step 1: Authentication

Authentication is the first facet of the three security elements, and it provides a basis for the remaining two components. Authentication provides the "who" in the AAA model. Like journalists who ask themselves the questions they must answer to make their story good (Who?, What?, Where?, When?, and How?), administrators need to ask who is involved in their system, one of the fundamental pieces of information they need to set up their system. Unfortunately, in computing, as in non-computing situations, it can be fairly simple to lie about one's identity.

In order to facilitate the authentication process, most systems require both a username and a password—hopefully, the password will be maintained in confidence in order to preclude the potential of compromise. By requiring two elements of identity, the computer-based system doubles the likelihood that the user is accurately identified.

However, it is possible to obtain, lie, or guess both pieces of information. The likelihood of accurate authentication is stronger if there is a physical element added. In non-computing situations, this may include a passport or driver's license, while in the computer world it may include a token-based device. As presented in the CiscoSecure section of this chapter, there are many products that can provide this service as a software receiver of the physical code card data.

Step 2: Authorization

Once the identity of the user has been established, a decision must be made regarding what rights that user can exercise. This is called *authorization*, and is assigned by the administrator based on the requirements and business policies of the organization. An example of authorization would include permissions to access a remote access device or the ability to print a file. Because authentication and authorization are so involved and dependent on each other, they are regarded as a single security component in most environments.

Step 3: Accounting

While authentication and authorization work to prevent unauthorized access, *accounting* provides a means of verifying that only authorized users obtain access. In addition, accounting may be used to audit the actions of an authorized user. In the near future, it is likely that more companies will add charge-back and billing to the accounting function—this will allow the network administrators to charge for actual usage instead of unlimited service.

An accounting record relies on the authenticity of the authentication process—a fraudulent user might provide a valid login, but the accounting feature provides the audit trail required to assess the damage. This log provides a record of when an activity occurred and what action was performed—connecting to a router, for example.

Router Access Modes

A Cisco router may be accessed using one of two access modes. These are broadly categorized as character mode and packet mode. In essence, the differences between these modes can be best understood by looking at the commands that configure character and packet modes, shown in the following sections. Readers should understand the difference in the modes and use this section as an introduction to the configuration command syntax.

Character Mode Connections

Character mode connections describe character-based access, including access via the VTY, TTY, AUX (auxiliary), and CON (console) ports. While such access may be through a packet-based network—Telnet, for example—the connection is still viewed as being character-based. The AAA commands that configure character mode access are as follows:

- login
- exec
- nasi
- connection
- arap
- enable
- command

Character mode access usually includes only connections to the router or network device. Table 11.1 includes explanations of these commands.

TABLE 11.1   Character Mode Authentication and Authorization Commands

Command	Description
`aaa authentication enable default tacacs+ enable`	Determines if the user can access enabled mode.
`aaa authorization exec tacacs+ local`	Determines if the user is allowed access to the EXEC shell. This example provides for TACACS+ authentication, and, should TACACS+ fail, it permits authorization via the local database. The local database is populated with the username command.
`aaa authorization command N tacacs+ local`	Runs authorization for all commands at privilege level *N* (a number between 0 and 15). Every line entered by a user can be controlled and authorized by TACACS+, although performance can suffer.
`Username user password password`	Creates or adds to the local database with a username of *user* and the password of *password*. This database is stored in the router's configuration file in NVRAM (nonvolatile random access memory), and it can be accessed upon authentication failure depending on configuration.

Packet Mode Connections

Packet mode connections include most dial-up connections, including the following:

- `async`
- `group-async`

- serial

- ISDN BRI

- ISDN PRI

Packet mode connections typically secure connections that pass through the network device. You use the `ppp`, `network`, and `arap` AAA commands to control packet mode connections. Table 11.2 offers a list with explanations of these commands.

NOTE These sections do not provide a complete breakdown of all possible commands, but instead they introduce the more common commands. Please refer to the documentation specific to your version of the IOS for a current listing of all commands and options, or use the incorporated help function.

TABLE 11.2 Packet Mode Authentication Commands

Command	Description
aaa authentication ppp user if-needed tacacs+	AAA is used for PPP packet mode challenges. The list user is used first, and if unsuccessful, TACACS+ will be used.
aaa authorization network tacacs+ if-authenticated	TACACS+ is used to determine if the user is permitted to make packet mode connections if the user is authenticated.
interface async16 ppp authentication chap user	This is a new command for this chapter in that it associates an AAA function with an interface. Specifically, line async16 is instructed to use the list user for CHAP authentication. Note that an AAA server (RADIUS, etc.) is not used.

Configuring AAA

While AAA was designed to centralize access control, it still requires configuration on each and every network device. Fortunately, once AAA is configured, there are few instances when the administrator will need to alter this configuration—for example, when the encryption key is changed. Aside from such minor alterations, all changes, including those for user accounts, are invoked at the security server. This configuration process teaches the router or access device about the type of security to be used, the location of the security server, and the passwords or other information needed to facilitate communications.

In addition to these configuration commands, the administrator must establish network level connectivity between the access device and the access server. This might require access-list modification or route entries.

Table 11.3 outlines some of the AAA commands, including those for authentication and accounting. The configurations that relate to these commands are shown in the following sections.

TABLE 11.3   Overview of AAA Commands and Configuration

Command	Description
`aaa new-model`	Enables AAA services on the router. New-model reflects changes from the initial implementation, which is no longer supported.
`aaa authentication login default tacacs+ enable`	Configures TACACS+ to be used for login level access.
`aaa authentication enable default tacacs+ enable`	Configures TACACS+ to be used for enable level access.
`aaa accounting exec start-stop tacacs+`	Starts the accounting process, logging the start and stop times of each access.

TABLE 11.3 Overview of AAA Commands and Configuration *(continued)*

Command	Description
tacacs-server host 10.1.98.36	Specifies the IP address of the TACACS+ server. The single-connection parameter may be used to improve performance by maintaining a single TCP session as opposed to starting a separate session for each authentication.
tacacs-server key tjelkprp	Specifies the encryption key to be used for communications between the router and server.

This command goes on all routers

Authentication Configuration

Authentication is configured differently on Cisco routers and switches; however, the general parameters are similar. In broad terms, the administrator must first instruct the device to use an authentication protocol, then provide the IP address for communications.

Router Configuration

The following is parsed from the full configuration file of the router to highlight the commands used for AAA configuration:

```
aaa new-model
aaa authentication login default tacacs+ enable
aaa authentication enable default tacacs+ enable
aaa accounting exec start-stop tacacs+
tacacs-server host 10.1.98.36
tacacs-server host 10.1.5.36
tacacs-server key tjelkprp
```

The preceding output is an example of a typical router configuration. This output starts the AAA service, establishes authentication services for both login and enable processes, and audits the start and end times of the access.

AAA is a standard throughout the industry

The two TACACS+ servers noted here are defined and the pre-shared key is assigned.

In detail, this example (which uses TACACS+), the `aaa authentication` command is used to define the type of authentication protocol. The `enable` keyword allows the local enable password to be used if network connectivity is lost between the access server and router; however, this also may be considered a security risk. This risk is minor, considering that the attacker would have to physically access the router or compromise the internal network sufficiently to change routes or block packets. Here, the `tacacs-server` command is being used to define the IP address. In this example, the server key is being used to provide basic security over the authentication protocol. Note that this configuration includes an `aaa accounting` command, which instructs the router to log the start and stop times of an exec session to the TACACS+ server.

NOTE

Readers should note that each of these commands is documented at the end of the chapter.

Catalyst Switch Configuration

On the Catalyst switch platform, the authentication commands present themselves differently, but the resulting behavior is the same. The following configuration, like the router configuration, uses TACACS+ for login and enable (privileged) mode:

```
#tacacs+
set tacacs server 10.1.98.36 primary
set tacacs server 10.1.5.36
set tacacs attempts 3
set tacacs directedrequest disable
set tacacs key tjelkprp
set tacacs timeout 5
set authentication login tacacs enable
set authentication login local enable
set authentication enable tacacs enable
set authentication enable local enable
```

This gets around the security server if it goes down

Can be used as spisef in password

Again, this configuration file is an excerpt from the Catalyst switch configuration file—displayed with the `show running-configuration` command. There are two TACACS+ servers defined, however, notice that one is defined as primary. On the router the first server listed is defaulted to primary, but the switch allows for configuration using the keyword. Don't be too concerned with understanding the switch configuration—the test objectives only focus on the router-based commands. It is provided here so readers who have not previously experienced Catalyst commands can become familiar with them. The remainder of this chapter will only focus on the router commands.

The switch commands in this chapter are based on version 4.5.5 of the Catalyst code. There may be minor differences with other versions. `show configuration` or `write terminal` is often used to show the configuration information.

Authorization Configuration

Authorization defines the network services that are available to an individual or group. It provides an easy means of allowing privileged-mode (enable mode) access while restricting the commands that may be executed. For example, you may wish to isolate most enable commands to a single administrator or manager, while allowing operators to perform limited diagnostic functions. More experienced operators would be granted higher levels of authorization—for example, they may be permitted to shut down an interface. The unrestricted enable mode administrator would be required for additional functions.

Use care in restricting administrative rights to the router. While this is a helpful option when allocating rights to vendors and other parties, too restrictive a policy will lead to the distribution of the unrestricted account information, which can create a larger security risk.

A Sample TACACS+ Configuration File

The easiest way to understand the authorization function is to examine a configuration file that controls authorized services. Take a look at the following sample configuration file that controls authorized services:

```
#TACACS+ V2.1 configuration file
#created 5/14/96
#edited 8/20/99
#
#If user doesn't appear in the config file user/etc/
password
default authentication = file /etc/passwd
accounting file = /home1/logs/tacacs+.accounting
#Must be same as router IOS "tacacs-server key"
key = tjelkprp
#
user=netops {
   member=operator
   login=cleartext dilbert
}
user=rpadjen {
   # Robert Padjen
   default service=permit
   login=cleartext yummy
}
group=operator {
   name="Network Operator"
   cmd=debug {
      permit .*
   }
   cmd=write {
      permit terminal
   }
   cmd=clear {
      permit .*
   }
   cmd=show {
   #permit show commands
   permit .*
   }
}

user=tlammle {
```

```
                    # Todd Lammle
                    member=operator_plus
                    login=cleartext flatshoe
                }
            group=operator_plus {
                name="Network Operator Plus"
                cmd=debug {
                    permit .*
                }
                cmd=write {
                    permit terminal
                }
                cmd=clear {
                    permit .*
                }
                    #permit show commands
                cmd=show {
                    permit .*
                }
                cmd=configure {
                    permit terminal
                }
                cmd=interface {
                    permit .*
                }
                cmd=shutdown {
                    permit .*
                }
                cmd=no {
                    permit shutdown
                }
            }
```

This file establishes a number of user accounts and authorization rights. The first group, operators, is provided with basic diagnostic and administrative functions, while the operators_plus group is enhanced with **shutdown**, **interface**, and **configure** commands. All commands are available to one administrator. Note that Todd is a member of operators_plus, while Rob is allowed full access.

Pay particular attention to a few additional items about this specific, and somewhat dated, configuration file. First, the passwords are in clear-text—meaning that anyone with access to the server can obtain them. Second, observe that restrictions can be quite granular and could include functions such as Ping while blocking extended Ping.

 Please refer to the documentation that accompanies your server for syntax and configuration instructions specific to your installation.

Authorization Commands

Recall that authorization is the AAA process responsible for granting permission to access particular components in the network. The administrator will need to define these permissions based on corporate policy and user privileges. It is important to note that while a TACACS+ file was included in the previous section to illustrate authentication, the actual authorization controls were not included.

The commands associated with authorization include parameters for the protocols that are to be used. These commands are used after the authentication phase of AAA, and they are described in Table 11.4.

TABLE 11.4 AAA Authorization Commands

Command	Function
aaa authorization network	Performs authorization security on all network services, including SLIP, PPP, and ARAP.
aaa authorization exec	Authorizes the EXEC process with AAA.
aaa authorization commands level 15	All EXEC commands at the specified level (0–15). In this example, this is level 15, which is regarded as full authorization and normally associated with enable mode.

TABLE 11.4 AAA Authorization Commands *(continued)*

Command	Function
aaa authorization config-commands	Use AAA authorization for configuration mode commands.
aaa authorization reverse-access	Uses AAA authorization for reverse Telnet connections.
aaa authorization if-authenticated	Permits the user to use the requested function only if the user is authenticated.
aaa authorization local	Uses the local database for authorization. This database is stored on the router's configuration in NVRAM.
aaa authorization radius	Uses RADIUS for authorization.
aaa authorization tacacs+	Uses TACACS+ for authorization.

Accounting Configuration

The accounting function records who did what and for how long. Because of this, it relies upon the authentication process to provide part of the audit trail. For this reason, it is recommended that accounts be established with easily identified usernames—typically a last-name, first-initial configuration.

The configuration of accounting is fairly simple, but there are a few choices that should be considered. Table 11.5 provides a subset of the more common commands. Administrators will need to balance the desire to obtain complete accounting records against the overhead incurred.

TABLE 11.5 AAA Accounting Commands

Command	Description
aaa accounting command level	Audits all commands. If specified, only commands at the specified privilege level (0–15) are included.

TABLE 11.5 AAA Accounting Commands *(continued)*

Command	Description
aaa accounting connection	Audits all outbound connections including Telnet and rlogin.
aaa accounting exec	Audits the EXEC process.
aaa accounting network	Audits network service requests, including SLIP, PPP, and ARAP requests.
aaa accounting system	Audits system-level events. This includes reload, for example. Because a router reload is one of the ultimate denial-of-service attacks, it would be useful to know what user identification was used to issue the command.
aaa accounting start-stop	Documents the start and stop of a session. Audit information is sent in the background, negating any delay for the user.
aaa accounting stop-only	Sends a stop accounting notice at the end of a user process.
aaa accounting wait-start	Similar to aaa accounting start-stop, this command documents the start of a session. However, the user is not permitted to continue until the accounting server acknowledges the log entry. This can delay user access.
aaa accounting {tacacs+ | radius}	Enables TACACS+ or RADIUS accounting.

One area in which accounting transcends security is charge-back. If accurate start and stop times are recorded, a company could charge users for their time on the system to offset the cost. Internet Service Providers (ISPs) have long considered this as an alternative to the flat-rate model currently found in the United States.

Virtual Profiles

Virtual profiles and virtual templates provide ways to apply centralized, user-specific parameters to multiple access servers and their physical interfaces. This can greatly reduce the impact of changes to widely distributed access points.

As suggested by the name, there is a difference between a virtual profile and the element it replaces—the dialer profile. Dialer profiles maintain information on a single access server for specific users. The virtual profile adds the following:

- User specific configurations served from the AAA server

- An open methodology for defining both standards-based and vendor-specific parameters

Once the user authenticates the system, a virtual template is applied to the virtual access interface. User parameters are then obtained from the AAA server (security server) and applied to the virtual access interface. This solution allows for better scalability and easier administration than would be allowed with standard dialer profiles. As a result, the virtual profile is actually a culmination of the physical interface, generic information stored in a virtual template on the access server, and user specific parameters stored on the security server.

Readers who wish to expand their understanding of virtual profiles and their usage should refer to the Cisco Web site.

Summary

This chapter addressed the components of centralized security and the protocols that are often used to provide these services. Specifically, this chapter addressed the following:

- TACACS+

- RADIUS

- Cisco's AAA model, including authentication, authorization, and accounting

- The configuration of TACACS+ and RADIUS in product networks

- Virtual profiles

Key Terms

Before you take the exam, be certain you are familiar with the following terms:

access control

access servers

accounting

authentication

authentication, authorization, and accounting (AAA)

authorization

brute force attack

character mode connections

denial-of-service attack

Enhanced Terminal Access Controller Access Control System (TACACS+)

intruder detection

one-time challenge tokens

packet mode connections

Remote Access Dial-in User Service (RADIUS)

security policy

security server

Commands in This Chapter

Command	Description
`aaa accounting {tacacs+ | radius}`	Enables TACACS+ or RADIUS accounting.
`aaa accounting command level`	Audits all commands. If specified, only commands at the specified privilege level (0–15) are included.
`aaa accounting connection`	Audits all outbound connections including Telnet and rlogin.
`aaa accounting exec`	Audits the EXEC process.
`aaa accounting exec start-stop tacacs+`	Starts the accounting process, logging the start and stop times of each access.
`aaa accounting network`	Audits network service requests, including SLIP, PPP, and ARAP requests.
`aaa accounting start-stop`	Documents the start and stop of a session. Audit information is sent in the background, negating any delay for the user.
`aaa accounting stop-only`	Sends a stop accounting notice at the end of a user process.
`aaa accounting system`	Audits system-level events. This includes reload, for example.

`aaa accounting wait-start`	Similar to `aaa accounting start-stop`, this command documents the start of a session. However, the user is not permitted to continue until the accounting server acknowledges the log entry. This can delay user access.
`aaa authentication enable default tacacs+ enable`	Determines if the user can access enabled mode.
`aaa authentication login default tacacs+ enable`	Configures TACACS+ to be used for login level access.
`aaa authentication ppp user if-needed tacacs+`	AAA is used for PPP packet mode challenges. The list user is used first, and if unsuccessful, TACACS+ will be used.
`aaa authorization command n tacacs+ local`	Runs authorization for all commands at privilege level (n). Every line entered by a user can be controlled and authorized by TACACS+, although performance can suffer.
`aaa authorization commands level 15`	All EXEC commands at the specified level (0–15). In this example, this is level 15.
`aaa authorization config-commands`	Use AAA authorization for configuration mode commands.
`aaa authorization exec`	Authorize the EXEC process with AAA.
`aaa authorization exec tacacs+ local`	Determines if the user is allowed access to the EXEC shell. This example provides for TACACS+ authentication, and, should TACACS+ fail, permits authorization via the local database. The local database is populated with the `username` command.

`aaa authorization if-authenticated`	Permits the user to use the requested function only if the user is authenticated.
`aaa authorization local`	Uses the local database for authorization. This database is stored on the router's configuration in NVRAM.
`aaa authorization network`	Perform authorization security on all network services, including SLIP, PPP, and ARAP.
`aaa authorization network tacacs+ if-authenticated`	TACACS+ is used to determine if the user is permitted to make packet mode connections if the user is authenticated.
`aaa authorization radius`	Uses RADIUS for authorization.
`aaa authorization reverse-access`	Use AAA authorization for reverse Telnet connections.
`aaa authorization tacacs+`	Uses TACACS+ for authorization.
`aaa new-model`	Enables AAA services on the router. `New-model` reflects changes from the initial implementation, which is no longer supported.
`interface async16 ppp authentication chap user`	This is a new command for this chapter in that it associates an AAA function to an interface. Specifically, `line async16` is instructed to use the list user for CHAP authentication. Note that an AAA server (RADIUS, etc.) is not used.

`tacacs-server host` `10.1.98.36`	Specifies the IP address of the TACACS+ server. The single-connection parameter may be used to improve performance by maintaining a single TCP session as opposed to starting a separate session for each authentication.
`tacacs-server key tjelkprp`	Specifies the encryption key to be used for communications between the router and server.
`username` *user* `password` *password*	Creates or adds to the local database with a username of user and the password of password. This database is stored in the router's configuration file in NVRAM and can be accessed upon authentication failure depending on configuration.

Written Lab

1. What command starts the AAA process?

2. What is the command to define the IP address 192.168.72.5 as the TACACS+ server?

3. Write the command used to specify the TACACS+ shared encryption key using the password key.

4. What is the command to define the use of RADIUS for accounting services?

5. In order to make certain that each session is logged with a start time, the administrator would use what command?

6. It is important to audit significant events in the network, including the reload command. To configure this, which command would the administrator use?

7. What command would the administrator use to create a local database entry for George with the password curious?

8. What command would be used to define a TACACS+ server at address 192.168.2.1 and a standby server of 192.168.90.1?

9. Question 5 asked for the generic command to configure wait-start accounting. How would you alter this command to use TACACS+?

10. What parameters and sequence would be used to configure the access server for RADIUS, and, when this failed, what command would be used (using TACACS+) for enable mode authentication

Hands-on Lab

In this lab, you will configure AAA services using TACACS+. You do not need an actual TACACS+ server, although it might be helpful to configure that portion of the connection.

Lab 11.1 Configuring TACACS+

1. Configure the router to perform the following authentication, authorization, and accounting against your TACACS+ server. Accounting should be configured so that all session starts are logged to the server before the user may continue. Use the shared key of "class" and an IP address of 192.168.1.1 for the server unless otherwise instructed. Audit outbound Telnet sessions as well.

```
aaa new-model
aaa accounting exec wait-start tacacs+
aaa accounting connection start-stop tacacs+
aaa authentication enable default tacacs+ enable
aaa authentication login default tacacs+ enable
aaa authorization tacacs+
tacacs-server host 192.168.1.1
tacacs-server key class
```

Review Questions

1. What component of AAA is responsible for tracking the time a user disconnected from the system?

   A. Authentication

   B. Authorization

   C. Accounting

   D. Auditing

2. The administrator wishes to restrict access to commands even if the user is in enable mode.

   A. This is possible.

   B. This is possible; however, the user must not be given the enable password.

   C. This is possible; however, each router must be configured with the restriction command locally.

   D. This is not possible.

3. CiscoSecure operates on which of the following operating systems?

   A. Unix

   B. Windows 95/98

   C. Macintosh

   D. Windows NT

4. What component of AAA is responsible for determining the identity of a user?

   A. Authentication

   B. Authorization

   C. Accounting

   D. Auditing

5. Login and enable are associated with which of the following?

   A. Packet mode

   B. Character mode

   C. Binary mode

   D. Hex mode

6. CiscoSecure provides which of the following?

   A. RADIUS and TACACS+ servers

   B. A Web-based management console

   C. A centralized, relational, database-based access management system

   D. All of the above

7. Authorization requires information from which AAA component?

   A. Authentication

   B. Accounting

   C. Auditing

   D. Access

8. Which of the following is an advantage of using a security server?

   A. All user and password information is propagated to every access server and router automatically.

   B. Security information may be stored in a central location, similar to the way DNS stores host names centrally.

   C. Users must first authenticate to the security server and then to the access device—this adds an extra authentication step that results in a more secure system.

   D. None of the above.

9. Which of the following is a method of scaling and simplifying the distribution of user specific configuration information?

   A. Virtual parameters

   B. Virtual routing

   C. Parameter servicing

   D. Virtual profiles

10. What command is used to log the beginning and end of a user session?

    A. `aaa accounting begin-end`

    B. `aaa auditing start-stop`

    C. `aaa accounting start-stop`

    D. `accounting ppp start-stop`

11. The command to define the shared secret encryption key for connections with a TACACS+ server is:

    A. `aaa tacacs-server key` *key*

    B. `aaa server-key tacacs` *key*

    C. `tacacs-server key` *key*

    D. `aaa shared-secret tacacs` *key*

12. Which AAA component might be used to establish a charge-back system?

    A. Authorization

    B. Accounting

    C. Administration

    D. Authentication

13. Which of the following is not true regarding CiscoSecure?

    A. The server runs on NT or Unix.

    B. Profiles are stored in a relational database, such as Oracle or Sybase.

    C. Clients must run Windows NT.

    D. It supports TACACS+ and RADIUS.

14. The implementation of intrusion detection can lead to which of the following?

    A. Improved security with service impacting risk

    B. The potential for an attacker to use the function for a denial-of-service attack

    C. Simplified administration

    D. Improved security from required token-based authentication

15. The wait-start parameter on the aaa accounting command results in which of the following?

    A. The access server waits for the user's remote profile, stored on their PC, to be uploaded.

    B. The access server waits for the AAA server to acknowledge receipt of the start log entry.

    C. The access server waits for acknowledgment of all AAA communications.

    D. None of the above.

16. Which of the following are examples of client protocols?

    A. CHAP

    B. PPP

    C. TACACS+

    D. RADIUS

17. Which of the following are examples of server (central site) protocols?

    A. TACACS+

    B. PAP

    C. Kerberos V

    D. L2F

18. If the TACACS+ protocol fails to find a server, the user or administrator is always locked out of the access device unless which of the following is true?

    A. They have the enable secret password.

    B. The `enable` keyword was used.

    C. They press CTRL+ALT+DEL on their workstation

    D. Telnet from a pre-authorized host is used.

19. TACACS+ communicates via which of the following?

    A. TCP

    B. UDP

    C. SPX

    D. CDP

20. It is possible to select multiple authentication methods. For example, the administrator could configure TACACS+ to be used, but upon failure the access server's local database could be used. Is the previous statement accurate?

    A. Yes, with the `enable` keyword.

    B. Yes, with the `tacacs failure` command.

    C. Yes, with the `backup authentication` command.

    D. No, it is not possible, and administrators should maintain a backup TACACS+ server.

Answers to Written Lab

1. `aaa new-model`

2. `tacacs-server host 192.168.72.5`

3. `tacacs-server key password`

4. `aaa accounting radius`

5. `aaa accounting wait-start`

6. `aaa accounting system`

7. `username George password curious`

8. `tacacs-server host 192.168.2.1`
   `tacacs-server host 192.168.90.1`

9. `aaa accounting exec wait-start tacacs+`

10. `aaa authentication enable radius tacacs+`

Answers to Review Questions

1. C. Recall that while the function provides an audit trail, the service is called accounting. Cisco is not above slight word alterations on their exams.

2. A. A TACACS+ server can be configured to restrict enable commands on a per-user basis. Note that TACACS+ is not required.

3. A and D. Unfortunately, this is one of those need-to-memorize questions. If you needed to guess, it is important to remember that most Cisco products support Unix and NT.

4. A. Authentication obtains the username and validates the user's identity with a password or other authentication process.

5. B. Recall that packet mode is generally used for pass-through packets, such as PPP. Character mode is associated with login and enable services.

6. D. CiscoSecure is Cisco's AAA server, providing all of the noted services.

7. A. In order to authorize access, the system must identify the user. Authentication provides this service.

8. B. Recall that usernames and other information may be stored on the router locally—the benefit of security servers is centralization.

9. D. Again, part of this question is tricky because of like words. Virtual profiles allow for interface and user-specific configuration options.

10. C. There are two tricks to this question. The first requires knowing the name of the service that provides logging—accounting. The second requires knowing the parameter that governs the service—start-stop. Note that this question is useful for teaching a common trick in test guessing. Look at the repetition found in the answers—auditing and begin-end appear only once, which makes them unlikely. Answer D adds ppp, which was not part of the question.

11. C. Unlike the previous question, this one is just tough. You may have been tricked into thinking that the aaa prefix was necessary simply because it appeared in three choices. Answer A is also a trick because the command is correct except for this prefix.

12. B. By recording the duration of access, a company could implement a charge-back billing system.

13. C. CiscoSecure has no such restriction on clients. Since the server can use NT or Unix, this answer choice is also unlikely.

14. B. Administrators need to be cautious when they are deploying aggressive intrusion detection methods because they can lead to denial-of-service.

15. B. This question could be regarded as tricky, but you remembered the syntax of the commands in the chapter—right?

16. A and B. TACACS+ and RADIUS are server protocols. One clue for this question was the use of the plural *examples*. This usually denotes more than one answer (although the exam will tell you the exact number). Remember that CHAP operates over PPP, so if you remembered CHAP as a client protocol, PPP also must also included.

17. A and C. PAP and L2F are not server protocols because they operate between the client and server.

18. B. The enable keyword allows the local TACACS+ service to timeout and then use the local enable password. Note that the administrator could also reload the router and break in locally.

19. A. TACACS+ uses a connection-oriented IP protocol.

20. A. The enable keyword allows the enable password to be used in the event of TACACS+ server failure.

Appendix

A

Practice Exam

Practice Exam Questions

1. The Cisco 804 router provides which of the following?

    A. A well positioned central office router

    B. A high-density remote branch router

    C. An inexpensive telecommuter router that runs the Cisco IOS

    D. A low-density, high-capacity, VPN central office termination

2. How many D channels does an ISDN PRI in New York City have?

    A. 1

    B. 2

    C. 23

    D. 24

3. Which of the following is true regarding X.25?

    A. It provides more bandwidth than Frame Relay.

    B. It provides less bandwidth than Frame Relay.

    C. It is equal to Frame Relay because X.25 uses Frame Relay as a carrier.

    D. It is equal to Frame Relay because Frame Relay uses X.25 as a carrier.

4. Which of the following is not a remote access selection criterion?

   A. Availability

   B. Cost

   C. Manageability

   D. Security

   E. All of these are remote access selection criteria.

5. The odds favor locating which of the following connections available for remote access?

   A. X.25

   B. Asynchronous dial-up

   C. Frame Relay

   D. ISDN BRI

6. What does the acronym UART stand for?

   A. Uniform Analog Response Terminal

   B. Universal Asynchronous Receiver/Transmitter

   C. United Asynchronous Real-Time Token

   D. Universal Analog Receiver/Transmitter

7. Reverse Telnet requires a minimum of which two commands?

   A. `modem inout` and `transport input all`

   B. `modem out` and `transport output all`

   C. `transport modem inout` and `transport input all`

   D. None of the above

8. The administrator who is using reverse Telnet and is connecting with port 6 on the router would use which port number?

   A. 2001

   B. 2006

   C. 2600

   D. 4606

9. Which of the following is an analog connection?

   A. DTE to DTE

   B. DTE to DCE

   C. DCE to DCE

   D. Router to modem

10. The default interface configuration will permit which of the following connections?

    A. SLIP

    B. PPP

    C. EXEC

    D. All of the above

11. When displaying the output of ICMP pings, which of the following will the router present the PPP packets for this traffic as?

    A. TCPCP

    B. CDPCP

    C. IPCP

    D. LCP

12. Compression can be distributed with which two of the following?

    A. VIP 2 technology

    B. An RSP7000 engine

    C. The Supervisor III engine

    D. The compression service adapter

13. PPP security can be improved with which two of the following?

    A. PPP callback

    B. CHAP

    C. TCP header compression

    D. DHCP

14. To automate post-login functions, a user might use which of the following?

    A. Multilink

    B. PPP

    C. Scripting

    D. None of the above

15. When you connect to a Cisco remote access device, the designer should plan to use which of the following? (Select two.)

    A. CHAP

    B. PPP

    C. SLIP

    D. ARA

16. Which of the following commands is used to set the switch type on a Cisco BRI? (Choose all that apply.)

    A. Router(config)#**switch-type**

    B. Router(config-if)#**switch-type**

    C. Router(config)#**isdn switch-type**

    D. Router(config-if)#**isdn switch-type**

17. What is a TE2?

    A. Terminal Editor Twice, used to edit ISDN parameters on a router up to two times

    B. Terminal Equipment Today, used for today's ISDN standards

    C. Terminal Equipment Type 2, which is a non-ISDN device

    D. Terminal Equipment Type 2, which is an ISDN standard device

18. What is an R reference point used for?

    A. Defines the reference point between non-ISDN equipment (TE2) and a TA

    B. Defines the reference point between non-ISDN equipment (TE1) and a TA

    C. Connects to a U interface of a RJ-45 demarcation location

    D. Connects non-ISDN standards to 4-wire ISDN standards

19. Which ISDN protocol specifies switching?

    A. E

    B. R

    C. Q

    D. P

20. What ISDN command will bring up the second BRI at 50 percent load?

    A. `load balance 50`

    B. `load share 50`

    C. `dialer load-threshold 125`

    D. `dialer idle-timeout 125`

21. Bonding provides what function?

    A. Improved security

    B. Passive routing

    C. Circuit aggregation

    D. IP addressing

22. ClickStart and Fast Step provide which of the following?

    A. Simplified configuration and management of 700 series routers

    B. Examples of e-commerce solutions that use the 700 series routers

    C. Network modeling and billing services

    D. None of the above

23. To conserve addresses in a dynamic network, such as a field office where users bring in laptop computers for a short period of time, the architect might use which 700 series router feature?

    A. DHCP

    B. Bonding

    C. Compression

    D. Snapshot routing

24. Which of the following would not be a reason to use the 700 series router?

A. Support for ISDN BRI

B. Identical configuration commands with the 7513 router

C. Support for IP and IPX routing

D. Low cost

25. Which of the following is an advantage to using ISDN BRI?

A. Voice and data support on the same wire

B. Support for 1.544Mbps downloads

C. Always-on connections

D. Quality of service integration

26. Which of the following information relating to X.25 is provided by using the `show interface serial` command?

A. REJs, SABMs, and RNRs

B. FRMRs, RESTARTs, and DISCs

C. SABMs, FRMRs, and RESTARTs

D. All of the above.

27. A Packet Switched Network provider (PSN) assigns an NTN within how many digits?

A. From 1 to 15

B. From 8 to 15

C. From 8 to 11

D. Any numerical value

28. Which of the following Data Network Identification Codes (DNICs) identifies that the network resides in the United States?

   A. 310–316

   B. 400–412

   C. 252–265

   D. 655 only

29. Which of the following devices is used to identify X.25 responsibilities over a WAN connection? (Choose the best two answers.)

   A. Switch

   B. DTE

   C. DCE

   D. Dumb terminal

30. At what OSI Reference Layer does LAPB operate?

   A. Layer 1 (Physical Layer)

   B. Layer 2 (Data Link Layer)

   C. Layer 3 (Network Layer)

   D. Layer 4 (Transport Layer)

31. Which of the following is a valid command for applying a map class to a VC?

   A. RouterA(config-if)#`frame-relay class name`

   B. RouterA(config)#`frame-relay class name`

   C. RouterA(config)#`frame-relay traffic-shaping`

   D. RouterA(config-if)#`frame-relay traffic-shaping`

32. How many LMI types are available with Cisco routers?

    A. 2

    B. 3

    C. 10

    D. Unlimited

33. What will the frame switch send to a transmitting router if the switch is congested?

    A. Source-quench message

    B. BECNs

    C. FECNs

    D. Choke packet

34. If you have multipoint links and distance vector routing when using Frame Relay, some problems may be inherent. What would solve these problems?

    A. Frame Relay

    B. ATM

    C. ISDN

    D. Secondaries

    E. Subinterfaces

35. Which type of queuing shares bandwidth among all traffic types, giving priority to low-volume traffic?

    A. WFQ

    B. Priority

    C. Custom

    D. Link

36. Which type of queuing will always process the highest priority traffic first?

A. WFQ

B. Priority

C. Custom

D. Link

37. Which type of queuing processes all queues equally?

A. WFQ

B. Priority

C. Custom

D. Link

38. What is accomplished by the following configuration?

```
Router_C(config)#priority-list 1 protocol ip high gt 256
Router_C(config)#interface serial 0
Router_C(config-if)#priority-group 1
Router_C(config-if)#^Z
Router_C#
```

A. IP is held to a packet size of less than 256.

B. Priority list 1 is applied to serial interface 0 and permits packet sizes less than 256.

C. IP packets with sizes greater than 256 are assigned to the high-priority queue, and the list is applied to serial interface 0.

D. IP packets with sizes less than 256 are assigned a low priority, and the list is applied to serial interface 0.

39. Which of the following is used to establish a conversation for weighted fair queuing? (Choose all that apply.)

    A. Source address

    B. Destination address

    C. Packet size

    D. Port number

40. What type of compression compresses the data field and the header?

    A. Link

    B. Header

    C. Payload

    D. Predictor

41. When an inside network uses an IP addressing scheme that is used by another company, what type of network is this known as?

    A. Second network

    B. Overlapping network

    C. Overloading network

    D. Secondary network

42. Which of the following commands would you apply to the inside network interface to enable NAT translation?

    A. `set nat enable`

    B. `configure nat enable`

    C. `enable nat inside`

    D. `ip nat inside`

43. Which of the following will a router configured for PAT process if the traffic type is addressed for the PAT border router itself?

A. DHCP

B. SNMP

C. Ping

D. All of the above

44. Which of the following commands would be used if NAT, although configured properly, was failing to provide translations?

A. ip nat enable

B. clear ip nat translation

C. ip nat restart

D. debug ip nat

45. Which of the following commands enables PAT on a Cisco 700 series router?

A. set ip pat on

B. ip pat on

C. ip pat enable

D. All of the above

46. What does the acronym RADIUS stands for?

A. Radical User System

B. Reliable Authentication Daemon Interface User Security

C. Remote Access Dial-in User Service

D. Redundant Authorization Domain—International User Security

47. Management wishes to log the beginning and ending of all router access sessions. This would be implemented with which of the following?

    A. Accounting

    B. Authorization

    C. Auditing

    D. Logging

48. Why would an administrator wish to configure a centralized security server in the AAA model?

    A. To integrate DNS information throughout the network

    B. To provide firewall services

    C. To customize access lists

    D. To reduce the administrative overhead associated with security.

49. To enable radius authorization, the administrator would use which of the following?

    A. `ppp authorization radius`

    B. `aaa radius authorization`

    C. `aaa authorization radius`

    D. `aaa sercure server protocol radius`

50. Virtual profiles can effectively replace what element?

    A. Dialer profiles

    B. AAA services

    C. The TACACS+ protocol

    D. None of the above

Answers to Practice Exam

1. C. The 800 series routers are generally the lowest cost, IOS-based systems.

2. A. All ISDN connections, BRI and PRI, European and American, have a single D channel.

3. B. X.25 provides less bandwidth than Frame Relay, in large part due to the extra overhead incurred with error checking.

4. E. All remote access solutions need to consider availability, cost, manageability, and security.

5. B. Asynchronous dial-up is the most ubiquitous connection type. ISDN, Frame Relay, and X.25 are all services that are generally found only once a need has been identified. Asynchronous dial-up is found in virtually every home, hotel, and business.

6. B. Unfortunately, this answer requires memorization, although you would most likely only need to understand the function based on either the term UART or Universal Asynchronous Receiver/Transmitter.

7. A. This question is tricky. Answer C looks correct; however, the answer is A—the modem needs to be configured for inout and the transport must be configured for input.

8. B. Reverse Telnet TCP ports start at 2000, with the physical port number providing the specific last number.

9. C. Modem-to-modem connections are DCE to DCE analog connections.

10. C. It is important to note that this problem frequently stumps administrators. Always note the default interface configuration—remember that the configuration file does not (most of the time) contain an entry for default options. The default is exec mode.

11. C. ICMP is a function of IP, so IPCP would be reported as the protocol in the PPP traffic flow.

12. A, D. Both the compression service adapter and the VIP 2 carrier cards can offload compression services.

13. A, B. Both PPP callback and CHAP can be used to improve security on PPP connections.

14. C. Scripts may be used with any protocol and provide a means of automating post-login functions. Multilink and PPP do not provide this service.

15. A and B. Of the choices provided, CHAP is virtually required for secure authentication, and PPP is required for CHAP. SLIP and ARA are both limited protocols that are rarely used.

16. C, D. The command `isdn switch-type` can be used in either global configuration mode or interface configuration mode.

17. C. TE2s define a device that does not understand ISDN signaling techniques.

18. A. The R reference point is the point in the ISDN network between a non-standard connection, like a serial interface on a Cisco router, to a terminal adapter, which changes the digital signaling to ISDN standards.

19. C. The ISDN protocol that specifies switching is Q.

20. C. The `dialer load-threshold 125` command tells the router to bring up the second BRI at 50 percent load.

21. C. Bonding makes two or more connections appear as a single logical link.

22. A. ClickStart and Fast Step are different programs offered by Cisco to aid in the configuration and management of 700 series routers.

23. A. DHCP is a means to conserve IP addresses because the pool of machines is substantially greater than the number of concurrent users.

24. B. The 700 series does not use the Cisco IOS that is found on the 7500 series routers.

25. A. ISDN BRI supports two B channels, each of which may be used for voice services.

26. D. The `show interface serial` command displays information on REJs, which are the number of rejects; SABMs, which are the number of Set Asynchronous Balance Mode requests; RNRs, which are the number of Receiver Not Ready events; FRMRs, which are the number of protocol frame errors; RESTARTs, which are the number of restarts; and DISCs, which are the number of disconnects.

27. C. The NTN is a numerical value between 8 and 11 digits that is assigned by a PSN.

28. A. A three-digit DNIC in the range of 310 to 316 identifies a network residing in the United States.

29. B, C. The DTE and the DCE are used to identify the responsibilities of X.25 over a WAN connection. The DTE device resides on the customer's side of an X.25 link and the DCE lies on the PSN side of an X.25 link.

30. B. The LAPB uses frames and is used at the Data Link Layer of the OSI Reference Model.

31. A. The command `frame-relay class name` sets the map class on a VC. The `frame-relay traffic-shaping` command must first be enabled on the interface.

32. B. Cisco routers support three LMI types: Cisco, ANSI, and q933a.

33. B. The frame switch will send Backward Explicit Congestion Notification (BECN) messages if the switch is congested.

34. E. Subinterfaces will automatically fix spit-horizon issues associated with routing protocols.

35. A. WFQ was designed to stop large file transfers from hogging the bandwidth of a serial link.

36. B. The highest priority queues will always be processed first with priority queuing.

37. C. Unlike priority queuing, custom queuing processes all queues equally. However, the administrator bases the queues on traffic types.

38. C. A priority queue list was created and assigned to serial 0, which assigns any packet larger than 256 bytes to a high-priority queue.

39. A, B, D. Source and destination address, as well as port number, are used to establish a conversation for WFQ.

40. A. Link compression compresses both the header and data field of the packet.

41. B. An overlapping network is a network that uses a globally routable IP range already in use on the Internet. This is possibly the cause of changing ISPs and receiving a new, valid, globally routable IP address.

42. D. The `ip nat inside` command is used to enable NAT on the interface connected to the inside network on the NAT border router.

43. D. A PAT border router will not allow DHCP, SNMP, or Ping (ICMP) destined to an inside address but will still process packets for those protocols destined for the router itself.

44. B. Occasionally, NAT will discontinue working properly even though it has been configured properly. Clearing the NAT table usually resolves the issue.

45. A. On a Cisco 700 series router, the command that enables PAT on a router is `set ip pat on` and must be used before the `set ip pat porthandler` command is used.

46. C. It is always a good idea to know what various acronyms stand for. RADIUS stands for Remote Access Dial-in User Service.

47. A. Accounting is the AAA service that provides auditing services. It is recommended that readers know the three services that comprise AAA.

48. D. Security servers only control authentication, authorization and accounting services. They do not incorporate DNS, firewall or access-list services.

49. C. The `aaa authorization radius` command instructs the router to use the RADIUS protocol for AAA authorization.

50. A. Virtual profiles allow centralized user permissions—dialer profiles allow only local settings. This makes virtual profiles more scalable.

Appendix

B

Commands in This Study Guide

This appendix is a compilation of the "Commands in This Chapter" lists at the end of the chapters.

Command	Meaning	Chapter
`aaa accounting {tacacs+ | radius}`	Enables TACACS+ or RADIUS accounting.	11
`aaa accounting command level`	Audits all commands. If specified, only commands at the specified privilege level (0–15) are included.	11
`aaa accounting connection`	Audits all outbound connections including Telnet and rlogin.	11
`aaa accounting exec`	Audits the EXEC process.	11
`aaa accounting exec start-stop tacacs+`	Starts the accounting process, logging the start and stop times of each access.	11
`aaa accounting network`	Audits network service requests, including SLIP, PPP, and ARAP requests.	11
`aaa accounting start-stop`	Documents the start and stop of a session. Audit information is sent in the background, negating any delay for the user.	11
`aaa accounting stop-only`	Sends a stop accounting notice at the end of a user process.	11
`aaa accounting system`	Audits system-level events. This includes reload, for example.	11
`aaa accounting wait-start`	Similar to `aaa accounting start-stop`, this command documents the start of a session. However, the user is not permitted to continue until the accounting server acknowledges the log entry. This can delay user access.	11

Command	Meaning	Chapter
`aaa authentication enable default tacacs+ enable`	Determines if the user can access enabled mode.	11
`aaa authentication login default tacacs+ enable`	Configures TACACS+ to be used for login level access.	11
`aaa authentication ppp user if-needed tacacs+`	AAA is used for PPP packet mode challenges. The list user is used first, and if unsuccessful, TACACS+ will be used.	11
`aaa authorization command n tacacs+ local`	Runs authorization for all commands at privilege level (n). Every line entered by a user can be controlled and authorized by TACACS+, although performance can suffer.	11
`aaa authorization commands level 15`	All EXEC commands at the specified level (0–15). In this example, this is level 15.	11
`aaa authorization config-commands`	Use AAA authorization for configuration mode commands.	11
`aaa authorization exec`	Authorizes the EXEC process with AAA.	11
`aaa authorization exec tacacs+ local`	Determines if the user is allowed access to the EXEC shell. This example provides for TACACS+ authentication, and, should TACACS+ fail, permits authorization via the local database. The local database is populated with the `username` command.	11

Command	Meaning	Chapter
aaa authorization if-authenticated	Permits the user to use the requested function only if the user is authenticated.	11
aaa authorization local	Uses the local database for authorization. This database is stored on the router's configuration in NVRAM.	11
aaa authorization network	Performs authorization security on all network services, including SLIP, PPP, and ARAP.	11
aaa authorization network tacacs+ if-authenticated	TACACS+ is used to determine if the user is permitted to make packet mode connections if the user is authenticated.	11
aaa authorization radius	Uses RADIUS for authorization.	11
aaa authorization reverse-access	Uses AAA authorization for reverse Telnet connections.	11
aaa authorization tacacs+	Uses TACACS+ for authorization.	11
aaa new-model	Enables AAA services on the router. New-model reflects changes from the initial implementation, which is no longer supported.	11
access-list	Configures a standard IP access list for the inside network.	10
backup delay	Sets the amount of time that the BRI interface will dial the remote end after the primary interface drops. Also sets the amount of time before the secondary link drops when the primary link comes back up.	5

Command	Meaning	Chapter
`backup interface`	Sets an interface to use a BRI interface if the main link fails.	5
`backup load`	Adds bandwidth to a primary link if it is saturated.	5
`cd lan`	Enters LAN configuration mode.	6
`channel-group`	Configures the amount of channels that are used on a PRI interface.	5
`clear frame-relay-inarp`	Deletes the dynamically assigned PVC to Network Layer addresses.	8
`clear ip nat translation`	Clears all NAT-table entries.	10
`clear ip nat translation inside`	Clears all inside NAT-table simple translation entries.	10
`clear ip nat translation outside`	Clears all outside NAT-table simple translation entries.	10
`compress [predictor	stac	mppc	[ignore-pfc]]`	The `compress` command is used to select the type of compression desired on a PPP link.	3
`compress predictor`	Turns on predictor compression.	9
`custom-queue-list`	Assigns a custom queue to an interface.	9
`debug ip nat`	Displays IP NAT debugging information.	10
`debug isdn q921`	Shows the commands and responses exchanged during peer-to-peer communication carried over the D channel.	5

Command	Meaning	Chapter
debug isdn q931	Displays information about call setup and teardown of ISDN network connections between the local router and the network.	5
debug lapb	Provides debug information for the LAPB protocol.	7
debug ppp authentication	Enables debug messages for authentication processes under PPP, including CHAP and PAP.	3
debug ppp negotiation	This **debug** command provides information about the PPP call establishment process.	3
debug ppp packet	Shows the administrator each packet that is encapsulated into PPP for transport.	3
debug x25 events	Provides debugging information on X.25 statistics.	7
default-router ip address	The **default-router** command configures the default gateway entry in DHCP leases.	3
dialer hold-queue	Specifies the length of the queue for packets waiting for the line to come up.	5
dialer idle-timeout	Tells a BRI interface to drop the line after a specified amount of seconds that interesting traffic is not found on the link.	5
dialer load-threshold	Specifies at what traffic load the BRI will bring up the second B channel. Also tells the interface when to bring down the second B channel. Used with multilink PPP.	5

Command	Meaning	Chapter
`dialer map`	Describes to an interface what number to dial based on IP packet characteristics.	5
`dialer pool`	Binds a dialer interface to a dialer pool configured with the `dialer remote-name` command.	5
`dialer pool-member`	Tells a BRI interface that it is part of a dialer pool.	5
`dialer string`	Defines the destination router's phone number and supports optional map classes.	5
`dialer-group`	Configures a dialer list that defines interesting packets to trigger a call for DDR.	5
`dialer-list`	Creates a list of interesting traffic based on protocol type.	5
`dns-server ip address`	Uses the `dns-server` command to configure the name servers to be used by DHCP clients.	3
`domain-name domain name`	DNS servers are defined with this command.	3
`encapsulation frame-relay`	Sets an interface to use Frame Relay.	8
`encapsulation ppp`	Enables the PPP protocol on the interface.	3, 5
`encapsulation x25`	Sets the encapsulation method to DTE or DCE.	7
`fair-queue`	Enables or disables fair-queuing on a routing interface.	9

Command	Meaning	Chapter
`flowcontrol`	May be followed with hardware or software settings. Typically, hardware is allowed to provide control over the data flow. Software flowcontrol is not recommended.	2
`frame-relay adaptive-shaping becn`	Sets bandwidth usage for protocols.	8
`frame-relay class name`	Assigns the map-class to a VC.	8
`frame-relay custom-queue-list`	Creates a queue list to be applied to a VC.	8
`frame-relay de-group`	Assigns the DE-list to an interface.	8
`frame-relay de-list`	Creates a list of protocols or applications that will be set with the DE bit on.	8
`frame-relay interface-dlci`	Sets a DLCI number on an interface.	8
`frame-relay intf-type dce`	Sets an interface as a DCE Frame Relay switch.	8
`frame-relay map`	Creates a static PVC to Network Layer mapping.	8
`frame-relay priority-group`	Creates a queue list to be applied to a VC.	8
`frame-relay route`	Creates static maps on a Frame Relay switch.	8
`frame-relay switching`	Turns your router into a Frame Relay switch.	8

Command	Meaning	Chapter
`frame-relay traffic-rate`	Changes the traffic rates on a Cisco router Frame Relay interface.	8
`frame-relay traffic-shaping`	Aligns the map-class to an interface.	8
`framing`	Configures a PRI interface with the type of framing that the provider's switch is using.	5
`int s0.16 point-to-point`	Creates a point-to-point subinterface.	8
`interface async16 ppp authentication chap user`	Associates an AAA function to an interface. Specifically, `line async16` is instructed to use the list user for CHAP authentication. Note that an AAA server (RADIUS, etc.) is not used.	11
`interface dialer`	Creates a logical interface. Used instead of dialer map statements.	5
`ip dhcp database`	Enters the database configuration mode.	3
`ip dhcp pool 0`	DHCP uses pools to categorize entries. This command example establishes the first pool, which generally contains global DHCP configurations.	3
`ip nat inside`	Enables NAT on the inside NAT interface.	10
`ip nat inside source list`	Maps an access list to the IP NAT pool.	10
`ip nat inside source static`	Configures the static NAT IP addresses to be used for translation.	10

Command	Meaning	Chapter
`ip nat outside`	Enables NAT on the outside NAT interface.	10
`ip nat pool`	Configures an IP pool of addresses for the inside network.	10
`ip tcp header-compression`	This command enables TCP header compression services.	3, 9
`isdn spid1`	Configures the first B channel on a BRI interface.	5
`isdn spid2`	Configures the second B channel on a BRI interface.	5
`line N`	Cisco routers refer to asynchronous ports as lines. N is equal to the number of the port and is used before the rest of the commands in this table.	2
`linecode`	Sets the type of line coding in a PRI interface that the provider's switch is using.	5
`login`	Is required in order to permit a connection.	2
`map-class frame-relay`	Creates a map-class on a Cisco router to perform traffic shaping.	8
`modem`	Is used to define the type of call allowed. By default, the modem will allow dial-in or incoming calls. However, for reverse Telnet or dial-out connections in addition to dial-in, the administrator would use the `inout` keyword.	2

Command	Meaning	Chapter
`netbios-name-server ip address`	Configures the WINS server entry that will be forwarded in the DHCP lease.	3
`network ip address mask`	The `network` command within the `ip dhcp pool` command defines the scope for the DHCP process.	3
`no debug all`	Stops all debugging functions.	7
`no debug x25 events`	Stops only X.25 events' debugging functions.	7
`password`	Establishes the password to be used on the line.	2
`ppp authentication {chap	chap pap	pap chap	pap} [if-needed][list-name	default] [callin]`	The `ppp authentication` command defines the type of authentication that should be used.	3
`ppp authentication chap`	Configures an interface to use CHAP authentication.	5
`ppp authentication pap`	Configures an interface to use PAP authentication.	5
`ppp multilink`	Specifies that this dialer interface uses multilink PPP.	3, 5
`priority-group`	Assigns a priority queue to an interface.	9
`priority-list`	Creates a priority queue list.	9
`queue-list`	Creates a custom queue list.	9
`service dhcp`	Establishes a DHCP server on the router.	3

Command	Meaning	Chapter
`set 1 dir directory-number`	The directory number is usually the last seven digits of the SPID number, not including the service bits. It may also be regarded as the prefix and identifier of the number in the North American Dialing Plan (NADP). This command defines the phone number of the connection, which may differ from the SPID.	6
`set 1 spid spid-number`	Defines the number to be associated with the first BRI channel. The number 2 would be substituted for the second BRI channel.	6
`set active profile_name`	Configures a profile to be active. The reverse of this command is `set inactive profile_name`.	6
`set bridging off`	Disables bridging services. As with most commands presented, the opposite keyword is used to reverse the setting—`set bridging on`, for example. This differs from the IOS, which typically uses the no prefix.	6
`set caller id on`	Allows receipt of caller ID information on the interface. It is important to note that this service must be provided by the local phone company. In addition, it is possible to block caller ID information—it is recommended that administrators install and test the connection without ID services and then add it to a working configuration.	6

Command	Meaning	Chapter
`set callisdnreceive number`	Ensures that calls from the specified number will be authenticated. The corollary is also true—calls from other numbers will not be authenticated.	6
`set default`	Is the same as `write erase` in the IOS—it clears the configuration from NVRAM. Unlike the IOS, a `reload` command is not required after NVRAM is cleared.	6
`set dhcp address 10.20.30.2 254`	Defines the starting and ending addresses in the DHCP pool. In this case, addresses from 10.20.30.2 through 10.20.30.254 are part of the scope.	6
`set dhcp dns primary 10.10.1.51`	Specifies the DNS address for DHCP clients.	6
`set dhcp gateway primary 10.20.30.1`	Defines the default gateway to be assigned as part of the DHCP lease.	6
`set dhcp netmask 255.255.255.0`	Specifies the subnet mask for the pool.	6
`set dhcp server`	Enables the DHCP server functionality on the Cisco 700 router.	6
`set dhcp wins primary 10.10.1.51`	Defines the WINS server to be used by DHCP clients.	6
`set ip address 192.168.2.1`	Sets the IP address for the Ethernet interface to the value provided; in this case, 192.168.2.1.	6

Command	Meaning	Chapter
`set ip netmask 255.255.255.0`	Configures a 24-bit netmask for the previously entered IP address. The IOS combines this with the `ip address` command.	6
`set ip pat on`	Enables PAT on Cisco 700 series routers.	10
`set ip pat port`	Allows all PAT services on Cisco 700 series routers.	10
`set ip pat tcptimeout 30`	Defines the timer used by the router to age TCP sessions—the router will remove the entry from the PAT table if no packets matching the entry are seen in the timeout window.	6
`set ip pat udptimeout 5`	Defines the timer used by the router to age UDP sessions—the router will remove the entry from the PAT table if no packets matching the entry are seen in the timeout window.	6
`set ip routing on`	Enables IP routing.	6
`set ppp authentication incoming [chap | pap | none ]`	Enables CHAP authentication for incoming connections when the chap keyword is used. All the options may be used, which will operate in the order chap, pap, and none.	6
`set ppp authentication outgoing [ chap | pap | none ]`	Enables CHAP authentication for outgoing connections. This is an optional item.	6
`set ppp secret client`	Sets the client CHAP secret password.	6

Command	Meaning	Chapter
`set ppp secret host`	Must match the secret client of the opposing router. Host is used to authenticate to the remote router.	6
`set switch 5ess`	Sets the 700 router to work with AT&T basic rate switches (U.S.).	6
`set switch dms`	Sets the 700 router to work with Nortel DMS-100 switch (North America).	6
`set switch net3`	Sets the 700 router to work with switches found in the United Kingdom and other European countries.	6
`set switch ni-1`	Sets the 700 router to work with National ISDN-1 (North America) switches.	6
`set systemname name`	Configures a name for the router.	6
`set user profile_name`	Enters user mode and defines the profile name.	6
`show dialer`	Shows information statistics for incoming and outgoing calls.	5
`show frame-relay lmi`	Shows the LMI information on the router.	8
`show frame-relay map`	Shows the dynamic and static mappings of DLCI to Network Layer addresses.	8
`show frame-relay pvc`	Shows the configured PVC on the router.	8
`show frame-relay route`	Shows the routes configured on the Frame Relay switch.	8

Command	Meaning	Chapter
`show interface`	Displays the line, encapsulation DLCI, and LMI information of an interface.	7, 8
`show interface serial`	Displays the serial interfaces' configuration and statistics.	7
`show ip configuration [all]`	With the `all` keyword, this command displays the IP configuration for all profiles. Without the keyword, the current profile's IP configuration will be displayed.	6
`show ip filter [all]`	While not a routing command, many times routing problems will appear as a result of an IP filter, or an access list in IOS terms. This command will display the filter for the current profile or, with the `all` keyword, all configured filters.	6
`show ip nat statistics`	Shows NAT statistics.	10
`show ip pat`	Displays PAT monitoring information.	10
`show ip route [all]`	With the `all` keyword, this command displays all static IP routes. Without the keyword, the current profile's routes will be displayed.	6
`show isdn status`	Displays information about memory and Layer 2 and 3 timers as well as the status of the channels.	5

Command	Meaning	Chapter
show line	Shows the status of a line on an access server. Usually requires that the connection be established to provide useful diagnostic data.	4
show nat translations	Shows NAT translations in the NAT table.	10
show queue	Displays more detailed information about queuing on an interface.	9
show queueing	Displays the current queuing configuration.	9
show running-config	Shows the current IOS configuration.	7
speed	Establishes the maximum speed to be used between the modem and access server or router. It defines the speed of both transmit and receive, which are noted in bits per second (bps). Note that the modem and access server can negotiate a slower speed or data rate.	2
stopbits	Are sent in asynchronous connections to define the end of a byte. Typically, the stopbit value is set to 1 because there is little reason to send additional bits; however, values of 1.5 and 2 are also allowed.	2

Command	Meaning	Chapter
`tacacs-server host 10.1.98.36`	Specifies the IP address of the TACACS+ server. The single-connection parameter may be used to improve performance by maintaining a single TCP session as opposed to starting a separate session for each authentication.	11
`tacacs-server key tjelkprp`	Specifies the encryption key to be used for communications between the router and server.	11
`transport input`	Defines the protocol to use in reverse Telnet connections. This may be LAT, MOP, NASI, PAD, RLOGIN, Telnet, or v120; however, administrators typically use the `all` keyword to allow all connection types. This is potentially less secure, as a hacker could use one of these protocols to gain access or deny service to the router. For example, if there is no business need to use RLOGIN, why leave the access available to allow repeated access attempts from an outsider?	2
`undebug all`	Stops all debugging functions.	7
`upload`	Views the saved configuration of the 700 series router.	6
`username`	Sets the name and password used to communicate with authentication to the remote router.	5
`username name password secret`	The `username` command places an entry in the router's user database.	3

Command	Meaning	Chapter
`username user password password`	Creates or adds to the local database with a username of user and the password of password. This database is stored in the router's configuration file in NVRAM and can be accessed upon authentication failure depending on configuration.	11
`x25 address`	Assigns an X.25 address to an interface.	7
`x25 hic circuit-number`	Sets the highest incoming VC number. Valid number range VC 1–4095.	7
`x25 hoc circuit-number`	Sets the highest outgoing-only VC number. Valid number range VC 1–4095.	7
`x25 htc circuit-number`	Sets the highest two-way VC number. Valid number range VC 1–4095.	7
`x25 ips`	Sets the maximum input packet size. Valid number range VC 1–4095.	7
`x25 lic circuit-number`	Sets the lowest incoming VC number. Valid VC number range 1–4095.	7
`x25 loc circuit-number`	Sets the lowest outgoing VC number. Valid VC number range 1–4095.	7
`x25 ltc circuit-number`	Sets the lowest two-way VC number. Valid number range VC 1–4095.	7
`x25 map`	Sets the LAN protocols–to–remote host mappings.	7

Command	Meaning	Chapter
x25 modulo	Sets the sliding window sequence count to 8 or 128.	7
x25 ops	Sets the output packet size.	7
x25 pvc	Configures PVC encapsulation information.	7
x25 win	Changes the incoming window size.	7
x25 wout	Changes the outgoing window size.	7

Appendix C

References

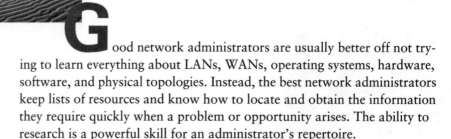ood network administrators are usually better off not trying to learn everything about LANs, WANs, operating systems, hardware, software, and physical topologies. Instead, the best network administrators keep lists of resources and know how to locate and obtain the information they require quickly when a problem or opportunity arises. The ability to research is a powerful skill for an administrator's repertoire.

This appendix includes various references to assist network administrators.

Not all of these sources were used in researching material for this book.

Web-Based Resources

The following sections list some of the resources available on the Internet. The lists are by no means intended to be exhaustive.

While every effort has been made to provide an accurate list, the dynamic nature of the Internet and the static nature of this text will likely result in invalid references over time.

WAN Technologies

Organization	URL
DSL Forum	www.adsl.com
DSL Life	www.dsllife.com
Frame Relay Forum	www.frforum.com
The ATM Forum	www.atmforum.com/index.html
Commercial Communications Standards	www-comm.itsi.disa.mil/isdn/index.html
The North American ISDN Users' Forum	www.niuf.nist.gov/

Operating Systems

Organization	URL
Apple	www.apple.com
Novell	www.novell.com
Microsoft	www.microsoft.com
CNET: WinFiles	www.winfiles.com
Linux	www.linux.org

Other Resources

Organization	URL
Cisco Systems	www.cisco.com
CMP Tech Web	teledotcom.com
Consortium for School Networking	www.cosn.org
Distributed Management Task Force	www.dmtf.org
GlobalNet Training Solutions	www.lammle.com

IBM	www.networking.ibm.com
Internet Traffic Statistics	whatis.com/itraffic.htm
Todd Lammle	www.lammle.com
L0PHT Heavy Industries	www.l0pht.com
NetFix: Used Cisco gear	www.netfix.com
Network World Fusion	www.nwfusion.com
NewBridge	www.newbridge.com
Nortel Networks	www.nortelnetworks.com
OpenView Forum International	www.ovforum.org
PC Week	www.pcweek.com
Pittsburgh Supercomputing Center	www.psc.edu/networking
RouterSim	www.routersim.com
Sean Odom	www.TheQuestForCertification.com
Securitywatch.com	www.securitywatch.com
Slashdot	www.slashdot.org
Sun Microsystems	docs.sun.com
Ziff-Davis	www.zdnet.com

Certification Study Groups

Organization	URL
NetCerts	www.netcerts.com
Cisco Professional Association Worldwide (CPAW)	www.ciscopaw.com
Boson Software: Practice tests	www.boson.com
GroupStudy.com	www.groupstudy.com
Network Study Guides	www.networkstudyguides.com

Users Groups

Organization	URL
Capital District Cisco Users Group	www.cdcug.org
Cisco Users Group for Central Iowa	www.cisco.knis.com
Dallas/Ft. Worth Cisco Users Group	www.cisco-users.org
Denver Cisco Users Group	www.twpm.com/dcug/
Kansas Cisco Users Group	www.cugkansas.com/home.cfm
New England Cisco Systems Users Group	www.ciscousers.com
Northern California Cisco Users Group	www.csecnet.com/cisco/index.htm
Omaha Cisco User Group	www.teklnk.com
Sacramento/Placer County Cisco Users Group	www.cisco-cert.org

San Diego Cisco Users Group	`www.sdvar.com/SDCUG/`
South Carolina Cisco Users Group	`www.angelfire.com/sc/cisco`
Southern California Cisco Users Group	`www.sccug.org`

Standards Organizations

Organization	URL
American National Standards Institute (ANSI)	`www.ansi.org`
Electronic Industries Alliance (EIA)	`www.tiaonline.org`
Gigabit Ethernet Alliance	`www.gigabit-ethernet.org`
High-Speed Token Ring Alliance	`www.hstra.com`
Institute for Electrical and Electronics Engineers (IEEE)	`www.ieee.org`
International Organization for Standardization (ISO)	`www.iso.ch`
International Telecommunication Union Telecommunication Standardization Sector (ITU-T)	`www.itu.int`
Internet Engineering Task Force (IETF)	`www.ietf.org`
National Committee for Information Technology Standards (NCITS)	`www.t11.org`

Job Search Web Sites

jobs.statestreet.com

talentmarket.monster.com

www.1-jobs.com

www.brainpower.com

www.brilliantpeople.com

www.careercast.com

www.computerjobs.com

www.dice.com

www.guru.com

www.headhunter.net

www.hotjobs.com

www.incpad.com

www.joboptions.com

www.modisit.com

www.monster.com

www.realrates.com

www.skillsvillage.com

www.techies.com

www.vault.com

Hands-on Schooling

Organization	URL
e-Business Process Solutions	www.e-bps.com
GlobalNet Training Solutions	www.lammle.com
Mentor Labs	www.mentorlabs.com
Router University	www.routeru.com

RFCs

It would be inappropriate to reprint the entire RFC index in this text. Several Web sites provide this information in a continually updated manner. This list is intended to highlight some of the more important and frequently referenced RFCs.

1055—SLIP

1483—ATM AAL5, Multiprotocol Encapsulation

1487—LDAP

1490—Multiprotocol Connect over Frame Relay

1492—TACACS

1577—ATM ARP

1586—OSPF on Frame Relay

1631—NAT

1661—PPP

1700—IP Assigned Numbers

1918—Private IP v.4 Address Space

1925—The 12 Networking Truths (the most important RFC?)

1990—PPP Multilink Protocol

2002—IP Mobility

2132—DHCP Options

2281—HSRP

2324—Hyper Text Coffee Pot Control Protocol (really)

2328—OSPF v.2

2338—VRRP

2676—OSPF QoS

2740—OSPF IP v.6

Glossary

A&B bit signaling Used in T1 transmission facilities and sometimes called "24th channel signaling." Each of the 24 T1 subchannels in this procedure uses one bit of every sixth frame to send supervisory signaling information.

AAA Authentication, authorization and accounting: A Cisco description of the processes that are required to provide a remote access security solution. Each is implemented separately but relies on the others for functionality.

AAL ATM Adaptation Layer: A service-dependent sublayer of the Data Link Layer, which accepts data from other applications and brings it to the ATM layer in 48-byte ATM payload segments. CS and SAR are the two sublayers that form AALs. Currently, the four types of AAL recommended by the ITU-T are AAL1, AAL2, AAL3/4, and AAL5. AALs are differentiated by the source-destination timing they use, whether they are CBR or VBR, and whether they are used for connection-oriented or connectionless mode data transmission. *See also: AAL1, AAL2, AAL3/4, AAL5, ATM,* and *ATM layer.*

AAL1 ATM Adaptation Layer 1: One of four AALs recommended by the ITU-T, it is used for connection-oriented, time-sensitive services that need constant bit rates, such as isochronous traffic and uncompressed video. *See also: AAL.*

AAL2 ATM Adaptation Layer 2: One of four AALs recommended by the ITU-T, it is used for connection-oriented services that support a variable bit rate, such as voice traffic. *See also: AAL.*

AAL3/4 ATM Adaptation Layer 3/4: One of four AALs (a product of two initially distinct layers) recommended by the ITU-T, supporting both connectionless and connection-oriented links. Its primary use is in sending SMDS packets over ATM networks. *See also: AAL.*

AAL5 ATM Adaptation Layer 5: One of four AALs recommended by the ITU-T, it is used to support connection-oriented VBR services primarily to transfer classical IP over ATM and LANE traffic. This least complex of the AAL recommendations uses SEAL, offering lower bandwidth costs and simpler processing requirements but also providing reduced bandwidth and error-recovery capacities. *See also: AAL.*

AARP AppleTalk Address Resolution Protocol: The protocol in an AppleTalk stack that maps data-link addresses to network addresses.

AARP probe packets Packets sent by the AARP to determine whether a given node ID is being used by another node in a nonextended AppleTalk network. If the node ID is not in use, the sending node appropriates that node's ID. If the node ID is in use, the sending node will select a different ID and then send out more AARP probe packets. *See also: AARP.*

ABM Asynchronous Balanced Mode: When two stations can initiate a transmission, ABM is an HDLC (or one of its derived protocols) communication technology that supports peer-oriented, point-to-point communications between both stations.

ABR Area Border Router: An OSPF router that is located on the border of one or more OSPF areas. ABRs are used to connect OSPF areas to the OSPF backbone area.

access control Used by Cisco routers to control packets as they pass through a router. Access lists are created and then applied to router interfaces to accomplish this.

Access Layer One of the layers in Cisco's three-layer hierarchical model. The Access Layer provides users with access to the internetwork.

access link Is a link used with switches and is only part of one Virtual LAN (VLAN). Trunk links carry information from multiple VLANs.

access list A set of test conditions kept by routers that determines "interesting traffic" to and from the router for various services on the network.

access method The manner in which network devices approach gaining access to the network itself.

access rate Defines the bandwidth rate of the circuit. For example, the access rate of a T-1 circuit is 1.544Mbps. In Frame Relay and other technologies, there may be a fractional T-1 connection—256Kbps, for example—however, the access rate and clock rate are still 1.544Mbps.

access server Also known as a "network access server," it is a communications process connecting asynchronous devices to a LAN or WAN through network and terminal emulation software, providing synchronous or asynchronous routing of supported protocols.

acknowledgment Verification sent from one network device to another signifying that an event has occurred. May be abbreviated as ACK. *Contrast with: NAK.*

accounting One of the three components in AAA. Accounting provides auditing and logging functions to the security model.

ACR allowed cell rate: A designation defined by the ATM Forum for managing ATM traffic. Dynamically controlled using congestion control measures, the ACR varies between the minimum cell rate (MCR) and the peak cell rate (PCR). *See also: MCR and PCR.*

active monitor The mechanism used to manage a Token Ring. The network node with the highest MAC address on the ring becomes the active monitor and is responsible for management tasks such as preventing loops and ensuring tokens are not lost.

address learning Used with transparent bridges to learn the hardware addresses of all devices on an internetwork. The switch then filters the network with the known hardware (MAC) addresses.

address mapping By translating network addresses from one format to another, this methodology permits different protocols to operate interchangeably.

address mask A bit combination descriptor identifying which portion of an address refers to the network or subnet and which part refers to the host. Sometimes simply called the mask. *See also: subnet mask.*

address resolution The process used for resolving differences between computer addressing schemes. Address resolution typically defines a method for tracing Network Layer (Layer 3) addresses to Data Link Layer (Layer 2) addresses. *See also: address mapping.*

adjacency The relationship made between defined neighboring routers and end nodes, using a common media segment, to exchange routing information.

administrative distance A number between 0 and 225 that expresses the value of trustworthiness of a routing information source. The lower the number, the higher the integrity rating.

administrative weight A value designated by a network administrator to rate the preference given to a network link. It is one of four link metrics exchanged by PTSPs to test ATM network resource availability.

ADSU ATM Data Service Unit: The terminal adapter used to connect to an ATM network through an HSSI-compatible mechanism. *See also: DSU.*

advertising The process whereby routing or service updates are transmitted at given intervals, allowing other routers on the network to maintain a record of viable routes.

AEP AppleTalk Echo Protocol: A test for connectivity between two AppleTalk nodes where one node sends a packet to another and receives an echo, or copy, in response.

AFI Authority and Format Identifier: The part of an NSAP ATM address that delineates the type and format of the IDI section of an ATM address.

AFP AppleTalk Filing Protocol: A Presentation Layer protocol, supporting AppleShare and Mac OS File Sharing, that permits users to share files and applications on a server.

AIP ATM Interface Processor: Supporting AAL3/4 and AAL5, this interface for Cisco 7000 series routers minimizes performance bottlenecks at the UNI. *See also: AAL3/4 and AAL5.*

algorithm A set of rules or process used to solve a problem. In networking, algorithms are typically used for finding the best route for traffic from a source to its destination.

alignment error An error occurring in Ethernet networks, in which a received frame has extra bits; that is, a number not divisible by eight. Alignment errors are generally the result of frame damage caused by collisions.

all-routes explorer packet An explorer packet that can move across an entire SRB network, tracing all possible paths to a given destination. Also known as an all-rings explorer packet. *See also: explorer packet, local explorer packet,* and *spanning explorer packet.*

AM   Amplitude Modulation: A modulation method that represents information by varying the amplitude of the carrier signal. *See also: modulation.*

AMI   Alternate Mark Inversion: A line-code type on T1 and E1 circuits that shows zeros as "01" during each bit cell, and ones as "11" or "00," alternately, during each bit cell. The sending device must maintain ones density in AMI but not independently of the data stream. Also known as binary-coded, alternate mark inversion. *Contrast with: B8ZS. See also: ones density.*

amplitude   An analog or digital waveform's highest value.

analog connection   Provides signaling via an infinitely variable waveform. This differs from a digital connection in which a definite waveform defines values. Traditional phone service is an analog connection.

analog transmission   Signal messaging whereby information is represented by various combinations of signal amplitude, frequency, and phase.

ANSI   American National Standards Institute: The organization of corporate, government, and other volunteer members that coordinates standards-related activities, approves U.S. national standards, and develops U.S. positions in international standards organizations. ANSI assists in the creation of international and U.S. standards in disciplines such as communications, networking, and a variety of technical fields. It publishes over 13,000 standards, for engineered products and technologies ranging from screw threads to networking protocols. ANSI is a member of the IEC and ISO.

anycast   An ATM address that can be shared by more than one end system, allowing requests to be routed to a node that provides a particular service.

AppleTalk   Currently in two versions, the group of communication protocols designed by Apple Computer for use in Macintosh environments. The earlier Phase 1 protocols supports one physical network with only one network number that resides in one zone. The later Phase 2 protocols support more than one logical network on a single physical network, allowing networks to exist in more than one zone. *See also: zone.*

Application Layer   Layer 7 of the OSI reference network model, supplying services to application procedures (such as electronic mail or file transfer) that are outside the OSI model. This layer chooses and determines the availability of communicating partners along with the resources necessary to make the connection, coordinates partnering applications, and forms a consensus on procedures for controlling data integrity and error recovery.

ARA   AppleTalk Remote Access: A protocol for Macintosh users establishing their access to resources and data from a remote AppleTalk location.

area   A logical, rather than physical, set of segments (based on either CLNS, DECnet, or OSPF) along with their attached devices. Areas are commonly connected to others using routers to create a single autonomous system. *See also: autonomous system.*

ARM   Asynchronous Response Mode: An HDLC communication mode using one primary station and at least one additional station, in which transmission can be initiated from either the primary or one of the secondary units.

ARP   Address Resolution Protocol: Defined in RFC 826, the protocol that traces IP addresses to MAC addresses. *See also: RARP.*

ASBR   Autonomous System Boundary Router: An area border router placed between an OSPF autonomous system and a non-OSPF network that operates both OSPF and an additional routing protocol, such as RIP. ASBRs must be located in a non-stub OSPF area. *See also: ABR, non-stub area, and OSPF.*

ASCII   American Standard Code for Information Interchange: An 8-bit code for representing characters, consisting of seven data bits plus one parity bit.

ASICs   Application-Specific Integrated Circuits: Used in Layer 2 switches to make filtering decisions. The ASIC looks in the filter table of MAC addresses and determines which port the destination hardware address of a received hardware address is destined for. The frame will be allowed to traverse only that one segment. If the hardware address is unknown, the frame is forwarded out all ports.

ASN.1 Abstract Syntax Notation One: An OSI language used to describe types of data that is independent of computer structures and depicting methods. Described by ISO International Standard 8824.

ASP AppleTalk Session Protocol: A protocol employing ATP to establish, maintain, and tear down sessions, as well as sequence requests. *See also: ATP.*

AST Automatic Spanning Tree: A function that supplies one path for spanning explorer frames traveling from one node in the network to another, supporting the automatic resolution of spanning trees in SRB networks. AST is based on the IEEE 802.1 standard. *See also: IEEE 802.1 and SRB.*

asynchronous connection Defines the start and stop of each octet. As a result, each byte in asynchronous connections requires two bytes of overhead. Synchronous connections use a synchronous clock to mark the start and stop of each character.

asynchronous dial-up Is interchangeable with analog dial-up. Both terms refer to traditional modem-based connections.

asynchronous transmission Digital signals sent without precise timing, usually with different frequencies and phase relationships. Asynchronous transmissions generally enclose individual characters in control bits (called start and stop bits) that show the beginning and end of each character. *Contrast with: isochronous transmission* and *synchronous transmission.*

ATCP AppleTalk Control Program: The protocol for establishing and configuring AppleTalk over PPP, defined in RFC 1378. *See also: PPP.*

ATDM Asynchronous Time-Division Multiplexing: A technique for sending information, it differs from normal TDM in that the time slots are assigned when necessary rather than preassigned to certain transmitters. *Contrast with: FDM, statistical multiplexing,* and *TDM.*

ATG Address Translation Gateway: The mechanism within Cisco DECnet routing software that enables routers to route multiple, independent DECnet networks and to establish a user-designated address translation for chosen nodes between networks.

ATM Asynchronous Transfer Mode: The international standard, identified by fixed-length 53-byte cells, for transmitting cells in multiple service systems, such as voice, video, or data. Transit delays are reduced because the fixed-length cells permit processing to occur in the hardware. ATM is designed to maximize the benefits of high-speed transmission media, such as SONET, E3, and T3.

ATM ARP server A device that supplies logical subnets running classical IP over ATM with address-resolution services.

ATM endpoint The initiating or terminating connection in an ATM network. ATM endpoints include servers, workstations, ATM-to-LAN switches, and ATM routers.

ATM Forum The international organization founded jointly by Northern Telecom, Sprint, Cisco Systems, and NET/ADAPTIVE in 1991 to develop and promote standards-based implementation agreements for ATM technology. The ATM Forum broadens official standards developed by ANSI and ITU-T and creates implementation agreements before official standards are published.

ATM layer A sublayer of the Data Link Layer in an ATM network that is service independent. To create standard 53-byte ATM cells, the ATM layer receives 48-byte segments from the AAL and attaches a 5-byte header to each. These cells are then sent to the Physical Layer for transmission across the physical medium. *See also: AAL.*

ATMM ATM Management: A procedure that runs on ATM switches, managing rate enforcement and VCI translation. *See also: ATM.*

ATM user-user connection A connection made by the ATM layer to supply communication between at least two ATM service users, such as ATMM processes. These communications can be uni- or bidirectional, using one or two VCCs, respectively. *See also: ATM layer* and *ATMM.*

ATP AppleTalk Transaction Protocol: A transport-level protocol that enables reliable transactions between two sockets, where one requests the other to perform a given task and to report the results. ATP fastens the request and response together, assuring a loss-free exchange of request-response pairs.

attenuation In communication, weakening or loss of signal energy, typically caused by distance.

AURP AppleTalk Update-based Routing Protocol: A technique for encapsulating AppleTalk traffic in the header of a foreign protocol that allows the connection of at least two noncontiguous AppleTalk internetworks through a foreign network (such as TCP/IP) to create an AppleTalk WAN. The connection made is called an AURP tunnel. By exchanging routing information between exterior routers, the AURP maintains routing tables for the complete AppleTalk WAN. *See also: AURP tunnel.*

AURP tunnel A connection made in an AURP WAN that acts as a single, virtual link between AppleTalk internetworks separated physically by a foreign network such as a TCP/IP network. *See also: AURP.*

authentication The first component in the AAA model. Users are typically authenticated via a username and password, which is used to uniquely identify them.

authority zone A portion of the domain-name tree associated with DNS for which one name server is the authority. *See also: DNS.*

authorization The act of permitting access to a resource based on authentication information in the AAA model.

auto duplex A setting on Layer 1 and 2 devices that sets the duplex of a switch or hub port automatically.

automatic call reconnect A function that enables automatic call rerouting away from a failed trunk line.

autonomous confederation A collection of self-governed systems that depend more on their own network accessibility and routing information than on information received from other systems or groups.

autonomous switching The ability of Cisco routers to process packets more quickly by using the cisco-Bus to switch packets independently of the system processor.

autonomous system (AS) A group of networks under mutual administration that share the same routing methodology. Autonomous systems are subdivided by areas and must be assigned an individual 16-bit number by the IANA. *See also: area.*

autoreconfiguration A procedure executed by nodes within the failure domain of a Token Ring, wherein nodes automatically perform diagnostics, trying to reconfigure the network around failed areas.

auxiliary port The console port on the back of Cisco routers that allows you to dial the router and make console configuration settings.

AVVID Architecture for Voice, Video, and Integrated Data. This is a Cisco marketing term to group their convergence efforts. Convergence is the integration of historically distinct services into a single service.

B8ZS Binary 8-Zero Substitution: A line-code type, interpreted at the remote end of the connection, that uses a special code substitution whenever eight consecutive zeros are transmitted over the link on T1 and E1 circuits. This technique assures ones density independent of the data stream. Also known as bipolar 8-zero substitution. *Contrast with: AMI. See also: ones density.*

backbone The basic portion of the network that provides the primary path for traffic sent to and initiated from other networks.

back end A node or software program supplying services to a front end. *See also: server.*

bandwidth The gap between the highest and lowest frequencies employed by network signals. More commonly, it refers to the rated throughput capacity of a network protocol or medium.

baseband A feature of a network technology that uses only one carrier frequency, for example Ethernet. Also named "narrowband." *Compare with: broadband.*

Basic Management Setup Used with Cisco routers when in setup mode. Only provides enough management and configuration to get the router working so someone can telnet into the router and configure it.

baud Synonymous with bits per second (bps), if each signal element represents one bit. It is a unit of signaling speed equivalent to the number of separate signal elements transmitted per second.

B channel Bearer channel: A full-duplex, 64Kbps channel in ISDN that transmits user data. *Compare with: D channel, E channel, and H channel.*

beacon An FDDI device or Token Ring frame that points to a serious problem with the ring, such as a broken cable. The beacon frame carries the address of the station thought to be down. *See also: failure domain.*

bearer service   Used by service providers to provide DS0 service to ISDN customers. A DS0 is one 64K channel. An ISDN bearer service provides either two DS0s, called two bearer channels for a Basic Rate Interface (BRI), or 24 DS0s called a Primary Rate Interface (PRI).

BECN   Backward Explicit Congestion Notification: BECN is the bit set by a Frame Relay network in frames moving away from frames headed into a congested path. A DTE that receives frames with the BECN may ask higher-level protocols to take necessary flow control measures. *Compare with: FECN.*

BGP4   BGP Version 4: Version 4 of the interdomain routing protocol most commonly used on the Internet. BGP4 supports CIDR and uses route-counting mechanisms to decrease the size of routing tables. *See also: CIDR.*

binary   A two-character numbering method that uses ones and zeros. The binary numbering system underlies all digital representation of information.

BIP   Bit Interleaved Parity: A method used in ATM to monitor errors on a link, sending a check bit or word in the link overhead for the previous block or frame. This allows bit errors in transmissions to be found and delivered as maintenance information.

BISDN   Broadband ISDN: ITU-T standards created to manage high-bandwidth technologies such as video. BISDN presently employs ATM technology along SONET-based transmission circuits, supplying data rates between 155Mbps and 622Mbps and beyond. Contrast with N-ISDN. *See also: BRI, ISDN, and PRI.*

bit-oriented protocol   Regardless of frame content, the class of Data Link Layer communication protocols that transmits frames. Bit-oriented protocols, as compared with byte-oriented, supply more efficient and trustworthy, full-duplex operation. *Compare with: byte-oriented protocol.*

BoD   Bandwidth on Demand: This function allows an additional B channel to be used to increase the amount of bandwidth available for a particular connection.

Boot ROM   Used in routers to put the router into bootstrap mode. Bootstrap mode then boots the device with an operating system. The ROM can also hold a small Cisco IOS.

border gateway   A router that facilitates communication with routers in different autonomous systems.

border router   Typically defined within Open Shortest Path First (OSPF) as a router that connects an area to the backbone area. However, a border router can be a router that connects a company to the Internet as well.

BPDU   Bridge Protocol Data Unit: A Spanning-Tree Protocol initializing packet that is sent at definable intervals for the purpose of exchanging information among bridges in networks.

BRI   Basic Rate Interface: The ISDN interface that facilitates circuit-switched communication between video, data, and voice; it is made up of two B channels (64Kbps each) and one D channel (16Kbps). *Compare with: PRI. See also: BISDN.*

bridge   A device for connecting two segments of a network and transmitting packets between them. Both segments must use identical protocols to communicate. Bridges function at the Data Link Layer, Layer 2 of the OSI reference model. The purpose of a bridge is to filter, send, or flood any incoming frame, based on the MAC address of that particular frame.

bridging   Bridging is a Layer 2 process to block or forward frames based on MAC layer addresses. Bridges are lower-speed, lower-port density switches.

broadband   A transmission methodology for multiplexing several independent signals onto one cable. In telecommunications, broadband is classified as any channel with bandwidth greater than 4kHz (typical voice grade). In LAN terminology, it is classified as a coaxial cable on which analog signaling is employed. Also known as wideband. *Contrast with: baseband.*

broadcast   A data frame or packet that is transmitted to every node on the local network segment (as defined by the broadcast domain). Broadcasts are known by their broadcast address, which is a destination network and host address with all the bits turned on. Also called "local broadcast." *Compare with: directed broadcast.*

broadcast domain   A group of devices receiving broadcast frames initiating from any device within the group. Because they do not forward broadcast frames, broadcast domains are generally surrounded by routers.

broadcast storm An undesired event on the network caused by the simultaneous transmission of any number of broadcasts across the network segment. Such an occurrence can overwhelm network bandwidth, resulting in time-outs.

brute force attack Bombards the resource with attempted connections until successful. The most common brute force attack repeatedly tries different passwords until finding a match that is then used to compromise the network.

buffer A storage area dedicated to handling data while in transit. Buffers are used to receive/store sporadic deliveries of data bursts, usually received from faster devices, compensating for the variations in processing speed. Incoming information is stored until everything is received prior to sending data on. Also known as an information buffer.

bursting Some technologies, including ATM and Frame Relay, are considered burstable. This means that user data can exceed the bandwidth normally reserved for the connection but cannot exceed the port speed. An example of this would be a 128Kbps Frame Relay CIR on a T-1—depending on the vendor, it may be possible to send more than 128Kbps for a short time.

bus topology A linear LAN architecture in which transmissions from various stations on the network are reproduced over the length of the medium and are accepted by all other stations. *Compare with: ring* and *star.*

bus Any physical path, typically wires or copper, through which a digital signal can be used to send data from one part of a computer to another.

BUS broadcast and unknown servers: In LAN emulation, the hardware or software responsible for resolving all broadcasts and packets with unknown (unregistered) addresses into the point-to-point virtual circuits required by ATM. *See also: LANE, LEC, LECS,* and *LES.*

BX.25 AT&T's use of X.25. *See also: X.25.*

bypass mode An FDDI and Token Ring network operation that deletes an interface.

bypass relay A device that enables a particular interface in the Token Ring to be closed down and effectively taken off the ring.

byte-oriented protocol Any type of data-link communication protocol that, in order to mark the boundaries of frames, uses a specific character from the user character set. These protocols have generally been superseded by bit-oriented protocols. *Compare with: bit-oriented protocol.*

cable modem Is not actually an analog device, like an asynchronous modem, but is, rather, a customer access device for linking to a broadband cable network. These devices are typically bridges that have a coax connection to link to the cable network and a 10BaseT Ethernet connection to link to the user's PC.

cable range In an extended AppleTalk network, the range of numbers allotted for use by existing nodes on the network. The value of the cable range can be anywhere from a single to a sequence of several touching network numbers. Node addresses are determined by their cable range value.

CAC Connection Admission Control: The sequence of actions executed by every ATM switch while connection setup is performed in order to determine if a request for connection is violating the guarantees of QoS for established connections. Also, CAC is used to route a connection request through an ATM network.

call admission control A device for managing of traffic in ATM networks, determining the possibility of a path containing adequate bandwidth for a requested VCC.

call priority In circuit-switched systems, the defining priority given to each originating port; it specifies in which order calls will be reconnected. Additionally, call priority identifies which calls are allowed during a bandwidth reservation.

call set-up time The length of time necessary to effect a switched call between DTE devices.

CBR Constant Bit Rate: An ATM Forum QoS class created for use in ATM networks. CBR is used for connections that rely on precision clocking to guarantee trustworthy delivery. *Compare with: ABR and VBR.*

CD Carrier Detect: A signal indicating that an interface is active or that a connection generated by a modem has been established.

CDP Cisco Discovery Protocol: Cisco's proprietary protocol that is used to tell a neighbor Cisco device about the type of hardware, software version, and active interfaces that the Cisco device is using. It uses a SNAP frame between devices and is not routable.

CDVT Cell Delay Variation Tolerance: A QoS parameter for traffic management in ATM networks specified when a connection is established. The allowable fluctuation levels for data samples taken by the PCR in CBR transmissions are determined by the CDVT. *See also: CBR and PCR.*

cell In ATM networking, the basic unit of data for switching and multiplexing. Cells have a defined length of 53 bytes, including a 5-byte header that identifies the cell's data stream and 48 bytes of payload. *See also: cell relay.*

cell payload scrambling The method by which an ATM switch maintains framing on some medium-speed edge and trunk interfaces (T3 or E3 circuits). Cell payload scrambling rearranges the data portion of a cell to maintain the line synchronization with certain common bit patterns.

cell relay A technology that uses small packets of fixed size, known as cells. Their fixed length enables cells to be processed and switched in hardware at high speeds, making this technology the foundation for ATM and other high-speed network protocols. *See also: cell.*

Centrex A local exchange carrier service, providing local switching that resembles that of an on-site PBX. Centrex has no on-site switching capability. Therefore, all customer connections return to the CO. *See also: CO.*

CER Cell Error Ratio: The ratio in ATM of transmitted cells having errors to the total number of cells sent in a transmission within a certain span of time.

challenge Provides authentication in CHAP as part of the handshake process. This numerically unique query is sent to authenticate the user without sending the password unencrypted across the wire.

channelized E-1 Operating at 2.048Mbps, an access link that is sectioned into 29 B-channels and one D-channel, supporting DDR, Frame Relay, and X.25. *Compare with: channelized T-1.*

channelized T-1 Operating at 1.544Mbps, an access link that is sectioned into 23 B-channels and 1 D-channel of 64Kbps each, where individual channels or groups of channels connect to various destinations, supporting DDR, Frame Relay, and X.25. *Compare with: channelized E-1.*

CHAP Challenge Handshake Authentication Protocol: Supported on lines using PPP encapsulation, it is a security feature that identifies the remote end, helping keep out unauthorized users. After CHAP is performed, the router or access server determines whether a given user is permitted access. It is a newer, more secure protocol than PAP. *Compare with: PAP.*

character mode connections Are typically terminated at the access server, and include Telnet and console connections.

checksum A test for ensuring the integrity of sent data. It is a number calculated from a series of values taken through a sequence of mathematical functions, typically placed at the end of the data from which it is calculated, and then recalculated at the receiving end for verification. *Compare with: CRC.*

choke packet When congestion exists, it is a packet sent to inform a transmitter that it should decrease its sending rate.

CIDR Classless Interdomain Routing: A method supported by classless routing protocols, such as OSPF and BGP4, based on the concept of ignoring the IP class of address, permitting route aggregation and VLSM that enable routers to combine routes in order to minimize the routing information that needs to be conveyed by the primary routers. It allows a group of IP networks to appear to other networks as a unified, larger entity. In CIDR, IP addresses and their subnet masks are written as four dotted octets, followed by a forward slash and the numbering of masking bits (a form of subnet notation shorthand). *See also: BGP4.*

CIP Channel Interface Processor: A channel attachment interface for use in Cisco 7000 series routers that connects a host mainframe to a control unit. This device eliminates the need for an FBP to attach channels.

CIR Committed Information Rate: Averaged over a minimum span of time and measured in bps, a Frame Relay network's agreed-upon minimum rate of transferring information.

circuit switching Used with dial-up networks such as PPP and ISDN. Passes data, but needs to set up the connection first—just like making a phone call.

Cisco FRAD Cisco Frame-Relay Access Device: A Cisco product that supports Cisco IPS Frame Relay SNA services, connecting SDLC devices to Frame Relay without requiring an existing LAN. May be upgraded to a fully functioning multiprotocol router. Can activate conversion from SDLC to Ethernet and Token Ring, but does not support attached LANs. *See also: FRAD.*

CiscoFusion Cisco's name for the internetworking architecture under which its Cisco IOS operates. It is designed to "fuse" together the capabilities of its disparate collection of acquired routers and switches.

Cisco IOS software Cisco Internet Operating System software. The kernel of the Cisco line of routers and switches that supplies shared functionality, scalability, and security for all products under its Cisco-Fusion architecture. *See also: CiscoFusion.*

CiscoView GUI-based management software for Cisco networking devices, enabling dynamic status, statistics, and comprehensive configuration information. Displays a physical view of the Cisco device chassis and provides device-monitoring functions and fundamental troubleshooting capabilities. May be integrated with a number of SNMP-based network management platforms.

Class A network Part of the Internet Protocol hierarchical addressing scheme. Class A networks have only 8 bits for defining networks and 24 bits for defining hosts on each network.

Class B network Part of the Internet Protocol hierarchical addressing scheme. Class B networks have 16 bits for defining networks and 16 bits for defining hosts on each network.

Class C network Part of the Internet Protocol hierarchical addressing scheme. Class C networks have 24 bits for defining networks and only 8 bits for defining hosts on each network.

classical IP over ATM Defined in RFC 1577, the specification for running IP over ATM that maximizes ATM features. Also known as CIA.

classless routing Routing that sends subnet mask information in the routing updates. Classless routing allows Variable-Length Subnet Mask (VLSM) and supernetting. Routing protocols that support classless routing are RIP version 2, EIGRP, and OSPF.

CLI Command Line Interface: Allows you to configure Cisco routers and switches with maximum flexibility.

clocking Used in synchronous connections to provide a marker for the start and end of data bytes. This is similar to the beat of a drum, with a person speaking only when the drum is silent.

CLP Cell Loss Priority: The area in the ATM cell header that determines the likelihood of a cell being dropped during network congestion. Cells with CLP = 0 are considered insured traffic and are not apt to be dropped. Cells with CLP = 1 are considered best-effort traffic that may be dropped during congested episodes, delivering more resources to handle insured traffic.

CLR Cell Loss Ratio: The ratio of discarded cells to successfully delivered cells in ATM. CLR can be designated a QoS parameter when establishing a connection.

CO Central Office: The local telephone company office where all loops in a certain area connect and where circuit switching of subscriber lines occurs.

collapsed backbone A nondistributed backbone where all network segments are connected to each other through an internetworking device. A collapsed backbone can be a virtual network segment at work in a device such as a router, hub, or switch.

collision The effect of two nodes sending transmissions simultaneously in Ethernet. When they meet on the physical media, the frames from each node collide and are damaged. *See also: collision domain.*

collision domain The network area in Ethernet over which frames that have collided will spread. Collisions are propagated by hubs and repeaters, but not by LAN switches, routers, or bridges. *See also: collision.*

composite metric   Used with routing protocols, such as IGRP and EIGRP, that use more than one metric to find the best path to a remote network. IGRP and EIGRP both use bandwidth and delay of the line by default. However, Maximum Transmission Unit (MTU), load, and reliability of a link can be used as well.

compression   A technique to send more data across a link than would be normally permitted by representing repetitive strings of data with a single marker.

configuration register   A 16-bit configurable value stored in hardware or software that determines how Cisco routers function during initialization. In hardware, the bit position is set using a jumper. In software, it is set by specifying specific bit patterns used to set startup options, configured using a hexadecimal value with configuration commands.

congestion   Traffic that exceeds the network's ability to handle it.

congestion avoidance   To minimize delays, the method an ATM network uses to control traffic entering the system. Lower-priority traffic is discarded at the edge of the network when indicators signal it cannot be delivered, thus using resources efficiently.

congestion collapse   The situation that results from the retransmission of packets in ATM networks where little or no traffic successfully arrives at destination points. It usually happens in networks made of switches with ineffective or inadequate buffering capabilities combined with poor packet discard or ABR congestion feedback mechanisms.

connection ID   Identifications given to each Telnet session into a router. The show sessions command will give you the connections a local router will have to a remote router. The show users command will show the connection IDs of users telnetted into your local router.

connectionless   Data transfer that occurs without the creating of a virtual circuit. No overhead, best-effort delivery, not reliable. *Contrast with: connection-oriented. See also: virtual circuit.*

connection-oriented   Data transfer method that sets up a virtual circuit before any data is transferred. Uses acknowledgments and flow control for reliable data transfer. *Contrast with: connectionless. See also: virtual circuit.*

console port   Typically an RJ-45 port on a Cisco router and switch that allows Command-Line Interface capability.

control direct VCC   One of three control connections defined by Phase I LAN Emulation; a bi-directional virtual control connection (VCC) established in ATM by an LEC to an LES. *See also: control distribute VCC.*

control distribute VCC   One of three control connections defined by Phase 1 LAN Emulation; a unidirectional virtual control connection (VCC) set up in ATM from an LES to an LEC. Usually, the VCC is a point-to-multipoint connection. *See also: control direct VCC.*

convergence   The process required for all routers in an internetwork to update their routing tables and create a consistent view of the network, using the best possible paths. No user data is passed during a convergence time.

Core Layer   Top layer in the Cisco three-layer hierarchical model, which helps you design, build, and maintain Cisco hierarchical networks. The Core Layer passes packets quickly to Distribution Layer devices only. No packet filtering should take place at this layer.

cost   Also known as path cost, an arbitrary value, based on hop count, bandwidth, or other calculation, that is typically assigned by a network administrator and used by the routing protocol to compare different routes through an internetwork. Routing protocols use cost values to select the best path to a certain destination: the lowest cost identifies the best path. Also known as path cost. *See also: routing metric.*

count to infinity   A problem occurring in routing algorithms that are slow to converge where routers keep increasing the hop count to particular networks. To avoid this problem, various solutions have been implemented into each of the different routing protocols. Some of those solutions include defining a maximum hop count (defining infinity), route poising, poison reverse, and split horizon.

CPCS   Common Part Convergence Sublayer: One of two AAL sublayers that is service-dependent, it is further segmented into the CS and SAR sublayers. The CPCS prepares data for transmission across the ATM network; it creates the 48-byte payload cells that are sent to the ATM layer. *See also: AAL and ATM layer.*

CPE Customer Premises Equipment: Items such as telephones, modems, and terminals installed at customer locations and connected to the telephone company network.

crankback In ATM, a correction technique used when a node somewhere on a chosen path cannot accept a connection setup request, blocking the request. The path is rolled back to an intermediate node, which then uses GCAC to attempt to find an alternate path to the final destination.

CRC Cyclical Redundancy Check: A methodology that detects errors, whereby the frame recipient makes a calculation by dividing frame contents with a prime binary divisor and compares the remainder to a value stored in the frame by the sending node. *Contrast with: checksum.*

CSMA/CD Carrier Sense Multiple Access Collision Detect: A technology defined by the Ethernet IEEE 802.3 committee. Each device senses the cable for a digital signal before transmitting. Also, CSMA/CD allows all devices on the network to share the same cable, but one at a time. If two devices transmit at the same time, a frame collision will occur and a jamming pattern will be sent; the devices will stop transmitting, wait a predetermined amount of time, and then try to transmit again.

CSU Channel Service Unit: A digital mechanism that connects end-user equipment to the local digital telephone loop. Frequently referred to along with the data service unit as CSU/DSU. *See also: DSU.*

CTD Cell Transfer Delay: For a given connection in ATM, the time period between a cell exit event at the source user-network interface (UNI) and the corresponding cell entry event at the destination. The CTD between these points is the sum of the total inter-ATM transmission delay and the total ATM processing delay.

custom queuing Used by the Cisco router IOS to provide a queuing method to slower serial links. Custom queuing allows an administrator to configure the type of traffic that will have priority over the link.

cut-through frame switching A frame-switching technique that flows data through a switch so that the leading edge exits the switch at the output port before the packet finishes entering the input port. Frames will

be read, processed, and forwarded by devices that use cut-through switching as soon as the destination address of the frame is confirmed and the outgoing port is identified.

data compression *See: compression.*

data direct VCC A bidirectional point-to-point virtual control connection (VCC) set up between two LECs in ATM and one of three data connections defined by Phase 1 LAN Emulation. Because data direct VCCs do not guarantee QoS, they are generally reserved for UBR and ABR connections. *Compare with: control distribute VCC and control direct VCC.*

data frame Protocol Data Unit encapsulation at the Data Link Layer of the OSI reference model. Encapsulates packets from the Network Layer and prepares the data for transmission on a network medium.

datagram A logical collection of information transmitted as a Network Layer unit over a medium without a previously established virtual circuit. IP datagrams have become the primary information unit of the Internet. At various layers of the OSI reference model, the terms *cell, frame, message, packet,* and *segment* also define these logical information groupings.

Data Link Control Layer Layer 2 of the SNA architectural model, it is responsible for the transmission of data over a given physical link and compares somewhat to the Data Link Layer of the OSI model.

Data Link Layer Layer 2 of the OSI reference model, it ensures the trustworthy transmission of data across a physical link and is primarily concerned with physical addressing, line discipline, network topology, error notification, ordered delivery of frames, and flow control. The IEEE has further segmented this layer into the MAC sublayer and the LLC sublayer. Also known as the Link Layer. Can be compared somewhat to the Data Link Control Layer of the SNA model. *See also: Application Layer, LLC, MAC, Network Layer, Physical Layer, Presentation Layer, Session Layer,* and *Transport Layer.*

DCC Data Country Code: Developed by the ATM Forum, one of two ATM address formats designed for use by private networks. *Compare with: ICD.*

DCE   data communications equipment (as defined by the EIA) or data circuit-terminating equipment (as defined by the ITU-T): The mechanisms and links of a communications network that make up the network portion of the user-to-network interface, such as modems. The DCE supplies the physical connection to the network, forwards traffic, and provides a clocking signal to synchronize data transmission between DTE and DCE devices. *Compare with: DTE.*

D channel   1) Data channel: A full-duplex, 16Kbps (BRI) or 64Kbps (PRI) ISDN channel. *Compare with: B channel, E channel, and H channel.* 2) In SNA, anything that provides a connection between the processor and main storage with any peripherals.

DDP   Datagram Delivery Protocol: Used in the AppleTalk suite of protocols as a connectionless protocol that is responsible for sending datagrams through an internetwork.

DDR   dial-on-demand routing: A technique that allows a router to automatically initiate and end a circuit-switched session per the requirements of the sending station. By mimicking keepalives, the router fools the end station into treating the session as active. DDR permits routing over ISDN or telephone lines via a modem or external ISDN terminal adapter.

DE   Discard Eligibility: Used in Frame Relay networks to tell a switch that a frame can be discarded if the switch is too busy. The DE is a field in the frame that is turned on by transmitting routers if the Committed Information Rate (CIR) is oversubscribed or set to 0.

DE bit   Marks a frame as discard-eligible on a Frame Relay network. If a serial link is congested and the Frame Relay network has passed the Committed Information Rate (CIR), then the DE bit will always be on.

default route   The static routing table entry used to direct frames whose next hop is not spelled out in the dynamic routing table.

delay   The time elapsed between a sender's initiation of a transaction and the first response they receive. Also, the time needed to move a packet from its source to its destination over a path. *See also: latency.*

demarc   The demarcation point between the customer premises equipment (CPE) and the telco's carrier equipment.

demodulation   A series of steps that return a modulated signal to its original form. When receiving, a modem demodulates an analog signal to its original digital form (and, conversely, modulates the digital data it sends into an analog signal). *See also: modulation.*

demultiplexing   The process of converting a single multiplex signal, comprising more than one input stream, back into separate output streams. *See also: multiplexing.*

denial-of-service attack   Also known as a DoS. Blocks access to a network resource by saturating the device with attacking data. Typically this is targeted against the link (particularly lower bandwidth links) or the server. DDoS attacks, or distributed denial-of-service attacks, use multiple originating attacking resources to saturate a more capable resource.

designated bridge   In the process of forwarding a frame from a segment to the route bridge, the bridge with the lowest path cost.

designated port   Used with the Spanning-Tree Protocol (STP) to designate forwarding ports. If there are multiple links to the same network, STP will shut a port down to stop network loops.

designated router   An OSPF router that creates LSAs for a multiaccess network and is required to perform other special tasks in OSPF operations. Multiaccess OSPF networks that maintain a minimum of two attached routers identify one router that is chosen by the OSPF Hello protocol, which makes possible a decrease in the number of adjacencies necessary on a multiaccess network. This in turn reduces the quantity of routing protocol traffic and the physical size of the database.

destination address   The address for the network devices that will receive a packet.

dial backup   Dial backup connections are typically used to provide redundancy to Frame Relay connections. The backup link is activated over an analog modem.

digital   A digital waveform is one where distinct ones and zeros provide the data representation. *Compare with: analog.*

directed broadcast A data frame or packet that is transmitted to a specific group of nodes on a remote network segment. Directed broadcasts are known by their broadcast address, which is a destination subnet address with all the bits turned on.

discovery mode Also known as dynamic configuration, this technique is used by an AppleTalk interface to gain information from a working node about an attached network. The information is subsequently used by the interface for self-configuration.

distance-vector routing algorithm In order to find the shortest path, this group of routing algorithms repeats on the number of hops in a given route, requiring each router to send its complete routing table with each update, but only to its neighbors. Routing algorithms of this type tend to generate loops, but they are fundamentally simpler than their link-state counterparts. *See also: link-state routing algorithm and SPF.*

Distribution Layer Middle layer of the Cisco three-layer hierarchical model, which helps you design, install, and maintain Cisco hierarchical networks. The Distribution Layer is the point where Access Layer devices connect. Routing is performed at this layer.

DLCI Data-Link Connection Identifier: Used to identify virtual circuits in a Frame Relay network.

DNS Domain Name System: Used to resolve host names to IP addresses.

DSAP Destination Service Access Point: The service access point of a network node, specified in the destination field of a packet. *See also: SSAP and SAP.*

DSL Digital Subscriber Line: Provides broadband services over a single copper pair, typically to residential customers. Most vendors are providing DSL services at up to 6Mbps downstream; however, the technology can support 52Mbps service.

DSR Data Set Ready: When a DCE is powered up and ready to run, this EIA/TIA-232 interface circuit is also engaged.

DSU Data Service Unit: This device is used to adapt the physical interface on a data terminal equipment (DTE) mechanism to a transmission facility such as T1 or E1 and is also responsible for signal timing. It is commonly grouped with the channel service unit and referred to as the CSU/DSU. *See also: CSU.*

DTE data terminal equipment: Any device located at the user end of a user-network interface serving as a destination, a source, or both. DTE includes devices such as multiplexers, protocol translators, and computers. The connection to a data network is made through data channel equipment (DCE) such as a modem, using the clocking signals generated by that device. *See also: DCE.*

DTR data terminal ready: An activated EIA/TIA-232 circuit communicating to the DCE the state of preparedness of the DTE to transmit or receive data.

DUAL Diffusing Update Algorithm: Used in Enhanced IGRP, this convergence algorithm provides loop-free operation throughout an entire route's computation. DUAL grants routers involved in a topology revision the ability to synchronize simultaneously, while routers unaffected by this change are not involved. *See also: Enhanced IGRP.*

DVMRP Distance Vector Multicast Routing Protocol: Based primarily on the Routing Information Protocol (RIP), this Internet gateway protocol implements a common, condensed-mode IP multicast scheme, using IGMP to transfer routing datagrams between its neighbors. *See also: IGMP.*

DXI Data Exchange Interface: Described in RFC 1482, DXI defines the effectiveness of a network device such as a router, bridge, or hub to act as an FEP to an ATM network by using a special DSU that accomplishes packet encapsulation.

dynamic entries Used in Layer 2 and 3 devices to create a table of either hardware addresses or logical addresses dynamically.

dynamic routing Also known as adaptive routing, this technique automatically adapts to traffic or physical network revisions.

dynamic VLAN An administrator will create an entry in a special server with the hardware addresses of all devices on the internetwork. The server will then assign dynamically used VLANs.

E-1 Generally used in Europe, a wide-area digital transmission scheme carrying data at 2.048Mbps. E-1 transmission lines are available for lease from common carriers for private use.

E.164 1) Evolved from standard telephone numbering system, the standard recommended by ITU-T for international telecommunication numbering, particularly in ISDN, SMDS, and BISDN. 2) Label of field in an ATM address containing numbers in E.164 format.

E channel Echo channel: A 64Kbps ISDN control channel used for circuit switching. Specific description of this channel can be found in the 1984 ITU-T ISDN specification, but was dropped from the 1988 version. *See also: B, D,* and *H channels.*

edge device A device that enables packets to be forwarded between legacy interfaces (such as Ethernet and Token Ring) and ATM interfaces based on information in the Data Link and Network Layers. An edge device does not take part in the running of any Network Layer routing protocol; it merely uses the route description protocol in order to get the forwarding information required.

EEPROM Electronically Erasable Programmable Read-Only Memory: Programmed after their manufacture, these nonvolatile memory chips can be erased if necessary using electric power and reprogrammed. *See also: EPROM, PROM.*

EFCI Explicit Forward Congestion Indication: A congestion feedback mode permitted by ABR service in an ATM network. The EFCI may be set by any network element that is in a state of immediate or certain congestion. The destination end-system is able to carry out a protocol that adjusts and lowers the cell rate of the connection based on value of the EFCI. *See also: ABR.*

EIGRP *See: Enhanced IGRP.*

EIP Ethernet Interface Processor: A Cisco 7000 series router interface processor card, supplying 10Mbps AUI ports to support Ethernet Version 1 and Ethernet Version 2 or IEEE 802.3 interfaces with a high-speed data path to other interface processors.

ELAN Emulated LAN: An ATM network configured using a client/server model in order to emulate either an Ethernet or Token Ring LAN. Multiple ELANs can exist at the same time on a single ATM network and are made up of an LAN emulation client (LEC), an LAN Emulation Server (LES), a Broadcast and Unknown Server (BUS), and an LAN Emulation Configuration Server (LECS). ELANs are defined by the LANE specification. *See also: LANE, LEC, LECS,* and *LES.*

ELAP EtherTalk Link Access Protocol: In an EtherTalk network, the link-access protocol constructed above the standard Ethernet Data Link Layer.

encapsulation The technique used by layered protocols in which a layer adds header information to the protocol data unit (PDU) from the layer above. As an example, in Internet terminology, a packet would contain a header from the Physical Layer, followed by a header from the Network Layer (IP), followed by a header from the Transport Layer (TCP), followed by the application protocol data.

encryption The conversion of information into a scrambled form that effectively disguises it to prevent unauthorized access. Every encryption scheme uses some well-defined algorithm, which is reversed at the receiving end by an opposite algorithm in a process known as decryption.

Enhanced IGRP Enhanced Interior Gateway Routing Protocol: An advanced routing protocol created by Cisco, combining the advantages of link-state and distance-vector protocols. Enhanced IGRP has superior convergence attributes, including high operating efficiency. *See also: IGP, OSPF,* and *RIP.*

enterprise network A privately owned and operated network that joins most major locations in a large company or organization.

EPROM Erasable Programmable Read-Only Memory: Programmed after their manufacture, these nonvolatile memory chips can be erased if necessary using high-power light and reprogrammed. *See also: EEPROM, PROM.*

error correction Uses a checksum to detect bit errors in the data stream.

ESF Extended Superframe: Made up of 24 frames with 192 bits each, with the 193rd bit providing other functions including timing. This is an enhanced version of SF. *See also: SF.*

Ethernet A baseband LAN specification created by the Xerox Corporation and then improved through joint efforts of Xerox, Digital Equipment Corporation, and Intel. Ethernet is similar to the IEEE 802.3 series standard and, using CSMA/CD, operates over various types of cables at 10Mbps. *Also called: DIX (Digital/Intel/Xerox) Ethernet. See also: 10BaseT, Fast Ethernet, and IEEE.*

EtherTalk A data-link product from Apple Computer that permits AppleTalk networks to be connected by Ethernet.

excess rate In ATM networking, traffic exceeding a connection's insured rate. The excess rate is the maximum rate less the insured rate. Depending on the availability of network resources, excess traffic can be discarded during congestion episodes. *Compare with: maximum rate.*

expansion The procedure of directing compressed data through an algorithm, restoring information to its original size.

expedited delivery An option that can be specified by one Protocol Layer, communicating either with other layers or with the identical Protocol Layer in a different network device, requiring that identified data be processed faster.

explorer packet An SNA packet transmitted by a source Token Ring device to find the path through a source-route-bridged network.

extended IP access list IP access list that filters the network by logical address, protocol field in the Network Layer header, and even the port field in the Transport Layer header.

extended IPX access list IPX access list that filters the network by logical IPX address, protocol field in the Network Layer header, or even socket number in the Transport Layer header.

Extended Setup Used in setup mode to configure the router with more detail than Basic Setup mode. Allows multiple-protocol support and interface configuration.

failure domain The region in which a failure has occurred in a Token Ring. When a station gains information that a serious problem, such as a cable break, has occurred with the network, it sends a beacon frame that includes the station reporting the failure, its NAUN, and everything between. This defines the failure domain. Beaconing then initiates the procedure known as autoreconfiguration. *See also: autoreconfiguration* and *beacon.*

fallback In ATM networks, this mechanism is used for scouting a path if it isn't possible to locate one using customary methods. The device relaxes requirements for certain characteristics, such as delay, in an attempt to find a path that meets a certain set of the most important requirements.

Fast Ethernet Any Ethernet specification with a speed of 100Mbps. Fast Ethernet is ten times faster than 10BaseT, while retaining qualities like MAC mechanisms, MTU, and frame format. These similarities make it possible for existing 10BaseT applications and management tools to be used on Fast Ethernet networks. Fast Ethernet is based on an extension of IEEE 802.3 specification (IEEE 802.3u). *Compare with: Ethernet. See also: 100BaseT, 100BaseTX, and IEEE.*

fast switching A Cisco feature that uses a route cache to speed packet switching through a router. *Contrast with: process switching.*

FDM Frequency-Division Multiplexing: A technique that permits information from several channels to be assigned bandwidth on one wire based on frequency. *See also: TDM, ATDM,* and *statistical multiplexing.*

FDDI Fiber Distributed Data Interface: An LAN standard, defined by ANSI X3T9.5 that can run at speeds up to 200Mbps and uses token-passing media access on fiber-optic cable. For redundancy, FDDI can use a dual-ring architecture.

FECN Forward Explicit Congestion Notification: A bit set by a Frame Relay network that informs the DTE receptor that congestion was encountered along the path from source to destination. A device receiving frames with the FECN bit set can ask higher-priority protocols to take flow-control action as needed. *See also: BECN.*

FEIP Fast Ethernet Interface Processor: An interface processor employed on Cisco 7000 series routers, supporting up to two 100Mbps 100BaseT ports.

firewall A barrier purposefully erected between any connected public networks and a private network, made up of a router or access server or several routers or access servers, that uses access lists and other methods to ensure the security of the private network.

Flash Electronically Erasable Programmable Read-Only Memory (EEPROM). Used to hold the Cisco IOS in a router by default.

flash memory Developed by Intel and licensed to other semiconductor manufacturers, it is nonvolatile storage that can be erased electronically and repro-grammed, physically located on an EEPROM chip. Flash memory permits software images to be stored, booted, and rewritten as needed. Cisco routers and switches use flash memory to hold the IOS by default. *See also: EPROM, EEPROM.*

flat network Network that is one large collision domain and one large broadcast domain.

flooding When traffic is received on an interface, it is then transmitted to every interface connected to that device with exception of the interface from which the traffic originated. This technique can be used for traf-fic transfer by bridges and switches throughout the network.

flow control A methodology used to ensure that receiving units are not overwhelmed with data from sending devices. Pacing, as it is called in IBM net-works, means that when buffers at a receiving unit are full, a message is transmitted to the sending unit to temporarily halt transmissions until all the data in the receiving buffer has been processed and the buffer is again ready for action.

FRAD Frame Relay Access Device: Any device affording a connection between a LAN and a Frame Relay WAN. *See also: Cisco FRAD, FRAS.*

fragment Any portion of a larger packet that has been intentionally segmented into smaller pieces. A packet fragment does not necessarily indicate an error and can be intentional. *See also: fragmentation.*

fragmentation The process of intentionally seg-menting a packet into smaller pieces when sending data over an intermediate network medium that can-not support the larger packet size.

FragmentFree LAN switch type that reads into the data section of a frame to make sure fragmentation did not occur. Sometimes called modified cut-through.

frame A logical unit of information sent by the Data Link Layer over a transmission medium. The term often refers to the header and trailer, employed for synchronization and error control, that surround the data contained in the unit.

Frame Relay A more efficient replacement of the X.25 protocol (an unrelated packet relay technology that guarantees data delivery). Frame Relay is an industry-standard, shared-access, best-effort, switched Data Link Layer encapsulation that services multiple virtual circuits and protocols between con-nected mechanisms.

Frame Relay bridging Defined in RFC 1490, this bridging method uses the identical spanning–tree algorithm as other bridging operations but permits packets to be encapsulated for transmission across a Frame Relay network.

Frame Relay switching Router at a service provider that provides packet switching for Frame Relay packets.

framing Encapsulation at the Data Link Layer of the OSI model. It is called framing because the packet is encapsulated with both a header and a trailer.

FRAS Frame Relay Access Support: A feature of Cisco IOS software that enables SDLC, Ethernet, Token Ring, and Frame Relay-attached IBM devices to be linked with other IBM mechanisms on a Frame Relay network. *See also: FRAD.*

frequency The number of cycles of an alternating current signal per time unit, measured in hertz (cycles per second).

FSIP Fast Serial Interface Processor: The Cisco 7000 routers' default serial interface processor, it provides four or eight high-speed serial ports.

FTP File Transfer Protocol: The TCP/IP protocol used for transmitting files between network nodes, it supports a broad range of file types and is defined in RFC 959. *See also: TFTP.*

full duplex The capacity to transmit information between a sending station and a receiving unit at the same time. *See also: half duplex.*

full mesh A type of network topology where every node has either a physical or a virtual circuit linking it to every other network node. A full mesh supplies a great deal of redundancy but is typically reserved for network backbones because of its expense. *See also: partial mesh.*

GNS Get Nearest Server: On an IPX network, a request packet sent by a customer for determining the location of the nearest active server of a given type. An IPX network client launches a GNS request to get either a direct answer from a connected server or a response from a router disclosing the location of the service on the internetwork to the GNS. GNS is part of IPX and SAP. *See also: IPX and SAP.*

GRE Generic Routing Encapsulation: A tunneling protocol created by Cisco with the capacity for encapsulating a wide variety of protocol packet types inside IP tunnels, thereby generating a virtual point-to-point connection to Cisco routers across an IP network at remote points. IP tunneling using GRE permits network expansion across a single-protocol backbone environment by linking multiprotocol subnetworks in a single-protocol backbone environment.

Group of Four Used by Cisco Local Management Interface on Frame Relay networks to manage the PVCs.

guard band The unused frequency area found between two communications channels, furnishing the space necessary to avoid interference between the two.

half duplex The capacity to transfer data in only one direction at a time between a sending unit and receiving unit. *See also: full duplex.*

handshake Any series of transmissions exchanged between two or more devices on a network to ensure synchronized operations.

H channel High-speed channel: A full-duplex, ISDN primary rate channel operating at a speed of 384Kbps. *See also: B, D, and E channels.*

HDLC High-Level Data Link Control: Using frame characters, including checksums, HDLC designates a method for data encapsulation on synchronous serial links and is the default encapsulation for Cisco routers. HDLC is a bit-oriented synchronous Data Link Layer protocol created by ISO and derived from SDLC. However, most HDLC vendor implementations (including Cisco's) are proprietary. *See also: SDLC.*

helper address The unicast address specified, which instructs the Cisco router to change the client's local broadcast request for a service into a directed unicast to the server.

hierarchical addressing Any addressing plan employing a logical chain of commands to determine location. IP addresses are made up of a hierarchy of network numbers, subnet numbers, and host numbers to direct packets to the appropriate destination.

HIP HSSI Interface Processor: An interface processor used on Cisco 7000 series routers, providing one HSSI port that supports connections to ATM, SMDS, Frame Relay, or private lines at speeds up to T3 or E3.

holddown The state a route is placed in so that routers can neither advertise the route nor accept advertisements about it for a defined time period. Holddown is used to surface bad information about a route from all routers in the network. A route is generally placed in holddown when one of its links fails.

hop The movement of a packet between any two network nodes. *See also: hop count.*

hop count A routing metric that calculates the distance between a source and a destination. RIP employs hop count as its sole metric. *See also: hop and RIP.*

host address Logical address configured by an administrator or server on a device. Logically identifies this device on an internetwork.

HSCI High-Speed Communication Interface: Developed by Cisco, a single-port interface that provides full-duplex synchronous serial communications capability at speeds up to 52Mbps.

HSRP Hot Standby Router Protocol: A protocol that provides high network availability and provides nearly instantaneous hardware fail-over without administrator intervention. It generates a Hot Standby router group, including a lead router that lends its services to any packet being transferred to the Hot Standby address. If the lead router fails, it will be replaced by any of the other routers—the standby routers—that monitor it.

HSSI High-Speed Serial Interface: A network standard physical connector for high-speed serial linking over a WAN at speeds of up to 52Mbps.

hubs Physical Layer devices that are really just multiple port repeaters. When an electronic digital signal is received on a port, the signal is reamplified or regenerated and forwarded out all segments except the segment from which the signal was received.

ICD International Code Designator: Adapted from the subnetwork model of addressing, this assigns the mapping of Network Layer addresses to ATM addresses. HSSI is one of two ATM formats for addressing created by the ATM Forum to be utilized with private networks. *See also: DCC.*

ICMP Internet Control Message Protocol: Documented in RFC 792, it is a Network Layer Internet protocol for the purpose of reporting errors and providing information pertinent to IP packet procedures.

IEEE Institute of Electrical and Electronics Engineers: A professional organization that, among other activities, defines standards in a number of fields within computing and electronics, including networking and communications. IEEE standards are the predominant LAN standards used today throughout the industry. Many protocols are commonly known by the reference number of the corresponding IEEE standard.

IEEE 802.1 The IEEE committee specification that defines the bridging group. The specification for STP (Spanning-Tree Protocol) is IEEE 802.1d. The STP uses SPA (spanning-tree algorithm) to find and prevent network loops in bridged networks. The specification for VLAN trunking is IEEE 802.1q.

IEEE 802.3 The IEEE committee specification that defines the Ethernet group, specifically the original 10Mbps standard. Ethernet is a LAN protocol that specifies Physical Layer and MAC sublayer media access. IEEE 802.3 uses CSMA/CD to provide access for many devices on the same network. FastEthernet is defined as 802.3u, and Gigabit Ethernet is defined as 802.3q. *See also: CSMA/CD.*

IEEE 802.5 IEEE committee that defines Token Ring media access.

IGMP Internet Group Management Protocol: Employed by IP hosts, the protocol that reports their multicast group memberships to an adjacent multicast router.

IGP Interior Gateway Protocol: Any protocol used by the Internet to exchange routing data within an independent system. Examples include RIP, IGRP, and OSPF.

ILMI Integrated (or Interim) Local Management Interface. A specification created by the ATM Forum, designated for the incorporation of network-management capability into the ATM UNI. Integrated Local Management Interface cells provide for automatic configuration between ATM systems. In LAN emulation, ILMI can provide sufficient information for the ATM end station to find an LECS. In addition, ILMI provides the ATM NSAP (Network Service Access Point) prefix information to the end station.

in-band management In-band management is the management of a network device "through" the network. Examples include using Simple Network Management Protocol (SNMP) or Telnet directly via the local LAN. *Compare with: out-of-band management.*

in-band signaling Configuration of a router from within the network. Examples are Telnet, SNMP, or an NMS station.

insured burst In an ATM network, it is the largest, temporarily permitted data burst exceeding the insured rate on a PVC and not tagged by the traffic policing function for being dropped if network congestion occurs. This insured burst is designated in bytes or cells.

interarea routing Routing between two or more logical areas. *Contrast with: intra-area routing. See also: area.*

interface processor Any of several processor modules used with Cisco 7000 series routers. *See also: AIP, CIP, EIP, FEIP, HIP, MIP,* and *TRIP.*

Internet The global "network of networks," whose popularity has exploded in the last few years. Originally a tool for collaborative academic research, it has become a medium for exchanging and distributing information of all kinds. The Internet's need to link disparate computer platforms and technologies has led to the development of uniform protocols and standards that have also found widespread use within corporate LANs. *See also: TCP/IP* and *MBONE.*

internet Before the rise of the Internet, this lowercase form was shorthand for "internetwork" in the generic sense. Now rarely used. *See also: internetwork.*

Internet protocol Any protocol belonging to the TCP/IP protocol stack. *See also: TCP/IP.*

internetwork Any group of private networks interconnected by routers and other mechanisms, typically operating as a single entity.

internetworking   Broadly, anything associated with the general task of linking networks to each other. The term encompasses technologies, procedures, and products. When you connect networks to a router, you are creating an internetwork.

intra-area routing   Routing that occurs within a logical area. *Contrast with: interarea routing.*

intruder detection   These systems operate by monitoring the data flow for characteristics consistent with security threats. In this manner, an intruder can be monitored or blocked from access. One trigger for an intruder detection system is multiple Ping packets from a single resource in a brief period of time.

Inverse ARP   Inverse Address Resolution Protocol: A technique by which dynamic mappings are constructed in a network, allowing a device such as a router to locate the logical network address and associate it with a permanent virtual circuit (PVC). Commonly used in Frame Relay to determine the far-end node's TCP/IP address by sending the Inverse ARP request to the local DLCI.

IP   Internet Protocol: Defined in RFC 791, it is a Network Layer protocol that is part of the TCP/IP stack and allows connectionless service. IP furnishes an array of features for addressing, type-of-service specification, fragmentation and reassembly, and security.

IP address   Often called an Internet address, this is an address uniquely identifying any device (host) on the Internet (or any TCP/IP network). Each address consists of four octets (32 bits), represented as decimal numbers separated by periods (a format known as "dotted-decimal"). Every address is made up of a network number, an optional subnetwork number, and a host number. The network and subnetwork numbers together are used for routing, while the host number addresses an individual host within the network or subnetwork. The network and subnetwork information is extracted from the IP address using the subnet mask. There are five classes of IP addresses (A–E), which allocate different numbers of bits to the network, subnetwork, and host portions of the address. *See also: CIDR, IP,* and *subnet mask.*

IPCP   IP Control Program: The protocol used to establish and configure IP over PPP. *See also: IP* and *PPP.*

IP multicast   A technique for routing that enables IP traffic to be reproduced from one source to several endpoints or from multiple sources to many destinations. Instead of transmitting only one packet to each individual point of destination, one packet is sent to a multicast group specified by only one IP endpoint address for the group.

IPX   Internetwork Packet Exchange: Network Layer protocol (Layer 3) used in Novell NetWare networks for transferring information from servers to workstations. Similar to IP and XNS.

IPXCP   IPX Control Program: The protocol used to establish and configure IPX over PPP. *See also: IPX and PPP.*

IPX spoofing   Provides IPX RIP/SAP traffic without requiring a connection to the opposing network. This allows a per-minute tariffed link, such as ISDN or analog phone, to support IPX without requiring the link to remain active.

IPXWAN   Protocol used for new WAN links to provide and negotiate line options on the link using IPX. After the link is up and the options have been agreed upon by the two end-to-end links, normal IPX transmission begins.

ISDN   Integrated Services Digital Network: Offered as a service by telephone companies, a communication protocol that allows telephone networks to carry data, voice, and other digital traffic. *See also: BISDN, BRI,* and *PRI.*

ISL routing   Inter-Switch Link routing is a Cisco proprietary method of frame tagging in a switched internetwork. Frame tagging is a way to identify the VLAN membership of a frame as it traverses a switched internetwork.

isochronous transmission   Asynchronous data transfer over a synchronous data link, requiring a constant bit rate for reliable transport. *Compare with: asynchronous transmission* and *synchronous transmission.*

ITU-T   International Telecommunication Union Telecommunication Standardization Sector: This is a group of engineers that develops worldwide standards for telecommunications technologies.

LAN Local Area Network: Broadly, any network linking two or more computers and related devices within a limited geographical area (up to a few kilometers). LANs are typically high-speed, low-error networks within a company. Cabling and signaling at the Physical and Data Link Layers of the OSI are dictated by LAN standards. Ethernet, FDDI, and Token Ring are among the most popular LAN technologies. *Compare with: MAN.*

LANE LAN emulation: The technology that allows an ATM network to operate as a LAN backbone. To do so, the ATM network is required to provide multicast and broadcast support, address mapping (MAC-to-ATM), SVC management, in addition to an operable packet format. Additionally, LANE defines Ethernet and Token Ring ELANs. *See also: ELAN.*

LAN switch A high-speed, multiple-interface transparent bridging mechanism, transmitting packets between segments of data links, usually referred to specifically as an Ethernet switch. LAN switches transfer traffic based on MAC addresses. Multilayer switches are a type of high-speed, special-purpose, hardware-based router. *See also: multilayer switch,* and *store-and-forward packet switching.*

LAPB Link Accessed Procedure, Balanced: A bit-oriented Data Link Layer protocol that is part of the X.25 stack and has its origin in SDLC. *See also: SDLC and X.25.*

LAPD Link Access Procedure on the D channel. The ISDN Data Link Layer protocol used specifically for the D channel and defined by ITU-T Recommendations Q.920 and Q.921. LAPD evolved from LAPB and is created to comply with the signaling requirements of ISDN basic access.

latency Broadly, the time it takes a data packet to get from one location to another. In specific networking contexts, it can mean either 1) the time elapsed (delay) between the execution of a request for access to a network by a device and the time the mechanism actually is permitted transmission, or 2) the time elapsed between when a mechanism receives a frame and the time that frame is forwarded out of the destination port.

Layer-3 switch *See also: multilayer switch.*

layered architecture Industry standard way of creating applications to work on a network. Layered architecture allows the application developer to make changes in only one layer instead of the whole program.

LCP Link Control Protocol: The protocol designed to establish, configure, and test data link connections for use by PPP. *See also: PPP.*

leaky bucket An analogy for the basic cell rate algorithm (GCRA) used in ATM networks for checking the conformance of cell flows from a user or network. The bucket's "hole" is understood to be the prolonged rate at which cells can be accommodated, and the "depth" is the tolerance for cell bursts over a certain time period.

learning bridge A bridge that transparently builds a dynamic database of MAC addresses and the interfaces associated with each address. Transparent bridges help to reduce traffic congestion on the network.

LE ARP LAN Emulation Address Resolution Protocol: The protocol providing the ATM address that corresponds to a MAC address.

leased lines Permanent connections between two points leased from the telephone companies.

LEC LAN Emulation Client: Software providing the emulation of the Link Layer interface that allows the operation and communication of all higher-level protocols and applications to continue. The LEC client runs in all ATM devices, which include hosts, servers, bridges, and routers. The LANE client is responsible for address resolution, data transfer, address caching, interfacing to the emulated LAN, and driver support for higher-level services. *See also: ELAN and LES.*

LECS LAN Emulation Configuration Server: An important part of emulated LAN services, providing the configuration data that is furnished upon request from the LES. These services include address registration for Integrated Local Management Interface (ILMI) support, configuration support for the LES addresses and their corresponding emulated LAN identifiers, and an interface to the emulated LAN. *See also: LES and ELAN.*

LES   LAN Emulation Server: The central LANE component that provides the initial configuration data for each connecting LEC. The LES typically is located on either an ATM-integrated router or a switch. Responsibilities of the LES include configuration and support for the LEC, address registration for the LEC, database storage and response concerning ATM addresses, and interfacing to the emulated LAN *See also: ELAN, LEC, and LECS.*

link compression   *See: compression.*

link-state routing algorithm   A routing algorithm that allows each router to broadcast or multicast information regarding the cost of reaching all its neighbors to every node in the internetwork. Link-state algorithms provide a consistent view of the network and are therefore not vulnerable to routing loops. However, this is achieved at the cost of somewhat greater difficulty in computation and more widespread traffic (compared with distance-vector routing algorithms). *See also: distance-vector routing algorithm.*

LLAP   LocalTalk Link Access Protocol: In a Local-Talk environment, the data link-level protocol that manages node-to-node delivery of data. This protocol provides node addressing and management of bus access, and it also controls data sending and receiving to assure packet length and integrity.

LLC   Logical Link Control: Defined by the IEEE, the higher of two Data Link Layer sublayers. LLC is responsible for error detection (but not correction), flow control, framing, and software-sublayer addressing. The predominant LLC protocol, IEEE 802.2, defines both connectionless and connection-oriented operations. *See also: Data Link Layer and MAC.*

LMI   An enhancement to the original Frame Relay specification. Among the features it provides are a keepalive mechanism, a multicast mechanism, global addressing, and a status mechanism.

LNNI   LAN Emulation Network-to-Network Interface: In the Phase 2 LANE specification, an interface that supports communication between the server components within one ELAN.

local explorer packet   In a Token Ring SRB network, a packet generated by an end system to find a host linked to the local ring. If no local host can be found, the end system will produce one of two solutions: a spanning explorer packet or an all-routes explorer packet.

local loop   Connection from a demarcation point to the closest switching office.

LocalTalk   Utilizing CSMA/CD, in addition to supporting data transmission at speeds of 230.4Kbps, LocalTalk is Apple Computer's proprietary baseband protocol, operating at the Data Link and Physical Layers of the OSI reference model.

LSA   link-state advertisement: Contained inside of link-state packets (LSPs), these advertisements are usually multicast packets, containing information about neighbors and path costs, that are employed by link-state protocols. Receiving routers use LSAs to maintain their link-state databases and, ultimately, routing tables.

LUNI   LAN Emulation User-to-Network Interface: Defining the interface between the LAN Emulation Client (LEC) and the LAN Emulation Server, LUNI is the ATM Forum's standard for LAN Emulation on ATM networks. *See also: LES and LECS.*

LZW algorithm   A data compression process named for its inventors, Lempel, Ziv, and Welch. The algorithm works by finding longer and longer strings of data to compress with shorter representations.

MAC   Media Access Control: The lower sublayer in the Data Link Layer, it is responsible for hardware addressing, media access, and error detection of frames. *See also: Data Link Layer and LLC.*

MAC address   A Data Link Layer hardware address that every port or device needs in order to connect to a LAN segment. These addresses are used by various devices in the network for accurate location of logical addresses. MAC addresses are defined by the IEEE standard and their length is six characters, typically using the burned-in address (BIA) of the local LAN interface. Variously called hardware address, physical address, burned-in address, or MAC-layer address.

MacIP   In AppleTalk, the Network Layer protocol encapsulating IP packets in Datagram Delivery Protocol (DDP) packets. MacIP also supplies substitute ARP services.

MAN Metropolitan-Area Network: Any network that encompasses a metropolitan area; that is, an area typically larger than a LAN but smaller than a WAN. *See also: LAN.*

Manchester encoding A method for digital coding in which a mid-bit–time transition is employed for clocking, and a 1 (one) is denoted by a high voltage level during the first half of the bit time. This scheme is used by Ethernet and IEEE 802.3.

maximum burst Specified in bytes or cells, the largest burst of information exceeding the insured rate that will be permitted on an ATM permanent virtual connection for a short time and will not be dropped even if it goes over the specified maximum rate. *Compare with: insured burst. See also: maximum rate.*

maximum rate The maximum permitted data throughput on a particular virtual circuit, equal to the total of insured and uninsured traffic from the traffic source. Should traffic congestion occur, uninsured information may be deleted from the path. Measured in bits or cells per second, the maximum rate represents the highest throughput of data the virtual circuit is ever able to deliver and cannot exceed the media rate. *Compare with: excess rate. See also: maximum burst.*

MBS Maximum Burst Size: In an ATM signaling message, this metric, coded as a number of cells, is used to convey the burst tolerance.

MBONE multicast backbone: The multicast backbone of the Internet, it is a virtual multicast network made up of multicast LANs, including point-to-point tunnels interconnecting them.

MCDV Maximum Cell Delay Variation: The maximum two-point CDV objective across a link or node for the identified service category in an ATM network. The MCDV is one of four link metrics that are exchanged using PTSPs to verify the available resources of an ATM network. Only one MCDV value is assigned to each traffic class.

MCLR Maximum Cell Loss Ratio: The maximum ratio of cells in an ATM network that fail to transit a link or node compared with the total number of cells that arrive at the link or node. MCDV is one of four link metrics that are exchanged using PTSPs to verify the

available resources of an ATM network. The MCLR applies to cells in VBR and CBR traffic classes whose CLP bit is set to zero. *See also: CBR, CLP, and VBR.*

MCR Minimum Cell Rate: A parameter determined by the ATM Forum for traffic management of the ATM networks. MCR is specifically defined for ABR transmissions and specifies the minimum value for the allowed cell rate (ACR). *See also: ACR and PCR.*

MCTD Maximum Cell Transfer Delay: In an ATM network, the total of the maximum cell delay variation and the fixed delay across the link or node. MCTD is one of four link metrics that are exchanged using PNNI topology state packets to verify the available resources of an ATM network. There is one MCTD value assigned to each traffic class. *See also: MCDV.*

MIB Management Information Base: Used with SNMP management software to gather information from remote devices. The management station can poll the remote device for information, or the MIB running on the remote station can be programmed to send information on a regular basis.

MIP Multichannel Interface Processor: The resident interface processor on Cisco 7000 series routers, providing up to two channelized T1 or E1 connections by serial cables connected to a CSU. The two controllers are capable of providing 24 T1 or 30 E1 channel groups, with each group being introduced to the system as a serial interface that can be configured individually.

mips millions of instructions per second: A measure of processor speed.

MLP Multilink PPP: A technique used to split, recombine, and sequence datagrams across numerous logical data links.

MMP Multichassis Multilink PPP: A protocol that supplies MLP support across multiple routers and access servers. MMP enables several routers and access servers to work as a single, large dial-up pool with one network address and ISDN access number. MMP successfully supports packet fragmenting and reassembly when the user connection is split between two physical access devices.

modem modulator-demodulator: A device that converts digital signals to analog and vice-versa so that digital information can be transmitted over analog communication facilities, such as voice-grade telephone lines. This is achieved by converting digital signals at the source to analog for transmission and reconverting the analog signals back into digital form at the destination. *See also: modulation* and *demodulation.*

modemcap database Stores modem initialization strings on the router for use in auto-detection and configuration.

modem eliminator A mechanism that makes possible a connection between two DTE devices without modems by simulating the commands and physical signaling required.

modulation The process of modifying some characteristic of an electrical signal, such as amplitude (AM) or frequency (FM), in order to represent digital or analog information. *See also: AM.*

MOSPF Multicast OSPF: An extension of the OSPF unicast protocol that enables IP multicast routing within the domain. *See also: OSPF.*

MP bonding Multipoint bonding is the process of linking two or more physical connections into a single logical channel. This may use two or more analog lines and two or more modems, for example.

MPOA Multiprotocol over ATM: An effort by the ATM Forum to standardize how existing and future Network Layer protocols such as IP, Ipv6, AppleTalk, and IPX run over an ATM network with directly attached hosts, routers, and multilayer LAN switches.

MTU maximum transmission unit: The largest packet size, measured in bytes, that an interface can handle.

multicast Broadly, any communication between a single sender and multiple receivers. Unlike broadcast messages, which are sent to all addresses on a network, multicast messages are sent to a defined subset of the network addresses; this subset has a group multicast address, which is specified in the packet's destination address field. *See also: broadcast, directed broadcast.*

multicast address A single address that points to more than one device on the network by specifying a special non-existent MAC address specified in that particular multicast protocol. Identical to group address. *See also: multicast.*

multicast send VCC A two-directional point-to-point virtual control connection (VCC) arranged by an LEC to a BUS, it is one of the three types of informational link specified by phase 1 LANE. *See also: control distribute VCC* and *control direct VCC.*

multilayer switch A highly specialized, high-speed, hardware-based type of LAN router, the device filters and forwards packets based on their Layer 2 MAC addresses and Layer 3 network addresses. It's possible that even Layer 4 can be read. Sometimes called a Layer 3 switch. *See also: LAN switch.*

multiplexing The process of converting several logical signals into a single physical signal for transmission across one physical channel. *Contrast with: demultiplexing.*

NAK negative acknowledgment: A response sent from a receiver, telling the sender that the information was not received or contained errors. *Compare with: acknowledgment.*

NAT Network Address Translation: An algorithm instrumental in minimizing the requirement for globally unique IP addresses, permitting an organization whose addresses are not all globally unique to connect to the Internet, regardless, by translating those addresses into globally routable address space.

NBP Name Binding Protocol: In AppleTalk, the transport-level protocol that interprets a socket client's name, entered as a character string, into the corresponding DDP address. NBP gives AppleTalk protocols the capacity to discern user-defined zones and names of mechanisms by showing and keeping translation tables that map names to their corresponding socket addresses.

NCP Network Control Protocol: A protocol at the Logical Link Control sublayer of the Data Link Layer used in the PPP stack. It is used to allow multiple Network Layer protocols to run over a nonproprietary HDLC serial encapsulation.

neighboring routers Two routers in OSPF that have interfaces to a common network. On networks with multiaccess, these neighboring routers are dynamically discovered using the Hello protocol of OSPF.

NetBEUI NetBIOS Extended User Interface: An improved version of the NetBIOS protocol used in a number of network operating systems including LAN Manager, Windows NT, LAN Server, and Windows for Workgroups, implementing the OSI LLC2 protocol. NetBEUI formalizes the transport frame not standardized in NetBIOS and adds more functions. *See also: OSI.*

NetBIOS Network Basic Input/Output System: The API employed by applications residing on an IBM LAN to ask for services, such as session termination or information transfer, from lower-level network processes.

NetView A mainframe network product from IBM, used for monitoring SNA (Systems Network Architecture) networks. It runs as a VTAM (Virtual Telecommunications Access Method) application.

NetWare A widely used NOS created by Novell, providing a number of distributed network services and remote file access.

network address Used with the logical network addresses to identify the network segment in an internetwork. Logical addresses are hierarchical in nature and have at least two parts: network and host. An example of a hierarchical address is 172.16.10.5, where 172.16 is the network and 10.5 is the host address.

Network Layer In the OSI reference model, it is Layer 3—the layer in which routing is implemented, enabling connections and path selection between two end systems. *See also: Application Layer, Data Link Layer, Physical Layer, Presentation Layer, Session Layer,* and *Transport Layer.*

NFS Network File System: One of the protocols in Sun Microsystems' widely used file system protocol suite, allowing remote file access across a network. The name is loosely used to refer to the entire Sun protocol suite, which also includes RPC, XDR (External Data Representation), and other protocols.

NHRP Next Hop Resolution Protocol: In a non-broadcast multiaccess (NBMA) network, the protocol employed by routers in order to dynamically locate MAC addresses of various hosts and routers. It enables systems to communicate directly without requiring an intermediate hop, thus facilitating increased performance in ATM, Frame Relay, X.25, and SMDS systems.

NHS Next Hop Server: Defined by the NHRP protocol, this server maintains the next-hop resolution cache tables, listing IP-to-ATM address maps of related nodes and nodes that can be reached through routers served by the NHS.

NIC network interface card: An electronic circuit board placed in a computer. The NIC provides network communication to a LAN.

NLSP NetWare Link Services Protocol: Novell's link-state routing protocol, based on the IS-IS model.

NMP Network Management Processor: A Catalyst 5000 switch processor module used to control and monitor the switch.

node address Used to identify a specific device in an internetwork. Can be a hardware address, which is burned into the network interface card or a logical network address, which an administrator or server assigns to the node.

nondesignated port The Spanning-Tree Protocol tells a port on a Layer 2 switch to stop transmitting and creating a network loop. Only designated ports can send frames.

non-stub area In OSPF, a resource-consuming area carrying a default route, intra-area routes, interarea routes, static routes, and external routes. Non-stub areas are the only areas that can have virtual links configured across them and exclusively contain an anonymous system boundary router (ASBR). *Compare with: stub area. See also: ASBR* and *OSPF.*

NRZ Nonreturn to Zero: One of several encoding schemes for transmitting digital data. NRZ signals sustain constant levels of voltage with no signal shifting (no return to zero-voltage level) during a bit interval. If there is a series of bits with the same value (1 or 0), there will be no state change. The signal is not self-clocking. *See also: NRZI.*

NRZI Nonreturn to Zero Inverted: One of several encoding schemes for transmitting digital data. A transition in voltage level (either from high to low or vice-versa) at the beginning of a bit interval is interpreted as a value of 1; the absence of a transition is interpreted as a 0. Thus, the voltage assigned to each value is continually inverted. NRZI signals are not self-clocking. *See also: NRZ.*

NT1 network termination 1: Is an ISDN designation to devices that understand ISDN standards.

NT2 network termination 2: Is an ISDN designation to devices that do not understand ISDN standards. To use a NT2, you must use a terminal adapter (TA).

NVRAM Non-Volatile RAM: Random-access memory that keeps its contents intact while power is turned off.

OC Optical Carrier: A series of physical protocols, designated as OC-1, OC-2, OC-3, and so on, for SONET optical signal transmissions. OC signal levels place STS frames on a multimode fiber-optic line at various speeds, of which 51.84Mbps is the lowest (OC-1). Each subsequent protocol runs at a speed divisible by 51.84. *See also: SONET.*

octet Base-8 numbering system used to identify a section of a dotted decimal IP address. Also referred to as a byte.

100BaseT Based on the IEEE 802.3u standard, 100BaseT is the Fast Ethernet specification of 100Mbps baseband that uses UTP wiring. 100BaseT sends link pulses (containing more information than those used in 10BaseT) over the network when no traffic is present. *See also: 10BaseT, Fast Ethernet,* and *IEEE 802.3.*

100BaseTX Based on the IEEE 802.3u standard, 100BaseTX is the 100Mbps baseband Fast Ethernet specification that uses two pairs of UTP or STP wiring. The first pair of wires receives data; the second pair sends data. To ensure correct signal timing, a 100BaseTX segment cannot be longer than 100 meters.

ones density Also known as pulse density, this is a method of signal clocking. The CSU/DSU retrieves the clocking information from data that passes through it. For this scheme to work, the data needs to be encoded to contain at least one binary 1 for each eight bits transmitted. *See also: CSU* and *DSU.*

one-time challenge tokens Provide a single-use password. This prevents replay attacks and snooping; however, it also requires the user to have a device that provides the token. This physical component of the security model prevents hackers from guessing or obtaining the user's password.

OSI Open System Interconnection: International standardization program designed by ISO and ITU-T for the development of data networking standards that make multivendor equipment interoperability a reality.

OSI reference model Open System Interconnection reference model: A conceptual model defined by the International Organization for Standardization (ISO), describing how any combination of devices can be connected for the purpose of communication. The OSI model divides the task into seven functional layers, forming a hierarchy with the applications at the top and the physical medium at the bottom, and it defines the functions each layer must provide. *See also: Application Layer, Data Link Layer, Network Layer, Physical Layer, Presentation Layer, Session Layer,* and *Transport Layer.*

OSPF Open Shortest Path First: A link-state, hierarchical IGP routing algorithm derived from an earlier version of the IS-IS protocol, whose features include multipath routing, load balancing, and least-cost routing. OSPF is the suggested successor to RIP in the Internet environment. *See also: Enhanced IGRP, IGP,* and *IP.*

OUI Organizationally Unique Identifier: Is assigned by the IEEE to an organization that makes network interface cards. The organization then puts this OUI on each and every card they manufacture. The OUI is 3 bytes (24 bits) long. The manufacturer then adds a 3-byte identifier to uniquely identify the host on an internetwork. The total length of the address is 48 bits (6 bytes) and is called a hardware address or MAC address.

out-of-band management Management "outside" of the network's physical channels. For example, using a console connection not directly interfaced through the local LAN or WAN or a dial-in modem. *Compare to: in-band management.*

out-of-band signaling Within a network, any transmission that uses physical channels or frequencies separate from those ordinarily used for data transfer. For example, the initial configuration of a Cisco Catalyst switch requires an out-of-band connection via a console port.

packet In data communications, the basic logical unit of information transferred. A packet consists of a certain number of data bytes, wrapped or encapsulated in headers and/or trailers that contain information about where the packet came from, where it's going, and so on. The various protocols involved in sending a transmission add their own layers of header information, which the corresponding protocols in receiving devices then interpret.

packet mode connections Are typically passed through the router or remote access device. This includes PPP sessions.

packet switch A physical device that makes it possible for a communication channel to share several connections, its functions include finding the most efficient transmission path for packets.

packet switching A networking technology based on the transmission of data in packets. Dividing a continuous stream of data into small units—packets—enables data from multiple devices on a network to share the same communication channel simultaneously but also requires the use of precise routing information.

PAD packet assembler/disassembler: Is used to buffer incoming data that is coming in faster than the receiving device can handle it. Typically, it is only used in X.25 networks.

PAP Password Authentication Protocol: In Point-to-Point Protocol (PPP) networks, a method of validating connection requests. The requesting (remote) device must send an authentication request, containing a password and ID, to the local router when attempting to connect. Unlike the more secure CHAP (Challenge Handshake Authentication Protocol), PAP sends the password unencrypted and does not attempt to verify whether the user is authorized to access the requested resource; it merely identifies the remote end. *See also: CHAP.*

parity checking A method of error-checking in data transmissions. An extra bit (the parity bit) is added to each character or data word so that the sum of the bits will be either an odd number (in odd parity) or an even number (even parity).

partial mesh A type of network topology in which some network nodes form a full mesh (where every node has either a physical or a virtual circuit linking it to every other network node), but others are attached to only one or two nodes in the network. A typical use of partial-mesh topology is in peripheral networks linked to a fully meshed backbone. *See also: full mesh.*

PAT Port Address Translation: Allows a single IP address to represent multiple resources by altering the source TCP or UDP port number.

payload compression Reduces the number of bytes required to accurately represent the original data stream. Header compression is also possible. *See also: compression.*

PCR Peak Cell Rate: As defined by the ATM Forum, the parameter specifying, in cells per second, the maximum rate at which a source may transmit.

PDN Public Data Network: Generally for a fee, a PDN offers the public access to computer communication network operated by private concerns or government agencies. Small organizations can take advantage of PDNs, aiding them creating WANs without investing in long-distance equipment and circuitry.

PGP Pretty Good Privacy: A popular public-key/private-key encryption application offering protected transfer of files and messages.

Physical Layer The lowest layer—Layer 1—in the OSI reference model, it is responsible for converting data packets from the Data Link Layer (Layer 2) into electrical signals. Physical Layer protocols and standards define, for example, the type of cable and connectors to be used, including their pin assignments and the encoding scheme for signaling 0 and 1 values. *See also: Application Layer, Data Link Layer, Network Layer, Presentation Layer, Session Layer,* and *Transport Layer.*

ping packet Internet groper: A Unix-based Internet diagnostic tool, consisting of a message sent to test the accessibility of a particular device on the IP network. The acronym (from which the "full name" was formed) reflects the underlying metaphor of submarine sonar. Just as the sonar operator sends out a signal and waits to hear it echo ("ping") back from a submerged object, the network user can ping another node on the network and wait to see if it responds.

pleisochronous Nearly synchronous, except that clocking comes from an outside source instead of being embedded within the signal as in synchronous transmissions.

PLP Packet Level Protocol: Occasionally called X.25 Level 3 or X.25 Protocol, a Network Layer protocol that is part of the X.25 stack.

PNNI Private Network-Network Interface: An ATM Forum specification for offering topology data used for the calculation of paths through the network, among switches and groups of switches. It is based on well-known link-state routing procedures and allows for automatic configuration in networks whose addressing scheme is determined by the topology.

point-to-multipoint connection In ATM, a communication path going only one way, connecting a single system at the starting point, called the "root node," to systems at multiple points of destination, called "leaves." *See also: point-to-point connection.*

point-to-point connection In ATM, a channel of communication that can be directed either one way or two ways between two ATM end systems. *See also: point-to-multipoint connection.*

poison reverse updates These update messages are transmitted by a router back to the originator (thus ignoring the split-horizon rule) after route poisoning has occurred. Typically used with DV routing protocols in order to overcome large routing loops and offer explicit information when a subnet or network is not accessible (instead of merely suggesting that the network is unreachable by not including it in updates). *See also: route poisoning.*

polling The procedure of orderly inquiry, used by a primary network mechanism, to determine if secondary devices have data to transmit. A message is sent to each secondary, granting the secondary the right to transmit.

POP 1) Point Of Presence: The physical location where an interexchange carrier has placed equipment to interconnect with a local exchange carrier. 2) Post Office Protocol (currently at version 3): A protocol used by client e-mail applications for recovery of mail from a mail server.

port density Reflects the capacity of the remote access device regarding the termination of interfaces. For example, the port density of an access server that serves four T-1 circuits is 96 analog lines (non-ISDN PRI).

port security Used with Layer 2 switches to provide some security. Not typically used in production because it is difficult to manage. Allows only certain frames to traverse administrator-assigned segments.

POTS Plain Old Telephone Service: Refers to the traditional analog phone service found in most installations.

PDU Protocol Data Unit: Is the name of the processes at each layer of the OSI model. PDUs at the Transport Layer are called segments; PDUs at the Network Layer are called packets or datagrams; and PDUs at the Data Link Layer are called frames. The Physical Layer uses bits.

PPP Point-to-Point Protocol: The protocol most commonly used for dial-up Internet access, superseding the earlier SLIP. Its features include address notification, authentication via CHAP or PAP, support for multiple protocols, and link monitoring. PPP has two layers: the Link Control Protocol (LCP) establishes, configures, and tests a link; and then any of various Network Control Programs (NCPs) transport traffic for a specific protocol suite, such as IPX. *See also: CHAP, PAP, and SLIP.*

PPP callback The point-to-point protocol supports callback to a predetermined number to augment security.

Predictor A compression technique supported by Cisco. *See also: compression.*

Presentation Layer Layer 6 of the OSI reference model, it defines how data is formatted, presented, encoded, and converted for use by software at the Application Layer. *See also: Application Layer, Data Link Layer, Network Layer, Physical Layer, Session Layer, and Transport Layer.*

PRI Primary Rate Interface: A type of ISDN connection between a PBX and a long-distance carrier, which is made up of a single 64Kbps D channel in addition to 23 (T1) or 30 (E1) B channels. *See also: ISDN.*

priority queuing A routing function in which frames temporarily placed in an interface output queue are assigned priorities based on traits such as packet size or type of interface.

process switching   As a packet arrives on a router to be forwarded, it's copied to the router's process buffer, and the router performs a lookup on the Layer 3 address. Using the route table, an exit interface is associated with the destination address. The processor forwards the packet with the added new information to the exit interface, while the router initializes the fast-switching cache. Subsequent packets bound for the same destination address follow the same path as the first packet.

PROM   programmable read-only memory: ROM that is programmable only once, using special equipment. *Compare with: EPROM.*

propagation delay   The time it takes data to traverse a network from its source to its destination.

protocol   In networking, the specification of a set of rules for a particular type of communication. The term is also used to refer to the software that implements a protocol.

protocol stack   A collection of related protocols.

PSE   Packet Switch Exchange: The X.25 term for a switch.

PSN   packet-switched network: Any network that uses packet-switching technology. Also known as packet-switched data network (PSDN). *See also: packet switching.*

PSTN   Public Switched Telephone Network: Colloquially referred to as "plain old telephone service" (POTS). A term that describes the assortment of telephone networks and services available globally.

PVC   permanent virtual circuit: In a Frame-Relay network, a logical connection, defined in software, that is maintained permanently. *Compare with: SVC. See also: virtual circuit.*

PVP   permanent virtual path: A virtual path made up of PVCs. *See also: PVC.*

PVP tunneling   permanent virtual path tunneling: A technique that links two private ATM networks across a public network using a virtual path; wherein the public network transparently trunks the complete collection of virtual channels in the virtual path between the two private networks.

QoS   Quality of Service: A set of metrics used to measure the quality of transmission and service availability of any given transmission system.

queue   Broadly, any list of elements arranged in an orderly fashion and ready for processing, such as a line of people waiting to enter a movie theater. In routing, it refers to a backlog of information packets waiting in line to be transmitted over a router interface.

queuing   A quality of service process that allows packets to be forwarded from the router based on administratively defined parameters. This may be used for time-sensitive protocols, such as SNA.

R reference point   Used with ISDN networks to identify the connection between an NT1 and an S/T device. The S/T device converts the 4-wire network to the two-wire ISDN standard network.

RADIUS   Remote Access Dial-In User Service: A protocol that is used to communicate between the remote access device and an authentication server. Sometimes an authentication server running RADIUS is called a RADIUS server.

RAM   random access memory: Used by all computers to store information. Cisco routers use RAM to store packet buffers and routing tables, along with the hardware addresses cache.

RARP   Reverse Address Resolution Protocol: The protocol within the TCP/IP stack that maps MAC addresses to IP addresses. *See also: ARP.*

rate queue   A value, assigned to one or more virtual circuits, that specifies the speed at which an individual virtual circuit will transmit data to the remote end. Every rate queue identifies a segment of the total bandwidth available on an ATM link. The sum of all rate queues should not exceed the total available bandwidth.

RCP   Remote Copy Protocol: A protocol for copying files to or from a file system that resides on a remote server on a network, using TCP to guarantee reliable data delivery.

redistribution   Command used in Cisco routers to inject the paths found from one type of routing protocol into another type of routing protocol. For example, networks found by RIP can be inserted into an IGRP network.

redundancy In internetworking, the duplication of connections, devices, or services that can be used as a backup in the event that the primary connections, devices, or services fail.

reference point Used to define an area in an ISDN network. Providers use reference points to find problems in the ISDN network.

reliability The measure of a connection's quality. It is one of the metrics that can be used to make routing decisions.

reload An event or command that causes Cisco routers to reboot.

remote access A generic term that defines connectivity to distant resources using one of many technologies, as appropriate.

reverse Telnet Maps a Telnet port to a physical port on the router or access device. This allows the administrator to connect to a modem or other device attached to the port.

RFC Request for Comments: Present and define standards in the networking industry.

RIF Routing Information Field: In source-route bridging, a header field that defines the path direction of the frame or token. If the Route Information Indicator (RII) bit is not set, the RIF is read from source to destination (left to right). If the RII bit is set, the RIF is read from the destination back to the source, so the RIF is read right to left. It is defined as part of the Token Ring frame header for source-routed frames, which contains path information.

ring Two or more stations connected in a logical circular topology. In this topology, which is the basis for Token Ring, FDDI, and CDDI, information is transferred from station to station in sequence.

ring topology A network logical topology comprising a series of repeaters that form one closed loop by connecting unidirectional transmission links. Individual stations on the network are connected to the network at a repeater. Physically, ring topologies are generally organized in a closed-loop star. *Compare with: bus topology* and *star topology.*

RIP Routing Information Protocol: The most commonly used interior gateway protocol in the Internet. RIP employs hop count as a routing metric. *See also: Enhanced IGRP, IGP, OSPF,* and *hop count.*

RIP version 2 Newer, updated version of Routing Information Protocol (RIP). Allows VLSM.

RJ connector registered jack connector: Is used with twisted-pair wiring to connect the copper wire to network interface cards, switches, and hubs.

robbed bit signaling Used in Primary Rate Interface clocking mechanisms.

ROM read-only memory: Chip used in computers to help boot the device. Cisco routers use a ROM chip to load the bootstrap, which runs a power-on self test, and then find and load the IOS in flash memory by default.

root bridge Used with the Spanning-Tree Protocol to stop network loops from occurring. The root bridge is elected by having the lowest bridge ID. The bridge ID is determined by the priority (32,768 by default on all bridges and switches) and the main hardware address of the device. The root bridge determines which of the neighboring Layer 2 devices' interfaces become the designated and nondesignated ports.

routed protocol Routed protocols (such as IP and IPX) are used to transmit user data through an internetwork. By contrast, routing protocols (such as RIP, IGRP, and OSPF) are used to update routing tables between routers.

route poisoning Used by various DV routing protocols in order to overcome large routing loops and offer explicit information about when a subnet or network is not accessible (instead of merely suggesting that the network is unreachable by not including it in updates). Typically, this is accomplished by setting the hop count to one more than maximum. *See also: poison reverse updates.*

route summarization In various routing protocols, such as OSPF, EIGRP, and IS-IS, the consolidation of publicized subnetwork addresses so that a single summary route is advertised to other areas by an area border router.

router A Network Layer mechanism, either software or hardware, using one or more metrics to decide on the best path to use for transmission of network traffic. Sending packets between networks by routers is based on the information provided on Network Layers. Historically, this device has sometimes been called a gateway.

routing The process of forwarding logically addressed packets from their local subnetwork toward their ultimate destination. In large networks, the numerous intermediary destinations a packet might travel before reaching its destination can make routing very complex.

routing domain Any collection of end systems and intermediate systems that operate under an identical set of administrative rules. Every routing domain contains one or several areas, all individually given a certain area address.

routing metric Any value that is used by routing algorithms to determine whether one route is superior to another. Metrics include such information as bandwidth, delay, hop count, path cost, load, MTU, reliability, and communication cost. Only the best possible routes are stored in the routing table, while all other information may be stored in link-state or topological databases. *See also: cost.*

routing protocol Any protocol that defines algorithms to be used for updating routing tables between routers. Examples include IGRP, RIP, and OSPF.

routing table A table kept in a router or other internetworking mechanism that maintains a record of only the best possible routes to certain network destinations and the metrics associated with those routes.

RP Route Processor: Also known as a supervisory processor, a module on Cisco 7000 series routers that holds the CPU, system software, and most of the memory components used in the router.

RSP Route/Switch Processor: A processor module combining the functions of RP and SP used in Cisco 7500 series routers. *See also: RP and SP.*

RTS Request To Send: An EIA/TIA-232 control signal requesting permission to transmit data on a communication line.

S reference point ISDN reference point that works with a T reference point to convert a 4-wire ISDN network to the 2-wire ISDN network needed to communicate with the ISDN switches at the network provider.

sampling rate The rate at which samples of a specific waveform amplitude are collected within a specified period of time.

SAP 1) Service Access Point: A field specified by IEEE 802.2 that is part of an address specification. 2) Service Advertising Protocol: The Novell NetWare protocol that supplies a way to inform network clients of resources and services availability on network, using routers and servers. *See also: IPX.*

SCR Sustainable Cell Rate: An ATM Forum parameter used for traffic management, it is the long-term average cell rate for VBR connections that can be transmitted.

scripts Predefines commands that should be issued in sequence, typically to complete a connection or accomplish a repetitive task.

SDLC Synchronous Data Link Control: A protocol used in SNA Data Link Layer communications. SDLC is a bit-oriented, full-duplex serial protocol that is the basis for several similar protocols, including HDLC and LAPB. *See also: HDLC and LAPB.*

security policy Documents that define the business requirements and processes to protect corporate data. A security policy might be as generic as no file transfers allowed or as specific as FTP puts allowed only to server X.

security server A centralized device that authenticates access requests, typically via a protocol such as TACACS+ or RADIUS.

seed router In an AppleTalk network, the router that is equipped with the network number or cable range in its port descriptor. The seed router specifies the network number or cable range for other routers in that network section and answers to configuration requests from nonseed routers on its connected AppleTalk network, permitting those routers to affirm or modify their configurations accordingly. Every AppleTalk network needs at least one seed router physically connected to each network segment.

server Hardware and software that provide network services to clients.

set-based Set-based routers and switches use the `set` command to configure devices. Cisco is moving away from set-based commands and is using the Command-Line Interface (CLI) on all new devices.

Session Layer Layer 5 of the OSI reference model, responsible for creating, managing, and terminating sessions between applications and overseeing data exchange between Presentation Layer entities. *See also: Application Layer, Data Link Layer, Network Layer, Physical Layer, Presentation Layer,* and *Transport Layer.*

setup mode Mode that a router will enter if no configuration is found in nonvolatile RAM when the router boots. Allows the administrator to configure a router step-by-step. Not as robust or flexible as the Command-Line Interface.

SF super frame: A super frame (also called a D4 frame) consists of 12 frames with 192 bits each, and the 193rd bit providing other functions including error checking. SF is frequently used on T1 circuits. A newer version of the technology is Extended Super Frame (ESF), which uses 24 frames. *See also: ESF.*

signaling packet An informational packet created by an ATM-connected mechanism that wants to establish connection with another such mechanism. The packet contains the QoS parameters needed for connection and the ATM NSAP address of the endpoint. The endpoint responds with a message of acceptance if it is able to support the desired QoS, and the connection is established. *See also: QoS.*

silicon switching A type of high-speed switching used in Cisco 7000 series routers, based on the use of a separate processor (the Silicon Switch Processor, or SSP). *See also: SSE.*

simplex The mode at which data or a digital signal is transmitted. Simplex is a way of transmitting in only one direction. Half duplex transmits in two directions but only one direction at a time. Full duplex transmits both directions simultaneously.

sliding window The method of flow control used by TCP, as well as several Data Link Layer protocols. This method places a buffer between the receiving application and the network data flow. The "window" available for accepting data is the size of the buffer minus the amount of data already there. This window increases in size as the application reads data from it and decreases as new data is sent. The receiver sends the transmitter announcements of the current window size, and it may stop accepting data until the window increases above a certain threshold.

SLIP Serial Line Internet Protocol: An industry standard serial encapsulation for point-to-point connections that supports only a single routed protocol, TCP/IP. SLIP is the predecessor to PPP. *See also: PPP.*

SMDS Switched Multimegabit Data Service: A packet-switched, datagram-based WAN networking technology offered by telephone companies that provides high speed.

SMTP Simple Mail Transfer Protocol: A protocol used on the Internet to provide electronic mail services.

SNA System Network Architecture: A complex, feature-rich, network architecture similar to the OSI reference model but with several variations; created by IBM in the 1970s and essentially composed of seven layers.

SNAP Subnetwork Access Protocol: SNAP is a frame used in Ethernet, Token Ring, and FDDI LANs. Data transfer, connection management, and QoS selection are three primary functions executed by the SNAP frame.

snapshot routing Takes a point-in-time capture of a dynamic routing table and maintains it even when the remote connection goes down. This allows the use of a dynamic routing protocol without requiring the link to remain active, which might incur per-minute usage charges.

socket 1) A software structure that operates within a network device as a destination point for communications. 2) In AppleTalk networks, an entity at a specific location within a node; AppleTalk sockets are conceptually similar to TCP/IP ports.

SOHO Small Office/Home Office: A contemporary term for remote users.

SONET Synchronous Optical Network: The ANSI standard for synchronous transmission on fiber-optic media, developed at Bell Labs. It specifies a base signal rate of 51.84Mbps and a set of multiples of that rate, known as Optical Carrier levels, up to 2.5Gbps.

SP Switch Processor: Also known as a ciscoBus controller, it is a Cisco 7000 series processor module acting as governing agent for all CxBus activities.

span A full-duplex digital transmission line connecting two facilities.

SPAN Switched Port Analyzer: A feature of the Catalyst 5000 switch, offering freedom to manipulate within a switched Ethernet environment by extending the monitoring ability of the existing network analyzers into the environment. At one switched segment, the SPAN mirrors traffic onto a predetermined SPAN port, while a network analyzer connected to the SPAN port is able to monitor traffic from any other Catalyst switched port.

spanning explorer packet Sometimes called limited-route or single-route explorer packet, it pursues a statically configured spanning tree when searching for paths in a source-route bridging network. *See also: all-routes explorer packet, explorer packet,* and *local explorer packet.*

spanning tree A subset of a network topology, within which no loops exist. When bridges are interconnected into a loop, the bridge, or switch, cannot identify a frame that has been forwarded previously, so there is no mechanism for removing a frame as it passes the interface numerous times. Without a method of removing these frames, the bridges continuously forward them—consuming bandwidth and adding overhead to the network. Spanning trees prune the network to provide only one path for any packet. *See also: Spanning-Tree Protocol and spanning tree algorithm.*

spanning-tree algorithm (STA) An algorithm that creates a spanning tree using the Spanning-Tree Protocol (STP). *See also: spanning-tree* and *Spanning-Tree Protocol.*

Spanning-Tree Protocol (STP) The bridge protocol (IEEE 802.1d) that enables a learning bridge to dynamically avoid loops in the network topology by creating a spanning tree using the spanning-tree algorithm. Spanning-tree frames called bridge protocol data units (BPDUs) are sent and received by all switches in the network at regular intervals. The switches participating in the spanning tree don't forward the frames; instead, they're processed to determine the spanning-tree topology itself. Cisco Catalyst series switches use STP 802.1d to perform this function. *See also: BPDU, learning bridge, MAC address, spanning tree,* and *spanning-tree algorithm.*

SPF Shortest Path First algorithm: A routing algorithm used to decide on the shortest-path spanning tree. Sometimes called Dijkstra's algorithm and frequently used in link-state routing algorithms. *See also: link-state routing algorithm.*

SPID Service Profile Identifier: A number assigned by service providers or local telephone companies and assigned by administrators to a BRI port. SPIDs are used to determine subscription services of a device connected via ISDN. ISDN devices use SPID when accessing the telephone company switch that initializes the link to a service provider.

split horizon Useful for preventing routing loops, a type of distance-vector routing rule where information about routes is prevented from leaving the router interface through which that information was received.

spoofing 1) In dial-on-demand routing (DDR), where a circuit-switched link is taken down to save toll charges when there is no traffic to be sent, spoofing is a scheme used by routers that causes a host to treat an interface as if it were functioning and supporting a session. The router pretends to send "spoof" replies to keepalive messages from the host in an effort to convince the host that the session is up and running. *See also: DDR.* 2) The illegal act of sending a packet labeled with a false address, in order to deceive network security mechanisms such as filters and access lists.

spooler A management application that processes requests submitted to it for execution in a sequential fashion from a queue. A good example is a print spooler.

SPX Sequenced Packet Exchange: A Novell NetWare transport protocol that augments the datagram service provided by Network Layer (Layer 3) protocols, it was derived from the Switch-to-Switch Protocol of the XNS protocol suite.

SQE Signal Quality Error: In an Ethernet network, a message sent from a transceiver to an attached machine that the collision-detection circuitry is working.

SRB Source-Route Bridging: Created by IBM, the bridging method used in Token-Ring networks. The source determines the entire route to a destination before sending the data and includes that information in route information fields (RIF) within each packet. *Contrast with: transparent bridging.*

SRT source-route transparent bridging: A bridging scheme developed by IBM, merging source-route and transparent bridging. SRT takes advantage of both technologies in one device, fulfilling the needs of all end nodes. Translation between bridging protocols is not necessary. *Compare with: SR/TLB.*

SR/TLB source-route translational bridging: A bridging method that allows source-route stations to communicate with transparent bridge stations aided by an intermediate bridge that translates between the two bridge protocols. Used for bridging between Token Ring and Ethernet. *Compare with: SRT.*

SSAP Source Service Access Point: The SAP of the network node identified in the Source field of the packet. *See also: DSAP and SAP.*

SSE Silicon Switching Engine: The software component of Cisco's silicon switching technology, hard-coded into the Silicon Switch Processor (SSP). Silicon switching is available only on the Cisco 7000 with an SSP. Silicon-switched packets are compared to the silicon-switching cache on the SSE. The SSP is a dedicated switch processor that offloads the switching process from the route processor, providing a fast-switching solution, but packets must still traverse the backplane of the router to get to the SSP and then back to the exit interface.

SS-7 signaling Signaling System 7: The current standard for telecommunications switching-control signaling. This is an out-of-band signaling that establishes circuits and provides billing information.

Stac A compression method developed by Stacker Corporation for use over serial links.

standard IP access list IP access list that uses only the source IP addresses to filter a network.

standard IPX access list IPX access list that uses only the source and destination IPX address to filter a network.

star topology A LAN physical topology with end-points on the network converging at a common central switch (known as a hub) using point-to-point links. A logical ring topology can be configured as a physical star topology using a unidirectional closed-loop star rather than point-to-point links. That is, connections within the hub are arranged in an internal ring. *See also: bus topology and ring topology.*

startup range If an AppleTalk node does not have a number saved from the last time it was booted, then the node selects from the range of values from 65280 to 65534.

state transitions Digital signaling scheme that reads the "state" of the digital signal in the middle of the bit cell. If it is five volts, the cell is read as a one. If the state of the digital signal is zero volts, the bit cell is read as a zero.

static route A route whose information is purposefully entered into the routing table and takes priority over those chosen by dynamic routing protocols.

static VLANs Static VLANs are manually configured port-by-port. This is the method typically used in production networks.

statistical multiplexing Multiplexing in general is a technique that allows data from multiple logical channels to be sent across a single physical channel. Statistical multiplexing dynamically assigns bandwidth only to input channels that are active, optimizing available bandwidth so that more devices can be connected than with other multiplexing techniques. Also known as statistical time-division multiplexing or stat mux.

STM-1 Synchronous Transport Module Level 1. In the European SDH standard, one of many formats identifying the frame structure for the 155.52Mbps lines that are used to carry ATM cells.

store-and-forward packet switching A technique in which the switch first copies each packet into its buffer and performs a cyclical redundancy check (CRC). If the packet is error-free, the switch then looks up the destination address in its filter table, determines the appropriate exit port, and sends the packet.

STP   1) Shielded Twisted Pair: A two-pair wiring scheme, used in many network implementations, that has a layer of shielded insulation to reduce EMI. 2) Spanning-Tree Protocol.

stub area   An OSPF area carrying a default route, intra-area routes, and interarea routes, but no external routes. Configuration of virtual links cannot be achieved across a stub area, and stub areas are not allowed to contain an ASBR. *See also: non-stub area, ASBR,* and *OSPF.*

stub network   A network having only one connection to a router.

STUN   Serial Tunnel: A technology used to connect an HDLC link to an SDLC link over a serial link.

subarea   A portion of an SNA network made up of a subarea node and its attached links and peripheral nodes.

subarea node   An SNA communications host or controller that handles entire network addresses.

subchannel   A frequency-based subdivision that creates a separate broadband communications channel.

subinterface   One of many virtual interfaces available on a single physical interface.

subnet   *See: subnetwork.*

subnet address   The portion of an IP address that is specifically identified by the subnet mask as the subnetwork. *See also: IP address, subnetwork,* and *subnet mask.*

subnet mask   Also simply known as mask, a 32-bit address mask used in IP to identify the bits of an IP address that are used for the subnet address. Using a mask, the router does not need to examine all 32 bits, only those selected by the mask. *See also: address mask* and *IP address.*

subnetwork   1) Any network that is part of a larger IP network and is identified by a subnet address. A network administrator segments a network into subnetworks in order to provide a hierarchical, multilevel routing structure, and at the same time protect the subnetwork from the addressing complexity of networks that are attached. Also known as a subnet. *See also: IP address, subnet mask,* and *subnet address.* 2) In OSI networks, the term specifically refers to a collection of ESs and ISs controlled by only one administrative domain, using a solitary network connection protocol.

SVC   switched virtual circuit: A dynamically established virtual circuit, created on demand and dissolved as soon as transmission is over and the circuit is no longer needed. In ATM terminology, it is referred to as a switched virtual connection. *See also: PVC.*

switch   1) In networking, a device responsible for multiple functions such as filtering, flooding, and sending frames. It works using the destination address of individual frames. Switches operate at the Data Link Layer of the OSI model. 2) Broadly, any electronic/mechanical device allowing connections to be established as needed and terminated if no longer necessary.

switch fabric   Term used to identify a Layer 2 switched internetwork with many switches.

switched LAN   Any LAN implemented using LAN switches. *See also: LAN switch.*

synchronous transmission   Signals transmitted digitally with precision clocking. These signals have identical frequencies and contain individual characters encapsulated in control bits (called start/stop bits) that designate the beginning and ending of each character. *See also: asynchronous transmission* and *isochronous transmission.*

T reference point   Used with an S reference point to change a 4-wire ISDN network to a 2-wire ISDN network.

T-1   Digital WAN that uses 24 DS0s at 64K each to create a bandwidth of 1.536Mbps, minus clocking overhead, providing 1.544Mbps of usable bandwidth.

T-3   Digital WAN that can provide bandwidth of 44.763Mbps.

TACACS+   Terminal Access Control Access Control System: An enhanced version of TACACS, this protocol is similar to RADIUS.

tag switching   Based on the concept of label swapping, where packets or cells are designated to defined-length labels that control the manner in which data is to be sent, tag switching is a high-performance technology used for forwarding packets. It incorporates Data Link Layer (Layer 2) switching and Network Layer (Layer 3) routing and supplies scalable, high-speed switching in the network core.

tagged traffic   ATM cells with their cell loss priority (CLP) bit set to 1. Also referred to as discard-eligible (DE) traffic. Tagged traffic can be eliminated in order to ensure trouble-free delivery of higher priority traffic, if the network is congested. *See also: CLP.*

TCP   Transmission Control Protocol: A connection-oriented protocol that is defined at the Transport Layer of the OSI reference model. Provides reliable delivery of data.

TCP header compression   A compression process that only compresses the TCP header information, which is typically repetitive. This does not compress the user data. *See also: compression.*

TCP/IP   Transmission Control Protocol/Internet Protocol. The suite of protocols underlying the Internet. TCP and IP are the most widely known protocols in that suite. *See also: IP and TCP.*

TDM   time division multiplexing: A technique for assigning bandwidth on a single wire, based on preassigned time slots, to data from several channels. Bandwidth is allotted to each channel regardless of a station's ability to send data. *See also: ATDM, FDM, and multiplexing.*

TE   terminal equipment: Any peripheral device that is ISDN-compatible and attached to a network, such as a telephone or computer. TE1s are devices that are ISDN-ready and understand ISDN signaling techniques. TE2s are devices that are not ISDN-ready and do not understand ISDN signaling techniques. A terminal adapter must be used with a TE2.

TE1   A device with a four-wire, twisted-pair digital interface is referred to as terminal equipment type 1. Most modern ISDN devices are of this type.

TE2   Devices known as terminal equipment type 2 do not understand ISDN signaling techniques, and a terminal adapter must be used to convert the signaling.

telco   A common abbreviation for the telephone company.

Telnet   The standard terminal emulation protocol within the TCP/IP protocol stack. Method of remote terminal connection, enabling users to log in on remote networks and use those resources as if they were locally connected. Telnet is defined in RFC 854.

10BaseT   Part of the original IEEE 802.3 standard, 10BaseT is the Ethernet specification of 10Mbps baseband that uses two pairs of twisted-pair, Category 3, 4, or 5 cabling—using one pair to send data and the other to receive. 10BaseT has a distance limit of about 100 meters per segment. *See also: Ethernet and IEEE 802.3.*

terminal adapter   A hardware interface between a computer without a native ISDN interface and an ISDN line. In effect, a device to connect a standard async interface to a non-native ISDN device, emulating a modem.

terminal emulation   The use of software, installed on a PC or LAN server, that allows the PC to function as if it were a "dumb" terminal directly attached to a particular type of mainframe.

TFTP   Conceptually, a stripped-down version of FTP, it's the protocol of choice if you know exactly what you want and where it's to be found. TFTP doesn't provide the abundance of functions that FTP does. In particular, it has no directory browsing abilities; it can do nothing but send and receive files.

Thicknet   Also called 10Base5. Bus network that uses a thick cable and runs Ethernet up to 500 meters.

Thinnet   Also called 10Base2. Bus network that uses a thin coax cable and runs Ethernet media access up to 185 meters.

token   A frame containing only control information. Possessing this control information gives a network device permission to transmit data onto the network. *See also: token passing.*

token bus   LAN architecture that is the basis for the IEEE 802.4 LAN specification and employs token passing access over a bus topology. *See also: IEEE.*

token passing   A method used by network devices to access the physical medium in a systematic way based on possession of a small frame called a token. *See also: token.*

Token Ring   IBM's token-passing LAN technology. It runs at 4Mbps or 16Mbps over a ring topology. Defined formally by IEEE 802.5. *See also: ring topology and token passing.*

toll network WAN network that uses the Public Switched Telephone Network (PSTN) to send packets.

trace IP command used to trace the path a packet takes through an internetwork.

traffic shaping Used on Frame Relay networks to provide priorities for data.

transparent bridging The bridging scheme used in Ethernet and IEEE 802.3 networks, it passes frames along one hop at a time, using bridging information stored in tables that associate end-node MAC addresses within bridge ports. This type of bridging is considered transparent because the source node does not know it has been bridged, because the destination frames are sent directly to the end node. *Contrast with: SRB.*

Transport Layer Layer 4 of the OSI reference model, used for reliable communication between end nodes over the network. The Transport Layer provides mechanisms used for establishing, maintaining, and terminating virtual circuits, transport fault detection and recovery, and controlling the flow of information. *See also: Application Layer, Data Link Layer, Network Layer, Physical Layer, Presentation Layer, and Session Layer.*

TRIP Token Ring Interface Processor: A high-speed interface processor used on Cisco 7000 series routers. The TRIP provides two or four ports for interconnection with IEEE 802.5 and IBM media with ports set to speeds of either 4Mbps or 16Mbps set independently of each other.

trunk link Link used between switches and from some servers to the switches. Trunk links carry information about many VLANs. Access links are used to connect host devices to a switch and carry only VLAN information that the device is a member of.

TTL Time To Live: A field in an IP header, indicating the length of time a packet is valid.

TUD Trunk Up-Down: A protocol used in ATM networks for the monitoring of trunks. Should a trunk miss a given number of test messages being sent by ATM switches to ensure trunk line quality, TUD declares the trunk down. When a trunk reverses direction and comes back up, TUD recognizes that the trunk is up and returns the trunk to service.

tunneling A method of avoiding protocol restrictions by wrapping packets from one protocol in another protocol's packet and transmitting this encapsulated packet over a network that supports the wrapper protocol. *See also: encapsulation.*

UART Universal Asynchronous Receiver/Transmitter: A chip that governs asynchronous communications. Its primary function is to buffer incoming data; however, it also buffers outbound bits.

U reference point Reference point between a TE1 and an ISDN network. The U reference point understands ISDN signaling techniques and uses a 2-wire connection.

UDP User Datagram Protocol: A connectionless Transport Layer protocol in the TCP/IP protocol stack that simply allows datagrams to be exchanged without acknowledgements or delivery guarantees, requiring other protocols to handle error processing and retransmission. UDP is defined in RFC 768.

unnumbered frames HDLC frames used for control-management purposes, such as link startup and shutdown or mode specification.

UTP unshielded twisted-pair: Copper wiring used in small-to-large networks to connect host devices to hubs and switches. Also used to connect switch to switch or hub to hub.

VBR Variable Bit Rate: A QoS class, as defined by the ATM Forum, for use in ATM networks that is subdivided into real time (RT) class and non-real time (NRT) class. RT is employed when connections have a fixed-time relationship between samples. Conversely, NRT is employed when connections do not have a fixed-time relationship between samples, but still need an assured QoS.

VCC Virtual Channel Connection: A logical circuit that is created by VCLs. VCCs carry data between two endpoints in an ATM network. Sometimes called a virtual circuit connection.

VIP 1) Versatile Interface Processor: An interface card for Cisco 7000 and 7500 series routers, providing multilayer switching and running the Cisco IOS software. The most recent version of VIP is VIP2. 2) Virtual IP: A function making it possible for logically separated switched IP workgroups to run Virtual Networking Services across the switch ports of a Catalyst 5000.

virtual circuit Abbreviated VC, a logical circuit devised to assure reliable communication between two devices on a network. Defined by a virtual path connection (VPC)/virtual path identifier (VCI) pair, a virtual circuit can be permanent (PVC) or switched (SVC). Virtual circuits are used in Frame Relay and X.25. Known as virtual channel in ATM. *See also: PVC and SVC.*

virtual ring In an SRB network, a logical connection between physical rings, either local or remote.

VLAN Virtual LAN: A group of devices on one or more logically segmented LANs (configured by use of management software), enabling devices to communicate as if attached to the same physical medium, when they are actually located on numerous different LAN segments. VLANs are based on logical instead of physical connections and thus are tremendously flexible.

VLSM variable-length subnet mask: Helps optimize available address space and specify a different subnet mask for the same network number on various subnets. Also commonly referred to as "subnetting a subnet."

VPN Virtual Private Network: This is a method of encrypting point-to-point logical connections across a public network, such as the Internet. This allows secure communications across a public network.

VTP VLAN Trunk Protocol: Used to update switches in a switch fabric about VLANs configured on a VTP server. VTP devices can be a VTP server, client, or transparent device. Servers update clients. Transparent devices are only local devices and do not share information with VTP clients. VTPs send VLAN information down trunked links only.

WAN wide area network: Is a designation used to connect LANs together across a DCE (data communications equipment) network. Typically, a WAN is a leased line or dial-up connection across a PSTN network. Examples of WAN protocols include Frame Relay, PPP, ISDN, and HDLC.

weighted fair queuing Default queuing method on serial links for all Cisco routers.

wildcard Used with access-list, supernetting, and OSPF configurations. Wildcards are designations used to identify a range of subnets.

windowing Flow-control method used with TCP at the Transport Layer of the OSI model.

WinSock Windows Socket Interface: A software interface that makes it possible for an assortment of applications to use and share an Internet connection. The WinSock software consists of a Dynamic Link Library (DLL) with supporting programs such as a dialer program that initiates the connection.

workgroup switching A switching method that supplies high-speed (100Mbps) transparent bridging between Ethernet networks as well as high-speed translational bridging between Ethernet and CDDI or FDDI.

X.25 An ITU-T packet-relay standard that defines communication between DTE and DCE network devices. X.25 uses a reliable Data Link Layer protocol called LAPB. X.25 also uses PLP at the Network Layer. X.25 has mostly been replaced by Frame Relay.

X.25 protocol First packet-switching network, but now mostly used in Europe. Replaced in U.S. by Frame Relay.

ZIP Zone Information Protocol: A Session Layer protocol used by AppleTalk to map network numbers to zone names. NBP uses ZIP in the determination of networks containing nodes that belong to a zone. *See also: ZIP storm and zone.*

ZIP storm A broadcast storm occurring when a router running AppleTalk reproduces or transmits a route for which there is no corresponding zone name at the time of execution. The route is then forwarded by other routers downstream, thus causing a ZIP storm. *See also: broadcast storm and ZIP.*

zone A logical grouping of network devices in AppleTalk. *See also: ZIP.*

Index

Note to the Reader: Page numbers in **bold** indicate the principal discussion of a topic or the definition of a term. Page numbers in *italic* indicate illustrations.

M

R